BUFFALO
RIVER
HANDBOOK

By the same author:
- *The Buffalo River Country*
- *Illinois River*
- *Sawmill*
- Layout and text for maps,
    Buffalo National River, West Half
    Buffalo National River, East Half

Cover and title page:
Roark Bluff is the most accessible
of the high cliffs along the Buffalo,
in plain view for canoers, campers,
hikers, horseback riders, and casual
sightseers at Steel Creek.

BUFFALO
RIVER
HANDBOOK

KENNETH L. SMITH

The OZARK
SOCIETY
FOUNDATION
Little Rock

BUFFALO RIVER HANDBOOK

Book design, page layouts: Kenneth L. Smith
Editor: Ainslie Gilligan
Publisher: Ozark Society Foundation, Box 3503, Little Rock, AR 72203

The Ozark Society Foundation publishes regional books and guides on nature and the environment. These are distributed by the University of Arkansas Press, McIlroy House, 201 McIlroy Avenue, Fayetteville, AR 72701 (800-626-0090; fax 479-575-6044; www.uapress.com).

The Library of Congress has cataloged an earlier edition as follows: 2005298813

First Edition, Third Printing
Printed in Canada   ISBN-13: 978-0-912456-23-2

CONTENTS

Part 2 **RIVER**

Part 3 **TRAILS**

OUTCOMES

In remembrance of my father,
who shared with me
his love of travel and the outdoors.

Acknowledgments

It would not have been possible to write this book without the knowledge and help of many people, those named below and others not named here. To each of them I offer heartfelt thanks.

Persons are listed for their principal contributions, though often their help extended to other areas.

LAND: Geologists Raymond Suhm (original mentor); Margaret Guccione, Walter Manger, and Doy Zachry (University of Arkansas, Fayetteville); Mark Hudson (U.S. Geological Survey); and John David McFarland III (Arkansas Geological Commission) read and commented on chapter drafts and stimulated discussion. Pete Lindsley and David Taylor shared knowledge of the Buffalo's caves.

LIFE: Biologists Jeffrey Barnes, Arthur Brown, Edward Dale, Johnnie Gentry, Douglas James, Cynthia Sagers, Blaine Schubert, and Frederick Spiegel (U. of A., Fayetteville); G. O. Graening (The Nature Conservancy); George Harp (Arkansas State University); Carl Dick and Michael Mathis (University of Central Arkansas); and Joseph Neal (U.S. Forest Service) helped with chapter drafts and specific topics. Geographers Malcolm Cleaveland and David Stahle (U. of A., Fayetteville) provided insights based on tree-ring dating.

PEOPLE: Archeologists-anthropologists Hester Davis, Randall Guendling, Jerry Hilliard, and George Sabo (Arkansas Archeological Survey); Michael Hoffman (U. of A., Fayetteville); Carol Spears (SPEARS, Inc.); and Don Dickson (Historic Preservation Associates) reviewed and assisted with writing about Native Americans.

Fred McCraw and Charles Banks Wilson told me about their friend Thomas Hart Benton. Cyrus Sutherland (U. of A., Fayetteville) and Kenneth Story (Arkansas Historic Preservation Program) read and commented on the Boxley Valley tour guide. Fred Bell, Oxford Hamilton, Joan Vancuren Hobbs, Wilma Villines Sims, Kelly

Swofford, Elmarene Primrose Vancuren, and Arbie Henderson Villines provided historical information relating to the upper river. Searcy County historian James Johnston provided information for the middle river. Marian Burnes, Jane-Ellen Murphy, Robert Myers, and David Scott helped with history of the lower Buffalo.

PARK: Buffalo National River staff members providing assistance for this book included rangers Jeff West and Stuart West; interpreters Linda Bishop and Douglas Wilson; facilities manager Roger Dillard; administrative officer Mike Lively; natural-resource managers John Apel, Charles Bitting, Noel Mays, Faron Usrey, and especially David Mott; archeologist David Hayes; historians Jim Liles and Suzanne Rogers; and superintendent Ivan Miller. Ozark National Forest staff members included Terry Hope and Jan Self on the Buffalo District and Jim Steele on the Sylamore District.

RIVER & TRAILS: Many people were helpful. Local residents provided place names and historical background. River runners and hikers shared their special knowledge. They are listed according to the parts of the river with which they are most closely related.

River above Boxley: Bill Bates, Paul McCune, Dave Millsap, and Stewart Noland. *Boxley to Ponca:* Claude Clark, Eul Dean Clark, Bill Duty, Waymon Villines, George Watson, Walter Williams, Ott Young, Hubert Ferguson. *Ponca to Kyles Landing:* Bill Villines, Boyd Villines, Roy Wishon, Margaret Hedges, Jim Lochhead, Steve McAdams. *Erbie to Pruitt:* Loyd Brisco, Ray and Robert Hickman, Bill Houston, Richard Holland, Ernest Lamb, Faye Scroggins.

Carver area: Gene Waters, James Veadle Waters. *Mount Hersey:* Armon Mays, Jack McCutcheon. *Mount Hersey to Maumee:* river expert Jack Hensley. *Woolum to Highway 65:* Janis White Busbee, Marcia Donley, Dunford Elliott, E. G. Grinder, Doshia Hamm, E. J. Hamm, (Kenneth) Lee Hunter, Doyce Manes, Leon Manes, Ben Passmore, Ben Stills, Utah Switzer, Helen (Mrs. James E.) White, Vernon Williams. *Gilbert and vicinity:* Bill Baker, Loucille Moore Baker, Connell (C. J.) Brown, Kenneth Hubbard, Ray Jordan, Mrs. Ray Wheeler. *Maumee to Rush Creek:* Leon Somerville, Jr.

Maumee to Spring Creek: Lillie Patterson Baysinger, Blaine Beavers, Mike and Harold and Haskell Cash, Felix Clingings, Glen and Nelda Davenport, James Davenport, Cenith Still Jackson, Howard Marshall, Bill McClain, Ella Mae Passmore, Robert Robison, James Sanders, Haskell Sitton, Deward (D. C.) Still, Bernard Sullivan. *Dillards Ferry and vicinity:* Bobby Joe Baker, Joe

Barnes, John Dillard, Doretha Dillard Shipman, Leon Shipman, Sr. *Rush:* Al and David Bowman, Lee Davenport.

Rush Creek to Big Creek: Dale Laffoon, Leo (H. L.) Avey, Earl and Pearl Hays, Arwood B. Marberry. *Big Creek to White River:* Carlisle Beavers, Ben R. Boyd, Erma Boyd, Everett Boyd especially, Walton Cox, Clyde and Ruby Franks, Orville and Ruth Franks, Boyce Henderson, Baxter Hurst, Nora (Mrs. Roscoe) Jefferson, Annabelle Perry Odegard, Nellie (Mrs. Ralph) Perry, Raymond Rasor, Connie Rose, Dorothy White, Garland and Virginia Woods.

Others helped during trips at the river, and in gathering information: Lynn Armstrong, Bill Bates, Dale and Becky Burris, Joan and Layton Chambers, Farrel Couch, Bill and Jan Craig, Bob Cross, Terry Fredrick, Jason Harmon, Richard and Brenda Hempel, John and Margaret Heuston, Lewis Hevel, Don House, Rex Judice, Paul Moser, Lloyd Owen, Bill Riecken, Jimmie Rogers, Bill Saunders, Bill Sheppard, David and Laura Timby, David Trissel, Syvalene Unwer, Phillip Walrod, Joan and Dick Williams and family. The staff of the Mullins Library, University of Arkansas at Fayetteville, especially those in Special Collections and Interlibrary Loan. And of the Baxter County Library, the Marion County Library, the Riley-Hickingbotham Library at Ouachita Baptist University, the Arkansas Game and Fish Commission, the Arkansas Parks and Tourism Commission, and the Shiloh Museum of Ozark History.

Thanks also are due to Ozark Society Foundation trustees Jim Allen, Paula Davis, Tom Foti, Bob James, Steve Noland, and especially Dana Steward for their time spent on behalf of this book.

And thanks also to Scott Hunter, Scott Mattson, and Neil Shipley for their patient assistance toward having this book printed.

Finally, special thanks to Ainslie Gilligan, my caring and capable editor, who helped me improve this writing in so many ways.

Kenneth L. Smith

Illustration Credits (in order by page)

5: (bluff-and-bench) Neil Compton/Shiloh Museum of Ozark History; (miners' camp) Harley Myles Collection, courtesy Mrs. Harley Myles. 15: (geologic column) Mark R. Hudson/U.S. Geological Survey. 26: James Terry. 28: (lower photo) U.S. Geological Survey, *Geologic Atlas of the United States, Eureka Springs-Harrison Folio*, No. 202. 30: U.S. Geological Survey/Ozark Underground Laboratory/National Park Service. 32: Hurley Cook/National Park Service. 38 (crinoids) and 40: National Museum of

Natural History, Smithsonian Institution. 51: U.S. Forest Service. 55: (Jim Bluff) Joan Chambers. 64: Carol Bitting/The Nature Conservancy. 67: Revised and redrawn from similar diagram in *Fresh-Water Invertebrates of the United States,* third edition, by Robert W. Pennak. 68: (caddisfly, mayfly) Oregon State Game Commission; (stonefly) Leon A. Hausman. 80: From *Human Adaptation in the Ozark and Ouachita Mountains,* by George Sabo III and others, Arkansas Archeological Survey, Research Series No. 31. 82 (acorns) and 84: National Museum of the American Indian, Smithsonian Institution. 91: Doshia and E. J. (John) Hamm. 94: (upper) *Engineering and Mining Journal,* August 19, 1916; (lower) Juanita Norris Buell. 99: (upper) *Arkansas Historical Quarterly,* vol. 19 (1960), p. 364; (lower) *Newton County Times*/Shiloh Museum of Ozark History. 101: (upper) James D. and Louise Greenhaw; (lower) Ella Mae Passmore. 107: Thomas H. and Rita P. Benton Testamentary Trusts, UMB Bank, Administrator. 108: (top) Ellen Compton. 116: National Park Service. 119: (lower) National Park Service. 124: Jeffery West/National Park Service. 126: James N. Huckins. 133: Arkansas Water Resources Center, Publication No. MSC-170. 157, 159, 163: Thase Daniel Collection, Riley-Hickingbotham Library, Ouachita Baptist University. 161: (lower) William Roston/American Fisheries Society. 164: (upper) A. C. Haralson/Arkansas Department of Parks & Tourism; (lower) Arkansas Game and Fish Commission. 183: Richard Holland/Shiloh Museum of Ozark History. 185: Fred W. McCraw/Private collection. 191: James D. and Louise Greenhaw. 210: Stella Grinder Mason/National Park Service. 223: Haskell E. Sitton. 226: B. Anthony Stewart/NGS Image Collection. 228: Douglas McClenathan/National Park Service. 243: From *Pioneer Life and Pioneer Families of the Ozarks* by Earl Berry, courtesy Earl Berry. 250: Phyllis and Sam Speer. 257: Carl James. 261: (upper) Historic Arkansas Museum. 264: (upper) Roy Wishon; (lower) David L. Scott. 265: (lower) Matt Bradley. 266: (upper) Charles Banks Wilson. 266 (lower) and 267: Thomas H. and Rita P. Benton Testamentary Trusts, UMB Bank, Administrator. 277: Dale Burris. 281: Susan Green (Mrs. Wayne) Hartsfield. 308: Dale Burris. 314: From *The Lithographs of Thomas Hart Benton,* new edition, by Creekmore Fath, courtesy Creekmore Fath. 326: Robert Batson photo, courtesy Deborah Batson. 329: Matt Bradley. 334: Ralph Foster Museum, College of the Ozarks. 364: Marcia Donley. 365: Carl James. 381: Ray Jordan. 383: Carnegie Public Library, Eureka Springs, AR. 408: Wilburn Hiser/National Park Service. 412: The Field Museum, Chicago, IL. (Negative #19716). 414: *Engineering and Mining Journal,* February 16, 1918. Back cover: Joan Chambers.

All other illustrations are by the author.

INTRODUCTION

This book is for anyone wanting to know more about the Buffalo River in northern Arkansas—a river that includes much of the finest natural environment of the Ozarks.

The book is about Buffalo National River, a unit of the National Park System. It also covers the adjoining Leatherwood Wilderness, Upper Buffalo Wilderness, and Buffalo Scenic River on the Ozark National Forest. Its text is coordinated with a pair of detailed maps from National Geographic/Trails Illustrated (see next two pages).

Buffalo River Handbook is in three parts:

Part 1 summarizes what is known about the river's geology, biology, past history, and present management. Here are the essentials from many technical publications, historical writings, and personal interviews. Altogether, they offer an opportunity to learn about the river's natural and human history and about the Buffalo's parklands. Much of the information helps in understanding other parts of the Ozarks and areas beyond the region as well.

Part 2 is a mile-by-mile guide for floating the river, with descriptions keyed to the Trails Illustrated maps and to what is said in Part 1. So here's another opportunity for learning the river while enjoying the river, when being on the river.

Part 3 is a comprehensive guide to the river's walking trails and paths and cross-country hiking areas, also keyed to the maps and related to Part 1. Here's still another opportunity, for the land along the river can be as captivating as the river itself.

The *Handbook*'s descriptions of places tend to emphasize history and ecology. History is useful because what we see today is the result of what happened in the past (also there are some good stories). Ecology is useful because it deals with how living things, including humans, have interacted with one another and with the Buffalo River environment. The themes, history and ecology, themselves interact.

Going beyond the first-generation guides we use for identifying birds, trees, or flowers, this is a second-generation guidebook full of background information. Also, sources for still more information about the Buffalo are listed *(Continued on page 4)*

Within the protected areas of Scenic River, Wilderness, and National River, the Buffalo River meanders through the Ozarks of northern Arkansas. The National River and Wilderness areas are also depicted in detail on two Trails Illustrated maps published by National Geographic Maps: *Buffalo National River, West Half* (map #232) and *East Half* (map #233). The portion of the river covered by the *West Half* map appears on this page while that for the *East Half* map is on the facing page.

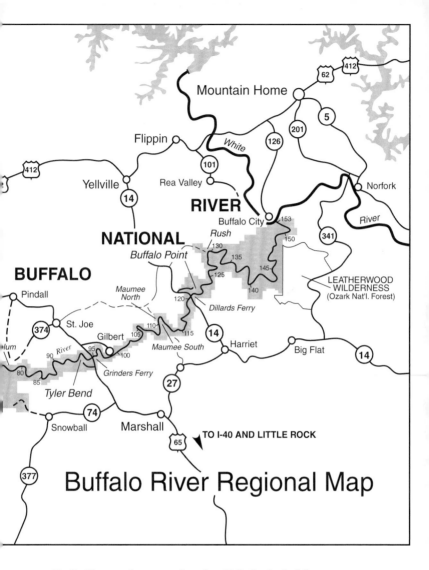

Buffalo River Regional Map

TO I-40 AND LITTLE ROCK

Trails Illustrated maps are based on U.S. Geological Survey topographic maps, with updated information on roads, trails, campgrounds, etc. These maps—on waterproof, tear-resistant plastic—are available at bookstores, outdoor stores, the river's float outfitters, and the area's Park Service and Forest Service sales outlets. The maps also can be purchased through Ozark Society Books, P.O. Box 3503, Little Rock, AR 72203; prices are shown at the Society's website: www.ozarksociety.net

on pages 423–424. And several organizations described on page 425 provide opportunities for learning outdoor skills. The Park Service and Forest Service contacts posted on page 424 offer up-to-date information on their regulations and facilities. (If not already familiar with the regulations, also take advantage of the agencies' road signs, bulletin boards, and visitor-center handouts. From these you actually can learn much more than just the regulations.)

Again concerning what *is* here in this book, we admit uncertainty about events of the past. Even the experts are unsure of—and argue about—past happenings for which there is a lack of hard evidence. Geologists differ widely about the how-and-when of Ozark uplifting and subsequent erosion. Paleobotanists debate how the Ozarks' vegetation survived the Ice Age. Archeologists vary in their interpretations of the uses of prehistoric sites. But scientists search for truth through observation, study, and experimentation, and indeed have gained much knowledge of most things related to the Buffalo.

The *Handbook* is a "fact book" like an encyclopedia. If reading it at home, you'll probably find it's better to browse than try to read straight through. Take it with you on the river or the trails, along with one or both of the Trails Illustrated maps, and when out there, look up whatever sparks your interest. The table of contents here in front may help you find what you're looking for. The index at the back can help even more.

Go on from there. Float another piece of the river; walk another part of the trails. Get off the river or trail and hike up a creek, down a ridge. Back home, find other reading material about your special interests—fishes, flowers, fossils, whatever. Get with others who share your likes and go to the river with them. In doing these things you can discover much more than this book can tell you.

Most essentially, *enjoy yourself.*

We hope that by enjoying and learning, you will begin to care…to take care of the river. Protect it from harm, for your own sense of fulfillment. And for your children. For all children.

But first, learn. And enjoy.

Insights:
the results of
understanding
the inner nature
of things.

Part 1

INSIGHTS

Top to bottom:
LAND—Bluff-and-bench
  mountainside, Boxley.
LIFE—Wild azalea
  blooms on Pine Ridge,
  near Gilbert.
PEOPLE—Miners' camp
  at Rush, about 1916.
PARK—Introducing kids
  to aquatic "bugs"
  at Buffalo Point.

Big Bluff. Almost the entire cliff is composed of the Buffalo's two most massive, widespread rock formations. The Everton is below the shadowed overhang area and the Boone is above it.

LAND

To a geologist, the Buffalo River country is Old Rock—geologically ancient bedrock. But it is a Young Landscape, appearing only in geologically recent times as erosion has shaped the rock to create hills, hollows, cliffs, caves, and much else we find so interesting about this uniquely scenic place.

Deep Time

To build and shape these landforms, geologic forces both "ancient" and "recent" took an almost inconceivably long time. We usually think of elapsed time in relation to human history—years, decades, centuries. But geologists think in terms of *deep time,* for geologic processes have been going on for millions…tens of millions…hundreds of millions of years. These processes are of immense antiquity and majesty. If we view this work of Creation in a spiritual sense, it is not only longer in duration, but larger in dimension and grander in conception than we may have ever realized.

The age of planet Earth is now thought to be about four and a half billion years. The first life known to have existed on Earth—simple, single-celled microscopic organisms—appeared about four billion years ago. The first complex, multicelled life forms came much later, around one billion years ago, and were soft-bodied sea-dwelling creatures, rarely preserved as fossils.

About 550 million years before the present (MYBP), the first animals developed with hard shells or skeletons, providing an abundance of fossils. Based on the appearance of various forms of life, geologic time from 550 MYBP to the present has been divided into three broad *eras*: Paleozoic ("old life"), about 550 to 250 MYBP; *Mesozoic* ("middle life"), 250 to 65 MYBP; and *Cenozoic* ("new life"), 65 MYBP to the present time.

During the Paleozoic Era, the bedrock of the Buffalo River country was first deposited as sediments, more recent layers on top of older ones. Paleozoic time is divided into seven *periods* based on changes in life forms, changes somewhat like those of the eras but smaller in scale. The oldest rock, seen near the river, was deposited about 480 MYBP during the Ordovician (Or-doh-VISH-un) Period. The youngest rock, seen today on the highest mountaintops overlooking the upper Buffalo, was deposited about 300 MYBP in the Pennsylvanian Period. All of the rock, then, that we see along the river was created during a time span of approximately 180 million years (see time scale, opposite).

Buried beneath the visible Ordovician rock are layers of still older sedimentary rock of the earlier Ordovician and Cambrian periods. Below that, and more than 2000 feet below the surface, is the Ozarks' Precambrian *basement rock,* more than a billion years old.

Rock Types

By observing how sediments accumulate in today's environments, geologists have been able to envision how the various kinds of Buffalo River rock originated under similar conditions during the Paleozoic Era. The Buffalo's limestone was formed from shells and skeletons of marine animals, but mainly from secretions by marine algae that caused a constant slow rain of microscopic bits of limy material falling to the sea bottom. Some of the river area's older, Ordovician-age limestones also became infiltrated by sea water bearing magnesium, resulting in chemical conversion of the limestone (composed mainly of calcium carbonate, the mineral calcite) to dolostone (calcium magnesium carbonate, the mineral dolomite). Though "dolostone" is perhaps more proper, the rock itself is usually called dolomite. Because both limestone and dolomite are composed of carbonate minerals, both are often called *carbonate rock.*

Many of the area's deposits of limestone and dolomite were infiltrated by another mineral in solution, silicon dioxide—commonly called silica—which came mainly from the secretions and skeletons of microscopic marine animals. The silica, which accumulated as layers or masses within beds of carbonate rock, is chemically identical to quartz and is called *chert* (see photo, page 57).

Beds of sandstone seen today near the river originated as beaches and shoreline dunes or as offshore deposits of sand along the margins of seas. Sandstone of the rimrock bluffs on the highest mountains flanking the river was deposited along braided (multichanneled) lowland rivers. Often the spaces between the grains of sand were infiltrated by calcite, which then cemented the grains together.

During the Pennsylvanian Period, fine particles of clay and silt that were deposited in still waters at river deltas and coastal marshes developed into shale, and into related types of fine-grained rock

GEOLOGIC TIME SCALE

ERAS	PERIODS	BUFFALO RIVER EVENTS
CENOZOIC	QUATERNARY 2	Ice Age. Valley-floor deposits.
CENOZOIC	TERTIARY	Erosion of earlier deposits. Rise of grasses, cereals, fruits. Mammals become predominant.
	65 million years ago	Dinosaurs extinct.
MESOZOIC	CRETACEOUS	Erosion of earlier deposits. Development of flowering plants. Zenith of dinosaurs.
MESOZOIC	144	
MESOZOIC	JURASSIC	Erosion of earlier deposits. Development of giant dinosaurs. First true birds.
MESOZOIC	208	
MESOZOIC	TRIASSIC	Erosion of earlier deposits. First dinosaurs. First mammals.
	245	
PALEOZOIC (Buffalo River rock deposited)	PERMIAN	Cooler, drier. Conifers abundant.
	286	Ouachita Mountains uplifted.
PALEOZOIC (Buffalo River rock deposited)	PENNSYLVANIAN	Primitive trees and ferns.
	320	
PALEOZOIC (Buffalo River rock deposited)	MISSISSIPPIAN	Limy, shaly deposits in warm seas teeming with life. Culmination of crinoids.
	360	
PALEOZOIC (Buffalo River rock deposited)	DEVONIAN	Many corals, fishes. First amphibians. Earliest forests spread over land.
	408	
PALEOZOIC (Buffalo River rock deposited)	SILURIAN	First air-breathing animals.
	438	
PALEOZOIC (Buffalo River rock deposited)	ORDOVICIAN	Life only in seas. Spread of mollusks. Creation of oldest rock formations visible along Buffalo River.
	505	
PALEOZOIC (Buffalo River rock deposited)	CAMBRIAN	First vertebrates (fishes). Many marine invertebrates.
	550	
	PRECAMBRIAN Includes several divisions of Era rank.	Over four billion years, about 88% of known geologic time. Earliest forms of life. Few fossils known.

known as mudstone and siltstone. Shale is composed of thin layers called laminations that split apart easily. Mudstone has the same fine grain size and smooth feel of shale but is massive and blocky, and lacks the laminations and ability to split. Siltstone, also lacking the ability to split, consists mostly of somewhat coarser silt grains.

Plate Tectonics

Much of the rock along the Buffalo River contains fossils of extinct species of marine animals. Today, similar species exist in warm tropical seas. While scientists have always believed the Paleozoic seas that covered today's Ozarks had to be warm bodies of water to support such an assemblage of marine life, they could not understand how any tropical environment could have existed in today's temperate zone. In the 1960s, though, they arrived at an explanation of how places such as northern Arkansas could at one time have been near the equator. The scientists' theory of *plate tectonics* is essentially that Earth's lithosphere (outer shell) is divided into large, slowly moving segments or plates, including several on which the continents ride in extremely slow motion, a phenomenon called *continental drift*. (In geology, "tectonics" means movement or structures caused by Earth's internal forces.) These plates, which may be about 75 miles thick, float atop the partially molten, plastic mantle below them. For hundreds of millions of years, the plates have moved over the surface of the planet.

Thus during the Paleozoic Era the portion of Earth's crust we now call the Ozarks was located some distance south of the equator. If what we now call the Ozarks moved across the face of Earth at only three-quarters of an inch a year—about the rate at which your fingernails grow—in 300 million years the Ozarks traveled 3500 miles. (And today the equator lies about 3200 miles south of the Ozarks.)

Deposition

At rates of deposition that have been measured at some places, shallow marine environments may produce a foot of sandstone in 500 years, a foot of shale in 1000 years, or a foot of limestone or dolomite in 2500 years. Thus a 100-foot layer of sandstone in a cliff overlooking the Buffalo could have been deposited in 50,000 years. The massive Boone Formation of limestone, 300 feet thick in many places along the river, could have been deposited in 750,000 years. If deposition were continuous—and it was not—all of the rock now existing along the Buffalo could have been laid down within a time span of about five million years.

As mentioned before, the accumulation took place during 180 million years. Deposition only occurred between many long interruptions. Repeatedly the Paleozoic seas advanced and then retreated. When the Ozark area was flooded, sediments were deposited. When the Ozarks were dry land, much of the previously deposited sediment (or rock) was removed by erosion.

Far more sedimentary rock was created than remains today. All of that eroded material took millions of years to accumulate and more millions to erode away. Today, only lines of contact between dissimilar rock strata provide evidence of gaps in the geologic record. In over a dozen different contacts between adjoining layers of Buffalo River rock, there are *unconformities* where erosion took material off the lower layer before sedimentation began to add a younger upper one (photo, page 53). The shallow, constantly shifting Paleozoic seas came and went at least that many times.

Moreover, the rock exposed along the Buffalo contains hundreds of *bedding planes*—not full-fledged erosional unconformities but visible dividing lines between beds (layers) of rock that indicate pauses or other changes of condition between episodes of deposition. Some of the pauses may have been brief; others may have lasted longer than the times of deposition of the adjoining beds. Altogether, those pauses represent a very long time.

Much of the Buffalo's rock of mid-Ordovician age lies in contact with rock that was deposited early in the Mississippian Period. There are only scattered outcrops of rock of the later Ordovician (which lasted about 25 million years) or of the Silurian Period (30 million years), and apparently no rock at all of the Devonian Period (48 million years). Whatever the amount of sediment deposited and rock created during this 100-million-year interval, the area was above water long enough for nearly all of it to be removed by erosion.

Why did the Paleozoic seas come and go so many times?

Earth scientists believe one answer is that during episodes of rapid motion of tectonic plates, high ridges were raised at plate boundaries under the oceans, displacing sea water that flooded lowland areas. When plate motion slowed or stopped, the ridges shrank or disappeared and water returned to the ocean basins. Also there were times when much of the world's water became frozen in gigantic ice sheets; ocean levels were lowered and land was exposed, only to be covered again when the next worldwide warming melted the ice. And at times, apparently, today's Ozark region was gently uplifted to become dry land, only to subside and again be inundated.

When inundated, the region evidently was part of a continental shelf, a shallow submarine plain. When land again, the same area lay close to sea level. Such conditions made it relatively easy for seas to spread over the land, or to retreat.

Rock Formations

Geologists have divided the various types of layered Buffalo River rock into named units (see chart, pages 14–15). Each principal body of rock, or *formation,* must be of considerable thickness and have characteristics that distinguish it from adjacent, underlying, or overlying rock units. The formation must also be continuous, spread over a large enough area that it extends beyond the limits of one seven-and-a-half-minute topographic map, and thick enough to be a visible area when drawn on the map.

A formation may be a single massive bed or layer of sedimentary rock such as limestone or sandstone. Or a formation may consist of consecutive thin beds of more than one rock type, but still distinctive enough to be named and mapped as a unit. If most or all of a formation is of one rock type, it may be called, for example, the Pitkin Limestone. If made up of several rock types, none predominant, the term "formation" is used in the name, such as the Hale Formation having beds of sandstone, shale, siltstone, and limestone.

The naming system allows for subdivisions. A prominent homogeneous unit within a formation may be designated a *member* of that formation. Thus the Newton Sandstone is a member of the Everton Formation, which also is composed of beds of dolomite and limestone with scattered traces of shale and chert.

Formations and members usually are named for the localities where they were first recognized and identified as separate units—Fayetteville Shale for the town of Fayetteville, Newton Sandstone for Newton County, St. Joe Limestone for the village of St. Joe in Searcy County. A formation extending beyond state boundaries, however, may be given a different name or names in each state. The Boone Formation of Arkansas has in Missouri been divided into several formations, none of them named Boone.

Finally, the identity of some rock units has changed as geologic knowledge has expanded. On the upper Buffalo, for instance, what was once believed to be the St. Peter Sandstone was discovered to be an older sandstone located within the underlying Everton Formation, and it was renamed the Newton Sandstone Member of the Everton. Also along the upper Buffalo, the massive sandstone cap rock of the Boston Mountains was long believed to be the basal (lowest) member of the Atoka Formation; after further investigation it is now considered a part of the next-lower unit, the Bloyd Formation, and is informally called the "middle Bloyd" sandstone (photo, page 58).

One reason for occasional errors in identifying rock units is that beds of rock or even entire formations become thicker or thinner over distance—or disappear, maybe to reappear somewhere else. Such interruptions of sedimentation over distance (or possibly erasure by erosion) are called *discontinuities.*

Even without discontinuities, a rock unit can, over distance, change in its chemistry, grain size, or other aspects. These variations in makeup of otherwise matching rock strata are known as *facies* (FAY-she-eez) changes. Over a small distance a bed of "pure" limestone, for example, can become sandy limestone, or limy sandstone, or dolomitic limestone. In any formation there are such "impure" types of rock as depositional conditions varied.

Ozark Uplifting

During the 180 million years when the Buffalo's rock formations were deposited, the Ozark region at times was gently uplifted, but uplift always was followed by erosion and then by inundation. Then, at some time after deposition of the Atoka Formation—the youngest rock now present in the Ozarks—the region was lifted up to become the elevated land area that it remains today.

The Ozarks' presumed "final" uplifting apparently was a result of a collision of the tectonic plate that included present-day North America with another plate or plates to the south. That collision crumpled Earth's crust along the south edge of the North American plate, evidenced today by compressed, folded, uptilted, and overturned rock strata in the Ouachita Mountains a hundred miles south of the Buffalo. This tectonic event that raised the Ouachitas is known as the Ouachita *orogeny* (oh-ROJ-e-nee, "mountain building," an episode of intense deformation of the rocks in a region). Across today's Arkansas Valley, to the north of the Ouachitas, rock layers were less deformed. In the Ozarks, still farther north, strata were only gently elevated. Thus the Ozark area at the continent's interior

THE BUFFALO RIVER'S ROCK FORMATIONS

Upper river (Ponca-to-Erbie canyon) has most of the river's major formations and several minor ones. A stratigraphic column (on facing page; rock types appear below) shows these formations in upward sequence from oldest to youngest, from Powell Dolomite at the river to the Bloyd Formation at mountaintops.

Sandstone

Cross-bedded sandstone

Shale, siltstone

Limestone

Dolomite

Chert

Upper & middle river (Boston Mtns. & Springfield Plateau) have the formations shown in the column, and others not in the Ponca-to-Erbie canyon. Text on the facing page describes these rock units. Major units, which together cover more than 90% of the land, are shown in capital letters. Formation thickness and other aspects vary over distance, so descriptions are generalized. Note that Point Peter Mountain is part of the Boston Mountains.

Middle & lower river (Springfield & Salem Plateaus) have no rock units above the Boone Formation. The following list of units from the Boone downward to the Powell includes several minor ones occurring only in limited areas:

BOONE FORMATION (Mississippian): See facing page.
   (The Buffalo River has no rock verified as from the
   Devonian Period, which preceded the Mississippian.)
Lafferty Limestone (Silurian): 0–30 ft, in Highway 65–Gilbert
   area. Gray with some orange or pink; upper beds gray.
St. Clair Limestone (Silurian): 0–34 ft, Tyler Bend to Little
   Rocky Creek. Coarse-grained; light gray to pinkish-gray.
Brassfield Limestone (Silurian): 0–38 ft, Highway 65 to
   Tomahawk Creek. Pinkish-gray to red-mottled; many fossils.
Cason Shale (Ordovician): 0–30 ft, Highway 65–Gilbert area.
   Seen as gray-green shale in bluff on Highway 333, 1 mile
   northwest of Gilbert.
Fernvale Limestone: See description on facing page.
PLATTIN LIMESTONE: See facing page.
Joachim Dolomite: 0–13 ft in one known exposure west of the
   mouth of Cedar Creek near river mile 132. Finely crystalline.
ST. PETER SANDSTONE, EVERTON FORMATION, and Powell
   Dolomite: These formations are described on the facing page.

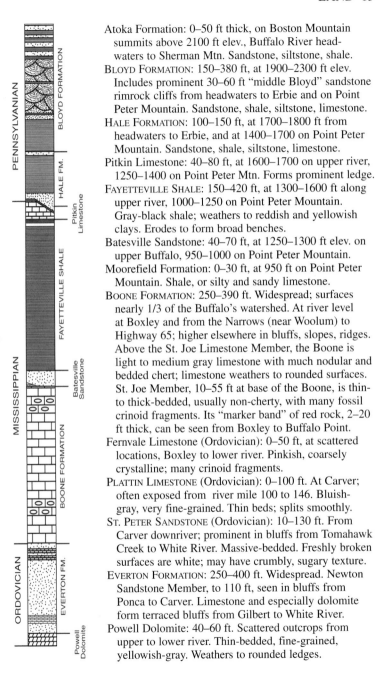

Atoka Formation: 0–50 ft thick, on Boston Mountain summits above 2100 ft elev., Buffalo River head-waters to Sherman Mtn. Sandstone, siltstone, shale.

BLOYD FORMATION: 150–380 ft, at 1900–2300 ft elev. Includes prominent 30–60 ft "middle Bloyd" sandstone rimrock cliffs from headwaters to Erbie and on Point Peter Mountain. Sandstone, shale, siltstone, limestone.

HALE FORMATION: 100–150 ft, at 1700–1800 ft from headwaters to Erbie, and at 1400–1700 on Point Peter Mountain. Sandstone, shale, siltstone, limestone.

Pitkin Limestone: 40–80 ft, at 1600–1700 on upper river, 1250–1400 on Point Peter Mtn. Forms prominent ledge.

FAYETTEVILLE SHALE: 150–420 ft, at 1300–1600 ft along upper river, 1000–1250 on Point Peter Mountain. Gray-black shale; weathers to reddish and yellowish clays. Erodes to form broad benches.

Batesville Sandstone: 40–70 ft, at 1250–1300 ft elev. on upper Buffalo, 950–1000 on Point Peter Mountain.

Moorefield Formation: 0–30 ft, at 950 ft on Point Peter Mountain. Shale, or silty and sandy limestone.

BOONE FORMATION: 250–390 ft. Widespread; surfaces nearly 1/3 of the Buffalo's watershed. At river level at Boxley and from the Narrows (near Woolum) to Highway 65; higher elsewhere in bluffs, slopes, ridges. Above the St. Joe Limestone Member, the Boone is light to medium gray limestone with much nodular and bedded chert; limestone weathers to rounded surfaces. St. Joe Member, 10–55 ft at base of the Boone, is thin- to thick-bedded, usually non-cherty, with many fossil crinoid fragments. Its "marker band" of red rock, 2–20 ft thick, can be seen from Boxley to Buffalo Point.

Fernvale Limestone (Ordovician): 0–50 ft, at scattered locations, Boxley to lower river. Pinkish, coarsely crystalline; many crinoid fragments.

PLATTIN LIMESTONE (Ordovician): 0–100 ft. At Carver; often exposed from river mile 100 to 146. Bluish-gray, very fine-grained. Thin beds; splits smoothly.

ST. PETER SANDSTONE (Ordovician): 10–130 ft. From Carver downriver; prominent in bluffs from Tomahawk Creek to White River. Massive-bedded. Freshly broken surfaces are white; may have crumbly, sugary texture.

EVERTON FORMATION: 250–400 ft. Widespread. Newton Sandstone Member, to 110 ft, seen in bluffs from Ponca to Carver. Limestone and especially dolomite form terraced bluffs from Gilbert to White River.

Powell Dolomite: 40–60 ft. Scattered outcrops from upper to lower river. Thin-bedded, fine-grained, yellowish-gray. Weathers to rounded ledges.

was only mildly affected by mountain building at what, in that long-ago time, was the continent's edge.

We assume that this last episode of Ozark uplift began during the Ouachita orogeny in Mid- or Late Pennsylvanian time, about 300 MYBP, and perhaps extended into or through the succeeding Permian Period. Whenever it occurred, it was not sudden; the process of uplifting may have taken tens of millions of years.

The Ozarks' uplifting resulted in very slightly inclined rock strata in the form of a shallow dome—the Ozark Dome—whose off-center core area is in the northeastern Ozarks, in the St. Francois Mountains about 75 miles southwest of St. Louis, Missouri. From that area the rock layers *dip* (slope; tilt) downward in all directions.

In northern Arkansas, farther from the core area of the Ozark Dome, the dip of rock strata decreases so that the layers are very nearly horizontal. Southward across the Buffalo River the angle of downward slope has been estimated to average only 19 minutes, about one-third of one degree, for an elevation decrease of about 29 feet per mile. At the Buffalo the land's surface is too eroded and uneven for the regional dip in underlying rock structure to be seen.

Along the Buffalo are also more localized changes in elevation of rock strata. The most pronounced changes involve the Everton and Boone Formations, alternating as the rock in view in riverside bluffs. The Everton, with its incised layers of dolomite or limestone, is visible all the way from Ponca to the White River, except where it dips out of sight below river level and is replaced in view by the Boone. Bluffs of Boone, its interbedded limestone and chert often having a rough, rubbly surface, can be seen at Camp Orr, at Erbie, and from the Narrows near Woolum to Highway 65. These "geologic lows" that bring the Boone down closer to the river may result from lows in underlying formations, possibly all the way down to the Precambrian. What originally caused these lows is not known.

The Ozarks' uplift caused rock strata to bend, to stretch, and to crack. Rock on one side of a break, or fault line, often moved downward past that on the other side. A number of these *normal faults* exist along the Buffalo. Most are hidden under loose rock and earth but one is visible as a break in the face of Welch Bluff below Pruitt (photo, opposite). And at several places along the Buffalo the Earth's crust subsided between two parallel faults (photos, page 18).

Faults, and localized vertical fractures known as *joints*, and horizontal cracks along bedding planes between rock layers, and pores in

At fault.
Welch Bluff below Pruitt is divided by a break in Earth's crust, the Buffalo River's most visible geologic fault. The downstream side of the fracture, to the right, was lifted nearly 100 feet. Tilted layers of rock at the break show the effects of drag as the two sides moved in opposition to each other. Rock close to the fault was also weakened and shattered, so that erosion proceeded more rapidly there, resulting in today's deep cut along the break.

the rock—all of these apparently provided passages for hot water deep within the Earth to carry dissolved lead and zinc minerals to areas along the Buffalo. It appears the minerals were injected at the time of the Ouachita orogeny, long before today's river and landscape took form. Near Ponca, along a zone of faulting running from southwest to northeast that has been called the Ponca lineament, lead and zinc were deposited in the Boone Formation and the overlying Batesville Sandstone. At scattered locations downriver but especially around Rush, zinc was injected into the Everton Formation, both in fractures and as extensive horizontally bedded deposits.

Geologists are puzzled about where the minerals originally came from. Some suggest the Arkansas Valley, which lay closer to the structural turmoil of the Ouachita Mountains' orogeny.

Ozark Erosion

Most if not all of today's geologic structure of the Buffalo River area—the sedimentary rock, uplifted and faulted—was completed

Jim Bluff graben.
From the Goat Trail across Big Bluff (left) to the ledge across Jim Bluff a half mile away (below), there's more than a 300-foot drop in elevation. But both ledges are at the base of the same flat-lying geologic unit, the St. Joe Limestone.

That's because Jim Bluff is within a _graben_ (German for "ditch"), a strip of Earth's crust that gradually slipped down between two parallel faults. The faults along this graben are about a quarter mile apart. The area between them, of course, slipped downward more than 300 feet.

The graben probably was created around 300 million years ago when the Ozarks area was subjected to uplift and other side effects of continental collision that raised the Ouachita Mountains to the south. But the Ozark landscape we see today has resulted from erosion during the subsequent 300 million years.

around 300 million years ago. From then on, by erosion, the rock would be worn down and shaped into today's landforms.

For a good view of the immensity of that work of erosion, walk the public trail circling the 2050-foot summit of Round Top Mountain near Jasper. Where the path extends to an overlook atop the "middle Bloyd" cap rock at the north end of the summit, look to the northeast, over a vast space to the far edge of the Buffalo's watershed (photo, page 60). There, twelve miles away, flat-topped 2213-foot Boat Mountain and several lower peaks stand along the horizon. Halfway between your viewpoint and Boat Mountain, and more than 1200 vertical feet below you, is the Buffalo River.

Barely recognizable in the distance but encircling the summit of Boat Mountain is a cliff of "middle Bloyd" sandstone—the same stuff as the cliff just below you on Round Top. But hundreds of vertical feet of solid rock that once lay between you and Boat Mountain, and beyond Boat to the distant horizon—and on far beyond that to the Missouri border and maybe even farther—have been rubbed and scraped, dissolved and broken and washed away by the forces of erosion. Boat and its sister peaks are the only surviving remnants of a once extensive higher land surface.

Erosion removed those hundreds of feet of rock during the 300 million years since the Ozark region last emerged from the sea. We are unable to describe the process, to say how the country looked 200 million years ago, or 100 million, because the physical evidence is gone. Where once was solid rock, now is thin air.

But still we wonder: How *did* the land change in that huge span of time, nearly 300 million years between creation of the youngest of the Old Rock and final shaping of this Young Landscape that we have today? When geologists believe the Colorado River carved the Grand Canyon in just 20 million years, how come the Buffalo River took 300 million to create a canyon not nearly as deep?

Geologists suggest several possibilities that may help to answer both questions. For one, more rock may have been deposited on top of the youngest rock remaining today, the Atoka Formation, and then stripped away by erosion. Such deposition and erosion of rock overlying the Atoka could have taken place during a sizeable portion of the 300-million-year time gap.

Of course, whether rock was deposited or not deposited above the Atoka Formation, there had to be an enormous volume of rock removed, both in depth and area—beds of rock that extended far to the northeast into present-day Missouri. Until weathering eventually cleared it away, this tremendous volume of rock could have underlain a high plain or tableland, scarcely affected by erosion.

At times the entire Ozark region may have seen little erosion at all. During the Permian Period, which followed the Pennsylvanian, it appears the region was a desert having little rainfall, little erosion. During the Mesozoic Era that followed—the time of dinosaurs—the region still lay at tropical or subtropical latitudes, probably with dense jungle that shielded the land from erosion by rainfall.

Even after nearly all of those 300 million years had passed since Pennsylvanian time, the details of Ozark landforms probably did not resemble ours of today. But some few million years ago—five million? eight million?—erosion may have begun to shape the Young Landscape, the Buffalo River country we know and recognize.

Many geologists believe that it took much less than five or eight million years to create today's hills and hollows, cliffs and caves. They believe the landforms we now recognize were shaped largely during the present geologic interval, the Quaternary Period (KWAH-ter-ner-ee or kwah-TERN-uh-ree), which began about two million years ago. They believe that abundant rainfall during the Quaternary helped with the work of sculpturing.

Though we have no direct clues about the sequence of erosional events that shaped the Ozarks, we do know the kinds of erosion that took place, even as they do today:

• *sheet erosion,* by heavy rainfall flowing across the ground in a thin layer (sheetwash) picking up and carrying with it small fragments of soil and rock;

• *rill erosion,* when sheetwash becomes concentrated in small channels to form tiny streams (rills);

• *downcutting*, deepening a valley by erosion of its stream bed. A swift-flowing stream in flood can carry sand, gravel, and even cobblestones and boulders that abrade and wear away bedrock in the bottom of the stream;

• *lateral erosion,* by streams eroding and undercutting their banks and valley walls;

• *headward erosion*, the slow uphill growth of a valley above its original source, through gullying, mass wasting, and sheet erosion;

• *mass wasting* (or mass movement), gravity-induced movement of bedrock, rock debris, or soil traveling downslope in bulk. Mass wasting includes creep (very slow movement) of soil or loose debris, slumping or sliding of earth and loose rock, and free falling of rock.

• *solution*, dissolving of carbonate rock (and carbonate cement when found in sandstone) by weak acid in rainwater.

Ozark Plateaus

All kinds of erosion have occurred in various combinations. And in varying degrees, too, for hard rock of course is more resistant to erosion than soft rock such as shale. On many hills and mountainsides, vertical ledges and cliffs of hard sandstone and limestone alternate with sloping terraces ("benches") that have developed on less resistant strata. Such bluff-and-bench topography is easily seen in winter, especially when benches are blanketed in snow while bluffs of hard rock are bare and appear almost black (photo, page 5).

Erosion has made the Ozarks a region having three dissected plateaus (map, page 23). "Dissected" means cut into and divided by streams. The term "plateau" is used because, over wide areas, the uplands between streams are at uniform elevations.

Actually, the highest of the Ozarks' three plateaus is made up of the relatively flat summits of the Boston Mountains. Within the area covered by the Trails Illustrated maps of the Buffalo River, for example, Boston Mountain summits are ridges often separated by valleys but of remarkably uniform elevation from one ridge to another. Over almost the entire Boston Mountain portion of the Buffalo River, which extends 25 straight-line miles from the river's headwaters downstream to Erbie, ridge elevations vary only from about 2100 to 2300 feet. The reason for this is that the ridges are capped by the massive horizontal bed of "middle Bloyd" sandstone, resistant to erosion. (Along the Buffalo's watershed divide at the headwaters, however, some areas have been even less affected by erosion. There, five inconspicuous hills rise to a little above the 2560-foot contour line and are the highest summits in the Ozarks.)

At Erbie the Buffalo River emerges from the Boston Mountains and flows eastward past their northern flank, where a series of ridges—Round Top Mountain, Judea Mountain, Lick Mountain, Horn Mountain, Point Peter Mountain—form part of the sinuous or winding Boston Mountains *escarpment,* steep mountainsides that overlook lower ridges and hollows to the north. The lower country is the Ozarks' next major division, the Springfield Plateau, extending into Missouri and named for that state's city of Springfield.

As on the Boston Mountains, for long distances the tops of ridges on the Springfield Plateau show little difference in elevation. Average elevations for Springfield ridges within about four miles' distance from the Buffalo are around 1400 to 1200 feet from Erbie to Pruitt; 1200 from Pruitt to Woolum; 900 to 950 from Woolum to Gilbert; and from 950 to 1150 from Gilbert to near the White River. Relatively low elevations from Woolum to Gilbert appear to be related to the mid-Buffalo "geologic low" mentioned earlier.

Most of the Springfield Plateau is surfaced with Mississippian-age rock of the Boone Formation. The Boone's massive limestone and especially its beds of hard, dense chert provide an erosion-resistant cap for Springfield ridges. The Boone Formation, however, is susceptible to wasting by solution, which will be described shortly.

The third plateau surface of the Ozarks, the Salem Plateau, widespread in Missouri and named for that state's town of Salem, is surfaced with Ordovician formations. On the Buffalo, the Salem exists mostly along the river's last five miles, below Cow Creek, where the Ordovician is present from river to tops of ridges. There, ridges often are capped by the massive, erosion-resistant St. Peter Sandstone.

The River's Course

Across the three Ozark plateaus—Boston Mountains, Springfield, and Salem—the Buffalo River has cut deeply, and twists and turns like the lower Mississippi. Apparently the Buffalo first established a meandering course early in its life, millions of years ago when it flowed across a level plain at about the elevation of today's Boston Mountains. These original meanders set the general pattern, but as the Buffalo cut downward it also eroded laterally, moving to one side or the other. There still were meanders, but not in the same positions as originally. For the Buffalo River, this combination of downcutting and lateral erosion has made what geologists call *ingrown meanders*, with bluffs on the outsides of the bends and gentler slopes on the insides. Along the upper river from Ponca to Erbie these twists and turns of the river are as much as 1200 feet below the plateau surface of the Boston Mountains.

While downcutting and lateral erosion have been important in shaping the Buffalo's valley, erosion of limestone by *solution* also has played a major part—with solution actually being corrosion: wearing away by chemical action. If you examine both geologic and topographic maps of the Buffalo country, you will find that where the surface rock along the river and its major tributaries is of the Boone

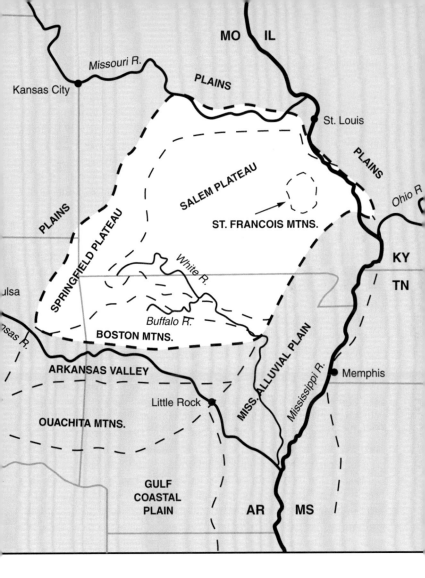

The Ozarks have four main divisions: St. Francois Mountains and the Salem, Springfield, and Boston Mountains Plateaus. The upper Buffalo is deeply entrenched in the Boston Mountains. Emerging from the mountains, the river meanders across the Springfield Plateau and, in its last miles to the White River, enters the Salem Plateau. Cutting into the surfaces of all three plateaus, the Buffalo exposes nearly twenty of the Ozarks' named rock formations created during some 180 million years.

Formation, the valley bottoms are much wider than elsewhere. The Boone's limestone was dissolved by weak carbonic acid in rainwater, and the formation's relatively thin layers of insoluble chert became isolated, broken apart, and carried away by floods. From Boxley to Ponca, on lower Richland Creek (photo, page 262), and along the Buffalo from the Narrows to Gilbert, removal of the Boone created today's open, pastoral valleys. In the seven-mile-long Boxley Valley, solution helped to remove an estimated 300 million cubic yards of the Boone Formation, in addition to erosion's taking away more than a billion yards of rock that lay above the Boone.

The River's Caves

More than half the Buffalo River's 1340-square-mile watershed is surfaced with carbonate rock. More than three-fourths of the 95,000-acre Buffalo National River has surface carbonate rock, nearly all of it in just two formations, the Everton and the Boone. In this carbonate rock—dolomite and especially limestone—solution has created hundreds of caves, most of them in the Boone Formation.

Geologists believe most of the caves have developed within the past ten million years; some think in the last two or three million. Many are still developing. As mentioned above, solution or dissolving of carbonate rock is caused by carbonic acid. Falling raindrops absorb carbon dioxide gas from the air, and as raindrops sink into the ground they absorb much more from soil gases (which are up to 10 percent carbon dioxide, from decaying organic matter and living soil organisms). The carbon dioxide combines with water to form weak carbonic acid, which dissolves calcite (limestone) or, to a lesser degree, dolomite (dolostone) as the acid water moves along joints and bedding planes in the rock. Water then carries away the dissolved material as it flows toward surface outlets (springs) at lower elevations. Thus the presence of caves indicates abundant—or at least adequate—rainfall during many, many centuries in the past.

The dissolving action that creates caves takes place primarily in the *phreatic* (FREE-at-ik) zone, the saturated region below the water table. (The water table is the upper limit or "surface" of the portion of the ground wholly saturated with water.) Eventually, as surface streams downcut and flow at lower elevations, the water table is lowered and caves may drain, becoming air-filled and thus part of the *vadose* (VAY-dos) zone above the water table. Even then, acidic rainwater in underground streams can enlarge the streams' channels. And water coming down vertical openings can create shafts and domepits.

Ground water entering a cave often drips from ceilings, oozes down walls, and trickles across floors. As each drop of water comes to rest, some of its dissolved carbon dioxide may escape to the cave's atmosphere, causing a microscopic amount of dissolved calcite to precipitate out of the water at the point of contact. Each succeeding drop adds more calcite to the earlier deposits. Over centuries and millenia, precipitated calcite builds up as *speleothems;* this name comes from Greek words meaning "cave deposits." Speleothems are the "cave formations"—stalactites, stalagmites, columns, flowstone, draperies—that most of us have seen, at least in photographs.

Interestingly, the Buffalo also has "cave formations" in broad daylight. Calcite-bearing water at times has trickled down the faces of the river's bluffs, and as the water has evaporated, the calcite has been deposited as draperies or even as stalactites on the cliffs.

Rarely, a speleothem underground will develop as (according to the most accepted theories) hydrostatic pressure forces a small amount of calcite-bearing water out of a pore in a cave wall. Carbon dioxide is lost and calcite is at first deposited around the pore. Water continues to seep through the opening and the pore becomes lengthened as an almost microscopic tube surrounded by calcite. Water continues flowing through this tube by capillary action, independent of gravity; the water may also be under slight hydrostatic pressure. Wedge-shaped calcite crystals form and stack around the end of the central canal and the speleothem usually takes an irregular form. Speleothems of this kind are called *helictites;* this name comes from "helix," or spiral. Helictites grow at all angles, even upward, to create twisted wormlike structures (photo, page 26).

Much more rarely, calcium sulfate (gypsum) speleothems will develop as flowerlike extrusions pushing out and growing from their base, or as twisted strands of fibrous threads resembling hair, or as thin needles growing upward from the floor. Speleothems of gypsum are relatively soft and extremely brittle (photo, page 126). The needles are so delicate they can be bent and broken by a person's breath. Several caves within Buffalo National River boundaries contain gypsum speleothems. Fitton Cave has all the forms described here.

Speleothems can grow—can be "alive"—only if ground water brings and releases dissolved mineral. Thus a cave or portions of a cave having moisture may have speleothems growing. A dry cave, or portions that are dry, may have them present but not growing.

Helictites.
Casting weird shadows, these rare three-inch speleothems stand on a ledge in Fitton Cave. Their name is from "helix," or spiral, because they grow in all directions as water deposits calcite at the outlets of microscopic capillary tubes.

Among spelunkers—cave explorers—some caves are famous for their speleothems. And some are notorious for their deposits of mud, tenaciously sticky or treacherously slick underfoot. The mud probably originated as an impurity in the carbonate rock whose solution created these caves; after the limestone dissolved away, fine-grained clay mud remained. Some mud has also washed in from outside.

More than 270 caves are known to exist within Buffalo National River boundaries, with "cave" being defined for the National Park Service's inventory as "a void or cavity in the earth at least 30 feet long or 30 feet deep and large enough to permit a person to enter." Fitton Cave, having the rare speleothems, is the longest—in fact, the longest known in Arkansas—with about ten miles of measured and mapped passages. The next longest (though not entirely within the National River) is Sherfield Cave, with 6666 feet. Next is John Eddings Cave, 6400 feet; next, Tom Watson Cave, 6130 feet. Behind these and a few other lengthy caves are many that are much shorter.

Among the short caves are vertical pits, at times having brief horizontal passages extending from the bottoms of their shafts. The deepest known vertical cave is named Mickey Mouse Pit. From a two-foot-diameter opening atop a wooded ridge, Mickey Mouse goes 180 feet down into the Boone Formation. Some of the other pit caves, usually shallow, are at the bottoms of funnel sinkholes.

Other Solution Features
Sinks occur where the ground has settled into voids in the underlying carbonate rock. Most of them along the Buffalo are shallow

bowl- or funnel-shaped depressions in woods or fields. There may be no visible opening at the bottom, but water poured into a sink can quickly disappear into the ground. At times sinks are aligned in rows along hidden subterranean fractures.

Areas underlain by the Boone Formation on the Springfield Plateau are often a maze of ravines or hollows, developed mainly by solution of Boone limestone along subterranean fractures and at the surface of bedrock beneath the mantle of soil and chert (photos, page 28). Buffalo National River has a number of these ravines along the trails at Tyler Bend and Buffalo Point. Highway 268, the road to Buffalo Point from Highway 14, winds along a ridge between the head ends of about a dozen of them. Beyond park boundaries both north and south of the river, Highway 14 follows ridges that overlook the head ends of many more. In any of these ravines, the abrupt head end resembles half a funnel sinkhole cut by a vertical plane.

The National River has other small valleys where it appears the roofs of long-ago caverns have fallen in. Lost Valley's narrow gorge in the Boone Formation is one such "collapse valley." The canyon of Indian Creek, developed in Boone limestone hundreds of feet thick, also must have been enlarged in the past by cave-ins after solution of the carbonate rock created immense voids having thin roofs.

Many of the Buffalo's tributary creeks flow on the surface when the creek bed is sandstone or shale, but become "sinking" or "losing" (disappearing) streams on arriving at areas of carbonate rock. Often a sinking stream will reappear as a *resurgence,* a spring, farther down the valley. A good example is Clark Creek, which ducks in and out of the Boone Formation at Lost Valley. Another is the creek that emerges from the Everton Formation's carbonate rock in the Indian Rockhouse at Buffalo Point, then immediately goes back underground, apparently to resurface at Pebble Spring, farther down the valley of Panther Creek.

Another sinking stream is the Buffalo River itself. At low flow in summer and fall, the much diminished river flows through subterranean passages in the Everton Formation or Boone Formation:

• from above the Highway 21 bridge at Boxley to the mouth of Arrington Creek, a mile down the river's surface channel;

• across Horseshoe Bend opposite Hemmed-in Hollow, leaving eight-tenths of a mile of the riverbed high and dry; and

• along a reach of the river from Woolum to White Springs, where four miles of the Buffalo become dry except for occasional pools.

Wooded hollows and pastured ridges (above) make a complex landscape on the Springfield Plateau two miles south of Gilbert. All is the work of acidic rainwater, penetrating and slowly dissolving thick beds of underlying limestone along fracture lines. Ground water carries away the dissolved rock, creating voids into which insoluble residues of chert and clay gradually settle. The result is V-bottomed ravines between rounded-off ridges. "Hills and hollers" of this sort occur on much of the Springfield, which has developed on the 300-foot-thick Boone Formation of limestone and chert.

The typical Springfield hollow or "solution valley" (below) has no sign of surface drainage. Rain sinks into fractures and moves underground toward a surface stream at lower elevation.

All of these solutional features—caves, sinks, underground streams—are components of *karst,* honeycombed landscape created by solution of carbonate rock. One unifying aspect of the Buffalo River's karst area is its complex and mostly unknown network of subterranean water channels, which often function independently of those above ground. Geologists have learned, for instance, that in the Boone limestone north of the river, water travels underground toward the Buffalo from outside the river's topographic, or "surface," watershed. This is true for waters feeding into Mill Creek, which runs to the Buffalo at Pruitt (map, page 30) and into Mitch Hill Spring, which flows into Mill Branch at Mount Hersey (photo, page 368).

After carbonate rock on or near the land's surface has been removed by solution, there usually is undissolved material left in place; this is called *regolith* (REG-uh-lith), or mantlerock. In Boone limestone country, including much of the Buffalo's watershed, regolith is broken chert in varying combination with clay that is colored rusty-red by iron oxide. In places this material is many feet deep. Even where all the Boone's gray limestone has weathered away and disappeared, broken chert rubble (local people call it flintrock) may cover the ground.

Pleistocene and Holocene

About two million years ago the present, or Quaternary, geologic period began. That also was the beginning of a subdivision of the Quaternary, the *Pleistocene* (PLYS-tuh-seen) Epoch, popularly called the Ice Age. Scientists believe that at least four times during the Pleistocene, ice sheets covered the northern United States and then melted back toward the Arctic. On one occasion the ice advanced to the Missouri River only 200 miles north of the Buffalo.

During the Pleistocene the Ozarks' climate fluctuated in response to the advance and retreat of the ice. Glacial advances undoubtedly brought lower temperatures. Their effect on rainfall is uncertain, though some geologists believe that during the past few million years there has been very heavy rainfall—enough to wash huge amounts of broken chert down the Buffalo, sharp hard rock that, as it was swept along, carved today's riverside cliffs. Abundant rainfall during the Pleistocene could also have helped to create the Buffalo's side canyons, its many caves, and other features of the Young Landscape.

The last glacial advance or series of advances—named the Wisconsin because it covered that state—began about 100,000 years

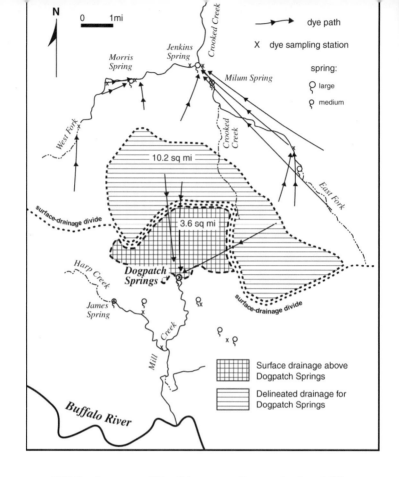

Mill Creek mystery. Why did water quality samples from Mill Creek, which flows into the Buffalo at Pruitt, have up to 25 times as much nitrate and phosphate pollution as the river itself?

Investigators then found the pollutants came from two springs flowing into the creek at the defunct Dogpatch amusement park at Marble Falls. But nitrates and phosphates usually come from farmlands, from animal manure. The watersheds of the springs were only 3.6 square miles in total area and were forested.

Just to the north, in Crooked Creek's watershed, were farms. And that area had sinkholes and losing streams. Into these the investigators poured dye, then sampled for dye appearing downstream in surface creeks and springs. As the map shows, they soon could delineate a 10.2-square-mile area—within Crooked Creek's surface watershed—from which ground water flows under the surface-drainage divide to the Dogpatch springs.

before the present (YBP) and may have reached its maximum as recently as 18,000 YBP. After 14,000 YBP the climate rapidly became warmer, the ice retreated, and by 10,000 YBP, Ozark temperatures, rainfall, and vegetative cover were much like they are today. The *Holocene,* or Recent, Epoch of geologic time had begun.

"Recent" is merely a label for these last 10,000 years when global climate has generally resembled that of today. There have been climatic swings of moisture and temperature but never the prolonged cold of the Pleistocene. From about 8000 to 5000 YBP the average temperature was higher than at present and drought prevailed over much of North America; this period is known as the *Hypsithermal,* or time of elevated temperatures.

Investigators in the 1980s learned some of the Buffalo's Holocene geology as they worked on archeological digs at Boxley, Erbie, and Rush. At that time they obtained radiocarbon dates for wood and charcoal found with Native American artifacts in deeply buried layers of flood plain sediment and near the surface of river terraces. From their findings and from work by others, we know that in the past 10,000 years the Buffalo River has deposited sediments across much of its valley floor, has changed its course in many areas, and in places has eroded downward more than ten feet.

At some locations the downcutting appears to have been rapid and nearly vertical. In most cases, though, the river eroded more slowly and shifted sidewise at the same time as it downcut. Cutting downward and sideways into a new and lower channel, it often left an earlier flood plain stranded at higher elevation and began to develop another flood plain along the new stream channel. During floods the new flood plain was covered by sediment as *overbank deposits.* Today many of the Buffalo's bottomlands have one or more abandoned flood plains recognizable as *stream terraces,* present as broad, nearly level steps above the river (photo, page 60).

The oldest, highest terraces along the Buffalo's narrow valley were deposited during the late Pleistocene, considerably more than 10,000 YBP. The lower terraces are always younger than higher terraces because the river is continually downcutting. At the Erbie campground the river moved to its present location between 7000 and 2000 YBP and began depositing sediment on its present flood plain between 5000 and 2000 YBP. At the Rush campground the river moved into its present channel about 2000 YBP and since that time has deposited about six and a half feet of overbank sediment on its

Record breaker. Floodwaters rush under the deck of the Highway 14 bridge, 60 feet above the river's normal level. Soon the Buffalo will crest at 65 feet—over the roadway.

This record-breaking flood on December 3, 1982, happened after eight inches of rain fell on the already saturated upper watershed.

Floods. Headwaters of the Buffalo and its largest tributaries are in the Boston Mountains and run off steep slopes of impervious sandstone and shale. The river's upper watershed also is fan-shaped—in a short reach of the main stream, several tributaries feed in. Mainly for these reasons, heavy rain causes flashy runoff. The Buffalo's fast rises also subside rapidly.

On the average a flood large enough to run at least bank-full and scour the river's channel occurs each 16 months (one and one-third years). At about half bank-full, hydrologists believe, the river undergoes "flow reversal." During lower flow the water is faster in riffles, slower in pools, but in higher flow the current moves faster in the pools, slower in the riffles. Floodwaters then scour the bottoms of the pools, washing out soft sediments, and deposit material at the riffles.

Scouring is most intense on the outsides of the bends. Within the bends the current is slower and drops its burden, depositing silt on flood plains and coarser material on gravel bars. Larger rocks normally settle first, at the heads of bars. Downstream, smaller rocks and finally sand may be deposited. But currents are capricious, and bars vary in their distribution of material.

During a succession of floods, water flow and landforms develop a harmony of balance. But if a disturbance occurs—a fallen tree blocks a riffle—the channel can be narrowed so the riffle washes out. The river's balance also can be upset by disturbances in the tributaries. Streambed gravel mining, for example, can release silt that moves down into the Buffalo, where it settles, smothering aquatic creatures that live on the bottom. Less desirable forms of life can then multiply and live in the sediment.

present flood plain. Though these changes cannot be dated precisely, their implication is clear: the Buffalo has shaped much of its valley bottom since the end of the Pleistocene.

At Rush in the past 2000 years the river has moved more than 300 feet across the narrow valley floor. At Erbie in 4000 years it has moved nearly 600 feet northward. At Boxley 5000 YBP the river ran close to where the Baptist church now stands, but since that time it has by stages migrated eastward more than 2000 feet, all the way across the valley. One or more of the Boxley Valley's ancient river alignments, known as *paleochannels,* can be seen today as swales across bottomlands along Highway 43 south of Ponca.

Today's Happenings

Compared with the whole of geologic time, the Holocene or Recent Epoch is but the blink of an eye. Against 10,000 years of Holocene, our human life spans are brief indeed. Occasionally, though, we may witness a major geologic event—for example the Buffalo's record-breaking flood of December 3, 1982, when the river rose more than 60 feet at Highway 14 (photo, opposite), wrecked the campground at Buffalo Point, dumped two feet of sand on campsites at Rush, and backed water more than a mile up Rush Creek.

Save for the rare cloudburst like that in 1982, today's rainfall is moderate, about 45 inches a year, not enough to bring sudden big changes to the landscape. Instead we have small, seemingly insignificant happenings: creep, slump, slide. We see where parts of the riverbank have sloughed off; we notice where pieces of bluff have fallen down. We remember only that from the 1970s to the 1990s the river below Ponca modified its channel and so bypassed two favorite canoeing hazards (Gray Rock; Wrecking Rock) but in the 1990s altered course and ran headlong onto a new peril (Killer Rock).

But minor changes can add up to major changes, even in our times. The middle river, with its broader valley and erodible bottomlands of deep alluvial soil, seems especially vulnerable. Consider:

• At Cash Bluff (river mile 77.6) a river channel in 1975 had become a dry wash by the 1990s, and at Love Hensley Bluff (mile 86.2) a dry wash had become the river's main channel.

• At the High Bank below Woolum (mile 80) since 1910, when the first detailed map was drawn, the river has moved a quarter mile north. During the 1990s the Buffalo chose to swing far around a hazardous ledge drop known by floaters as the Pouroff or Little Niagara.

• At Arnold Island (mile 91.1) after 1910 the river's meander channel west of the island was gradually replaced by a cutoff on the east. By the year 2000 the Buffalo had piled gravel across the upper end of the older channel and made it a backwater, like an oxbow lake. (But in 2001 some gravel washed out and canoers floated through.)

We talk about changes less easy to verify. Old-timers mourn the loss of fishing holes—filled up with gravel, they say—and assert that the river now is wider and shallower. We speculate that such changes originated with row-crop farming, with gully erosion of plowed fields that sent much soil and rock into the Buffalo.

We also speculate that gravel bars along the river are becoming smaller, or at least are becoming covered with bushes and trees. Aerial photographs made in 1941 show extensive bare gravel bars; photos made in the 1990s show these same areas covered with vegetation. Is vegetation taking hold because the bars are becoming more stable, perhaps because less gravel is washing onto them and smothering plant seedlings, perhaps because there is less erosion of fields once plowed but now woodland or pasture?

There may be truth in these opinions—a wider, shallower river now, with more stable (if not smaller) gravel bars. Or we may be just talking. Whatever is true, absolute proof is not yet with us.

We can keep talking, though, and keep an eye on the river. With attention and effort we can make new discoveries.

Watercolors. The blue-green or green color of the Buffalo River is caused by suspended particles in the water scattering light of different wavelengths. The most intense blue comes when particles are approximately the same size as the wavelength of blue light, 5/100,000 centimeter. Clay particles produce a blue color, dissolved organic matter imparts a yellow color, and blue and yellow together make green. A higher percentage of blue with green will result in blue-green, or turquoise. If clay particles are larger, the river only appears milky white or gray.

Particles may be composed of silica, calcium carbonate, iron oxides, clay, organic matter, or simply rock that has been ground up by stream action and weathering processes. Suspended matter increases when runoff is greater during the wet months, November through April, and the color of the river is more noticeable then. In summer, when the river is low, the water may appear clear, although reflections from streamside trees may impart a green color and the sky may be reflected as blue.

LIFE

Buffalo River discoveries?

They're as likely to be about life as about land, as much about animals and plants as about cliffs and caves.

And sometimes a bit offbeat. You may discover life in a piece of rock. You pick up a piece of broken limestone, look at it, and see something that resembles a little clam—a fossil (photo, page 37).

But that isn't the whole story. *All* of your piece of limestone came from living things. A small part of it may be shells or skeletons of sea animals. Most is made of the limy secretions of marine algae. So it is also for dolomite, the other type of carbonate rock.

That still isn't the entire story. You may next pick up a piece of chert, and it too is made mostly of things once alive, the siliceous (silica-bearing) skeletons of microscopic marine animals.

So consider this: Most of the rock that you see along the Buffalo River is limestone, dolomite, or chert. And almost all of it was created by extremely large numbers of extremely small living things.

Practically all the nonmicroscopic, visible fossils in Buffalo River rock are of marine animals. There were primitive kinds of plants, too, in those times several hundred million years ago, but they left very little fossil evidence. Occasionally an exposed face of Ordovician Period carbonate rock includes a stromatolite (stroh-MAT-o-lite), where layers of limy sediment accumulated on a mounded colony of shallow-water algae (photo, page 38). Sometimes Pennsylvanian-aged sandstone contains fossilized pieces of a *Lepidodendron* scale tree (LEP-i-doh-DEN-dron; photo, page 59). Scale trees are long extinct, but they had vascular tissue for conducting water and nutrients throughout the plant, just as most plants that we are familiar with have today.

Origins of Today's Life Forms

Vascular land-based plants, including ferns, horsetails, and cone-bearing species, originated in the Devonian Period around 380 MYBP (million years before the present; see time scale, page 9). Non-vascular forms—algae, fungi, liverworts, mosses, club mosses—appeared even earlier. If any of these plants existed in the Buffalo

River Ozarks during the Paleozoic Era, they could well have been removed by erosion. And, of course, 300 million years of erosion removed evidence of plants that lived from the Pennsylvanian Period to nearly the present time.

At a few localities in the surrounding region, however, historical ecologists have uncovered enticing clues to what existed at somewhat later times. Excavating at a site in west Tennessee, they found plant fossils from the late Cretaceous Period, about 70 MYBP, as flowering plants were beginning to develop. There they identified earlier forms of beech, buckthorn, cottonwood, hackberry, magnolia, maple, oak, persimmon, sassafras, walnut, and willow. All were species that could survive at midrange temperatures and would develop into the northern temperate deciduous forests, reaching around the globe and including the region we now call the Ozarks.

At a higher level of the west Tennessee excavation that dated from the early Tertiary Period, about 50 MYBP, the scientists recovered plant remains showing rapid advancement toward modern flowering species. Here the plant list included ash, bumelia, dogwood, hickory, Hercules'-club, pawpaw, pipe-vine, redbud, sweet gum, wahoo, and yellowwood. Most of these species have southern affinities; others found at this level of the excavation were related to present-day subtropical or tropical plants. Absent from this assortment were cool-weather species found at the site's lower level from Cretaceous time: beech, cottonwood, maple, oak, willow. Thus the investigators saw the Tertiary assemblage of plants as evidence of development by that time of a warm-moist, mixed deciduous forest.

Ice Age Plant Life

Warm climate appears to have continued and become even warmer through the Tertiary until about 25 MYBP. Then a gradual cooling began, a trend that culminated about 2 MYBP with the onset of the Pleistocene Epoch, or Ice Age, when continental glaciers advanced at least four times into the northern United States. Apparently each glacial stage lasted 100,000 years or longer, and each interglacial stage having warmer weather did also. Early in the Pleistocene the ice advanced to the northern edge of the Ozarks in Missouri, 200 air-line miles north of the Buffalo River. Later the ice pushed into southern Illinois about 250 miles northeast of the Buffalo. Toward the end, about 18,000 YBP (years before the present), the Wisconsin stage of glacial advance reached south-central Illinois 300 miles northeast of

Fossils. This brachiopod (BRAY-ke-oh-pod) was a marine animal having a soft body within a shell consisting of two halves. It resembled a clam, but its two half-shells were not alike in size or shape. "Brakes" lived attached to the sea floor by a flexible stalk. Very abundant during the Paleozoic Era, they gradually gave way to clams.

Above the penny is a faint whitish, fanlike network, the imprint of bryozoans, tiny aquatic animals that grew by budding into colonies, fan-shaped fronds cemented to an object on the bottom of the sea. These almost microscopic "moss animals" secreted calcite skeletal masses or crusts of lacy design.

the river. At these times the local climate of course became cooler.

We have no direct evidence of Pleistocene vegetation along the Buffalo but again can draw a few inferences from discoveries made elsewhere in deposits of fossil plant pollen. Such deposits are rare, usually occurring in ancient beds of peat trapped in sinkhole ponds, spring basins, or stream sediments. For example, at one such site near Toronto, Canada, scientists recovered fossil remains from a warm interglacial stage more than 100,000 YBP and learned they came from deciduous plant species. These included black locust, Osage orange, and sweet gum, which now exist only well to the south of Toronto. They also found that as the ice sheet had again advanced toward Toronto, the broad-leaved plants were replaced by spruce, fir, and hemlock. The findings from this Canadian site suggest that within one interglacial interval during the Pleistocene, the Buffalo River forest, too, could have changed in makeup from "northern" to "southern" and then back again as its plant species

Stromatolites, wavy laminations in Everton carbonate rock (beside the Mines Trail at Rush), were formed by mats of blue-green algae in shallow water. Particles of calcium carbonate sifted down, collected on the algae, and the algae grew upward to stay above the sediment. More sediment accumulated, algae grew on that layer and trapped still more sediment…and laminations developed.

Crinoids on the bottom of a shallow sea during the Mississippian Period resembled flowers on tall stems. Each "flower"— shown here in a museum diorama—was actually an animal related to today's starfishes. The head had organs to gather and digest food and to excrete wastes.

Crinoid heads were soft and very few have been preserved as fossils. The stems, broken into disks, are the most abundant fossils along the Buffalo (photo, page 55).

spread or died back in response to warmer or cooler temperatures.

From a site close to Memphis, Tennessee—about 180 miles from the Buffalo—investigators recovered pollen radiocarbon-dated at around 18,000 YBP, at the last glacial maximum when ice extended into south-central Illinois about 300 miles north of Memphis. The plants here were from a broad-leaved forest of such species as alder, ash, elm, hazel, hornbeam, oak, and willow. These were in marked contrast to northern pine and spruce that grew at the same time in southern Missouri, not far away. At Memphis, the scientists had found a *refugium* (place of refuge) where deciduous species had survived while much of the region was taken over by evergreens that today are confined to the northern United States and Canada.

Did parts of the Buffalo River valley, in the southern Ozarks and sheltered from blasts of cold air coming off the ice sheet, also serve as refugia for deciduous plants? Did cool-temperate species such as beech and maple survive in places along the Buffalo through the Ice Age? We do not know, for no fossil pollen deposits have been discovered along or near the river. Some scientists believe, though, that Ice Age refugia for at least the Ozarks' present warm-temperate species were located much nearer the Gulf Coast. At that time, 18,000 YBP during the glacial maximum, isolated patches of northern spruce grew as far south as Baton Rouge, Louisiana.

But northern and southern species often coexisted. Next to northern spruce and larch at Baton Rouge, there were bald cypress trees. Close to the sixty-percent-spruce forests in southeastern Missouri and northeastern Arkansas, there was that grove of deciduous trees near Memphis. Again, we wonder: What did the Buffalo River's woodlands look like during the Ice Age?

Ice Age Animals

Our uncertain knowledge of the Buffalo's Pleistocene plant life is based mostly on what existed outside the Ozarks. Knowledge of the animals, however, comes from evidence closer at hand. Caves in the Ozarks—including four in the Buffalo's own watershed—have provided stable, tomblike environments for preservation of faunal remains. Animals lived in these sheltered sites, or were carried or dragged in by predators intent on eating them. Investigators today have discovered their bones, teeth, tracks, and other clues.

What a strange mix of species! These Ice Age animals of the Ozarks included grazers, browsers, and grubbers: ground sloths,

Fearsome beast.
The saber-toothed cat roamed the Buffalo area during the Pleistocene. Big as an African lion and having daggerlike front teeth for slashing at prey, it was a match for even the largest animal, such as a mastodon. About 12,000 years ago the saber-toothed cat became extinct, perhaps because a warming climate wiped out its prey species.

tapirs, peccaries, horses of a species now extinct, armadillos three times as big as the present kind, and mastodons larger than elephants. And there were predators, meat eaters: jaguars, cheetahs, dire wolves the size of timber wolves, saber-toothed cats as large as African lions. And real lions of an American species, and black bears of an extinct form. And, most fearsome of all, giant short-faced bears over five feet tall at the shoulder and weighing up to 1500 pounds.

With these were smaller animals, down to the size of shrews. Among the small species, especially, were "northern" and "southern" ones that today live far apart. The Buffalo watershed's Conard Fissure and Peccary Cave both yielded such combinations of animal remains. These included species such as the eastern chipmunk, which lives here today, but also the least chipmunk (today in the West and in Canada), tapir (whose extant species are in Central and South America), musk ox (with an extant relative in the Far North), red squirrel (now farther north, into Canada and Alaska), and the yellow-cheeked vole (now only in northwestern Canada and Alaska).

The remains from Peccary Cave have been dated at about 16,000 YBP, around the time of the last glacial maximum. Some researchers believe the Ozarks at that time were a refugium for boreal (northern) animals that moved south, ahead of the advancing ice sheet. The region's summers apparently were much cooler than today, with more moisture. But winters were not extremely cold, so that year-round temperatures were more uniform. "Southern" species also could live here, in what is believed to have been a parkland of spruce and pine, grassy areas, and perhaps some deciduous trees.

But then the climate became warmer and the ice sheet retreated northward. Warming proceeded more rapidly. The region's temperatures began to show seasonal extremes of hot and cold. Plants and animals both became stressed. It appears that forage plants died off, and probably the large animals were especially sensitive to the high temperatures. Whatever the circumstances, around 12,000 YBP there occurred a series of die-offs of Pleistocene animals. Most of the large ones became extinct.

The die-offs occurred at about the same time over much of the world, which suggests that climatic change was the basic cause. Grazing or browsing species may have starved—and so also their predators such as the dire wolf, saber-toothed cat, and short-faced bear. Ancient man, dispersing across North America at around that time, could have hunted and killed the last of the big Pleistocene animals, completing the extinctions.

Holocene

About 16,000 YBP when the climate began to become warmer, the front of the ice retreated toward the north—at first gradually, then rapidly. Broad-leaved vegetation spread northward. (Some zoologists speculate that oak trees were helped ahead by blue jays. They say that the birds could have carried acorns beyond the forest's front edge to bury them out of reach of pilfering squirrels.)

By 10,000 YBP, at the beginning of the Holocene, or Recent, Epoch, a deciduous forest apparently had taken over the Buffalo area, with warm-temperate oaks and hickories dominant. Most of the other plants and animals we know today may also have become established—that is, if the climate had become reasonably humid. We know more about the climate of a later interval, from about 8000 to 5000 YBP, because pollens from that time that have been recovered at several sites surrounding the Buffalo area indicate prolonged dryness. Presumably drought also meant warmth; as mentioned in the preceding chapter, this Middle Holocene interval is known as the Hypsithermal, the time of elevated temperature.

During the Hypsithermal, as archeologists working in Missouri have learned, land snails and mussels diminished, indicating reduced rainfall and streamflow. (At the Conard Fissure, excavators found remains of ground squirrels, antelope, and other "western" animals, further evidence of less rainfall at some period.) The western Ozarks became open prairie. Along the Buffalo, woodlands on south- and west-facing slopes probably died out, to be replaced by annual weedy plants, prairie grasses, and drought-resistant trees such as blackjack oak and Ashe's juniper. Prairies or savannas may have developed on ridge tops. Forest cover survived only along perennial streams and in shaded ravines.

After 5000 YBP the climate moderated. With increased rainfall, deciduous forests spread north and westward, gradually replacing prairie. Warm-temperate species from the south, including shortleaf pine, colonized the Ozarks. The end result of this last, most recent transition was today's assemblage of plants and animals.

A Home for Many Species

As the Ozarks' climate changed over thousands of years, the region experienced distinct variations: cool-moist, cool-dry, warm-moist, warm-dry. Cool-moist climate tended to favor northern species such as spruce, which spread southward in front of slowly advancing Pleistocene ice sheets. Cool-dry favored northern pine and oak. Warm-moist encouraged colonization by magnolias, sweet gum, and spicebush; warm-dry worked to the advantage of dryland oaks, hickories, and grasses.

Climate changed, but its geographic effects were uneven. During intervals of dryness, species such as beech and magnolia survived in *microhabitats* having favorable *microclimates*—small areas still meeting their requirements for additional moisture. Similarly, during lengthy periods of humid climate, dryland plants such as Ashe's juniper and prickly pear (both of which probably had arrived during the dry Hypsithermal) survived in their own ecologic niches, sunny south-facing hillsides.

Moist slopes, sunny hillsides, and a variety of other kinds of habitats allowed special situations to develop. For example, the Ozarks have provided refugia in cool hollows and the mouths of caves for a *relict* (surviving) population of the wood frog, which must have colonized the region during the Ice Age and now is separated from its main population in the northeastern United States and across Canada. Other relicts along the Buffalo include small numbers of two western plants, a native mallow now 175 miles from the nearest of its species in Oklahoma, and a yellow monkey flower 700 miles from the nearest of its kind in Colorado. Their seed may have come to the Buffalo country via Native American trade routes. More probably, these plants spread to the Ozarks during a lengthy period of widespread favorable climate.

These species that are discontinuous, or *disjunct*, from their main populations also include several kinds of trees in the Ozarks. Basswood, beech, black locust, smoke tree, umbrella magnolia, and yellowwood all are widely separated from the same species living east of the Mississippi River. The past two centuries of land clearing along the Mississippi Valley may have increased the separation, but it probably began much earlier, perhaps during the Pleistocene when the Mississippi became a sprawling flood of glacial meltwater, its valley a near desert, whipped by cold winds. Or perhaps the trees' original range was divided even earlier, around 65 million years ago, when today's lower Mississippi Valley was an arm of the sea.

Other special situations include those for *endemic*, or local, species that apparently evolved and live in one specific area, sometimes quite small. A pretty blue wildflower, Moore's delphinium, is related to three other species of larkspur in Arkansas but is different in form from the others and is known from only four counties, including Newton and Searcy Counties on the Buffalo. Even more localized are two endemic species of millipedes, each known from only one locality near the Buffalo in Newton County, one of those places being Hemmed-in Hollow.

We can wonder, too, how long the endemics have existed. Did they evolve only in the last 10,000 years after the climate and the forest became similar to today's? Or did they develop before the Ice Age and then survive in Ozark refugia, or in places farther south?

Because the Ozarks provide a variety of habitats in a transition zone between the northern and southern United States, a large number of species live here. The region is at the northwestern limit of many species from the southeast, also at the southwestern limit of many others from the northeast. And there are many other plants and animals at the western limit of ranges that cover practically all the eastern United States. (Of all species present in the Ozarks, only a relative few also exist farther west in the drier, less varied habitats of the prairies and Great Plains.) Thus the Buffalo is home for northern red oak on shadier north-facing slopes, and for southern red oak on south-facing exposures where higher temperatures occur. In cooler places are northeastern species: sugar maple and Ohio buckeye. In warmer locations are southeastern ones: sweet gum and red buckeye.

Animals, being mobile, are not as limited in habitat requirements as plants. Still, the Indiana bat (an endangered species, by the way) is near the southwest end of its range, and the gray bat (also endangered) is near the west end. The southern bog lemming and the prairie vole are at or near the southern limits of their living spaces, the fulvous harvest mouse and brush mouse near the northern limits. The Swainson's warbler nests in cane thickets along the river, here at the northwestern limit of its range. The Harris' sparrow is found along the Buffalo near the eastern limit of its winter range in the southern plains. In other words, each of these species is faced with some direction in which under present conditions it can go no farther, but the Ozarks provide acceptable living space.

Most of the other Ozark animals at limits of their ranges are small ones—bats, mice, shrews. But even a number of the larger, far ranging ones colonized the Ozarks only after habitats became friendly. In terms of origins or affinities, the beaver is northern, the opossum and armadillo are southern, the woodchuck is eastern, the coyote is western. Other Buffalo River animals are so widespread across America that their places of origin are not obvious; these include the black bear, bobcat, mink, muskrat, raccoon, red fox, river otter, striped skunk, weasel, and white-tailed deer. After the Ice Age these widespread species must have entered the Ozarks from the east and southeast, as they exist also in the eastern deciduous forests.

Plant Communities

Today's Buffalo River forest is a mosaic or patchwork of many combinations of trees, shrubs, and herbaceous (nonwoody) plants. At any given locality the vegetation often forms a *community*, a recognizable combination of species that tends to repeat itself at other localities having the same type of site. It can be interesting—entertaining, actually—to travel through the woods and recognize the various communities of plants.

Several influences govern what grows at any particular site:

• *Moisture* is probably the most important one. Some plants require *hydric* (wet) conditions; water willow, for example, lives in shallow parts of the river (photo, page 160). Many other species prefer *mesic* (moderately moist) areas. Still others thrive in *xeric* (from the Greek *xeros*, dry) places such as south or west slopes.

• *Soil* (or substrate, the mineral material on which soil forms) is another major influence. Soils vary from wet to dry, fine-grained to coarse-grained, and basic (alkaline) to neutral to acidic. Buffalo River soils in sandstone, shale, or chert areas, generally in the uplands, are acidic and are low in important plant nutrients, primarily calcium and magnesium. Some species, however, including black gum, huckleberry, mountain azalea, red maple, and shortleaf pine, grow only on acid soils. Basic, or alkaline, soils occur on limestone or dolomite of the river's bluffs and have their own dependent vegetation such as Ashe's juniper and smoke tree. Soils of lower slopes and bottomlands are basic or neutral, rich in nutrients and moisture, and are home to many plant species.

• *Topography* (slope and exposure) can cause extremes in temperature and moisture. North- and east-facing slopes, protected from hot summer sun and from drying winds from the southwest, are cooler and damper than south- or west-facing ones. Ravines are less exposed to sun and wind than are ridges.

• *Other plants* (all kinds, including fungi and bacteria) can affect the makeup of the forest. Tall trees may form a dense canopy or overstory so that many understory plants—saplings, shrubs—cannot grow. This changes when a large canopy tree falls down; opportunistic plants then quickly begin to fill the vacant space.

• *Animals* (all kinds, including birds, insects, and earthworms) assist plants by transporting seeds and pollen and by working the soil. Or destroy plants by chewing them up (gypsy moths; oak borers) or cutting them down (beavers, humans).

We can devise a list of the Buffalo River's types of forest communities, classifying them according to landforms and "indicator" plants of easy-to-identify species that set each community apart from the others. Indicator plants often are specialists that require specific conditions of moisture, soil, topography, or air quality. (Many other species, of course, are generalists that can live under a variety of conditions; see photos, page 46.)

Here are recognizable forest communities along the Buffalo:

• *Gravel bars* often have Ward's willow, sandbar willow, and sycamores growing in thickets that are aligned with the flow of floodwaters. The trees' roots, which help to stabilize their part of the gravel bar, reach down to the water table so that the trees live in a hydric environment. Other areas of the bar are xeric, sunbaked but having a variety of smaller plants, mostly annual weeds.

• *Riverbanks* have several easily identified kinds of trees: black

A specialist...

Old-man's-beard hangs in gray-green wisps from junipers on the river's bluffs. Highly sensitive to air pollution, it dies off when air quality is poor.

Old-man's-beard is not "Spanish moss," as some people imagine, but instead is a species of lichen, depending on the tree for support and food.

Scientists know old-man's-beard as *Usnea longissima* and Spanish moss as *Tillandsia usneoides.* In both their names: *usne,* from the Arabic *ushnah,* moss.

...and a generalist.

Growing in a variety of places, poison ivy with its three leaves is the area's most widespread ground-cover vine. In the woods it also climbs trees; in open areas it can stand up like a shrub. It may be plentiful because free-ranging hogs once rooted almost everywhere, disturbing the soil—and ivy spreads onto disturbed ground.

The plant here with five leaves is often mistaken for poison ivy but is woodbine, or Virginia creeper, a harmless vine.

willow, catalpa, cottonwood, river birch, silver maple, and sycamore. Many have roots that reach down to water. The Buffalo's *riparian* (rih-PAIR-e-un, riverside) areas also support large patches of switch cane (also called giant cane, river cane, or pipe cane), which provide a special kind of habitat for wildlife.

• *Flood plains* are low areas behind the riverbanks that may be flooded at least once a year. Here are the riverbank species named above. Also present are American elm, box elder, green ash, and sweet gum. (And growing on moist alluvial soil, stinging nettle!)

• *Stream terraces* along the river and its larger tributaries have alluvial soil like the soil of flood plains but stand a bit higher in elevation. Wooded terraces are apt to have most of the flood plain trees along with black walnut, ironwood (blue beech; "muscle tree"), leatherwood, pawpaw, and spicebush. These rich, moist woodlands often have fine displays of wildflowers blooming in early-spring sunshine before the trees leaf out.

• *Bluffs and glades* harbor plants that can live on, or close to, bedrock. Most of the bluffs overlooking the river are limestone or dolomite, with pockets of soil influenced by the carbonate rock. Here is the only habitat acceptable to Ashe's juniper (photo, page 158) and to smoke tree, which has been called one of the rarest American trees. The glades, occurring as treeless or sparsely wooded areas along midbluff terraces and bluff tops, are usually xeric and have a variable mix of vegetation that may include both Ashe's juniper and eastern red cedar, and gum bumelia, or chittim-wood. Here too are patches of little bluestem and other prairie grasses, and Indian paintbrush and other prairie wildflowers. (These prairie plants may have arrived during the Hypsithermal, or earlier during an interglacial stage of the Ice Age. Today there is no true prairie along the Buffalo.) Where soil is very thin on top of bedrock, there are lichens, dryland ferns, and other small plants—attractive but fragile and easily crushed underfoot.

• *Beech woods* are found only in the Boston Mountains of the upper Buffalo, mainly at moist sites on north- and northeast-facing slopes. One of these places is Lost Valley, where the presence of beech and other "eastern" trees—basswood, cucumber magnolia, sugar maple, yellowwood—reminds plant geographers of woodlands in parts of the southern Appalachians, including the cove-hardwood forests of the Great Smokies. Plant scientists believe the Buffalo River's beech groves are surviving remnants of the beech forests of an earlier time when climate was more humid, wetter than it is today.

• *Mixed hardwoods* occupy what biologists call an *ecotone*, or transition zone, in limited areas between the Buffalo's lowland communities and the drier oak-hickory and oak-pine forests upslope. This habitat type may include many of the lowland hardwoods and some of the upland oaks and hickories, but rarely is any single species dominant. Mixed hardwoods are found usually in moist ravines close to the river and have a fairly well defined upper limit, where oaks and hickories begin to predominate.

• *Oak-hickory forest*, on soils varying from acidic to basic, covers much more area along the Buffalo and throughout the Ozarks than any other forest type. Oaks are dominant (most numerous) and hickories are more or less abundant. Oak-hickory woodlands can be divided into subtypes based on which species of oak predominate. White oak, combined with northern red oak, may prevail on north- or east-facing slopes having the most moisture. Black oak will occupy areas on ridges and upper east and west slopes, sometimes in combination with post oak, which signals a drier environment. Black oak or black oak–hickory is considered the most widespread of the oak-hickory subtypes. In still drier areas on south slopes, southern red oak may become dominant in combination with post oak and blackjack oak.

• *Oak-pine forest* occurs in patches on acid soils derived from sandstone, shale, or chert and having southern or western exposure. Shortleaf pines can form almost pure stands, but usually are mixed with upland oaks dominating and pines occupying 10 to 40 percent of the total forest composition (photo, page 370).

• *Post oak woodland* occupies drier areas having thin, rocky soil on south- or west-facing hillsides, and on top of Boston Mountain ridges. In these open woods, stunted post oaks can be predominant and blackjack oak may also be present. On the scale of moist to dry, post oak woods are next to open glades at the dry end.

• *Old fields* are former pastures or croplands that are reverting to forest. Even in 2002 as this book was written, a few woodland openings along the Buffalo remained as evidence of fields abandoned in the 1930s or earlier when unsuccessful homesteaders moved away.

But also by 2002, other old fields had been rapidly taken over by shrubbery and trees. After the National Park Service acquired land in the 1970s, for example, fields no longer in agricultural use began to undergo a series of fairly predictable replacements of plants and animals, a process called *old-field succession*. The first stage in the process is an invasion of annual, and then perennial, weedy plants. After a few years the field can become overgrown with blackberry, sumac, or hawthorn, and young trees such as persimmon, red cedar, sassafras, and winged elm. In time the cedars, especially, overtop and shade out grasses and shrubs. After more time, hardwoods may overtop and suppress the shade-intolerant cedars. In most areas, after a century or two, the successional climax may be reached with development of an old-growth hardwood forest with a full complement of woodland animals. Toward the end, even mature pines give way to the more aggressive hardwoods. If spared a major ecological disaster, the climax forest of hardwoods may persist indefinitely, for its plants and animals will be replaced by others of the same kinds.

A Look at Biodiversity

As described here, the climax hardwood forest has attained a point of balance with no important changes occurring. Such an ideal state may seldom be reached along the Buffalo, given all the possibilities for both human-caused and natural disasters: windstorms, wildfire, drought, insects, disease. These *disturbances*, as ecologists call them, can suddenly change or interrupt many aspects of forest succession and allow it to shape the forest community in new ways. In fact, a case can be made that the *lack* of one significant disturbance, wildfire, because of fire prevention through the twentieth century, has changed the Buffalo's forest ecosystem in many ways from what it was in the time of the Native Americans or of the first European-American settlers.

Aside from whatever has happened in the past, we now know that forest succession gradually increases the number of species in plant and animal communities, and ecologists regard that as a good thing. Complexity, biodiversity, the presence of many species rather than few, makes for greater ecological stability. The greatest biodiversity may in fact be attained not in the climax forest but in woodlands at the midrange of succession toward the climax—likely the state of the Buffalo River's woodlands now and for some time to come.

As this was written, the red oak borer had killed thousands of oaks along the Buffalo and hundreds of thousands on the adjacent Ozark National Forest. Biodiversity, the presence of many other, healthy species, assures that vacant spaces will quickly be filled. Thus the forested shorelands of the Buffalo are buffered from ecological upsets. The river's large number of plant and animal species is being maintained and enhanced by old-field succession, by protection of the river and shorelands from human disturbances, and importantly, by having a great variety of usable habitats.

How many kinds—or species—are there of plants and animals?

We do not know. By one estimate the Buffalo River's "macro" plants, large enough for us to see easily, number about 1200 species, counting the lichens, the visible fungi such as mushrooms, and more than 600 known kinds of green plants. Now we should also include the "micro" plants—fungi, algae, bacteria—but we have no idea how many kinds there are. The known species of microscopic plants that probably exist along the Buffalo may number over 2000. The ones not yet known to science—undiscovered, unclassified—may total that many more. (After all, about 500 species of bacteria are said to reside just in the human mouth.)

Among the animals, there are about 280 visible known vertebrate species, ranging in size from elk to minnows. These are the mammals, nesting birds (but not migrants or wintering species), reptiles, amphibians, and fishes. Beyond those are many others that we see but that are less known, or perhaps not even known to science. These others include representatives of the earthworms, tapeworms, snails, mussels, spiders, ticks, centipedes, and millipedes. A biologist found 46 kinds of mollusks—snails and their relatives—when searching one hillside at the Buffalo. Within the largest category of species, the insects, the Buffalo may have nearly 100 kinds of butterflies alone. Finally, to all the insects and other visible animals that might be found along the river, add a presently unknown number of forms of microscopic water-dwelling or parasitic animals called protozoa.

Sorting those many species of animals and plants by size of individuals, it is obvious that the smaller they are, the more species there are. The largest animals are of only five kinds: elk, deer, bear, coyote, and the elusive cougar (or six, counting the feral pig but still not counting domestic livestock). The next group, in size from raccoon and turkey vulture to squirrel, numbers about 40 species. The next, including rats, mice, songbirds, frogs, the smaller fishes, and so on, comes to about 230 species. Then, the insects and other animals of comparable size must number in the thousands, and microscopic animals in thousands more. And among the plants, the Buffalo's trees include about 80 species, the shrubs more than 100, the smaller

Twig girdler.

What cut off those limbs—the ones about as thick as a pencil, lying on the ground along the trail?

The culprit is the twig girdler, *Oncideres cingulata*, a beetle about one-half to three-quarters of an inch long. In early fall the adult female chews a groove around one of these small limbs, girdling it. Between the groove and the end of the limb she gnaws tiny cuts through the bark and lays eggs in the scars.

Soon the eggs hatch. The larvae cannot develop in healthy sap-wood—but that's taken care of because girdling kills the limb. Nor can the larvae live if the wood dries out—but the limb breaks off and falls to the ground, where there's more likely to be enough moisture. As one expert has said, it's a clever act but hard on trees. Especially hickories, which twig girdlers prefer. But also persimmon, oak, elm, gum, and other species.

Through the following seasons the larvae tunnel into and consume wood in the limb, developing as plump white grubs. The next July they pupate within the limb and in late summer and early fall they emerge as adults. The adults mate and the males die. Before dying also, the females girdle twigs and lay eggs to launch another life cycle.

Finally, consider this: Entomologists estimate there are five to ten *thousand* species of beetles along the Buffalo River, and each species has its own special plan for living and reproducing.

plants around 1000, the microscopic plants maybe several thousand.

So it is also with population counts for individual species: Smaller plants and animals exist in far greater numbers than larger ones. There are exceptional cases where a rare species of plant or animal exists in very small numbers, but among the Buffalo's animals, for example, we can easily imagine a population of ten bears along the river, or ten dozen raccoons, or ten thousand white-footed mice, or ten million black ants, or tens of billions of one kind of bacterium.

Smaller organisms, then, occur both in greater numbers of species and in greater numbers of individuals for each species. And as suggested already, the smaller they are, the less we know about them. Except for ones such as butterflies, katydids, ladybugs, and fireflies, we are ignorant or even contemptuous of the insects, for example, usually considering them a nuisance. As for the microscopic life forms—well, we can't see them. Out of sight, out of mind.

Facts of Life

Before looking at Buffalo River ecosystems, we need to recall some basic biology—that all living things can be divided into three categories:

• Green plants are the *producers*. They use radiant energy from the sun to convert carbon dioxide from the air—along with water and a few dissolved minerals from the soil—into food, fiber, and fuel. As a byproduct, plants supply the atmosphere with its oxygen.

• All animals are the *consumers*. The plant eaters are known as *herbivores*. The meat eaters, or *carnivores,* consume many of the herbivores and in some cases other carnivores. *Omnivores*, including human beings, consume both plants and animals.

• Scavengers, or *decomposers,* break down dead plants and animals—and wastes from living ones—and return the organic matter to the environment for reuse. These armies of organisms include animals such as vultures, earthworms, and many kinds of insects. Especially they include bacteria and fungi from the plant kingdom.

The idea of animals eating plants, and those animals being eaten in turn by other animals, is the concept of *food chains*. One type of food chain involves decomposers eating dead plants and animals; in this *detritus* (de-TRY-tus), or debris, food chain, the decomposers may be eaten in turn by other organisms.

The Most Complex Ecosystem

The role of insects, fungi, and bacteria as decomposers is vital. Grinding, chewing, dissolving, and digesting, they recycle Earth's limited supplies of carbon, hydrogen, oxygen, nitrogen, calcium, iron, phosphorus, and sulfur needed by all living things. Without the decomposers, life along the Buffalo River or anywhere else would be impossible.

Most decomposers live in, or on, the soil. Theirs has been called the most complex ecosystem on Earth. A few of the mammals (mice, moles, shrews) are a part of it, but essentially all decomposition is the work of great numbers of smaller *(Continued on page 61)*

Some Evidence
from Deep Time **LAND**

Creation of the ages, Painted Bluff at Buffalo Point displays two
of the Buffalo's major rock formations. The cliff's lower half is
Everton limestone, deposited in a shallow sea and then exposed
above water level. Erosion then shaped its uneven surface. Later
the sea returned and piled sand on the limestone; this eventually
became the St. Peter Sandstone, the upper half of the bluff.

Geologists call the wavy boundary between the limestone and
the sandstone an *unconformity,* marking the episode of erosion
between times of deposition. This uneven line between the
Everton Formation and the St. Peter Sandstone is the most easily
recognized of many geologic unconformities along the Buffalo.

A streak of red rock along Jim Bluff (above) is the "marker band" of the St. Joe Limestone, at the base of the Boone Formation. Hundreds of feet thick, the Boone ranks with the Everton Formation for dominant presence along the river.

Pieces of limestone from the upper Boone (right, under the penny) and the red St. Joe have buttonlike segments of crinoid stems, the river's most abundant fossils.

Everton or Boone rock is present in each of the river's bluffs.

The Everton Formation, to 400 feet thick, is seen in most of the river's cliffs. At Roark Bluff at Steel Creek (opposite), the water-streaked Newton Sandstone Member of the Everton looms high above. Below the Newton is gray, rough-surfaced Everton limestone. A narrow shelf marks the boundary between the two units.

Limestone and chert in alternating layers make up much of the Boone Formation. Where limestone dissolves away, chert layers break up and create rough surfaces, as at Blue Bluff (left) above Tyler Bend.

Limestone is dissolved by weak carbonic acid in rainwater. Dissolving (or *solution*) formed an "eye socket" at Skull Bluff above Woolum (right). Rain from the ground's surface may have come down a joint in the rock.

Boone chert takes varied forms. In this group of broken pieces, the ones at upper left and top are smooth, dense flint. At lower left is softer, porous rock. The piece at right has fossil imprints, including brachiopods. Where weathering has removed Boone limestone, the land is often littered with broken rubble of insoluble Boone chert. Buffalo residents call it "flintrock."

The Boone Formation can be pure, gray limestone, or it can be alternating layers of limestone and chert.

Layers of sandstone were deposited above the Boone Formation. In side canyons along the upper river, including Lost Valley, Boone limestone dissolved away and overlying beds of sandstone lost support and broke up. Over the ages, pieces of this less soluble sandstone have moved down to the bottoms of these canyons.

One of these pieces is beside the trail into Lost Valley (right). This boulder has been rounded off by breaking and weathering. Its edges and corners were less resistant to physical impact and offered more surface area for attack by acids from mosses and lichens.

The sandstones have few fossils—but one that is easily recognized is the diamond imprint from *Lepidodendron,* or scale-tree. This fossil is found in sandstones on the upper slopes of the Boston Mountains.

Above the Boone Formation: layers of shale and sandstone.

A slack-jawed monster (opposite) stands alone near McFerrin Point, long after its surrounding "middle Bloyd" sandstone has broken up and weathered away. On the highest ridges facing the river, this middle unit of the Bloyd Formation also forms rimrock cliffs—a prominent feature of the Boston Mountains.

From Round Top Mountain (above) near Jasper to flat-topped
Boat Mountain on the horizon 12 miles across the Buffalo River
valley, erosion during the last 300 million years has taken away
as much as 1000 feet of solid rock. Erosion also removed huge
amounts of rock to create the Springfield Plateau, now stretching
many miles past Boat Mountain to beyond the far horizon.

Erosion continues. Boxley's two-story community building
(below) stands on a *stream terrace,* a former flood plain of the
Buffalo. Around 10,000 years ago the river cut downward and
created a lower terrace, today the foreground field. Later the
Buffalo downcut again and moved all the way across the valley.

species with immense numbers of individuals, from insects down to bacteria that can be seen only with a powerful microscope. Just to list the *types* of organisms is daunting: ants, tiny spiders, beetles and their larvae, fly larvae (maggots) and wood lice. Earthworms, millipedes, centipedes, grubs and slugs and snails, springtails, mites, nematodes, pill bugs, sow bugs, pseudoscorpions, daddy longlegs. Molds and other fungi. Bacteria. Protozoa. Nearly all of these organisms are active in the detritus food chain, eating the forest's debris and then being eaten by other organisms.

Most of the life of the forest floor is composed of immense numbers of bacteria, protozoa, nematodes, and other microscopic creatures. A teaspoon of fertile soil can contain five billion of them. A pound of forest litter may contain over 30 billion bacteria. An acre of fertile woodland topsoil along the Buffalo may have five tons of very small below-ground soil organisms, including 5000 pounds of living and dead bacteria and over 1000 pounds of fungi. On that acre, the total number of these little plants and animals may be several million times the total of the more than six billion people on Earth.

That acre of Buffalo River woodland may have more than 4000 pounds per year of accumulating waste from plants and animals—an average of 2000 to 3000 pounds per year of leaf fall, plus fallen tree limbs (but not counting entire trees that fall), plus remains and wastes of animals. But at about the same rate as it falls, this waste is processed by the decomposers. The woodland acre can have as many as millions of earthworms, capable of eating up to 18 tons of debris in a year. The acre's good topsoil can contain 40 tons of organic matter from plants and animals, constantly being recycled through plants and animals. Most of the recycling is done by decomposers; they consume more than 90 percent of plant growth, while the creatures that eat living plant material consume less than 10 percent.

One obvious example of the work of decomposers is a rotting log on the forest floor. When the tree falls to the ground, it is attacked by battalions of shallow-boring grubs, deeper borers, termites, beetles, ants, centipedes, snails, slugs, and other small creatures—all busily eating, chewing the dead wood, cutting it into tiny shreds. Fungi spread over parts of the log, and the wood softens. Bacteria multiply and help break down the carcass. Where the rotting wood touches the moist ground, earthworms find bits that they carry into their tunnels, soften them in their digestive tracts, and pass out the remains.

The fungi grow on the dead wood and bark, and their excretions become a nursery for multiplying bacteria. Nematodes—tiny worms—multiply, eat, and excrete. Spiders and centipedes prey on the decomposers, and in turn add excretions to the growing accumulation of humus. The chief decomposers, however, are the many species of fungi and bacteria, scavenging the remains of the log and decomposing the lignin—the material that binds the wood fibers—so that the log breaks into smaller pieces more easily attacked by insects. The end result of all this work by hordes of organisms is that the log is converted into fine humus, organic material to become part of the underlying soil.

Decomposition involves so many species in so many interrelationships that it is impossible to describe them all—or even to know everything that goes on. But we do know some of the benefits:

• *Trash removal.* The rotting log, leaves, and limbs, dead animals and animal wastes—all disappear. Imagine what the forest would be like in only a few years if all that stuff were *not* removed by decomposers. (Fire also can remove forest debris and release nutrients, but fire is often not as acceptable as letting decomposers do their work.)

• *Soil conditioning.* Addition of decayed organic material, with churning and mixing by decomposing organisms, improves soil tex-

---

Oh, scat! A raccoon, probably, left its six-inch feces (opposite) on a ledge 700 feet inside Fitton Cave, thus contributing to the cave's ecosystem. Fungi of at least three kinds are feeding on decomposing vegetable matter in the scat. The cave's high humidity and moderate, constant temperature are ideal for this flourishing mix of fungi at all stages of growth.

What happens next? Probably small cave-adapted organisms—insects, millipedes—will feed on the fungi. Then small predators such as spiders or salamanders will feed on those organisms. The energy that came from plants is being, and will be, passed from the raccoon to other species.

The whole ecosystem is dependent on vegetable and animal matter washed or carried in from the outside. Food for cave species is therefore sparse, but a surprising number of life forms are able to exist at least part of the time in cave environments. Biologist G. O. Graening has identified 192 animal species that spend at least part of their lives in Buffalo River caves. Almost all are small, insect-sized. Almost all spend time outside. But 17 of these species are land-based *troglobites* or aquatic *stygobites,* which are adapted to spending their entire lives in total darkness.

ture and composition so that it can protect plant roots, retain moisture, and serve as a better growing medium for plant seedlings.

• *Nutrient cycling.* As mentioned above, decomposers convert the useful elements that are tied up in dead plants and animals to forms that can be absorbed by plants for their life processes. Decay bacteria return carbon dioxide to the atmosphere, where it again is available for intake by growing plants. Bacteria and fungi convert sulfur from forms that cannot be utilized to sulfates that can be absorbed and processed by green plants. Fungal *mycelia*—microscopic rootlike threads that extend everywhere through the soil—absorb, hold, and pass on nutrients to green plants. Mycelia of some fungi attach themselves to the tiny feeder roots of plants such as pine trees and beech trees, and the mycelia and plant roots exchange nutrients that each needs—a mutually beneficial relationship.

So life's activities in the soil continue, ignored by and almost unknown to us. Biologists, however, have come to realize that soil organisms are "the little things that run the world." Those little things go about their business unaware of us, not needing us except as we may protect them from destruction. If we human beings were to disappear from Earth, the soil creatures would go on without missing a beat and actually would benefit from the absence of human disturbance. Could we do the same, if all life in the soil were extinguished?

Life in the River

The Buffalo River has its own ecosystem, rivaling the soil's system for diversity of species and intensity of action. As in every other ecosystem, plants capture the sun's energy and then transfer it to animals (diagram, page 67). And as in other systems, smaller organisms far outnumber the larger ones.

But the river ecosystem is unlike any land-based one. Its supporting medium is moving water, conveying nutrients to organisms that live downstream. There is no longtime succession of species as in a maturing forest, only fast changes in populations and combinations of short-lived, rapidly reproducing life forms.

Life in the river is affected by many factors, including:

• daily and seasonal variations in temperature of the water and intensity of light;

• water level and flow rate, low to high, drought to flood (here are probably the most important influences on river organisms);

• water chemistry (for example, the Buffalo's headwaters, which flow over sandstone and shale, are acidic, but the lower river, on limestone and dolomite, is less so);

• levels of dissolved oxygen and levels and nature of nutrients;

• the shape and composition of the streambed, whether bedrock, boulders, gravel, sand, or silt;

• any human disturbance of streambed or watershed; and

• interactions among the river's own plants and animals (for instance, an excess of predators can affect species all the way down the food chain).

Despite those many chances for upsets, the river's biological communities tend to maintain dynamic equilibrium; population losses can be rapidly replaced. Biologists also see a "river continuum" of gradual but predictable changes in the mix of aquatic species, depending on changes in habitat and food availability as the river proceeds downstream from the headwaters. Though the continuum idea works better for the Buffalo's pool-dwelling species than for the ones along most of the river in riffles, the continuum helps explain the differences in life forms from the Buffalo's headwaters to the middle reaches and to the lower part of the river.

At its headwaters the Buffalo is narrow and lined with trees, too shady for aquatic plants such as algae, but it receives nutrient input from leaves, limbs, and other plant debris that fall or wash into the river. Aquatic insects and insect larvae act as "shredders," beginning to reduce coarse pieces of fallen leaves to tiny fragments. Fungi and bacteria digest and further reduce the fragments and also break down wood detritus. The end product is what aquatic biologists call fine particulate organic matter, or FPOM, which drifts downriver to be eaten by "collectors" such as the larvae of mayflies and midges and reduced to still finer particles.

Downstream the Buffalo becomes much wider, more open to the sun. Detritus from shoreland vegetation is much less important as a nutrient source, though FPOM drifting down from the headwaters is food for "filterer" organisms such as mussels. Having more sunlight, microscopic algae called diatoms grow abundantly. Together with bacterial matter, protozoa, and other organisms, diatom species produce living *biofilm* that coats every underwater surface. We know biofilm as slimy gel, slippery underfoot, but it is the most important food source for "grazers" or "scrapers," many of the small aquatic animals that themselves range down to microscopic size. These organisms are in turn important food for larger species. The river's middle reaches, sunlit and relatively shallow and with a variety of habitats, are likely to have the largest, most diverse number of species, most productive of life.

Farther downstream the Buffalo's pools become deeper, with less sunlight penetrating to the bottom, and algal production falls off. The smaller organisms here are mainly "collectors" of FPOM arriving from farther up the river and from tributaries. The species here can be completely different from those of the upper river. Here as elsewhere, the small animals become food for larger ones.

The Buffalo supports many hundreds of living species, with much yet to be learned about them. Cataloging the river's algae, biologists in the 1970s identified 274 kinds, including more than 100 species of diatoms. They also found that the microscopic diatoms, attached to rocks or drifting in suspension, are a more important food source than the "mossy" algal species that we see and recognize.

Algae vary greatly with the seasons. In the wintertime diatoms are dominant, colonizing sunny parts of the stream and forming golden brown gelatinous biofilm on rocks. After silt-laden spring floods scour away the diatoms, another coating of them may develop, but of different species. In summer, at dry parts of the riverbed above Ponca, red algae remain dormant but alive. Downriver, microscopic algae attach to submerged parts of water willow; one species forms visible colonies. Microscopic plankton grows profusely in still water. Riffles support different species that hide below rocks.

So important in the Buffalo's ecosystem, algae are essentially invisible to us. If we notice at all, algae are annoying—the slippery stuff underfoot, or the *Spirogyra* whose slimy green filaments form dense tufts that local swimmers call "moss" (or "pond scum" if it floats on the surface).

Of the river organisms that feed on algae, other living plants, and detritus, almost all are small, from microscopic up to the size of minnows and crayfish. These consumers of plant food, along with a few carnivorous species, are of many kinds: microscopic or nearly microscopic rotifers, protozoa, bryozoans, copepods, water fleas, water mites, and bacteria. Freshwater sponges. Aquatic earthworms, sow bugs, and snails. Flatworms, nematodes. Crayfish, mussels. Scuds and sideswimmers, called "freshwater shrimp." And among the insects, larvae of damselflies, dragonflies, and dobsonflies, and larvae and adults of water beetles. And on the water surface, water striders and whirligig beetles.

Consumer species differ from pool to riffle. In pools, worms and insect larvae live in the bottom sediments; other species live on or among water plants in the shallows. In the riffles are mostly insect larvae, with each kind having its own way of dealing with fast water. Some are adapted to swim. Many hide in crevices under or between rocks. Others, with flat or streamlined bodies, live within the thin layer of calm water that occurs at the surfaces of stream-swept rocks, or stay in pockets of still water on the downstream sides. Usually these insect larvae are equipped with claws or grapples, friction pads, suckers, sticky secretions, or protective cases to help them hang on and wait for the current to bring particles of food.

Nearly all the insect larvae are of species that spend their adult lives out of water. And perhaps most important among the insects are four major groups of larvae: caddisflies, mayflies, stoneflies, and true flies. Members of these four groups are known to have specific tolerances for pollution. The larvae of true flies—including crane flies, black flies, and midges—are the most tolerant of pollution. Mayflies can stand a small degree of water impurity, caddisflies tolerate less than mayflies, and stoneflies generally cannot stand any at all. Mayflies, caddisflies, and stoneflies (illustration, page 68) are indicators of highest stream quality; they are the models for flies that fly fishermen tie. The relative abundance of members of the four

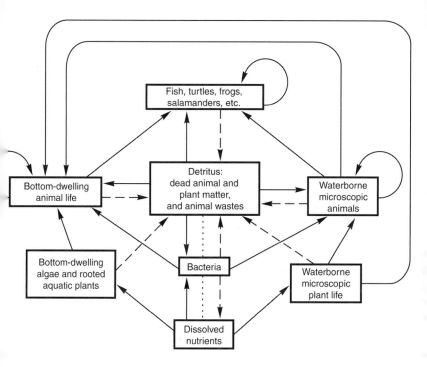

Major aspects of the Buffalo's aquatic food web are shown in
this diagram. (It applies as well to most freshwater ecosystems.)
Solid lines with arrowheads indicate what is used as food by
organisms higher up on the food chain. **Circled arrows** that both
begin and end at the three categories of animals indicate that
some species in each category feed on other animals of the same
category. **Dashed lines** show that organisms, as they die or
excrete, contribute to detritus or dissolved nutrients that are recycled into the food web. The **dotted line** indicates that some of
the detritus is converted by bacterial action to dissolved nutrients.

   Bottom-dwelling animal life includes insects and insect larvae
—and microscopic forms as well—that live on or in silt or mud,
on rocks, or on underwater parts of aquatic plants. *Bottom-
dwelling algae* include those—mainly diatoms—attached to or
living on silt, rocks, underwater parts of aquatic plants, or
aquatic animals. In this diagram, *bacteria* also includes molds.

   Waterborne microscopic animals (zooplankton) float or drift.
This category also includes miofauna—mid-size species somewhat larger than microscopic. *Waterborne microscopic plant life*
(phytoplankton) floats or drifts suspended on or beneath the
surface of the water. It, too, plays a part in the food web.

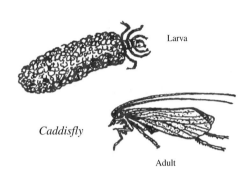

Larva

Caddisfly

Adult

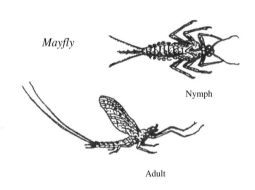

Mayfly

Nymph

Adult

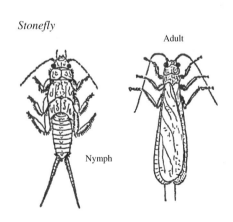

Stonefly

Adult

Nymph

Prime indicators of high quality streams are 3 large groups of insect species: the caddisflies, mayflies, and stoneflies. Many species of each are found in the Buffalo River. Illustrations here are not of local types but show their general characteristics.

Caddisfly: Caterpillar-like larva, up to 1"; 6 hooked legs in front, 2 hooks at back; many build portable protective cases of bits of wood, leaves, sand, or pebbles. Adult mothlike, usually dull-colored; long thread-like antennae; soft hairy wings folded tentlike over the insect's back.

Mayfly: Nymph up to 1"; single claw on each foot; usually 3 tails; leaflike gills along abdomen. Adult delicate with gauzy iridescent wings held vertically; long front legs point forward when insect is at rest.

Stonefly: Nymph 1/2" to 1-1/2"; 2 claws on each foot; usually 2 tails; smooth rear part of body. Adult looks much like nymph, but with 4 wings, clear and membranous, folded back over the body when at rest.

groups taken in samples from a stream such as the Buffalo can indicate any problems with pollution. If true flies have become more abundant in relation to larvae of the other three groups, the water is likely to be degraded.

Biologists collected and cataloged these organisms along the Buffalo for several seasons into the mid-1990s, identifying 30 kinds of mayflies, 30 of stoneflies, 35 of caddisflies, and 72 of true flies. Though the species count for true flies appears high, the overall balance among the four groups indicated a river having very high water quality. Of all streams in the United States sampled up to that time, only one in Georgia had a greater number of species of caddisflies.

In all, the biologists identified 232 species of macroinvertebrates ("macro" meaning visible to the naked eye and "invertebrates" meaning creatures not having a backbone, such as worms, insects, snails, crayfish, and mussels). Two or three species are known only from the Buffalo River watershed. The 232 species were from 50 families, including 45 families of insects, which were by far the most dominant group. All are eaten by predators farther up the river's food chains, including the fishes.

In truth, the smallmouth bass is much less a factor in the Buffalo's ecological stability than the aquatic insects and the still smaller organisms that feed the macroinvertebrates.

The River's Fishes

All the Buffalo's fishes are predators except perhaps for three small species that subsist on plant life. (A biologist describes one of these, the largescale stoneroller, which grows to about eight inches long, as "an herbivorous cow, grazing on algae.") In general, the small fishes consume macroinvertebrates, while the large ones eat both macros and small fishes.

Exactly how many kinds of fishes are there?

We don't know. Ichthyologists—fish biologists—collecting fish along the Buffalo from the 1930s to 1992 identified 67 species, including one hybrid sunfish. They found most species time after time at many sampling sites along the river. They found others at only one or two sites, or failed to find them during one or more rounds of sampling. The uncommon or no-show fishes amounted to about 16 species; some of them may no longer exist today along the Buffalo. People with the National Park Service have simply stated there are "fifty-nine recognized native fish species."

Fewer than a dozen species—the ones we call bass, sunfish, cat-fish, bluegill, and crappie—are considered game fish, to be caught for fun or frying pan. All these are among the 26 species that grow to ten inches or longer. The other 41 species, less than ten inches in size, include 29 forage or bait types under six inches full grown.

We tend to call any of these small fishes "minnows." Biologists, however, regard minnows as only certain species belonging to the minnow and carp family, *Cyprinidae*, a large family that in the Buffalo River includes fish with names identifying them as minnows, shiners, chubs, dace, or stonerollers. The small fishes also include representatives of other families: madtoms, studfish, topminnows, silversides, sculpins, perch, and, finally, darters of ten different kinds in the Buffalo (photo, page 161).

Among the 67 fish species collected from the river, about 13 are extremely adaptable, able to live both in clear upland streams including the Buffalo and in turbid lowland waters beyond the Ozarks. These include longnose gar and largemouth bass, green sunfish and bluegill, black bullhead and yellow bullhead, channel catfish and flathead catfish. At the other extreme are about 20 species, most of them small, that are so sensitive to pollution that they are restricted to the uplands. Actually that sensitivity, especially to silt and turbidity, applies to most of the Buffalo's fish species. Only the most adaptable ones—gar, catfish—can live long in muddy water.

Seven of the small species are endemic to the Interior Highlands (Ozarks and Ouachita Mountains) or to only the Ozarks: duskystripe shiner, wedgespot shiner, Ozark madtom, Ozark sculpin, Ozark bass, Arkansas saddled darter, and stippled darter. Three more—the checkered madtom, Ozark shiner, and yoke darter—are endemic to only the White River and its tributaries.

There also are eight disjunct species, small fishes whose populations in the Ozarks are split off from populations of the same species east of the Mississippi River. We can wonder how and when these populations became separated.

People sometimes guess that *all* the Buffalo's warm-water fish are isolated, cut off from the rest of the world by the White River's cold-water releases from Bull Shoals and Norfork Dams. Biologists, however, have collected some fifty of the Buffalo's fish species in the cold reach of the White from Bull Shoals downstream to Sylamore Creek. Presumably the collecting was done at times during winter cold spells when water from the dams could actually have been warmer than inflow from the Buffalo. The White in summer rarely becomes warmer than 72 to 75 degrees F and few native fish can survive in such cold water during the breeding season. Bass, for example, require summer temperatures 75 degrees F or higher.

The White's cold waters may have kept a few unwanted exotic species from traveling up the White and into the Buffalo. One time a biologist found common carp (originally from Asia and now widespread in the United States) in the White at the Buffalo's inflow, but none have been collected since.

At other times biologists have found new kinds of fish in the Buffalo itself. Golden shiners, probably leftover bait dumped by fishermen, turned up in several samples. The golden shiner tolerates pollution and turbidity but is not adapted to the clear, fast-moving water of the Buffalo, and it failed to show in subsequent collections. On the other hand, redear sunfish and black crappie, lowland game fishes that may have arrived among other species stocked by the Arkansas Game and Fish Commission in the 1970s, have been able to survive. In 1992 a biologist found crappie at several sampling sites located from the upper to the lower river.

And one winter in the 1990s a fisherman pulled one of the White River's hatchery-raised rainbow trout from the Buffalo at Tyler Bend, 59 miles above the river's confluence with the White. Rainbows have an inborn desire to travel and can tolerate water temperatures up to 77 degrees F for extended periods, so these wandering trout surely have gone even farther and stayed longer than any quick midwinter swim up the river to Tyler Bend.

Human-Caused Disturbances

Rainbows were stocked in the White River when cold water released from deep behind the dams caused habitat changes, doing away with spawning areas for warm-water fishes. The Buffalo and its shorelands also have undergone changes as people have farmed, logged, and mined, and built homes, roads, and campgrounds. Habitat for native plants and animals has diminished. On disturbed areas, space for non-native species has expanded.

Most obviously, natural habitat changed as the original forest was cut down. Woodland animals disappeared; open-country species took their places. Birdwatchers see the difference: forest-dwelling birds including cerulean warblers, wood thrushes, and Acadian flycatchers are replaced by open-habitat species such as bluebirds, mockingbirds, and meadowlarks. Robins have increased along the Buffalo so that in winter great flocks of more than 50,000 birds may gather to roost in sheltering thickets of cedars. About 1960, as more land was cleared, armadillos (photo, page 164), coyotes, and roadrunners spread into the Buffalo area from open country farther west.

Much less obvious are any changes in the river's aquatic species caused by gravel and fine sediments washed into the river during the more than 150 years since first settlement. Changes here are in fact barely knowable because there is no record of aquatic life forms in, say, the early nineteenth century. Even less known are the changes that human activity has caused in microscopic life in the soil. Since the first European settlers, there probably have been die-offs of native micro life and replacement by immigrant species. We do know that our common earthworm was introduced from Europe.

We know that humans killed off the largest wild animals. Buffalo were present until hunters did them in; the last one in Searcy County is said to have been killed in 1840. Elk were here, too, but they also were easy targets and probably were gone before 1840. Gray wolves were present in the early 1800s but then rapidly disappeared. The native red wolf lasted much longer, but in the 1920s its numbers were much reduced by bounty hunting. Then, around 1960, Arkansas Game and Fish Commission and U.S. Fish and Wildlife Service trappers focused on wolves and coyotes, and the red wolf was driven to near extinction. The few remaining wolves probably interbred with coyotes and with free-running dogs, and today occur only in wolf-coyote and wolf-dog-coyote hybrids, with coyotes genetically dominant. Coyotes had spread into Arkansas in the 1940s, benefiting from land clearing and not having competition from wolves.

People have done away with species. They have introduced others, sometimes with unexpectedly bad results. In the 1930s agricultural and wildlife agencies promoted multiflora rose, from Asia, as wildlife cover and as a natural hedge. The numerous rose hips were eaten by birds, which spread the seeds to places where the rosebushes became a pest. In the 1940s kudzu, another Asian import, was introduced for erosion control along road cuts—but then it was learned the fast-growing vines smothered other vegetation. Common privet from Europe and mimosa trees and Japanese honeysuckle from Asia were imported as ornamentals but soon escaped from gardens. Honeysuckle is shade tolerant and now covers old homesites and the surrounding woods where birds have spread its seeds.

Most pasture grasses, including fescue, sericea lespedeza, and bermuda grass, were brought from Europe or Asia, and they crowd out native grasses and are nearly impossible to eliminate. Many of the roadside wildflowers, including chickory, ox-eye daisy, and Queen Anne's lace, were imported from Europe and are here to stay.

We have imported and released undesirable species of birds, including the English sparrow (from Europe, 1852; introduced in Memphis, Tennessee, 1871) and the starling (to New York City about 1890; to northwest Arkansas by 1930). The rock dove, the cooing domestic pigeon of city buildings and Buffalo River cliffs, also came from Europe. Like other exotic, alien species, these birds have found niches they could occupy in local ecosystems and have thrived.

We have unwittingly unleashed plant diseases. Chestnut blight, apparently from Asiatic chestnut trees planted in New York City in 1904, first killed off American chestnuts in the eastern United States, then by the late 1930s spread to Arkansas and attacked a closely related tree, the Ozark chinquapin. Chestnut blight is a fungus that blocks the flow of moisture from the tree's roots, killing the tree above ground level but often allowing the roots to resprout; the sprouts are then killed in turn by the blight. Through the 1990s there were still decay-resistant carcasses of large chinquapins lying on the ground in Buffalo River woodlands.

From bad experiences we try to learn. In 1994 the imported gypsy moth—whose caterpillars have defoliated and killed thousands of acres of hardwoods in the Northeast—was discovered near the upper Buffalo. Biologists arranged to have the affected area sprayed, then set traps to see if any moths had survived and dispersed. A few had, in fact, but to the year 2002 there were no serious outbreaks.

Restorations and Recoveries

More encouraging are the efforts of wildlife agencies to restore populations of animals that along the Buffalo had been nearly or totally wiped out. As early as 1873, Arkansas citizens began the slow process of restoring game and fish populations by enacting and enforcing protective laws. But that wasn't enough; species had to be reintroduced—restocked where they had been wholly eliminated. In most cases restocking has been successful, and in a few other instances depleted species have been able to recover on their own.

Beaver were eliminated throughout Arkansas by 1900. Today they are present along the Buffalo and its tributaries, and visitors often find beaver-cut trees and limbs though the animals themselves stay out of sight. Restocking in Arkansas began in the 1940s.

Black bear were so reduced in numbers that all through the 1950s only three bears were seen anywhere in the Buffalo's watershed. Again they are present; people may see a bear, or bear sign. These animals are descended from bears the Arkansas Game and Fish Commission brought from northern Minnesota and Canada and released on the Ozark National Forest between 1959 and 1968.

Elk were eliminated throughout Arkansas by the 1840s; these were of the eastern subspecies, which later became extinct throughout its range. Today elk graze in plain view of travelers along Highway 43 near Ponca (photo, page 164). Between 1981 and 1986 the Game and Fish Commission brought 112 elk of the Rocky Mountain subspecies from Colorado and western Nebraska and released them at sites along the upper Buffalo. Despite poaching, and deaths from a parasitic brainworm transmitted from white-tailed deer, the elk herd had by the year 2000 increased to some 400 animals. Most had remained along the upper and middle river. In 1998 an annual regulated hunt was begun to control the size of the herd.

White-tailed deer were practically gone in Arkansas by 1920. As recently as the 1960s deer were scarce along the Buffalo, but by the 1990s their numbers had increased to such an extent that park visitors saw them in both the backcountry and developed areas. Restocking had begun in Arkansas in the 1930s and 1940s.

Turkey were all but exterminated in the Ozarks by 1910. Today backcountry visitors can see wild turkeys—at times a dozen or more at once in winter, when the birds gather in flocks. Restocking began in Arkansas in 1932.

By the 1960s bald eagles were disappearing, as DDT residues in their bodies prevented development of shells of their eggs. DDT was banned, eagle populations began to increase, and since the 1980s migrating eagles have wintered along the Buffalo. Hoping to restore a population of year-round residents, Game and Fish biologists and the National Park Service during the summers of 1982, 1983, and 1984 placed five orphaned eagle chicks in cages overlooking the river, fed them fish twice a day, and assumed they would become used to the river as their home territory. The birds were released when able to fly, but they failed to remain in the area to nest.

Ruffed grouse were not seen in northwestern Arkansas after the 1880s. In 1981 the Game and Fish Commission and the Park Service

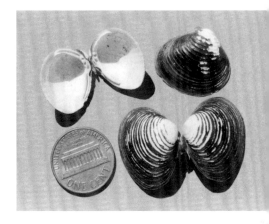

The invasive clam is an inch and a quarter wide when full grown. It reproduces rapidly and its shells, like these, can be found on many of the river's gravel bars.

Invasive species.

The Asian clam, *Corbicula fluminea,* was first found in Washington State in 1938 and in Arkansas in 1970. *Corbicula* now lives in nearly every major watershed in the U.S. The clam is sold as fish bait and its free-swimming microscopic larvae may travel in minnow buckets, so it may have been introduced on the Buffalo River by fishermen dumping unused bait. The clam's eggs or larvae may also attach themselves to boats and be carried upstream. Today *Corbicula* is present in every reach of the Buffalo except the headwaters.

Unlike the larvae of native mussels, larvae of the Asian clam do not need to attach themselves to fish as intermediate hosts. The clam produces a high number of fast-growing, fertile off-spring, adapted to a variety of habitats and tolerant of a wide range of water temperatures and of some degree of disturbance or pollution. In some eastern streams *Corbicula* occurs in the thousands per square meter.

During several years around 2000, Buffalo River researchers saw increasing densities of the clam, with the highest concentrations where habitat was disturbed and water quality degraded. Increasing densities appeared also to be related to declines in the diversity of surrounding communities of macroinvertebrates. The clam's effect on the Buffalo's native mussels was uncertain, but in other rivers the effect has been adverse because the clams compete with native bottom dwellers for limited food resources.

Besides its use as fish bait, the clam provides food for several species of native fish, as well as for flatworms, crayfish, wading birds, and raccoons. And, of course, the presence of large numbers of Asian clams serves as a useful signal of pollution.

released 50 birds along the Buffalo. Ruffed grouse require dense stands of saplings or brush for protection against predators, mainly hawks and owls. Because of inadequate habitat or for other reasons, the reintroduced grouse failed to take hold within Buffalo National River, though they may have done so within the Ozark National Forest at the river's headwaters.

River otter were trapped to near extinction by 1900. But today's Buffalo River canoer may see an otter, or possibly more than one, in the river or along its banks. There was no restocking program, but after 1970 the population of otters gradually increased.

The mountain lion (or catamount, cougar, panther, or puma) for a long time was at or near extinction in Arkansas from being aggressively hunted, or from scarcity of its main prey, white-tailed deer. With larger deer populations have come reports of the presence of mountain lions. Beginning in the 1990s, hikers have reported evidence of cougars along the Buffalo, though the animals themselves are secretive and stay out of sight. Whether these reported cougars are of wild stock, or simply are overgrown pets that people have released into the wild, is unknown.

Human intervention is everywhere. We even manage the wild animals. Is there *anything* along the Buffalo that people haven't changed? Some virgin forest, maybe?

Yes, at least we can say there is virgin forest, anywhere that exploitation was not undertaken. These bits of noncommercial woodland are found at glades, along the faces of bluffs, on infertile mountain tops, and in the bottoms of rugged canyons where the timber could not profitably be removed. The Buffalo's virgin forest exists in many, many small patches.

If that isn't enough undefiled country for you, take heart. Watch the woodlands along the Buffalo. And keep watching as they slowly return toward their primeval appearance.

Eventually, if those woods remain under strong legal protection, they will be there for us, our children, and their children to see and to marvel at—a vision of the original wild America.

PEOPLE

No less than any species of plant, or any other species of animal, human inhabitants along the Buffalo have, from earliest times until today, been dependent on what the land and its other life forms could provide. And—it must be obvious—as humans throughout time have learned more about what nature has offered, they have adapted, changing their ways of living.

NATIVE AMERICANS

Compared with the European Americans who came later, prehistoric Native Americans were few in number, had minimal impact on natural resources, and changed their lifeways only very slowly. Over thousands of years, however, they made changes that in many ways fitted a pattern of gradual advancement. After scientists became able to learn the ages of prehistoric sites through carbon-14 dating, the pattern of advancement became apparent. As archeologists learned more, they drew up an outline of prehistoric development of the Ozarks' Native Americans having four broad cultural stages within approximate dates:

• *Paleo-Indian,* 9500 to 8000 BC, the time of the earliest nomadic big-game hunters. Included in this stage is the Dalton Culture, 8500 to 8000 BC, a time of adaptation at the end of the Ice Age.

• *Archaic*, 8000 to 500 BC, when regionally distinctive foraging lifeways developed;

• *Woodland*, 500 BC to AD 900, when people first domesticated native plants for food and invented pottery; and

• *Mississippi*, AD 900 to 1500, when maize-based agriculture and temple-mound building societies were established in the southeastern United States and along the Mississippi River.

By the 1980s, however, archeologists were excavating more sites, dating more material, and discovering that the dates assigned to the four cultural stages weren't matching reality. Notably, they had found that domestication of plants and invention of pottery had taken place earlier, during the late Archaic stage instead of the Woodland. So today the four stages are considered as time periods, not as accurate indicators of cultural development. Another framework for the prehistoric inhabitants of the Buffalo River seems better fitted to their changing livelihoods:

• *Hunters,* small groups of people who lived almost entirely by following big game, migrating seasonally during Paleo-Indian times, 9500 to 8000 BC;

• *Foragers,* people who, by hunting and gathering, developed a more varied diet of both wild game and native plants during the early and middle Archaic, 8000 to 3000 BC;

• *Semi-sedentary cultivators,* people who added gardening to hunting and gathering and put up dwellings in which they remained at least part of the year, during late Archaic and Woodland times, 3000 BC to AD 900; and

• *Sedentary cultivators,* people who came to rely considerably more on cultivated crops, had year-round settlements, and were influenced to some extent by cultural developments beyond the Ozarks during the Mississippi period, AD 900 to 1500.

The following discussion of Native American cultural development will use the hunters-to-cultivators framework, but will refer as well to the Paleo-Indian-to-Mississippi time periods.

Hunters

According to prevalent belief, sometime between 20,000 and 40,000 years ago people crossed the Bering land bridge from Asia and began to disperse through North America. Around 11,000 years ago small groups of wandering hunters now known as Paleo-Indians ("old Indians") probably visited the Buffalo River country.

The Paleo-Indians arrived at the end of the Ice Age. For centuries they had followed the Pleistocene megafauna—large grazing animals—and even in the Ozarks they must have found musk oxen and mastodons. These people, widely dispersed in small groups, were so few in number there must have been no gender roles except that women bore children. Everyone took part in the hunt and in gathering usable parts of wild plants.

They carried few belongings and left practically nothing behind. We know of their presence from their unique chipped-stone dart and spear points having a channel or flute on each side at the base. An investigator in the 1970s was able to list only 13 of these fluted points that had been found in the Arkansas Ozarks; all were in private collections. Five of the points were from the Buffalo River's watershed. All 13 were isolated finds. Almost all were found on or near the surface of the ground, exposed by erosion or perhaps carried and dropped there by somebody who had found them elsewhere.

As the Pleistocene ice sheet retreated northward, the Ozarks' groves of northern spruce and jack pine died out and gradually were replaced by a mixed hardwood forest much like that of today. The big animals of the Ice Age disappeared. The musk ox retreated toward the Arctic. Mammoth and mastodon, through loss of food sources or because of overhunting, became extinct.

As new species of both plants and animals gradually spread northward into the Ozark region, Paleo-Indians adapted. Instead of the megafauna, they now hunted deer and elk and smaller animals and began to learn that parts of many of the new kinds of plants were edible. The Dalton Culture, the lifeway of these people during their transition to a post-Pleistocene environment, lasted about 500 years.

Like the Paleo-Indians, the Dalton people created their own distinctive type of chipped-stone point. The Dalton point, roughly triangular and having a concave base, has been found throughout the southeastern United States (drawing, page 80). Along the Buffalo, however, at least through the year 2000, archeologists had excavated only one site having evidence of Dalton presence.

Elsewhere in the Ozarks, archeologists have unearthed Dalton-age stone adzes and spokeshaves used to produce such items as weapon shafts and tool handles of wood. Bone awls and needles, and chipped-stone perforators and scrapers, all were employed in working with animal skins. Sandstone mortars and grinding stones undoubtedly were used to process nuts, berries, and seeds. While some of these implements may have been developed in Paleo-Indian times, others must have been devised by the Dalton people as their subsistence base changed.

Foragers

People of the ensuing Archaic period continued to develop new skills, invent new tools, and locate new sources of food. As always with Native Americans, hunting was the mainstay. Archaic people had the atlatl, or throwing stick (which probably came from the Paleo-Indians), enabling hunters to hurl darts or spears long distances with considerable power and accuracy. For the atlatl they created stone points of many shapes. Throughout the Ozarks, Archaic points have turned up in great variety.

Points not only served as tips for projectiles; many also were used

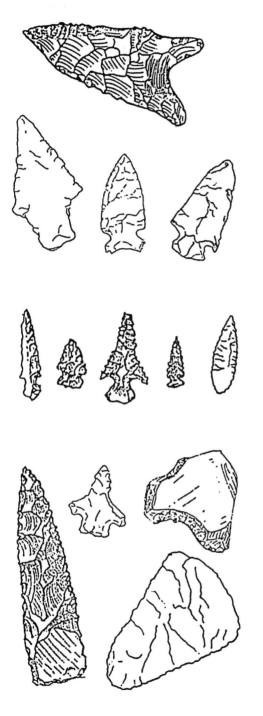

Native tool kit.
Stone implements created by Native Americans in the Ozarks are shown actual size in drawings.

One of the earliest types of projectile points (left, at top) is the diagnostic artifact of the Dalton period, 8500–8000 BC. In the subsequent Archaic and Woodland periods, 8000 BC–AD 900, native people created many more styles of points, including general forms designated as stemmed, notched, and corner-notched (second row, left to right). All were spear or dart points.

The bow and arrow, which came into use around AD 700, resulted in a variety of small tips for arrows (third row). An arrow point of the leaflike Nodena type (right end of row) found at Buffalo National River's Fitton Cave has been dated at AD 1500.

Natives fashioned special-purpose tools as well, including (bottom group, clockwise from left) knives, drills, spokeshaves, and endscrapers.

Projectile points also were used for cleaving, sawing, scraping, slicing, or whittling.

as knives and saws. Archaic people chipped and ground stone for other implements, too: blades, scrapers, chisels, axes, hammerstones, whetstones, abraders, drills, perforators, milling stones, atlatl weights. They split, drilled, and polished bone (harder than wood, less brittle than flint) to create flaking tools, weaving tools, awls, needles, pins, hoes, spades, handles, sickles, and projectile points.

Around 5000 BC or possibly earlier, the people also learned to twist fibers into twine and weave twine into bags, mats, sandals, fish nets, and other useful things. (Later they would learn to use split cane to make baskets. They would twist turkey-down feathers or rabbit fur around fiber cords, then weave the cords to produce warm capes and robes; see illustration, page 84.)

As foragers searching for food and provisions, they made ingenious use of whatever came to hand. At Ozark sites they left remains of woodchuck, bobcat, wood rat, fox, skunk, beaver, turkey vulture, box turtle, mussels, crayfish, and gar. They captured turkeys (in traps, maybe) and caught catfish and suckers (with nets, apparently). Venison was a staple; they may have formed hunting groups to drive or surround deer. They also killed bison, then present in the Ozarks, and elk and bear. Almost every part of the animal was used—meat, bones, bone marrow, skin, feathers.

In time the people learned about many more native plants that could provide food, fiber, or medicine. For example, they collected seedpods of the honey locust tree for their sweet pulp. During times of scarcity they used roots of greenbrier as a source of starch. They gathered quantities of small seeds for food. Investigators of prehistoric storage sites have found oily seeds of marsh elder, sumpweed, and sunflower, and starchy seeds of little barley, knotweed, pigweed, maygrass, canary grass, and giant ragweed.

This summary of Native American foraging activity includes some developments that came later than the Middle Archaic, but most are from that time. At Boxley, for example, excavators of a site dated at 4800 BC found two large grinding stones, together with many carbonized hickory nut shells broken into small pieces. Archeologists believe the nuts were dumped into water to separate shells from nutmeats that could provide dietary fat and protein.

Semi-Sedentary Cultivators

About 3000 BC, basic changes in native lifestyle took place. People no longer followed herds of grazing animals as they had during the

Fall-winter food.
Natives first parched or roasted acorns to prevent germination during storage and kill insect larvae inside the shells. When preparing acorns for eating, they shelled them, ground them to a pulp, and soaked or boiled the pulp to leach out the tannic acid. The end product was nourishing acorn meal.

Native pantry. Native Americans relied mainly on hunting wild game, but they also utilized many other sources for food. They collected and processed acorns (above, from a dry shelter in northwest Arkansas), grew miniature ears of corn (below, from Cob Cave), and may have harvested aquatic snails to eat (below, from another shelter cave near the Buffalo River).

Pleistocene. Instead, within a fairly small area, they found ample food—deer, elk, smaller animals, and the products of indigenous plants. Gradually people became more sedentary, remaining in one locality, camping there for a season or for several seasons.

One archeologist now suggests that disturbed topsoil at such a base camp probably provided a good spot for "weeds" to sprout and flourish—some of the same plants that the people had looked for and harvested in the wild. Observing this, these base-camp people of Late Archaic time became the first gardeners, disturbing soil, scattering seeds, domesticating useful indigenous plants.

Tending gardens was one more reason for staying in one place. Another was that, as the human population had increased, mobile or nomadic groups may have had territorial conflicts. In other words, being sedentary was less risky.

Evidence of the trend toward sedentarism turned up at Erbie in 1986. Excavators discovered what appeared to have been a base camp, dating from about 1300 BC, where child-rearing women, children, or old people could have remained while others went out to hunt and gather food. At this site they uncovered postmolds (holes where timber posts had been set in the ground) around an open hearth. Apparently people had erected a structure above a fire to smoke meat (probably fish) to be stored for future use.

Archeologists also have noticed that these Late Archaic campsites on stream terraces, and in rock shelters too, tend to be larger in extent than earlier sites, indicating longer stays or larger groups of people (or both) and more settled lifestyles.

Further evidence of the trend comes from a site at Rush dating from early Woodland time, about 200 BC. Postmolds and fragments of hardened clay plaster remained from a circular or conical structure. That, plus the remains of a wide range of animals and non-domesticated plants, and fragments of pottery, all suggest that the site was occupied as a multiseason base camp.

In the southeastern United States, pottery appears to have first been made in the Archaic period, when seeds were first gathered for food. Seeds required cooking, and so fired-clay pottery vessels were produced. Cooking was done by putting hot stones into pots filled with water and seeds; people had found that the clay pots broke when placed on an open fire.

Archeologists excavating another portion of this same site at Rush in 1988 found evidence of a related, major improvement in pottery

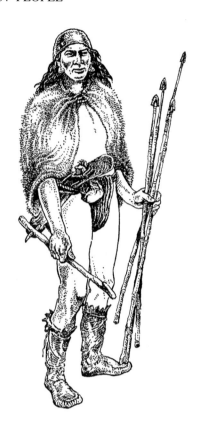

Native wardrobe.
The model is an Ozarker of about AD 600. He has a woven cap. His cape is probably of rabbit fur twisted around fiber cords that were woven together. His breechclout is grass fiber. Moccasins are deerskin with attached leggings of tanned deerskin.

Women probably wore similar clothing, though the breechclout would have been replaced by a skirt, probably of woven cords of grass fiber.

In this man's right hand is an atlatl, or spear thrower. The object tucked in his belt is an axe with a wood handle.

The drawing is based on study of specimens recovered from dry shelters in the early 1900s.

making. Around AD 700, someone had mixed bits of ground-up mussel shells with clay for pots, and unlike earlier ones, these pots could be used to boil water over cooking fires.

The Rush site also had evidence of another significant change around AD 700. Excavators found a few tiny carbonized kernels of maize—corn, arrived via trade routes from Mexico. Natives along the Buffalo would grow maize, though it would never become a major part of their diet. Investigators have seen that the people still relied mainly on hunting, even as they increased their use of wild and cultivated plant foods. And by one estimate most of their food came from the largest animals: deer, bison, elk, and bear. Deer alone constituted nearly half of their consumption of wild game.

The people who occupied the AD 700 campsite at Rush had put up a square or rectangular structure. They dug pits for storage of food;

such pits are often found at sites from this time period and are indicators of multiseason use. During a winter at Rush, it appears, the occupants consumed the stored food, and the following spring they cleaned up and dumped kitchen refuse into the emptied storage pits.

Native Americans around AD 700 had also acquired the bow and arrow. While the atlatl probably remained in use, a hunter with a bow could send arrows farther and with greater accuracy. Woodland people now made chipped-stone tips for arrows, the small points that some people today call "bird points."

By this time also, people had developed a regional trade network. Archeologists at Rush found evidence of this as they unearthed chert and quartzite of types occurring in Missouri, and refuse from quarrying quartz crystals from deposits nearby. The crystals had been removed; they may have been traded to peoples farther south.

Archeologists sense there was a widespread increase in Ozark population during Woodland times, perhaps causing greater pressure on resources such as wild game and a need for living groups to cooperate and share during times of shortage. At a Woodland site on the upper White River, though, excavators discovered evidence of violence—a human pelvis with an embedded projectile point.

Sedentary Cultivators

Excavators at Erbie in 1986 discovered remains of a house that they were able to date to AD 1350. Rows of closely spaced postmolds enclosed a rectangular area about 18 by 25 feet. Within the rectangle were an earthen hearth and a metate, or grinding stone (the domestic area), concentrations of flint chips (work areas), and an open space that may have had a low platform for sleeping.

At the house site, remains of a deer that was half grown indicated the animal was killed in the fall. The skull of another deer had a last-year's antler within days of being shed; this animal was killed in late winter or early spring. A collection of fish bones suggested that people also lived here during the spring or summer, the Southeastern Indians' season for fishing. From all evidence, this house at Erbie of the Mississippi period was occupied year round.

Also at the house site were fragments of pottery jars—ten-gallon jars, as sedentary as their maker!—and large storage pits containing corn, bean, and squash seeds. Sites of comparable age in the Boxley Valley had postmolds, a deep midden, or refuse pile, and carbonized corn, all providing evidence of year-round occupancy.

The Mississippi period was named for the cultural attainments of late prehistoric people along the Mississippi River, complex societies having large populations, extensive croplands, and sizeable towns. These people built massive earth mounds on which they erected religious structures and chiefs' houses. Along the Arkansas River, southwest of the Ozarks, Caddoan people of that period built similar groups of mounds. ("Caddoan" here means that the practices of the people along the Arkansas somehow resulted from interaction with the mound-building Caddo, who lived farther south.) They, or others who took up their practices, built groups of mounds along the upper White River and on War Eagle Creek, in northwest Arkansas, and a single large mound on the upper Buffalo near Ponca. (The Ponca mound was leveled in the 1920s by a landowner.)

Up to the year 2000, investigators had found no certain evidence of Caddoan influence along the Buffalo, nor any strong indication of influence from the Mississippi societies to the east. The Buffalo's people were a small, rather isolated population—perhaps no more than 100 people lived along the river at any given time—and it appears they had ample resources for living as they pleased while adopting some innovations from outside sources and not adopting others. They were not backward; they maintained contacts and trade with people beyond the Buffalo and generally went along with the advances made by people throughout the region.

Also to the year 2000, only one Buffalo River site carried a more recent radiocarbon date than the AD 1350 house at Erbie. In Fitton Cave, not far from Erbie, a spelunker in 1995 discovered a hidden cache: a pottery bowl, some charcoal, a few acorns, and an arrow point. The bowl is similar to varieties that may have originated in eastern Oklahoma. The arrow point is of the type called Nodena (drawing, page 80), also found in eastern Arkansas. These artifacts, with associations both east and west, are from about 1500.

From 1500 until the first direct contact with whites was made in the 1700s, the Buffalo had no native people that we know of; certainly no sign of them has yet been discovered. Did they die of disease, perhaps smallpox that originated with the DeSoto expedition through Arkansas in 1541, or with the Spanish living in Mexico or the Southwest in the 1500s and 1600s? Or did the Buffalo's people suffer from prolonged drought and move away, as did ancient peoples in the Southwest? We do know from tree-ring data that the Ozarks had a severe, prolonged drought between 1560 and 1590, when 20 to 25 years during that period were deficient in moisture. Drought could have left people malnourished, prey to disease.

Historic Indians

After 1700, Osage Indians came to the Ozarks of northern Arkansas each year on hunting trips from their villages in present-day Missouri. Even past 1800, they had semipermanent hunting camps in the hills of southern Missouri, but no physical evidence of the Osage has been found along the Buffalo.

In 1818 the Osage ceded their remaining lands in Arkansas and Missouri to the U.S. government. From 1817 to 1828 the Buffalo River's watershed lay within an area the government set aside by treaty for the Cherokee Indians, who were being moved west from their homeland in the Southeast. Cherokees are said to have established a town named Sequatchie on the lower Buffalo. If the town ever existed, it probably was no more than a scatter of log cabins and garden patches similar to those of more extensive Cherokee settlements along the Arkansas River during that time.

Or, as at least one historian believes, Sequatchie was not Cherokee at all, but peopled by Shawnee Indians. This is based partially on written accounts that about 1819 some two thousand Shawnee, who were allies of the Cherokee, were brought to the White River, where they established villages in the general vicinity of the Buffalo. Peter Cornstalk, identified by some as the Cherokee chief at Sequatchie, is said by others to have been Shawnee.

Whatever the case, the Cherokee or Shawnee would have lived on the Buffalo only a short time. In 1828, by order of another treaty with the United States, the Cherokee gave up their Arkansas lands and moved farther west to Indian Territory, present-day Oklahoma. The Buffalo country was now wholly open to Euro-American settlement.

EUROPEAN AMERICANS

The first Europeans to see the Buffalo River must have been French hunters or trappers who made their way up the White River from Arkansas Post, near the junction of the White with the Mississippi. These eighteenth-century adventurers bestowed names on the White's major tributaries—or perhaps they adopted names that local Indians were using. One of those names, translated to Spanish during the time present-day Arkansas was under Spanish rule, became recorded in a land grant made in 1793 to Arkansas Post commandant Joseph Vallière (portrait, page 261). *Rio Cibolos* formed one boundary of Vallière's grant. *Cibolo* (or the feminine form, *cibola*) is Spanish for American bison, or buffalo. This was the Buffalo River's first appearance on any known written document.

By 1806 there was an American trading company at Arkansas Post, and its agent, John Treat, described what he had heard about the White and its tributaries in a report he mailed to Washington, mentioning a tributary "of Buffaloes...the mouth of which is two hundred feet across." Four years later, the "Buffaloe Fork" of the White River was placed on the first American map of the region.

Already the first Anglo game hunters had worked their way up the White to the Buffalo. Soon afterward, hunter-herders brought livestock up the White and settled along its banks. During the winter of 1818–1819, when Henry R. Schoolcraft traveled along the White through northern Arkansas (and produced for us the first written eyewitness description of the region), he found about a dozen dwellings in one hundred miles of the river.

In his journey Schoolcraft bypassed the Buffalo but heard and commented that the river was "a region much resorted to by hunters on account of the abundance of game it affords." Concerning hunters along the White, he wrote:

Vast quantities of beaver, otter, raccoon, deer, and bear-skins are annually caught. These skins are carefully collected and preserved through the summer and fall, and taken down the river in canoes, to the mouth of the Great North Fork of White River, or to the mouth of Black River, where traders regularly come up with large boats to receive them. They also take down some wild honey, bear's bacon, and buffaloe-beef, and receive in return, salt, iron-pots, axes, blankets, knives, rifles, and other articles of first importance in their mode of life.

Schoolcraft's hunters were almost totally isolated, cut off. Even so, Schoolcraft could write that "we are beyond the pale of civilized society...but we are not beyond the influence of money, which is not confined by geographical boundaries." Indeed, the inhabitants' need for cash has continued throughout the history of the area.

Settlement, 1820s–1860

The first whites to settle along the Buffalo, if not hunters in Schoolcraft's time, were a few individuals, probably related to

Indians, who arrived during the years from 1817 to 1828, when the land belonged to the Cherokee. In the 1820s, Robert Adams of Kentucky built his cabin on Bear Creek in today's Searcy County; legend has it that a daughter of the Adams family married the Cherokee—or Shawnee—chief Peter Cornstalk. (By one report, Cornstalk was a nephew of Shawnee chief Tecumseh. As mentioned earlier, the Shawnee were allied with the Cherokee and lived among them in northern Arkansas, and in 1829 government surveyors found Shawnees living on Bear Creek.) In 1825, John and Nancy Brisco from Tennessee—she reputedly part Indian—were the first to locate on the upper Buffalo, below Erbie. About 1827, Mitchell and Nancy Hill from Tennessee settled near Mount Hersey. By that time also, according to Searcy County historian Orville McInturff, a scattering of settlers lived along both Bear Creek and Richland Creek.

In 1828, when by treaty the Cherokee were relocated to present-day Oklahoma, the Buffalo country became fully open to whites. A few immigrants arrived during the 1830s...many more in the 1840s...thousands more in the 1850s. The largest number came from Tennessee and Missouri. Some came from Virginia or North Carolina, pausing in Alabama, Kentucky, or Tennessee on their way toward settling west of the Mississippi.

Beginning in 1829, government surveyors divided off the land, locating and marking township and section lines, and recording on their plat maps the occasional clearings of the first settlers. Even in 1834, surveyors found fifteen families along Richland Creek, more than five miles above its confluence with the Buffalo.

Pioneers like these often moved onto public land in advance of the U.S. surveyors; there was no law prohibiting that. Also, in 1830 and succeeding years Congress passed pre-emption acts, so that these people had first right to purchase. Land usually was put on the market about five years (or more) after surveys were begun. The price was set at $1.25 an acre, so that a 40-acre block cost $50.00.

By one estimate, only one out of four of the original settlers along the Buffalo in the 1830s and 1840s filed for title to land. Many had little or no money. Many were restless, already thinking of moving somewhere else. In 1856, for example, James and Adeline Black, who had built their cabin at Leatherwood Creek near Ponca, gathered up their several children and went to Texas. In 1857 the widow and other relatives of Solomon Cecil, who had settled near Cecil Creek around 1830, loaded their wagons and headed for California.

By 1850 the surveyors had divided the Buffalo River valley into square-mile sections, with many of the sections divided into 40-acre blocks. Settlers had built cabins, cleared fields, opened primitive roads, built gristmills, and established churches, post offices, and a few log-cabin schools. County-seat villages took form: Jasper and Yellville, and Burrowsville, which soon would be renamed Marshall. Immigrants kept coming, looking for cheap land and elbow room. By 1860 more than 8000 people lived in the Buffalo River's watershed. They had taken all the best agricultural land along the river and its tributaries. Farms were small; in 1860 the average family had only 21 improved acres.

Although Arkansas allowed slavery, here in the mountainous northwestern part of the state only 1.6 percent of the white settlers were slaveholders. Along the Buffalo in 1860 there were 24 slaves in Newton County, 93 in Searcy County. Most of these slaves worked bottomland farms along the river and its larger tributaries.

Civil War, 1861–1865

Slavery, of course, had become a red-hot emotional issue by this time, one that helped ignite the Civil War in 1861. Then, even in the isolated Buffalo valley, people were forced to choose sides. A number of settlers preferred to be left alone and joined a secret organization called the Peace Society—but they were betrayed, rounded up, and taken to Little Rock, where they were offered a choice: either join the Confederate army or be tried for treason. One of these unfortunates was Peter A. Tyler of Tyler Bend, who was conscripted into the army and died during the war.

Like much of northern Arkansas, the Buffalo valley was a Confederate borderland having a divided population. Newton County was said to have been one-third Confederate, two-thirds Unionist. Communities, and even families, were divided. People at the upper end of the Boxley Valley were Confederates; those at the downstream end were Unionists. Upriver members of the extensive Villines family were on the Southern side, those downriver on the Northern side (photo, page 264). Among the Cecils who remained in Newton County, John became a Confederate captain but his brother Samuel made sergeant in the Union army.

During the early years of the war—1861 and 1862—Confederates controlled the Buffalo area. At several caves along the river they began to mine and process nitrogen-rich bat guano and cave earth to obtain saltpeter (potassium nitrate), needed in making gunpowder. News of this reached the Union army—present in northwest Arkansas by that time—and in January 1863, Union cavalry from Huntsville raided two "nitre works" in the Boxley Valley, destroying equipment and capturing laborers but not inflicting death or injury.

Events downriver only a week earlier were more typical of the Civil War. A Confederate force of 1600 men rode north toward the Buffalo, bent on what would become a successful raid into Missouri. When nearing the river, they were fired on by what one officer described as "about 100 notorious bushwhackers and deserters." Soldiers pursued the attackers, killed about 20, and captured 27. Six of the prisoners were Confederate deserters, and they and two other locals were court-martialed that evening at the army's campsite by the river. Three of the eight were sentenced to hard labor. The next morning the other five were taken out and shot.

Through 1863 and 1864, Union patrols to the Buffalo area from Fayetteville, Huntsville, and Yellville clashed with bands of locally recruited Confederates, "irregulars" or "home guards" who knew the country and fought aggressively. It became a standoff; neither side was able to control the area.

Tragically, neither side could protect the civilian population, caught in a no man's land with conditions worsening month by

Civil War, close up.
Lewis Brewer lived near the Buffalo River below Richland Creek. One day Brewer came home to find that a Confederate guerilla named Cordelle had robbed and beaten his wife, Martha, and left her to die—this was witnessed by their 11-year-old son. Brewer rode in pursuit, caught up with Cordelle, and disabled him. Then Brewer's gun failed to fire. He stabbed Cordelle to death.

month, prey to outlaws who robbed families, murdered old men and young boys, burned houses and left women and children without food or possessions. People hid food and livestock in the woods; men hid in caves; Unionists fled north to Springfield, Missouri, or beyond. From the upper river, Abraham Clark (for whom Clark Creek was named) and George Washington Steele (of Steele Creek) took their families north beyond danger and stayed till war's end.

Homesteading, 1865–1900s

Within a decade after 1865, the scars of war were erased, except for those who had suffered family losses. (Even today in the Buffalo River area one can find alignments that go back to the Civil War. Descendants of those on the Southern side have traditionally been Democrats. Descendants of Unionists vote Republican.) By 1870 the Buffalo's population had increased from what it had been in 1860. Settlers now could get free land through the Homestead Act of 1862, if only they would live on their acreage five years and make minimal improvements. Valley bottoms had been taken, of course, but second- and third-generation locals (many of whom wanted to remain near their kin) and a stream of newcomers staked claims on vacant land along mountainside benches and on tops of ridges.

For several decades, people continued searching for unclaimed public land to homestead. Historian Walter Lackey recalled that from 1900 to 1910, "Newton County was invaded by a horde of fur-riners…from many states, especially from Eastern states, and large cities in the East." One of Lackey's in-laws, Milas Wishon, remembered that some came for rest and relaxation in the wilderness while others sought to own a home for the first time. For $50, Milas would build a homesteader a one-room log house.

Another native, Walter Williams, says that homesteaders "was wanting a piece of land. They was here only to get the property."

Many of the homesteaders did make an effort. They cleared and fenced a few acres, planted gardens and fruit trees, and acquired hogs and a milk cow to run on free range in the surrounding woods. (Walter Williams: "The acorns just covered the ground. They never wanted for pork.") On better land, if they had any, homesteaders grew corn for livestock feed and sorghum cane to make molasses.

Farm families had plenty of food but continually struggled to obtain cash. Some trapped furs to sell. Others dug roots (mayapple, cohosh, black haw, bloodroot, goldenseal, ginseng) or collected bark (haw, sassafras, slippery elm) for which pharmaceutical dealers would pay. Most families, however, depended on growing an acre or two of cotton. After picking it and piling it into a wagon, they took it to the nearest cotton gin and sold it. If fortunate, they received enough money to pay the year's land taxes and buy the year's salt, coffee, cloth, horseshoes, and other needs.

Recalling those times, Noah Barnett of Searcy County says: "The money was scarce. No railroads, no automobiles…no market for [live]stock, only barter among neighbors. Cotton was about the only money crop."

During January 1880, in an attempt at cooperative marketing, farmers in and around Richland Valley organized a long train of wagons loaded with the previous season's harvest—cotton, corn, apples, and so on—and headed south 80 miles over the mountains to the railroad at Russellville. Day after day for two entire weeks the caravaners struggled along primitive tracks through the forest. They never repeated the trip.

In part because there was so little money to pay for goods or for labor, people were drawn together. They helped one another with harvests and house-raisings; they donated their work to improve roads and to build schools and churches. In the decades after the Civil War, communities took form, often centered on a one-room building that housed both school and church, often with a combined country store and post office nearby. Within the geographic limits of one community there might also be a gristmill, a sawmill, a sorghum mill, and a cotton gin. Everything was located within a few miles, within reach for these people who either rode horseback or walked.

Mining, 1880s–1920s

At times one source of cash income was from mining lead or zinc. Settlers discovered and mined lead ore near Lost Valley before the Civil War. Others later found lead or zinc ore at several places around Boxley and Ponca and at scattered sites along the upper and middle Buffalo as far downstream as Tomahawk Creek. On the lower river, prospectors located zinc at Rush Creek in the 1880s, and then at locations from Maumee to Cow Creek, near the White River. The most productive zinc mines along the Buffalo—and in all of northern Arkansas—were at or near Rush Creek.

Miners were active along the Buffalo from the 1880s until as recently as 1962, but the major ore discoveries were made before

Boomtown. During World War I the price of zinc skyrocketed, bringing hundreds of miners to Rush. By 1916 the town's population swelled to around 2000. "Main Street" (above) along Rush Creek was lined with shacks and tents. Phone wires had been strung and hillsides were laced with scaffolding for conveyors to bring zinc ore down from mines to concentrating mills.

Among the shack and tent dwellers were a few higher-ups, including John Conness Shepherd and his wife, Sarah, owners of the very first automobile in Rush, a Model-T Ford (below). J. C. Shepherd, with mining know-how and access to capital, bought or leased one mine after another until he became the leading zinc operator along the Buffalo. But by war's end in 1918 the price of ore was down to $10 a ton. Mining was unprofitable and mines closed. The Shepherds, and nearly everyone else, left town.

1900 and large-scale mining ended in 1918. At Rush there was inter-mittent activity from 1886 until 1918, with mining booms from 1899 to 1901 and from 1915 to 1917.

In 1899, when prices of ore increased, a mob of newcomers descended on Rush and soon used up local supplies of beef, chicken, eggs, and butter; people then had to eat salt pork. From 1915 to 1917, when ore prices soared from $14 to $160 per ton, the boom was big-ger still. Rush then became a sprawl of shacks and tents having more than 2000 inhabitants (photos, opposite and page 5). A Rush native, Lee Medley, remembered that "all the ground room available for building purposes was full up." Housing was crowded, sanitation poor. People got typhoid. And to provide fuel for home heating and cooking and for steam boilers at ore-processing mills, woodcutters stripped the surrounding hills of trees.

"Old Rush," a mile up Rush Creek around the Morning Star Mine (see photo, page 414), had since the 1890s been a fairly stable, cohe-sive community—brush arbor meetings, children in school. But "New Town," which sprang to life near the Buffalo at the beginning of World War I, was more lively. New Town had a school, a bakery, three hotels, restaurants, a hardware store. And there were shows, dance halls, pool halls. Bootleggers sold moonshine for 75 cents a pint. Men got drunk and had fights. Women had fights. The county court at Yellville stayed busy with cases from Rush.

There were jobs at the mines for almost everybody—drifters, local farmers between crops, even teenage boys (photo, page 264). When only 14 years old, Lee Medley got a job paying $2 for a nine-hour day, at that time considered good wages. Skilled workers received even higher pay, and Medley and all the others could work six days a week. There were no fringe benefits; there was no accident insur-ance. Fortunately very few miners were hurt or killed in accidents.

Upriver, Ponca also boomed during World War I, though on a smaller scale. By 1918, however, demand for lead and zinc had slacked off, prices were down, and boom became bust. Each year from 1915 to 1917 the Buffalo River mines produced several thou-sand tons of high-grade ore, mostly zinc. By 1920 production was near zero. Ponca and Rush again became backcountry villages.

Mine operators knew they had two major problems that would force shutdowns when ore prices fell. One was suggested as early as 1858 by Arkansas' first state geologist, David Dale Owen, after he looked at lead mines in Newton County. Owen wrote that ore occurred in small irregular deposits, "hence, mining operations will be attended with some uncertainty, and considerable labor and expense." Even the Morning Star Mine at Rush, once the most famous zinc mine in Arkansas, shut down when ore prices collapsed.

The other big problem was getting the ore to market. Dewey Clark, who hauled ore concentrates from the Boxley Valley in the early 1920s, recalled, "I used four mules, sometimes six on that mountain to get on top of it and on into Harrison. I was a wagon freighter." The round trip took three days.

At Rush, operators tried barging ore down the Buffalo to the White River, where steamboats could tow the barges to the railroad at Batesville. The passage down the Buffalo was hazardous and empty barges could not be brought back up the river, so instead the miners chose to haul the ore in wagons by road for eight rugged miles— "over one of the worst mountains in Marion County," says Lee Medley—to the White River at Buffalo City, where it was transferred to flatboats. At Buffalo City the wagon drivers also could pick up mining supplies and not have to return empty.

Promoters tried more than once to build a railroad to Rush, or to alter the Buffalo River's channel to allow small steamboats to ascend from the White River to Rush Creek, but nothing came of their efforts. In the late 1920s miners began to use trucks instead of wagons to haul ore from Rush to a railroad siding near Yellville, but by that time nearly all the major operations had shut down.

There was still another problem for many who sought riches in zinc mining. J. C. Shepherd (see *Boomtown,* page 94), described it to a newspaper reporter. Said Shepherd: "Ninety out of a hundred operations have been promotional schemes. There have been few real miners.... Promoters have built mills without a source of ore, and investors...have sunk their money in impossible ventures."

Today most evidence of the mining era is gone. The denuded hills around Rush are forested again. Vegetation has spread over waste piles and crumbling foundations of ore-processing mills, whose machinery was sold for scrap around 1940 and whose buildings were torn down or simply melted into the earth. (To visit Rush as it is today, see pages 409–417.)

Timbering, 1880s–1920s

More than zinc or cotton, timber proved to be a continuous source of cash income for people along the Buffalo. The forest was nearly everywhere, mainly hardwoods but also stands of pine and cedar. The timber market had its ups and downs but always there were buyers for one species of tree or another. As with mining, moving the product to market was a problem; in fact, timber could not be "sent outside" until there was access, by road or by river, to a railroad.

In 1882 the first railroad within reach of Buffalo River timber was opened to the town of Batesville, 88 miles down the White River from the Buffalo's confluence. Two years later Charles Robertson Handford established C. R. Handford & Company at Batesville to become "manufacturers of mountain red cedar, telegraph poles, railway piling, sawed and split fence posts, cedar shingles and pickets." Buyers at Handford's riverside cedar yard would pay cash for cedar logs. In response, Buffalo River farmers cut cedar trees, hauled logs to the river, nailed them together into floating rafts 100, 150, even 200 feet long, then got aboard with camping supplies and poled and steered their way down the Buffalo to the White River, then down the White to Handford's cedar yard. After collecting their money—probably about ten cents per log—the rafters walked home.

In 1897 a railroad was opened to the head of the White River valley at Pettigrew, about 25 miles southwest of Boxley. That presented an opportunity to "Boxley Joe" Villines, who began cutting black walnut lumber at his steam sawmill. Even at that time, walnut was highly valued for furniture, cabinetry, and gunstocks, and Villines sent wagonloads of it over primitive mountain roads to Pettigrew.

In 1902 another railroad, the Missouri & North Arkansas, was completed to the middle Buffalo at Gilbert. Within months investors installed a sawmill at Gilbert to produce seven-inch-long cedar slats to be sold to the Eagle Pencil Company as stock for making pencils, and organized a logging operation in Newton County to supply the raw material. Crews of tree cutters invaded the groves of cedar along the Buffalo (which often were on steep, rocky hillsides, still in the public domain). They felled the cedars, many of them nearly two feet in diameter, and sectioned them into twelve-foot logs. Another crew with mules dragged the logs to the river (photo, page 99).

All winter the crews cut cedar and piled logs along the banks of the Buffalo. Then, as the first spring flood began to recede, the call went out: "Roll 'em in!"

Soon a crew of rivermen had a huge raft of loose logs moving downstream. A cook paddled ahead with the supply boat, and the others followed in boats or waded or swam with the slowly moving mass of cedar, breaking up logjams. This crew stayed with the logs all the way to Gilbert, 18 days down the river when from Erbie, 22 days one time when from Boxley. Many of the men had no dry clothing the entire trip. Sometimes the water was warmer than the air and crewmen preferred to stay in the river.

At Gilbert the logs lodged behind a boom—a floating barrier stretched across the river. As the river crew departed, walking home, workers pulled logs from the Buffalo on an endless cleated chain and stacked them on shore to be run through the slat mill.

Thus from 1903 to 1909 several hundred men and boys were employed in cutting cedar until Newton County's merchantable virgin cedar had been shipped out of state to the pencil company.

Around 1900 the railroads were building trackage throughout the Midwest and Great Plains, creating a huge demand for crossties. In many areas along the Buffalo, tie hackers felled white oaks and shaped the logs with broadaxes to make standard-dimension ties. (A good tie hacker could produce eight to ten ties a day, for which he would be paid ten cents per tie.) They hauled the ties to the river, or to bluffs overlooking the Buffalo where they sent them down to the river in chutes or on cables. The ties were rafted to Gilbert, Buffalo City, or Batesville (photo, page 210). Rafting of ties—and cedar logs, too, on the lower Buffalo—continued until around 1920.

White oak also was the preferred wood for barrel staves. About 1920, as passable roads were opened, operators moved small stave mills from place to place in timbered areas, produced rough-cut staves and headings (the latter being short boards for ends of barrels), loaded them on wagons, and hauled them to railroad sidings. These "export staves" were shipped to Europe for beer, wine, or whiskey barrels (photo, opposite). In a decade or so, stave millers cut much of the virgin white oak, even from the rough, isolated hills along the lower river.

Diminishing Resources, after 1900

From 1900 to 1920 more than 21,000 people lived in the Bufffalo River's watershed: Population was at its maximum. Homesteading, mining, and timbering all were in full swing. Families were large. People scrambled to make a living (Ray Jordan of Gilbert: "Every forty acres, a house—somebody trying to exist").

For a living or sometimes only for amusement, people exploited natural resources with little thought about eventual outcomes. James

Cedar logs...
Daniel Boone Lackey and his mule Going Joe worked together, dragging logs to the river during removal of the upper Buffalo's virgin cedar around 1905. Often the cedars grew on very steep slopes above the river. Lackey recalled he snaked logs to the top of a bluff near today's Camp Orr, then rolled them off—and one time almost lost his "snake" mule off the edge.

...and stave bolts. Men and boys pause from cutting short lengths of oak logs, then splitting them into quarters (bolts) for further processing to make barrel staves. The place is near the upper Buffalo in Newton County; the time is around 1920. Two German men operated this logging camp to produce "export staves" to go to Europe for beer, wine, or whiskey barrels.

Villines of Ponca trapped beaver and otter—winning himself the nickname Beaver Jim—and completely eliminated them from his part of the Buffalo. Walter Isom on the lower river in 1901 took 50 deer hides and 100 cured deer hams to Batesville and sold them. And along the river, hunting wild bees became a competitive sport. It was said a good bee hunter could find eight or ten bee trees in a day, setting things up to kill the bees and rob the hives.

Two widely separated side canyons of the Buffalo are named Fishtrap Hollow. There, and at many other places along the river, neighboring farmers built V-dams at shoals during periods of drought. Fish moving downriver had to go through an opening at the apex of the V and into a holding pen. These traps caught fish by the hundreds. Other exploiters killed fish by dragging a gunnysack of crushed green walnut hulls through the river's pools in hot summertime, or by dropping in a half stick of dynamite. Then they gathered up the dead or stunned fish as they floated to the surface. (Says Gene Waters, a fourth-generation Buffalo River native: "There was no law. They used to do what they wanted to do.")

At the height of this era of careless exploitation of the Buffalo's natural bounty, one significant move was made in another direction. On March 6, 1908, President Theodore Roosevelt signed a proclamation setting aside 917,944 acres of public domain lands as the Ozark National Forest, the nation's first protected body of hardwood timber. The National Forest was to include a large area along the southern flank of the Buffalo's watershed, including headwaters of the river and several major tributaries.

Beyond the National Forest, the land provided less and less. After 1900, people began to move away. First to go were homesteaders and others who had "starved out" on the poorest land. (Walter Williams: "They seen they couldn't make a living, so they left.") In truth, these people became part of a much broader movement at that time, for others were abandoning failed homesteads in many parts of the United States (see *Exodus,* page 361).

During the 1930s Depression, however, the watershed's population increased: People moved back to scratch out a subsistence. Baxter Hurst of Buffalo City recalls seeing impoverished families at abandoned mines who were engaged in ore gouging, picking out pieces of zinc ore to sell.

From 1940 to 1960 people moved away in droves and the watershed's population fell by more than one-third (graph, page 103).

River crossings. The first Buffalo River bridge was opened at Pruitt in 1913. Responding to public demand, the county had a second bridge (above) installed at Carver about 1916.

The lower river had no bridge until 1958. Through the 1920s and 1930s travelers on the direct route between Marshall and Yellville could cross on the ferry at Maumee (below). About 1925, folks stand for a photograph while the ferry operator turns a windlass to make the river's current push the boat across.

During World War II they left for military service and defense plant jobs. After the war others left to find employment in towns and cities. Farm people along the river in Searcy and Marion Counties, for example, moved to escape the recurring floods, the isolation from schools and medical help, and what many saw as an unhealthy climate. (E. G. Grinder of St. Joe: "People didn't like to live on the river. They'd be sick. You'd take malaria.")

And after a century of row cropping, the soil was tired. (Janis White Busbee of St. Joe, whose forebears farmed along the Buffalo for generations, says: "The three Big C's raped and ruined it— Cotton, Corn, and Cane.")

Changes after World War II

World War II, 1941–1945, can be seen now as a watershed event, standing at the divide between the earlier Depression and later prosperity, and between the old, country life and a new, more urbanized one. Along the Buffalo just as everywhere else, the end of World War II marked the beginning of profound changes. For those who remained in the Buffalo country after the war, life became better.

The first large—and welcomed—change was rural electrification. The first electric lines were put up shortly before the war, and a major effort to extend lines was begun soon after. By the 1960s all but the most isolated households had electric power.

Then came better roads. Before the war only one paved highway, U.S. 65, reached the Buffalo River. Between 1945 and 1990 pavement was extended to the Buffalo on six state highways, five high-standard river bridges were built, and dozens of connecting county roads were improved. Better roads combined with loss of rural population brought other changes: Rural mail carriers replaced country post offices; consolidated schools supplanted the one-room variety. Moreover, Buffalo River people could live on the farm while traveling to town for work, for shopping, for sociability and entertainment.

One more fundamental change was near universal rural telephone service. Even in the early 1900s a few communities had local phone systems, but after the 1960s every community was connected to the long-distance network. In the 1990s some of the most isolated households were connected. For many, the telephone strengthened ties with kinfolk, friends, and sources of help—ties that had become threatened by the faster pace of life brought by other changes.

Another change. Farmers gave up traditional row crops—cotton,

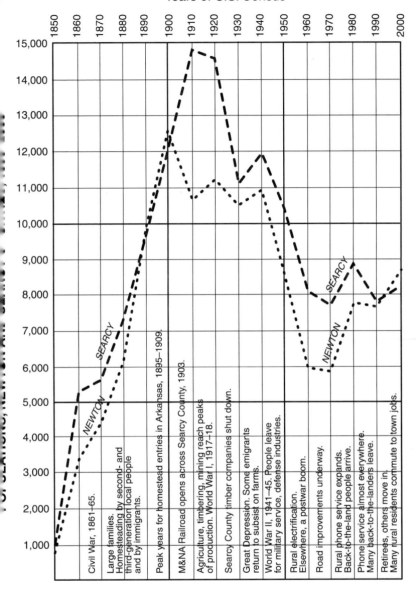

Years of U.S. Census

Chart showing population trends for Newton and Searcy Counties from 1850 to 2000, with annotations along the bottom:

- Civil War, 1861–65.
- Large families. Homesteading by second- and third-generation local people and by immigrants.
- Peak years for homestead entries in Arkansas, 1895–1909.
- M&NA Railroad opens across Searcy County, 1903.
- Agriculture, timbering, mining reach peaks of production. World War I, 1917–18.
- Searcy County timber companies shut down.
- Great Depression. Some emigrants return to subsist on farms.
- World War II, 1941–45. People leave for military service, defense industries.
- Rural electrification. Elsewhere, a postwar boom.
- Road improvements underway.
- Rural phone service expands. Back-to-the-land people arrive.
- Phone service almost everywhere. Many back-to-the-landers leave.
- Retirees, others move in. Many rural residents commute to town jobs.

Population trends in Newton and Searcy Counties from 1850 to 2000 closely parallel those in the Buffalo River's watershed. The river's drainage area comprises 75 percent of each of these two counties, and the counties embrace 83 percent of the watershed. (The other 17 percent is divided among seven other counties.)

Here, as elsewhere in the Ozarks, population was related to the exploitation of natural resources that peaked in the early 1900s.

corn, sorghum cane, wheat, oats—in favor of cattle and hay. At times, some had tried other cash crops: tomatoes for local canneries that were established in the 1920s and 1930s, strawberries in Searcy County in the 1960s. Tomatoes were wiped out by drought and blight; strawberries were abandoned when labor for handpicking became scarce. By the 1980s, though, a few people were specializing in organically grown vegetables. Others in the watershed area had dairy herds, or goats, or horses, or had hogs in confinement buildings. Overall, however, raising beef cattle became predominant wherever there was land for pasture.

Timber operations changed dramatically, first with logging trucks and then the bulldozer. Loggers tried trucks as early as the 1920s and 1930s, and by the 1940s abandoned wagon hauling entirely. After World War II they acquired bulldozers and began to build logging roads into country formerly too isolated or steep for mules and wagons. Around 1950 they replaced crosscut saws with chain saws. After the war also, the first power skidders replaced horses and mules to pull logs from the woods and load them onto trucks. By the 1980s practically all log handling was being done with power equipment.

Beginning in the 1930s, when improved roads and sturdier trucks meant easier transportation to markets, local sawmill operators selected different tree species for a variety of products. Before the war Jess Shroll of Ponca cut hickory stock, 2 by 2 by 50 inches, for golf clubs. After the war Arvel Casey at Boxley produced walnut blanks for rifle stocks, and hickory and oak pieces for furniture. Casey also cut beech, which previously had been without commercial value. Ash, black gum, sweet gum, persimmon—all had their special uses. Dogwood became shuttles for textile mills. Red oak was good for flooring, hickory for handles, elm for chair parts, maple for chair backs, ash for shovel and hoe handles. Pine became lumber and, more recently, log-cabin logs.

By the 1990s timber harvesting on any given tract of land seemed to take place every 20 to 40 years, at least on privately owned parcels outside the Ozark National Forest. Loggers cutting a tract on Running Creek near Ponca removed virgin white oak for wagon parts in the late 1930s; other species (cedar, hickory, oak, persimmon) over 14 inches in diameter about 1950; and all merchantable timber in 1994. As happened elsewhere, each successive cut was done with less waste of useable wood but from timber stands generally having smaller trees of lower quality.

Seed of Abraham.

Abraham, the family patriarch, was born in Virginia about 1777. By midlife he had married, sired six children, and acquired slaves and tobacco plantations in North Carolina. But around 1825 his wife Nancy died, and he had financial reverses and lost most of his land. Apparently Abraham then married his late wife's sister, Martha, and he and his family moved west. Over the next ten years he—or one or another of his grown children—touched down in Tennessee, Kentucky, Indiana, and Missouri.

Then, according to family legend, relatives returned from a trip to Arkansas bearing tales of an Ozark valley where good land was free for the taking. About 1837, Abraham and Martha, their oldest son Hezekiah (with wife and six children and a slave girl named Piety), their daughter Virginia and her husband, William Keith, and Abraham's two youngest sons, Hosea and Copeland, all came in a family caravan to the upper Buffalo. Abraham, Martha, and Copeland settled opposite Big Bluff below Ponca and the others took land in the Boxley Valley. In the early 1840s another son, Nathaniel, came with wife and children and located at Erbie. Only one son—William—stayed in Tennessee.

Abraham's five children along the Buffalo stayed with the nineteenth-century practice of having big families, producing 43 offspring of their own. Many lived to maturity. Among the males of Abraham's 43 grandchildren, two then had 9 children apiece, another had 13, another had 15, and another had 17.

Through marriage the family became related to nearly everyone for miles around. Over succeeding decades along and around the upper Buffalo, mailboxes and tombstones in increasing numbers bore Abraham's distinctive surname, *Villines* (which appears to have come to America with one Jean Vilain, a French Huguenot refugee who landed in Virginia in 1700). By the late twentieth century the surname had come down to the eighth generation beyond Abraham. In the 1990s a local phone book listed 74 Villines households. A directory for three counties to the west had 49 Villineses. One for Kansas City listed 14.

Without doubt, no other pioneer along the Buffalo has as many descendants as does that patriarch, Abraham Villines.

From 1960 to 1970 the watershed's population loss slowed to a walk. From 1970 to 1980 population increased, partly because of an influx of retirees. Local couples returned after years of employment elsewhere, and others came because of the Ozarks' moderate climate, scenic beauty, cheap land, and low taxes.

Younger people came also, part of a widespread back-to-the-land movement from urban to rural areas across the United States. Back-to-the-landers—often referred to as hippies—tended to be college educated and idealistic. Armed with how-to-do-it information from *Mother Earth News* magazine and books such as *Living the Good Life* by Helen and Scott Nearing, they erected shelters of various sorts (photo, page 364), started gardens…and learned that attaining the good life was not as easy as they may have imagined. Like the Eastern homesteaders of the early 1900s, most of them left, helping cause the watershed's loss of population between 1980 and 1990.

Some of the back-to-the-landers did take to country life, and they found ways to support themselves by growing organic crops, doing construction work or arts and crafts, working with computers, or serving in occupations such as teaching and health care. Many of the newcomers, and longtime local people as well, found it necessary to commute long distances from their rural homes to town jobs.

Some also found employment in serving recreationists along the Buffalo River. Even before 1930 the Buffalo had become known among avid fishermen as a beautiful smallmouth bass stream, and a few local men had become float-fishing guides. (Float-fishing, down Ozark rivers, apparently had originated in Missouri around 1900.) After World War II, as outboard motors came into wide use, float businesses expanded, catering mainly to well-to-do men. Most of the float activity was along the lower river, centered on Buffalo River State Park, which had opened in the late 1930s.

In the 1950s the first canoers arrived, and floating the Buffalo became more a family affair. By 1975 canoeing had become large-scale, attracting thousands from within and beyond Arkansas. New businesses catering to floaters were established and expanded to provide rental canoes, johnboats, and rafts, car shuttles and guide services, outdoor supplies for sale and housekeeping cabins for rent.

River Development

Running along with other past activity in the river's watershed was a series of proposals for dams and other government-funded devel-

Backwoods hotel.
Benton began his career in art as a newspaper cartoonist. That ability to emphasize and exaggerate essential character is evident in his sketch of the Whiteley Hotel at Ponca, made when he stayed there in the spring of 1926.

River lover.

Tom Benton grew up in the Ozarks at Neosho, Missouri. After years as an artist in Chicago, Paris, and New York, Benton decided to visit the Arkansas Ozarks and draw local scenes.

Sometime in May 1926 he arrived at Ponca, on the upper Buffalo. For a day or two he made sketches, then hiked down the river, visited people, and walked over the mountain to Jasper. Later he wrote that this trip was the beginning of his interest in studies of the American rural scene. In 1935, Thomas Hart Benton settled permanently in Kansas City, to become nationally known as a Midwest regionalist painter who focused on people of the American heartland.

In the decade before his death in 1975, Benton was on the Buffalo River nearly every year, sketching and painting. During that time controversy raged over whether to have the U.S. Army Corps of Engineers dam the river. Benton wrote to the Corps:

As a lover of the great scenic beauty of the Buffalo River I would like to add my name to those others which are lined up in protest, against plans to put a dam across its waters....

Man, hog tied as he largely is, with the steel tentacles of an increasingly mechanistic world, and with the prospect of being tied ever tighter, needs some areas of escape, of escape to the natural world from which he came. He'll need these all the more in the future.

The Buffalo River provides one of these areas.
I say, and I intend it emphatically, let the river be.
Sincerely yours
Thomas H. Benton

Life-changing.
For the young man standing in the johnboat, this Buffalo River fishing trip in the summer of 1932 was a beginning toward directions later in life. After medical school and service in World War II, Neil Compton returned to the Buffalo, came to know and love the river, and spent years toward protecting it as Buffalo National River.

A river at risk.
During the 1960s Dr. Compton and his allies campaigned to stop a proposed Army Corps of Engineers dam. Other developments, too, were threatening the Buffalo. At Pruitt, for example, there were newly erected charcoal kilns (below), and wooded land beside the river had become building lots (left).

opment on the Buffalo River, up to 1972, when Congress authorized establishment of Buffalo National River. Here are highlights:

1896. The U.S. Army Corps of Engineers surveyed the Buffalo from Rush Creek to the White River to learn how the Buffalo's channel might be opened to permit zinc ore to be barged downriver from the Rush mines. The Corps concluded that five locks and dams costing $750,000 would be needed—an expenditure not justified by the expected amount of river traffic. The Corps suggested that overhanging trees and limbs, and projecting rocks in the shoals, could be removed as a makeshift solution costing $3,500. Nothing was done.

1910. W. N. Gladson, an engineering professor at the University of Arkansas, surveyed the river from Boxley to the White to locate sites for hydroelectric development. Gladson then proposed that a 20-foot dam be built at the upstream end of the seven-mile bend downriver from present-day Buffalo Point. From the dam the river would be diverted through a half-mile tunnel across the narrow neck of the bend, to then drop about 40 feet and turn an electric generator. Nothing was done; there were better power sites elsewhere.

1938. Congress authorized the Corps of Engineers to build Lone Rock Dam on the Buffalo 3.6 miles above its junction with the White River. Justified as part of a flood control plan for the White River basin (for which the Corps would later build six dams on the White and its tributaries), the Lone Rock impoundment was to have a surface area of 11,000 acres when at maximum (flood control) level and extend about 55 river miles upstream from the dam to near Highway 65. At its lowest level, 121 feet below maximum, its surface area was to be 1350 acres.

1954. As the Corps dammed other Ozark rivers, it looked again at the Buffalo and now recommended construction of both Lone Rock Dam and a dam upriver near Gilbert. The Gilbert reservoir at maximum level was to cover 16,000 acres and extend about 40 miles upstream from the dam to Highway 7 at Pruitt. At low pool, 53 feet below maximum, its area was to be 6200 acres.

1956 and 1957. President Dwight Eisenhower twice vetoed bills having funds for construction of Lone Rock and Gilbert Dams, for reasons of economy.

1963. The National Park Service, after conducting studies of the river, recommended establishment of Buffalo National River to protect the natural attributes of the Buffalo.

1964. The Corps dropped its recommendation for Lone Rock Dam and instead proposed a high dam at the Gilbert site a mile upriver from U.S. Highway 65, combined with a low dam near the village of Gilbert and 3.6 miles downstream from the high dam. The two dams would make possible a pumped-storage scheme for generating electric power. During peak demand for electricity in daylight hours, water from the upstream reservoir would flow through generators at the high dam, producing electricity and then accumulating in the smaller, downstream reservoir. Late at night, when public demand for electricity slacks off, the generators would be reversed and run as pumps using surplus electric power to lift water from the downstream pool back into the reservoir behind the high dam.

1965. As the elected governor of Arkansas, Orval E. Faubus announced his opposition to damming the Buffalo. The Corps of Engineers therefore withdrew its proposal for the Gilbert project.

1966. The Federal Power Commission, in a report on potential dam sites in the region, suggested that pumped-storage power plants could also be built at Point Peter, using the reservoir behind Gilbert Dam as the lower pool; and at Hemmed-in Hollow, where the river could be dammed to create the lower pool.

1967. The first bills to authorize Buffalo National River were introduced in Congress.

1972. After ten years of controversy, Congress authorized establishment of Buffalo National River, without any dams. Local business people had wanted Gilbert Dam as an economic stimulant. Proponents of the National River saw the undammed river as having both economic and nonmaterial benefits.

PARK

In *Webster's New Collegiate Dictionary* one definition of "park" is "an area maintained in its natural state as a public property."

Webster's New World Dictionary adds to this definition, saying that a park can be "a large area known for its natural scenery and preserved for public recreation by a…national government."

By these definitions Buffalo National River is a park, for Congress in 1972 preserved the river in its natural state for public recreation. So also are those large, natural, scenic areas along the river that Congress in later years set aside as wilderness areas, three of them within the boundaries of Buffalo National River and two more on the adjoining Ozark National Forest. And so again are two segments of the headwaters stream that Congress in 1992 designated as the Buffalo Wild River and Buffalo Scenic River.

In the following pages we deal first with how the earliest and largest of these reservations, Buffalo National River, has been developed and how it is managed to fulfill its purposes set forth by Congress. Then we deal with the wilderness areas, administered by two government agencies acting separately toward the same goals. Finally we briefly describe the Wild River and the Scenic River, each with its own administrative requirements.

BUFFALO NATIONAL RIVER

On March 1, 1972 (which happened to be exactly 100 years after President U. S. Grant signed an Act of Congress that established Yellowstone, the world's first national park) President Richard Nixon signed an Act of Congress "to provide for the establishment of the Buffalo National River." That Act, Public Law 92-237, was

> for the purposes of conserving and interpreting an area containing unique scenic and scientific features, and preserving as a free-flowing stream an important segment of the Buffalo River in Arkansas for the benefit and enjoyment of present and future generations.

Thus the Buffalo would become part of a national park system comprising many of the nation's most significant natural, historical, and recreational areas. The National River would be administered by the National Park Service. Congress in 1916 had instructed the Park Service, in administering parks:

> to conserve the scenery and the natural and historic objects and the wildlife therein and to provide for the enjoyment of the same in such manner and by such means as will leave them unimpaired for the enjoyment of future generations.

Those instructions imply a balance between development ("provide for the enjoyment") and nondevelopment ("conserve"). The Park Service always has understood the Congressional mandate as one to plan and design any park facilities so as to have as little impact as possible on the natural surroundings. As much as in any other area in the national park system, such treatment would need to apply to Buffalo National River.

The National River Act of 1972 also specified that:

• the total area within the boundaries of Buffalo National River was not to exceed 95,730 acres.

• the National Park Service could acquire land by donation, purchase, or exchange, except that lands owned by the State of Arkansas could be acquired only by donation.

• except for property the Park Service needed for administration, development, access, or public use, the owners of a residence or farm within National River boundaries could elect to retain use and occupancy of such property for life, or, if electing a specific term in years, for a term of up to 25 years after the Park Service purchased the property.

• the Park Service was to pay the owners the fair market value of the property on the date of its purchase, less the fair market value of the term retained by the owner.

• hunting and fishing were to be permitted in accordance with federal and state laws, except at places and times where they had to be prohibited for reasons of public safety, administration, fish or wildlife management, or public use and enjoyment.

• there were to be no dams on the Buffalo, and no federal assistance to any water resources project that would have a direct and adverse effect on the river's natural qualities.

• the Park Service was to administer, protect, and develop Buffalo National River in accordance with the Act of August 25, 1916 (the Act that says "conserve" and "provide for the enjoyment").

• by March 1975, the Park Service was to review the area within

National River boundaries and identify and recommend any portion of that area suited for preservation as wilderness.

Land Acquisition

Soon after the 1972 Act was signed, the Park Service employed a private contractor to prepare a map of landholdings within National River boundaries. It turned out there were 1307 parcels of land to be acquired, from quarter-acre subdivision lots to large tracts of more than 1000 acres. The Park Service assembled a staff of appraisers and negotiators to buy land.

In the fall of 1973 the State of Arkansas donated 2021-acre Buffalo River State Park and 280-acre Lost Valley State Park. In 1985 the Arkansas Game and Fish Commission donated 853 acres of the Gene Rush/Buffalo River Wildlife Management Area and 120 acres of the Loafer's Glory Wildlife Management Area that lay within National River boundaries. The U.S. Forest Service transferred 2035 acres of similarly situated land from the Sylamore District of the Ozark National Forest and 28 acres from the Henry Koen Experimental Forest. The U.S. Bureau of Land Management transferred 723 acres in 15 parcels of the original public domain that had never been acquired by private interests—scattered pieces of land too steep and rocky for homes or farms (though in the past, on parts of this unprotected acreage, timber had been stolen whenever practicable). In all, then, 6060 acres of public land were transferred or donated to the care of the Park Service.

That left nearly 90,000 acres to be purchased from private owners. As specified in the 1972 Act, payments were to be fair market value, based on amounts willingly paid by buyers to willing sellers in recent sales of comparable properties in the surrounding area. As land purchases proceeded, disagreements about price between private owners and the government were resolved by having the courts determine the amounts to be paid. Court procedures also were employed to resolve uncertainties about ownership of land, and in a few cases, condemnation allowed the Park Service immediate possession where property was in immediate danger of private development. Some landowners were bitter about having to sell their homes. Most, however, simply sold for prices that the Park Service offered.

In terms of acreage, 95 percent of the land was purchased by 1981. Subsurface mining rights for some tracts were acquired after 1990, and land sell-backs and exchanges to protect the historic farming community in the Boxley Valley and the pastoral bottomlands of the Richland Valley were done as recently as 1992.

By 1994 the payments for purchases in fee (all rights acquired), for easements (only specified rights acquired), and for mineral rights totaled a little over $36,250,000. This did not include expenses for title work, surveys, mapping, appraisals, and staff payroll.

Private Ownership

About 5800 acres of land within National River boundaries are privately owned or leased for farming. These arrangements were first anticipated by the Park Service in 1963; in its initial study report favoring creation of the National River, the Service said that farmlands in the Boxley Valley and along Richland Creek should remain in private ownership. Subsequently, Congress also recognized that within limits, grazing or haying could continue, providing income to local residents and not interfering with recreational use of the river. Moreover, the Boxley and Richland Valley farms were historic; they had been there for 150 years (photos, pages 262, 268, and 366).

Private landowners now remain within National River boundaries under any of several arrangements. For most properties in the Boxley and Richland Valleys, for example, the Park Service purchased *scenic easements*—or, at Boxley, *preservation easements*—that allow existing single-family residences to remain, as well as gardens, orchards, haying, and grazing. Arts and crafts studios are allowed, and home-based bed-and-breakfast inns in historic houses. When purchasing easements, the Park Service acquired rights for confinement feeding of livestock and for other commercial operations that would disrupt the historic pastoral scene. Lands under easements are closed to public access; the easements are meant only to protect water quality in the river and views from the valley roads.

Another form of easement was written for the Boy Scouts' Camp Orr. The camp was established in 1955, well before creation of the park, and serves a broad sampling of youth from Arkansas and out of state. Therefore the Park Service purchased rights that provide for continued use of the camp by the Scouts but prevent commercial developments. Camp Orr's easement also permits hikers on the public-use Buffalo River Trail to enter the property. Along another path closer to the river, horseback riders are allowed when the camp is not in session for the Scouts.

As provided in the 1972 Act, owners of properties not needed by the Park Service as sites for development could retain *use and occupancy* for up to 25 years or *life estate* for the sellers' lifetimes. In other words, sellers could lease back their properties, with the rental charge deducted from the purchase price. A number of people chose use and occupancy for 25 years, which in most cases ran from dates of sale in the later 1970s; the last of these leases was written to expire in 2007. Very few chose life estate; after the year 2000 there were only three life estate contracts still in effect. Life estate and use and occupancy agreements specified that until the contracts expired, the properties were closed to public entry, for the contract holders had rights to use the land for private homes and for agriculture.

Elsewhere, a number of properties purchased by the Park Service included fields well suited for growing hay. These areas have become what the Park Service calls *hay leases,* rented to local farmers who cut and bale the hay for feeding to cattle located elsewhere.

In the Boxley Valley several tracts passed to public ownership but needed to be maintained as part of the pastoral, historic scene. For these properties the Park Service executed long-term (10–20 years) *historic property leases* with valley landowners to use these tracts for residences, haying, and grazing. Public entry is permitted in parts of these areas, but not camping or hunting.

A long-term, 50-year lease was written in 1992 with the nonprofit Gorgas Science Foundation to provide for interpreting the story of Boxley's water-powered mill (drawing, page 116). In the late 1980s a Park Service restoration crew had shored up and stabilized the mill's sagging building—which dates from 1870—but the Service lacked funds to prepare the mill's interior for public viewing. The Science Foundation installed walkways and interpretive displays, and in 2000 began guided tours on a limited basis.

Also at Boxley is the one continuously active, long established church within National River boundaries. The Boxley Baptist Church and its parsonage remain in private ownership, as does the adjacent Boxley Community Building; all serve the people living in and around the valley (photo, page 60).

Two cemeteries in the Boxley Valley, cemeteries at Erbie and at Pruitt on the upper river, and cemeteries in Richland Valley and Arnold Bend on the middle Buffalo still receive burials or at least are maintained by private individuals or organizations. These cemeteries remain in private ownership, but elsewhere about thirty small cemeteries, family plots, and single grave sites are on public property. A few of these long neglected burial places in the Lower Buffalo Wilderness are so well hidden in undergrowth that while their existence is known, their exact locations are uncertain. In the 1990s local youth groups began clearing and fencing the unmaintained plots.

Uses for Buildings

During the 1970s, as the Park Service acquired land having buildings—houses, barns, and other structures—each was evaluated for how it might best serve the purposes of the park.

Because several park rangers would need to live near their assigned areas, and seasonal employees and volunteers would have difficulty finding housing outside the park, more than a dozen existing houses, a mobile home, and a four-unit lodge were reserved for

The Boxley mill around 1900 was a community center where people brought corn to be ground for meal and wheat for flour.

Two men lean against the flume that carried water from the millpond to the boxed-in pit at the end of the building. Dropping into the pit, the water turned a turbine at the bottom, which by a system of gears, shafts, and pulleys turned machinery in the mill.

The lean-to room next to the pit was an "office" where the miller could retreat on cold days and warm himself by a stove.

their use. Several other buildings were kept to be used as ranger stations and as shop or storage space for park maintenance crews.

Many other buildings were of historical value. A number of the most significant ones have been stabilized to prevent further deterioration and their significance has been recognized by including them on the National Register of Historic Places. The Collier cabin and outbuildings at Tyler Bend, the Civilian Conservation Corps–built cabins, lodge, pavilion, and retaining walls at Buffalo Point, the Cold Springs Schoolhouse below Rush, and buildings at Boxley, Erbie, and Rush have all been placed on the National Register.

A few buildings not eligible for the National Register but of value for understanding local history have been stabilized. For example, park employees and volunteers have repaired the roof and front porch of the longtime home of Eva Barnes (Granny) Henderson (photos, pages 265 and 329), who lived in what is now the Ponca Wilderness. Granny's house was in good enough condition to be saved but her outbuildings had collapsed; these, and ruins of structures elsewhere in the park, have been left as "discovery sites."

Many of the purchased buildings were of no special historic significance and were not needed for park administration. Some of these buildings were salvaged, as part of the sale agreements, by owners who had sold the land to the Park Service. Others were sold to highest bidders who moved them outside the park or tore them down for materials. Stone or concrete foundations often remain.

Finally, there were nonhistoric buildings having no salvage value and in such poor condition they posed safety hazards, and park employees tore them down.

Park Planning

The Park Service's direction from Congress to combine preservation with development prompts the Service to move cautiously, with research and planning, before undertaking any important project or program. Much of this preliminary work at Buffalo National River has been done by the park staff, but often they look for help from knowledgeable employees at other parks, or from the National Park Service's planning and design office in Denver, Colorado, or from universities or private firms. The efforts of all these people on behalf of the Buffalo River have added up by now to a tall stack of research and planning reports, many of them to be mentioned here.

The first research project was begun barely a year after the 1972

Act when the Park Service employed a team of scientists from the University of Arkansas for a preliminary survey of the Buffalo River's water quality. The investigators found the river in good condition and their data provided a basis for comparison with water quality surveys in later years.

Then, as required by the 1972 Act, the Service in 1975 completed a study to locate areas that qualified for Congressional designation as wilderness. The recommendations of this study were embodied in wilderness legislation enacted by Congress in 1978, further described here on pages 135–136. In 1975 also, the Service completed a plan that sketched the locations and uses for developed and nondeveloped areas that exist today along the Buffalo, as well as a prospectus, or collection of ideas, for interpreting the river's natural and human history for park visitors.

Through the 1980s, plans followed one after another. A river use management plan written in 1983 was based on studies of floaters and their activity that had been made by a team from Texas A&M University. The plan's principal finding was that the numbers of canoers on various parts of the Buffalo did not exceed what appeared to be the river's carrying capacity, so there should be no restrictions on their numbers. (Actually, canoe use had peaked around 1980; see photos, opposite.)

During the 1980s, planning teams having members from the park, the Service's Southwest Regional Office, and the planning staff in Denver produced a series of proposals for facilities at specific sites in most of the development areas, from Lost Valley all the way downriver to Rush. Another plan, published in 1987, called for an extensive system of hiking and horseback riding trails.

These plans were generalized and conceptual, and as subsequent events have shown, somewhat overambitious. There was neither the funding nor the need for everything that was proposed in these conceptual plans, so the actual developments were scaled down. But the plans did reflect the best thinking at the time, and many of their proposals became actual, on-the-ground development.

Other plans emerged: in 1982 a Resources Management Plan; in 1985 a land use plan for protecting the historic character of the Boxley Valley; in 1986 a Road System Evaluation to determine whether to improve, maintain, or close each of dozens of existing roads and tracks throughout the park. In 1994 a plan for wilderness and backcountry management followed a series of public meetings in which interested parties expressed strongly differing beliefs: Some wanted more development of trails and others wanted less, and so on. Then in 1995 a Fisheries Management Plan—a joint effort of the Park Service, the U.S. Forest Service, and the Arkansas Game and Fish Commission—called for avoidance of artificial measures to introduce new fish species or to increase the numbers of native fish beyond the river's natural carrying capacity. The goal was to have self-sustaining populations of native fish. Fishing would be for the quality of the experience rather than for the numbers of fish caught.

As the Park Service acquired land and prepared plans, the planners

More people. The difference in the size of weekend crowds at the Ponca low-water bridge in 1965 (upper view) and ten years later (lower) suggests that around 1970 canoeing became a much more popular pastime. For the Park Service, the eternal question is: When does use become overuse, damaging both the river's natural resources and the canoers' quality of experience?

became much better acquainted with the river and its environs. They learned that, within park boundaries, a large number of buildings—257 in all—were historic or at least had value for explaining the river's history. These buildings tended to be concentrated in areas having roads, fences, and other bits and pieces that defined historic communities. Thus the Park Service recognized, and designated, several "culturally significant landscapes" worthy of protection. These areas, surrounding the National Register buildings named above, now comprise more than 10 percent of Buffalo National River. They vary in size from only a few acres around the Cold Springs Schoolhouse to 7900 acres encompassing the Boxley Valley.

Park Development

Sandwiched between park planning and subsequent development are two additional steps that result from mandates by Congress. Development sites on federal land, whether for a front-country campground or a backcountry trail, must be first surveyed for the presence of both archeological sites and botanical rarities. These requirements stem from realization that the public lands are the only places—given that there are private rights to unchecked development nearly everywhere else—where we might learn more of otherwise unknown prehistoric or historic peoples, or protect rare and endangered plant species that may prove useful to us for medicines or for other purposes. At Buffalo River development sites, archeological and botanical surveys have been done by qualified persons on the park staff or by outside contractors.

The first major development at an entirely new site began at Erbie in the late 1980s to improve the access road from Highway 7 and to construct the Erbie campground, the Cedar Grove picnic area, trails at Erbie, and the Buffalo River Trail from Kyles Landing past Erbie and to Ozark Campground. Then, around 1990, the Tyler Bend complex took form, with its three-mile entrance road, visitor center, campground, picnic area, pavilion, amphitheater, boat launch site, maintenance shops and storage area, loop trails, and Buffalo River Trail from Richland Valley to Gilbert.

Except for trail construction done by a Park Service crew, these major developments were handled by private contractors with oversight from engineers, architects, and landscape architects from the planning and design office in Denver. Smaller projects elsewhere have been carried out by the park's maintenance workers, who over the years have built, modified, and repaired camp and picnic sites, canoe launch ramps, bulletin boards, roads, trails—everything.

Trail construction has also been done by volunteers. Trail workers from the Student Conservation Association, Sierra Club, American Hiking Society, Ozark Society, and other organizations and individuals as well in the 1980s and 1990s built more than 20 miles of trails, including nearly all the Buffalo River Trail through difficult terrain from Boxley down the river to Kyles Landing.

Park Operations

Soon after 1972, as the Park Service acquired land and public use areas along the river, the Service divided the park into three operating districts: Upper River District, headquartered at Pruitt; Middle River District, to be based at Tyler Bend; and Lower River District, overseen from Buffalo Point. Each district was to be staffed with *park rangers, park interpreters,* and *maintenance mechanics.*

Out front and visible to the public when going their rounds, park

"America's First National River," the Buffalo is proclaimed. True—but how many other national rivers are there?

To the year 2002, only one, the New River Gorge National River in West Virginia. Two other rivers, the Big South Fork in Tennessee and the Mississippi in Minnesota, have the hybrid name "National River and Recreational Area." Among the 20 National Park Service areas focused on rivers, all the others have different designations, such as National Recreational Area, or Wild River, or Wild and Scenic River, or National Preserve. As the names suggest, these rivers vary from near-urban to far-from-anywhere. The Buffalo is about midway across the spectrum, or probably on the wilderness side of midway.

Buffalo National River was the second "river park" to be created by Congress, in 1972. The first, in 1964, was the Ozark National Scenic Riverways, on the Current River, and its Jacks Fork, in Missouri. Of all the river parks, the Ozark Riverways most resembles the Buffalo in acreage, stream mileage, geology, biological makeup and historical background. These two parks, however, have obvious and counterbalancing differences. The Ozark Riverways, fed by large springs, has more abundant water flow during summer's drought. But the Buffalo, with more extensive areas of wilderness and many high cliffs, has the edge on spaciousness and rugged scenery.

rangers have become symbolic of the Park Service, so much so that other park employees are often mistakenly called rangers. The park rangers, though, have two specific areas of responsibility: to safeguard the park and its resources and to protect the lives and safety of park visitors. In protecting resources and people, rangers have to deal with lawbreaking, which at Buffalo River may mean theft, trespass, vandalism, arson, poaching, public drunkenness, or traffic violations. They are trained to fight fires. They manage searches for lost hikers, and rescue the injured or evacuate the dead from isolated and dangerous places (photos, page 124). They patrol the river to warn canoers of coming high water (aided, in this case, by the park's network of rain gauges placed strategically to provide advance warning of floods). The rangers also have mutual-assistance agreements with others who deal with public safety—local sheriffs' deputies, highway patrolmen, firefighters, wildlife officers, Forest Service officers, and search-and-rescue volunteers—all of whom reciprocate for backup and assistance.

The park interpreters provide information at visitor centers, lead the guided hikes, and give the evening programs. Their job is to interpret (meaning to translate, to bring out the meaning of) the natural and historic aspects of the park. They may be assisted by volunteers—local people with intimate knowledge of the river can enliven any interpretive program. The interpreters also provide learning in the field for school classes (photos, pages 5 and 125) and give programs for groups outside the park.

A large number of park employees are charged with *facilities management*—maintaining the National River's buildings, utility systems, roads, and trails. A core group of maintenance mechanics is mostly employed year-round. Each of them has journeyman ratings in at least two skilled trades—carpentry, electrical work, plumbing, painting, heavy equipment operation (graders, backhoes), wastewater plant operation. Among them, they are capable of fully carrying out smaller construction projects as well as operation and maintenance of larger facilities. At Buffalo National River they are to maintain 135 miles of paved and unpaved road surfaces, more than 100 miles of trails, 283 buildings and structures, 20 water systems, three wastewater treatment plants, and about 200 acres of mowed areas along park roads, around buildings, and in campgrounds (photo, page 125).

The maintenance force doubles in size during the warm months, when seasonal workers are employed to take care of nearly all the visitor services such as bathroom cleaning, grounds maintenance, and trash collection. In all, year-round and seasonal maintenance activities require approximately half the park's staff and 50 percent of the park's total budget. (This also is the case throughout the National Park System.)

While most park employees out in the districts are seen by park visitors, others at the headquarters offices in town—Harrison, Arkansas—are much less visible to the public. There, supervisors for the rangers, interpreters, and maintenance force plan, budget, and provide overall direction. Administrative people exercise accounting controls over funds, purchase and store equipment and supplies, keep tabs on valuable property, administer contracts for construction and other services, assist other staffers having problems with their computers, and process personnel actions. One person oversees contracts with the park's licensed canoe-raft-johnboat concessioners and the operator of the restaurant and rental cabins at Buffalo Point, ensuring that these concessioners meet standards for safety of visitors and charge for services at prices comparable with those of other businesses in their neighborhoods.

Other headquarters employees include a team of natural-resource managers. A hydrologist and assistants work toward protecting the Buffalo River's water quality (see page 130). Resource managers also maintain an air quality monitoring station at Buffalo Point (where the air is so unpolluted that it is used as a standard for comparison with urban air monitored at other stations of the National Atmospheric Deposition Program). Among other duties, resource people maintain what is termed the Buffalo National River Hydrologic Data System, rain gauges placed around the river's watershed that transmit data to base stations and provide early warnings of flash floods (see page 424). Staffers also monitor, inventory, and protect rare and endangered plant and animal species, remove invasive alien plants, protect rare features in the park's caves (photo, page 126), and administer and monitor areas under private use permits, leases, and easements for hay cutting and grazing. They also carry out wildlife projects, for example quail habitat restoration by replacing sod grasses (fescue) with clump grasses (native species). Trained crews carry out controlled burns to remove buildups of flammable debris in old fields, keeping them open for wildlife, including elk. At other times the park's fire crews suppress wildfires, especially

Down and up.
To rescue victims of falls on cliffs and in caves, rangers and other park employees learn how to rappel down rock faces (left). Also to climb from ledges or pits (below) using rope-gripping devices called ascenders.

They train regularly. Employees advance from basic first aid to emergency medicine dealing with trauma from falls or auto accidents, with hypothermia or with heat exhaustion, with near drowning, or with cardiac arrest. Also they learn advanced methods to contain both structural and wildland fires and to rescue canoers stranded in swift floodwaters.

Three basic, visible functions of the National Park Service are protection of visitors and park resources, care of the park's facilities, and interpretation of the park's story.

Park care. Shortly before 7:00 a.m., two employees (opposite) get ready to mow a campground and chip brush. The National River has about 200 acres to be mowed—roadsides, camp and picnic areas, visitor centers, historic sites—and many other tasks to keep everything ready for use by park visitors. Here at Tyler Bend is one of the park's three facilities-maintenance centers.

"Doing bugs."

Park intepreters show pupils from area schools the basics of the aquatic ecosystem. One way is to catch macroinvertebrates—insect larvae—in a net and let the children identify the various kinds. One youngster studies a mayfly that lit on his little finger.

This "doing bugs" learning session is at Buffalo Point.

where fire is likely to spread onto private property outside the park.

At headquarters also are an archeologist and an historian. Both are cultural resource managers in that they are to inventory the National River's prehistoric and historic features and assure compliance with federal laws protecting these features. They also become interpreters, sharing their knowledge of the park's history or Native American prehistory when requested by schools and other organizations.

Finally, a park superintendent is in charge overall, directs park planning, and is the National River's principal representative in contacts and relations with outside groups and individuals wishing to influence park operations. As happens throughout the federal government, knowledgeable members of the park staff write the outgoing letters, but the superintendent signs the letters as an indication that they are written with his or her knowledge and approval.

In addition to the park's own employees, individuals and organizations in several categories have important roles in park operations. One category would be the various kinds of *contractors*: construction

Can't fix it.
Broken by a careless caver, a rare, fragile speleothem of gypsum lies on the floor of a low passage in Fitton Cave. Required to protect such irreplaceable natural features, the Park Service closed a section of the cave having delicate gypsum needles after some were broken off by a spelunker.

Fitton Cave's entrances have locked gates. To gain entry, visitors must be in small, properly equipped groups with qualified leaders. Those meeting the requirements can enter and explore.

firms, research groups, boundary surveyors, archeological and botanical investigators, and many others.

Another category could be labeled the *cooperators*, organizations whose own funded programs benefit the National River. These include the public safety agencies—sheriffs' offices, state police, volunteer fire departments, and others who assist park rangers. And the state and federal pollution control agencies and the Natural Resources Conservation Service of the U.S. Department of Agriculture, with programs to abate non–point source pollution of the Buffalo's tributaries. Cooperators include other federal agencies—the U.S. Geological Survey and even that former proponent of damming the river, the U.S. Army Corps of Engineers. State agencies are also cooperators—the highway department and especially the Game and Fish Commission. Private nonprofit organizations also have helped in game restoration programs: These include the Rocky Mountain Elk Foundation and the National Wild Turkey Federation. And several universities have cooperated in a variety of projects concerning the river's natural and historic resources.

Still another category: *volunteers*, a large number of people who as individuals or members of organizations have worked for a day or a week or for months as interpretive demonstrators, cave surveyors, archeological assistants, trail maintainers, historical researchers, campground hosts, litter removers, and in many other roles. Some volunteers live close by; others have come from far away. Around the year 2000, volunteers in total contributed more than 9000 hours annually toward the betterment of the park (photo, page 128).

In truth, the development, upkeep, and improvement of Buffalo National River has required the help of thousands.

River Care

The Arkansas Department of Environmental Quality has placed the Buffalo River on its short list of the state's Extraordinary Resource Waters—unpolluted, pristine. Both the state and the National Park Service want the river to remain pristine for reasons both aesthetic and economic. Any significant amount of pollution could have two bad consequences:

• It could play havoc with the river's pollution-intolerant fish and the insect larvae on which they feed. Many of the macroinvertebrates could disappear. Their predator fish, including the Buffalo's prized smallmouth bass, could also be relegated to history.

• It could shut down recreation. Pollution from domestic animals, for instance, can transmit any of thirteen diseases to humans through water. Swimming, even wading, would have to stop.

To detect any immediate problems and long-term trends in water quality, the Park Service since 1985 has carried on a monitoring program. Every other month, park technicians test the waters and take samples at nine locations along the Buffalo from Boxley to the White River, and at the inflows from 20 of the river's tributaries, and at three springs (photos, page 130). More than a dozen parameters, or characteristics, are measured—some to obtain general knowledge of the river but most because they can indicate any problem. And beginning in 1989, graduate students from the University of Central Arkansas sampled and studied the macroinvertebrates, many of which are indicators of the biological health of the river. The results of all this chemical and biological testing have been encouraging: Pollutants have generally remained well within safe limits.

Still, the record is not perfect. While water quality has been excellent most of the year with the river at base flow and replenished only by ground water, problems occur when the Buffalo is fed by surface

Volunteers.
Selfless citizens have built and maintained many of the river's more than 100 miles of hiking and horse trails. People help as individuals, as members of hiking and horse-riding groups, and as members of outdoor organizations that sponsor service trips. During the 1980s and 1990s, for example, the Ozark Society, Sierra Club, American Hiking Society, Boy Scouts, and Student Conservation Association sponsored hundreds of workers for Buffalo River trails.

runoff from rain or snow melt, which happens on an average of about 65 days a year. The river then becomes turbid (cloudy, muddy), its levels of nutrients (nitrates, phosphates) go up, and concentrations of fecal coliform bacteria can increase dramatically.

The Buffalo exhibits natural turbidity, or cloudiness, when flowing over shale formations near its headwaters and may become cloudy if nutrients in the water fertilize the growth of aquatic algae. Nearly all the turbidity, however, comes with runoff from bare earth of unpaved roads, logged-over areas, or construction sites, or when the river's channel or banks erode. Riverbank erosion has usually been most severe where, in the past, cropland was extended to the water's edge with no buffer of trees and brush having roots to anchor the soil.

The most rapidly eroding site, located below Woolum and known as the High Bank, had a 10-foot-high, 2200-foot-long vertical cutbank that from 1985 to 1991 retreated northward at an average rate of 14 feet per year. (In the previous 75 years it had moved northward a quarter mile.) On average each year, 8000 dump truck loads—40,000 tons—of soil broke loose here and washed down the river. Bank erosion here and elsewhere also widens and destabilizes the river's channel, not only at the eroding cutbanks but also upstream and down as the river works in complex ways to rebalance itself. The result is a shallower, wider stream, less attractive visually. Aquatic habitats are degraded and water quality is reduced by increased sediment loads and turbidity.

During the mid-1990s a Park Service work crew stabilized many of these erosion banks by sloping them back and laying and anchoring cedar trees along the river's edge (photo, page 131). The trees' many limbs shielded the banks from scouring flood waters and trapped sediments that became seedbeds for seeds that washed in. Along the banks and within a buffer strip behind these cedar revetments, workers planted river cane and tree seedlings—ash, cottonwood, oak, sweet gum, sycamore, and willow, all of them native riparian species—to grow and establish root systems to bind the soil.

Three of the cedar revetments were in areas exposed to the full force of floods and they were lost. The other eleven have held on and these former erosion banks have become covered with vegetation.

As mentioned above, surface runoff brings nitrate and phosphate nutrients into the river. These can originate from septic tank or sewage plant effluent, but predominantly they come in runoff from agricultural fertilizers or manure spread on pastures within the

River care.
A Park Service hydrologist takes measurements of cross-sectional area and flow velocity in the channel of a Buffalo River tributary. From this information he can calculate the stream's discharge in cubic feet per second. He takes water samples to learn the concentrations of contaminants such as sediment, nutrients, and fecal coliform bacteria. The concentration of a contaminant multiplied by the stream's discharge will indicate how much of that contaminant this tributary is putting into the Buffalo River.

A park technician holds a sensor probe in the river, and his instrument reads the percentage of dissolved oxygen in the water. His measurements taken here in the Lower Buffalo Wilderness will provide a standard for comparison with sites likely to be more affected by development.

Fish—especially the river's smallmouth bass—need adequate amounts of dissolved oxygen for survival.

watershed (or in subsurface flow from agricultural or residential areas outside the surface watershed of the river; see map, page 30). Nutrients, even in small amounts, can upset the diversity and stability of macroinvertebrate populations, and hence fish species, as macros sensitive to pollution die off and are replaced by tolerant but less desirable ones. Researchers have found this happening on parts of the middle river having increased levels of nutrients.

And as mentioned above, with surface runoff the coliform bacteria show up. Coliforms, which come from intestines of warmblooded animals, including humans, were first thought to be present in the river at heavily used camping and swimming areas, but only negligible numbers of them have been found in water samples from eleven of the most popular public use sites. Instead, the highest coliform counts have occurred at sampling sites affected by runoff from agricultural areas in the Boxley Valley and in tributary valleys draining into the middle Buffalo. These elevated bacteria counts come in rel-

Bank stabilization. In the 1990s the Park Service sloped back many of the river's erosion banks, pinned cedar trees along the water's edge, and planted native hardwoods on the slopes. By 2002 at the High Bank below Woolum, floods had left wads of leaves in the cedars and young hardwoods but the bank was holding. The cutbank in the background did not get treatment.

atively brief pulses after rainstorms. The highest concentrations of coliforms, at the mouths of creeks entering the middle river, have been 150 to 200 times the safe limit for water in which people swim.

In cooperation with the Park Service, Boxley Valley landowners have fenced off a buffer strip averaging 50 feet in width along the river where cattle are excluded and vegetation is allowed to grow so that it can filter runoff from pastures. The Natural Resources Conservation Service (the former Soil Conservation Service) has assisted dairy farmers along middle Buffalo tributaries to provide either holding ponds or roofed dry-storage areas for manure from their herds, alleviating contamination of the creeks. The state's pollution control agency has helped hog farmers on the southern edge of the Buffalo's watershed to better maintain waste treatment ponds. While these abatement measures seem to make no measurable improvement in the river's water quality, it appears there has been no degradation either, even as agricultural growth has continued.

From 1965 to 1992 about 93,000 acres of forest in the Buffalo's watershed were cleared for pasture, so that cleared agricultural land increased from 122,000 to 215,000 acres (maps, opposite). At the year 2000, farm animals in the watershed included about 40,000 beef and dairy cattle and calves, 5000 hogs and pigs, and about 200,000 chickens and 200,000 turkeys. The total output of animal wastes was equivalent to the human wastes of a city. With agriculture in the watershed likely to expand further, the Park Service and others depending on the Buffalo's good water quality will continue to monitor the river's condition and sound alarms when problems become evident. But reducing high bacteria counts or nutrient levels, which we now know are coming almost entirely from farm animals in the watershed, will be a long-term, costly undertaking.

About 60 percent of the Buffalo's watershed is in small private landholdings. (The other 40 percent in public ownership consists of National Forest 27 percent, National River 11 percent, and state wildlife management areas 2 percent.) The private landowners, particularly those with farm animals, are central in maintaining the river's quality. There are things they can do to reduce contamination of the tributaries: for example, by establishing buffer strips, improving pastures, and developing new, land-side stock-watering tanks to keep cattle out of creeks on their farms. But these small farmers cannot afford to do such things. Nor do they feel any strong reason to; they themselves do not perceive benefit from the Buffalo River.

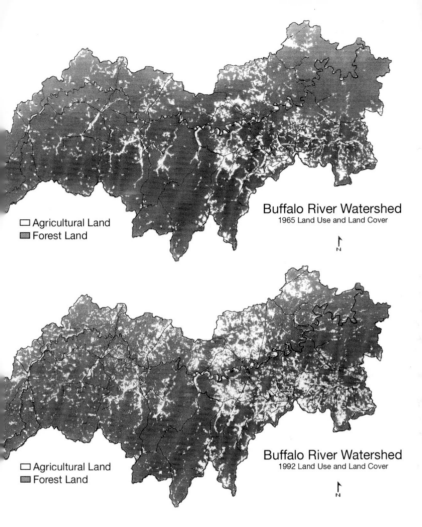

Watershed clearing. Two aerial photo-based maps show more "white space" in the more recent one, representing about 93,000 acres of forest cleared for pasture between 1965 and 1992.

Much of the clearing was on land underlain by the extensive Boone Formation, where weathering has removed limestone bedrock, leaving areas that could be stripped of trees and planted with grass. On the upper watershed, land on the Boone was cleared along Big Creek and Cave Creek and along Highway 123 north of Hasty. In the watershed's midsection, clearing was done mainly around St. Joe, in the drainages of Tomahawk and Calf Creeks, and on upper Big Creek east of Marshall.

This suggests that farm improvements toward protecting water quality will have to be at least a joint effort between farmers and the public—the taxpayers, if you will, who benefit from the pristine Buffalo River. In cost-sharing arrangements, farmers or others could provide labor and U.S. or state agencies could pay for contract work and materials. State or federal pollution control agencies might at times wield the stick (enforcement of laws or regulations to bring gross violators into compliance) as well as offer the carrot (payments for pasture improvements that can increase the farmers' income).

As said before, the development, upkeep, and improvement of Buffalo National River require the help of thousands. All those who live in the watershed, as well as many individuals and organizations outside, are automatically enrolled to assist.

Investigations and research continue. Mapping by the Geological Survey will provide a clearer picture of where underground flow is passing beneath the surface divide along the Buffalo watershed's north side, where the cavernous Boone Formation provides conduits for subterranean streams. Other studies are focused on controlling degradation of the river's channel, especially where the banks are eroding. Still others are about aquatic life and how it may be changing in response to human-caused alterations of the watershed.

THE WILDERNESS AREAS

On September 3, 1964, Congress enacted a law, the Wilderness Act, which began with a statement of policy:

> In order to assure that an increasing population, accompanied by expanding settlement and growing mechanization, does not occupy and modify all areas within the United States and its possessions, leaving no lands designated for preservation and protection in their natural condition, it is hereby declared to be the policy of the Congress to secure for the American people of present and future generations the benefits of an enduring resource of wilderness.

The Act then called for federally owned areas to be designated as "wilderness areas," to be administered "for the use and enjoyment of the American people in such manner as will leave them unimpaired for future use and enjoyment as wilderness."

Wilderness was then defined as "an area where the earth and its community of life are untrammeled [unrestrained, uncontrolled, unmanaged] by man, where man himself is a visitor who does not remain." Wilderness was further defined as an area of undeveloped federal land retaining its primeval character and influence, without permanent improvements or human habitation, and which (1) generally appears to have been affected primarily by the forces of nature, with man's imprint substantially unnoticeable; (2) has outstanding opportunities for solitude or a primitive and unconfined type of recreation; (3) has at least 5000 acres of land or is of sufficient size to make practicable its preservation and use in an unimpaired condition; and (4) may also contain ecological, geological, or other features of scientific, educational, scenic, or historical value.

Specifically prohibited within wilderness areas were permanent and temporary roads, motor vehicles and motorized equipment, other forms of mechanical transport, structures or installations, and commercial enterprises such as timbering and mining. The Act, however, permitted livestock grazing, actions taken (including use of motor vehicles) in emergencies involving the health and safety of persons within a wilderness area, and measures for control of fire, insects, and diseases. Owners of private land within wilderness areas were given rights to assure them adequate access to their land.

Wilderness areas were to be designated only by Acts of Congress. For several years after 1964, the areas so designated were large, pristine, and in the West. A debate arose. Citizens wanted wilderness areas set aside also in the eastern United States, closer to centers of population. But others argued that eastern areas, even if uninhabited, were too small and too degraded by evidence of abandoned roads, homesites, and other development.

Nearness to people eventually prevailed over purity of landscape. Congress began to designate eastern wilderness areas, with each one essentially complying with the requirements of the 1964 Wilderness Act. Thus in 1975, Congress created the Upper Buffalo Wilderness on the Ozark National Forest. Then in 1978, Congress followed up on a requirement of the Buffalo National River Act of 1972 and designated three wilderness areas within the National River: the 2200-acre Upper Buffalo Wilderness adjoining the National Forest's Upper Buffalo; the 11,300-acre Ponca Wilderness; and the 22,500-acre Lower Buffalo Wilderness. And in 1984, Congress established the 16,838-acre Leatherwood Wilderness on the National Forest adjoining the Lower Buffalo Wilderness, and enlarged the National Forest's Upper Buffalo Wilderness to its present size of 11,094 acres.

Here were five eastern wilderness areas, tiny compared with those hundred-thousand-acre preserves out West or the million-acre ones in Alaska. Furthermore, every one of the Buffalo River areas bore the marks of roadbuilding, timbering, and homesteading. The Park Service's Ponca and Upper Buffalo included vacant houses and barns; the Ponca and Lower Buffalo had abandoned mines; the Lower Buffalo even had the abandoned Cold Springs Schoolhouse, which would be placed on the National Register of Historic Places to be preserved into the future. Tucked away in the Lower Buffalo were half a dozen gutted hulks of 1950s-vintage cars; they too may be deemed historic and allowed to stay. And in the Forest Service's Leatherwood Wilderness at year 2002, two private inholdings remained, with their owners having legal rights of access by road.

At one extreme in distractions from wilderness purity is the Ponca unit, less than 18 square miles with 37 miles of maintained hiking and horseback trails—more than two miles of trail for each square mile of wilderness. The Ponca also has two scenic magnets that attract day-trippers: the Goat Trail across the upper face of Big Bluff and the 204-foot waterfall in Hemmed-in Hollow. At the Ponca's east boundary is the Boy Scouts' Camp Orr, from which each summer more than one thousand Scouts troop into the wilderness.

Most of the 13,000-acre combined Park Service/Forest Service Upper Buffalo Wilderness is much less accessible, and much less visited, than the Ponca. There are no maintained trails except for the one-and-a-half-mile path the Forest Service opened to channel a steady stream of day-hikers to what had become another prime destination, the rock overhang known as Whitaker Point or Hawksbill Crag. The overhang is a scenic eye-stopper and an easy photo-grab; its relation to wilderness is accidental. People walk down to it, stay a while, and then turn back toward their cars. Few go beyond.

For the Park Service's Lower Buffalo Wilderness, one more distraction: buzzing boat motors on the river, which bisects the area. Fishermen here have long made use of motors (which, however, are limited to ten horsepower), so the Buffalo River to its normal high water mark is excluded from the wilderness.

Actually, the final and truly universal blow to wilderness purity, for which wilderness is simply a blank spot on the map, is that such blank spots no longer exist. All the Buffalo River's wilderness, indeed every wilderness area in the United States including those in Alaska, is nicely displayed on topographic maps (and many are described at length in guidebooks such as this one).

So what can we say about Buffalo River wilderness living up to the 1964 Wilderness Act's statement about wilderness having "outstanding opportunities for solitude"?

Part of the answer is that the Act immediately expands that statement by adding "or a primitive and unconfined type of recreation." If not always utter solitude, at least the Buffalo's little wildernesses offer considerable space for wandering around on foot. Even the Ponca can be a quiet, lonely sort of place, off-trail if not on the trails. And though every wilderness acre is topographically charted, those maps do not reveal the details: the curiously eroded rock, the astonishingly big tree, the soothing sound of trickling water. With numberless nooks and crannies to explore, any of the Buffalo's wilderness areas can entertain for an entire day or for several days. The largest wilderness area, the combined Lower Buffalo/Leatherwood, has enough territory for many days of exploration. The combined area is nearly 40,000 acres, making it the second-largest wilderness reserve in the middle United States, surpassed in size only in the Boundary Waters Canoe Area of northern Minnesota.

Concerned people sought to establish wilderness areas along the Buffalo so as to put the brakes on development. While these areas bear evidence of human alteration of the land, there will not be any more such alteration, only the work of natural processes. Eventually—a century from now?—the buildings may be gone. Road grades and mine diggings will be largely blended into their surroundings. Barring catastrophe, the maturing forest will become much like the forest encountered by the first Euro-American settlers. In this world so likely to become ever more densely populated, more completely mechanized, more noisy and complex, the Buffalo's wildernesses will become not only preserves of nature but also places of refuge where people can go, and relax, and revive.

To care for the wilderness, the Park Service and Forest Service are to remain unobtrusive—or nonintrusive—letting nature take its course and doing only what is necessary to protect the land and promote its native life forms. They will control wildfires (with hand tools, if possible) and insect and disease outbreaks, largely to keep any of these from spreading onto private lands outside the wilderness. They will keep an eye on the condition of backcountry campsites, trails, and stream banks and try to mitigate the effects of human-caused erosion. They will encourage and carry out information gathering and research to increase understanding of the natural systems at work in wilderness and to learn about visitor activities, behavior, and perceived needs.

Trail construction or relocation would be only to prevent resource damage, not for hiker convenience. A single exception would be a trail that has been proposed to run downriver from Highway 14, if a portion of it is located within the Lower Buffalo area.

The wilderness areas are intended to allow the visitor spontaneity of use and freedom from regimentation. Controls on human movement are to be minimal, and for the foreseeable future there is to be no control on numbers of visitors to the wilderness areas. If controls ever come, they would be to disperse use because too many people, or too many at one time, are destroying popular campsites (the damage there is measurable) or interfering with others' desire for solitude (the damage here is subjective, inexact). Such controls usually mean having a system in which designated campsites must be reserved like hotel rooms, as they already are in wilderness areas having many visitors. The system of course curtails spontaneity and freedom even as it restricts the number of overnight visitors and spreads them out.

But the Buffalo River wildernesses are not on a reservation system, and as impure as these little areas may be, they can perform as perhaps only wilderness can perform in satisfying people's conscious or subconscious needs:

• to experience and to develop understanding and appreciation of unmodified natural ecosystems (which may be the most important of these needs);

• to escape personal pressures, in quiet places free of unnatural sights and sounds (this may be the second most important need);

• to keep fit, through physical and mental challenge;

• to gain freedom, in situations not involving obligations to others or social restrictions; and

• to achieve a sense of self-worth, through traveling and living without mechanized aids, successfully confronting nature "on its own terms" in surroundings where one succeeds or fails depending on one's own abilities and knowledge.

WILD AND SCENIC RIVER

Employing much the same philosophy written into the Wilderness Act of 1964 to protect natural landscapes, Congress in 1968 enacted the Wild and Scenic Rivers Act to protect some of the least developed waterways. In 1968 and in later years Congress designated a number of segments of rivers around the United States as "wild" (primitive surroundings, wilderness), "scenic" (basically natural surroundings), or "recreational" (readily accessible, populated). On April 22, 1992, Congress passed the Arkansas Wild and Scenic Rivers Act to protect several streams, including the Buffalo's headwaters on the Ozark National Forest.

The Arkansas Act designated as "wild" the 9.7-mile segment of the Buffalo within the Forest Service's Upper Buffalo Wilderness. There were to be restrictions on mining, timbering, and other commercial activities—a "second layer of protection," for these restrictions were already in effect for the Wilderness.

The 1992 Act designated as "scenic" a 6.4-mile stretch of the Buffalo extending up the river from the upstream boundary of the Upper Wilderness near Dixon Ford to a point located little more than a mile downstream from the river's farthest source (map, page 2). The "scenic" designation protects a strip of national forest land, averaging about one-fourth mile on each side of the river, from commercial activities such as quarrying and timbering. Woods roads along the river are blocked to motor vehicles but are open to hikers, horseback riders, and mountain bikers.

The Buffalo Scenic River above Dixon Ford is a small stream, labeled "Main Prong Big Buffalo Creek" on topographic maps. Scattered along its narrow valley are old farm clearings overgrown with non-native pasture grasses and multiflora rose, or with pine trees either planted around 1960 or colonizing naturally. In the 1990s the area lay within two of the Forest Service's woodland range grazing allotments and cattle occasionally could be seen in these old fields. Grazing was allowed in the 1992 Act.

In other respects the Forest Service manages the Scenic River corridor to prevent degradation of resources, including the quality of water in the stream. The forest is to develop toward old growth.

Of What Use, "Natural Areas"?

With Congressional designation of the Scenic River segment in 1992, practically the entire Buffalo River had been placed within a corridor of public land having special protection—Buffalo Scenic River and the Forest Service's Upper Buffalo Wilderness at the headwaters, Buffalo National River the rest of the way downstream. Largely undeveloped to begin with, or reverting to nature after past development, most of the river and its shorelands were placed on course toward becoming a "natural area" having old-growth forest.

Apart from the recreational and cultural values of a "natural" river, the fact that the Buffalo's protected corridor will largely regain some sense of the primeval could—or will—have some uses not as easily recognized. Namely, the Buffalo River natural area can serve as:

• *a standard for comparison with altered areas.* For example, researchers were wondering why planted shortleaf pine trees were sick—until they compared soil in the plantation with soil in an undisturbed pine forest. The plantation soil lacked the complex mix of soil organisms, the community of micro plant and animal species that contributed to fertility.

• *a chemical storehouse and gene pool of potentially useful plants and animals.* Undisturbed forests, for example, tend to harbor a far greater number of species of plants and animals than disturbed areas such as cutover woodlands. Each species of plant is a unique biochemical factory; many of our medicines have been, and will continue to be, discovered in plants. Among the many distinct species of insects, some have been discovered to be natural predators of other kinds of insects that damage food crops.

• *a nursery for wildlife.* A natural area can harbor not only large populations of game animals, but also such species as songbirds, whose surplus numbers tend to spread out and repopulate developed areas where the birds fail to reproduce enough to replace losses.

• *a place for learning.* With their variety of plants and animals in varied habitats, natural areas offer endless opportunity for teaching and learning about biology and the ecology of living organisms.

Learn. And enjoy.

Part 2

RIVER

Canoers' noon break
on the big gravel bar
at Toney Bluff.

Spring Creek Bluff overlooks the lower Buffalo, a spacious, gentle stream. Novice canoers can enjoy impressive scenery.

River Overview

From farthest source to eventual end, the Buffalo River goes for 153 miles. Recreationists have navigated the river for 146 of those miles, beginning just seven miles below the farthest source.

In 146 miles are opportunities for river trips by canoe, kayak, raft, johnboat, or other floating conveyance, on turbulent whitewater or lazy flat water, from two-hour excursions to ten-day expeditions. Clean gravel bars at frequent intervals on the river make good lunch spots and campsites; there also are several developed campgrounds about one day's float apart. And where the Buffalo River Trail runs parallel to the river, there are opportunities to combine river travel with hiking (see *Float-Hiking,* page 144).

Opportunities for river trips—float trips, as they are called on the Buffalo—depend mostly on rainfall. Springtime, with ample water levels, is ideal for floating the upper river: There is no place more beautiful in the spring than the Buffalo from Ponca to Pruitt. On the upper and middle river from Pruitt down to Tyler Bend, there's a longer season, usually into midsummer. From Tyler Bend downstream the season's still longer. Past Buffalo Point the river is easily navigated year-round except during severe drought.

There are other windows of opportunity. Experienced, properly equipped floaters run the river during warmer spells from late fall through early spring; temperatures are chilly but the river's flow is ample and solitude is guaranteed. And for brief periods, usually in the spring, the young river from Boxley to Ponca has enough water for a sporty run. For very brief periods—a day or so after heavy rainfall—experts can run the highest, wildest stretch of the Buffalo from Dixon Ford to Boxley.

Up-to-date information on river levels for floating can be obtained from the National Park Service (see page 424) and from many of the river's float outfitters.

Floating means getting people, boats, and other gear to the put-in point and away from the take-out. You can do it all yourself, bringing your own canoe, for example, and shuttling a car to the end point of your trip. There also are concessioners along the river who can rent you a canoe, raft, or johnboat; deliver your car to the take-out point or bring you and boat and duffel back to the put-in; and care for other needs. They are licensed by the Park Service and their prices are in line with those of similar businesses in the area. The National Park Service can provide a list of the Buffalo River's concessioners (see page 424 for information on obtaining the list).

On the following pages you will find the river divided into parts of convenient length for floating. The description of each segment includes its length in miles and average gradient in feet per mile. Length, of course, can suggest how long the float will take, and gradient can indicate difficulty. The gradient becomes less—that is, the current becomes slower, more gentle, with fewer drops or rapids—as the river progresses from the headwaters downstream into gentler terrain.

For any given part of the river, how long your trip will take depends on how fast the river is flowing, how hard you paddle, and other factors. The average paddler probably goes about two miles per hour, counting time for lunch and rest breaks. The average canoer can easily go eight to ten miles a day, which allows time also for moving people and equipment at put-in or take-out, or for setting up or taking down camp on a longer journey. Plan to go a shorter distance if you desire a leisurely trip. If you go much farther in your allotted time, the emphasis turns to just getting there.

At times we call your attention to places along the river that are hazards to floaters. Usually these are obstacles that show up where the current is swift. But the river keeps changing; yesterday's hazard may today be gone, and replaced by a new obstacle somewhere else. Just be aware that hazards exist, probably most often as fallen trees blocking the channel in swift water at the river's tightest bends. If you are not sure what you'll encounter around a blind curve, land

> *Float-Hiking* stretches two different sets of muscles, provides two views of the river, and can be done with only one car. Here's how: Drive with a canoe to a boat landing along the Buffalo River Trail. Leave the car there and canoe to the next landing. Land and secure the canoe (chain it to a tree), then hike back up the trail to get the car. Finally, drive downriver to retrieve the canoe. One-day float-hikes have to be done on fairly short stretches of river and trail, but can be on longer ones by starting early or by carrying a backpack and camping overnight before returning for the car. Such trips are best when the temperature is moderate, comfortable for both canoeing and hiking.

your boat, walk down the bank, and take a look—*If in doubt, scout.* Know how to control your boat and avoid the obstacles, even if it means getting out and walking the boat down the opposite bank.

The descriptions of the river that follow are related to what has been discussed in the first four chapters of this book: geology, plants and animals, human history, and park management. Admittedly, plants and animals aren't often mentioned, and evidence of park management isn't often seen along the river. But geology—the rock formations—can be seen in every bluff and on every gravel bar, so geologic features get talked about frequently.

And so do the historic features. People who lived along the river in the past gave names to practically every hole (pool), shoal, bluff, hill, and hollow. Local historians and old-timers have shared their knowledge of place names recorded in this river guide and displayed on the two Trails Illustrated maps that coordinate with the guide.

These names are now in print for several reasons. One was indicated by a Newton County outdoorsman, Roy Wishon. Recalling how people have described the river in terms of holes and shoals, Wishon says: "You talk to one of them old-timers, you tell him where you caught a big fish, he'd know right where it's at."

Another reason is that many of the old names come from the river's early settlers, and pioneers deserve to be remembered. A third reason is that while some of the names are commonplace, some are colorful—Redhorse Hole, Margaret White Bluff, the Judge Moore Whirl—with stories to tell about them.

These place names may also suggest a folk culture. Ten pools scattered along 82 miles of the river were named Blue Hole. While each was named for its color (blue-green, not true blue) it's interesting that at least ten scattered individuals acting independently all hit upon the same name. Coming from similar backgrounds, these people had minds that ran on the same track.

The culture is also there in people's creative spelling ("Sour" for "Sauer") and in names that changed as they were passed along by word of mouth (Robertson to Robinson; Sitton to Sutton to Setten). The isolation of people along the Buffalo, even from others in the same neighborhood, shows in different names that those of the same generation gave the same feature on the river. People on the south side of the Buffalo would have one name for a fishing hole; those on the north side, another name. Many places also were named for the landowners, and as ownership changed, so did names.

Nature also affects names. A hole along the river may fill up. A shoal may wash out, erasing the boundary between two holes. Human mortality surely has erased many more names from memory. Thus these pages show only the remembered names. At times this means more than one name for one place, in which case the more widely accepted or more descriptive name may be noted first.

The locations of holes of water and other features along the river are keyed to river mileage figures printed in black on the two Trails Illustrated maps, indicating distance downstream from the river's farthest source. (On the maps, figures in blue are distances upstream from the White River.) To make it easier to refer back and forth between guide and map, the mileages here in the guide are printed in **boldface**, for example **28.6–28.7**, the location of Blue Hole a quarter mile downstream from the Ponca low-water bridge.

Also, when a geographic feature is named both on the map and here in the guide, the name here is in **boldface**, as for example **Bee Bluff**, located half a mile downriver from above-named Blue Hole.

The Trails Illustrated maps are marked off in miles only, but the above-named Blue Hole—and most other features, too—occur between the mile marks. To place Blue Hole on the map, it may be easier to first visualize a point at 28.5, halfway between mile 28 and mile 29, then to place Blue Hole—or any other feature presently of interest—in relation to the half mile and the nearest mile mark.

Topography displayed on the Trails Illustrated maps, and on the U.S. Geological Survey's topo maps of the area, provide elevations used in calculating average gradients for each section of the river. The maps also were used to find the heights of the river's bluffs. This was done by determining—as closely as possible, within about ten feet—the elevation of each cliff's highest edge, then, within about five feet, the elevation of the river's water surface at the foot of the cliff, then subtracting the lower elevation from the higher one.

The Trails Illustrated maps are waterproof; one can be dropped in the river without harm. This book, however, is not waterproof—but here's an idea: When on the river, keep it in a clear plastic freezer bag, gallon size, about 11 inches square. The bags that have sliding zippers (Hefty OneZip, Ziploc Easy Zipper, or the equivalent) are the easiest to close. In the bag the book can stay open, so you can see the page you want to refer to as you float the river.

Dixon Ford to Boxley Bridge

River miles 7.0 to 22.3. Distance 15.3 miles. Average gradient 34 feet per mile. Challenging but rewarding for whitewater experts. Put-in at ford at end of Forest Route 1463 (Dixon Ridge Road) north of Fallsville. Take-out at Highway 21 bridge in Boxley Valley.

On June 15, 1974, five canoers put in at Dixon Ford—only seven miles downstream from the Buffalo River's farthest source—and became the first persons known to have navigated this highest, wildest reach of the river. During their trip a rain shower turned to hail the size of Ping-Pong balls. The trip's organizer, Margaret Hedges, later wrote about their hazard-filled journey in the *Ozark Society Bulletin* but identified the river only as the Upper Hailstone. She declared that she wanted "to protect the innocent."

Whitewater paddlers quickly deduced that "Upper Hailstone" meant the upper Buffalo. Today whenever heavy rainfall briefly changes this headwaters creek from trickle to torrent, the bold and fearless come and run the Hailstone.

The Hailstone trip goes the entire length of the two adjoining Upper Buffalo Wilderness areas and includes a series of drops totaling 525 feet. As canoeing instructor Bill Bates, who has made the trip several times, says, "It's not just a float stream. It's challenging whitewater...not altogether friendly. But it is beautiful, up there in that wilderness."

Bates agrees with whitewater expert Stewart Noland—who was on that first Hailstone trip in 1974—that this run should only be attempted by people who are comfortable running solid Class III water. (Whitewater textbooks describe Class III as "Rapids...often capable of swamping an open canoe...narrow passages that often require complex maneuvering.") Boats must be equipped with flotation, and equipment must include PFD, helmet, gear in dry bags, extra paddles, rescue rope, Z-drag, first-aid kit, and a waterproofed map. "The map is for keeping track of where you are," Bates says, "and for finding your way out—if you get a boat pinned that you can't even get loose, and you have to walk out."

Bates continues: "That river can be demanding, and it's capable of killing someone, even it it didn't in the first twenty-five years it was floated. But during that time some paddlers have run it repeatedly. The skill of experienced boaters has improved. Equipment has, too. For the experienced paddler it has become less of a challenge.

"What makes the Hailstone so difficult is its length—over fifteen miles from put-in to take-out. There's no way to shorten it, except by camping partway down and making it a two-day trip, but by the second day the water may be too low, and carrying camp stuff on whitewater is not very practical. For whitewater, it's a very long run and you've got all these river maneuvers to make. It wears you out. You just get arm-weary—your hands, forearms, shoulders.

"It's seldom floatable in warm weather, when it would be friendlier. Most often it isn't up and runnable till late fall, starting in November. And then through mid-April usually, when days are short, water's cold, temperature is often cold. So hypothermia is a threat. Most of the times it's runnable, you want to be in a wet suit.

"No one should run it alone or with just two boats. You need to look out for each other's safety—three or four boats to help one another in case someone gets pinned in the middle of the river.

"Most people take at least six hours to accomplish this run. With rescues and pinned boats it could be several hours more. If floaters in November take till ten a.m. to get on the river, they may not have enough time.

"Zero air space under the Ponca low-water bridge to one foot of water over the bridge is optimum for floating the Hailstone. Some prefer up to a foot under, but then the run is increasingly technical.

"If the river's more than a foot over the bridge or is rising, it can be dangerous. Before starting, boaters need to know how much it has rained in the upper watershed, and what's the forecast for rain. They need to take a second read, on conditions at Dixon Ford."

Bates describes the Hailstone in four sections:

7.0–12.0, Dixon Ford to Terrapin Branch, *5.0 mi., 41 ft./mi.* "After you put in, you hit open shelf rock, small falls. A couple of them funnel into powerful wave trains. Down trees also can block the only channel and you have very little time to react to them. In the first mile an old road runs along the right bank. Those having trouble should take out and hike back up the old road."

8.8 "Just after the mouth of **Pruitt Hollow**, there's False Double-Drop, with a waterfall on the left bank. Then Double-Drop, with a boulder blocking the channel except for a narrow slot, and two drops into a pool. Below Double-Drop it's almost continuous Class II or III with maneuvers to make, very short pools, to Terrapin Branch.

"Getting out and scouting would be a good idea, but there's too much to scout everything on the Hailstone. At least the major, Class III rapids should be scouted, unless the boater already knows them."

10.2 "At **Adkins Creek** it's open but a series of ledge drops, crosscurrents—called the Mixmaster [photo, page 257]. Then a rapids with no name but high standing waves. The worst place on this section is just above Terrapin Branch, a series of ledges in a tight S-curve, followed by an undercut bluff on river left. Water goes left, right, left, and under the bluff. You can pin boats in there, in a hole behind the column in the bluff. Some call it the Room of Doom. Others call it Lemming Falls, maybe because boaters can run in there like lemmings, headed for disaster."

12.0–15.5, Terrapin Branch to just above Whitaker Creek, *3.5 mi., 36 ft./mi.* "This section is still challenging and fast, Class II or II-plus, but it's not quite so technical. It's picked up some water from side canyons, the pools are a little longer, and you can relax a little."

15.5–20.7, Whitaker Creek to upper Luallen Field, *5.2 mi., 31 ft./mi.* "Just when you're getting tired and cramped up, here come some of the most demanding places—the biggest drops, the biggest boulders—from Whitaker past **Dug Hollow [17.0]**. For the first big one, the Keyhole, you go to the left of a large flat-topped boulder, then immediately go right, through a slot and over a five-foot drop.

"Farther along there's Deliverance Falls, through a slot between two big rocks and over a drop into a third rock that's more exposed at lower water levels. That's followed by the Cemetery, big rocks everywhere, some so large they block a view of the whole rapids. And drops, multiple drops. You have to read the route quickly and make the necessary moves. The water's still fairly continuous Class II-plus or III, with a few pools. One pool is wide and deep enough to have a name, the Bluff Hole [**18.5**]. Here's the highest bluff you will see, nearly a hundred feet.

"And there's one more place where boulders block the channel so there's complex maneuvering. Scouting beforehand can help.

"Then you come to the Pickle Hole [**20.0**]. The water's nearly ten feet deep, with huge rocks. About here the river lets up; it's Class II-plus." (The Pickle Hole—and Pickle Spring, about 150 yards down-river on the right—were named for W. P. "Pickle" Edgmon, who lived up the hill to the right. A long time after Edgmon sold out and moved to Oregon, the property became known as the Hedges place.)

Wilderness highway. Rocks in the riverbed below Dug Hollow mark a backpacker's route through the Upper Buffalo Wilderness during dry October. Big rains may soon make this stretch of the Buffalo a slalom course for expert whitewater paddlers. Elsewhere along the tiring 15-mile run are more difficult obstacles.

20.7–22.3, Upper Luallen Field to Boxley Bridge, *1.6 mi., 22 ft./mi.* "At the first field, you begin gravel-and-willow stuff, more like the river from Boxley to Ponca. This goes all the way to the take-out, the Boxley bridge, except maybe when you pass through the Baptizing Hole [**21.0**].

"So what's nice about the Hailstone? It's gorgeous. The river's gorgeous. The canyon's gorgeous. Pour-off waterfalls, even at river level. Views down the canyon. The rock—the massive proportions of some of the rock. You're in a magnificent wilderness. It's not a big wilderness, but you feel very remote, very isolated…and you are!"

Boxley Bridge to Ponca Low-Water Bridge

River miles 22.3 to 28.4. Distance 6.1 miles. Average gradient 16 feet per mile. A sporty run for intermediate and advanced paddlers. Put-in at Highway 21 bridge in Boxley Valley. Take-out at Ponca low-water bridge off Highway 43 near the Highway 74 junction.

The Buffalo, here in transition from the wild creek above Boxley to a tamer river below Ponca, still has frequent steep shoals, sometimes with shelf drop-offs. The river occasionally divides around islands and for short stretches has opened new channels and abandoned old ones. A narrow passage may twist among boulders and willows, with blind turns to be checked for down trees before entering. But unlike the Hailstone above Boxley, this six-mile run allows you time to scout for hazards ahead.

The river goes along the Boxley Valley, with fields and highway to the left, low bluffs and wooded hillsides to the right, and dense vegetation along both banks during the warm seasons. Scenery is unspectacular but pleasing—rock formations, springtime wildflowers, the river itself.

For the "Boxley run," there has to be enough water to float the first shoal below the Boxley bridge without hitting a rock; if so, there's enough water for the rest of the trip. (For much of the year the river at the Boxley bridge actually runs below-ground with no visible flow.) Or check the five-inch scale painted on the Ponca low-water bridge. Zero to 15 inches of air space under the low-water bridge is best for floating from Boxley.

Most of the farmland between the river and Highways 21 and 43 is private property. Enter private land only in case of emergency.

22.3 At the **Highway 21 Bridge** the river begins tumbling down a steep, boulder-filled channel, descending 25 feet in the first mile. A quarter mile below the bridge is the highest sheer cliff on this run, a 100-foot exposure of Boone Formation limestone and chert.

22.8 At **Beech Creek** is the first sizeable pool, over 100 yards long. Where the pool bends to the right, the creek enters from the left, providing an emergency exit to Highway 21 a short distance up Beech Creek.

23.5 **Arrington Creek**, coming from the right, was evidently named for John Arrington III and his wife, Nancy. A government survey map made in 1845 shows that the Arringtons had a pasture here along the river's left bank. The pool at Arrington Creek is the John Fults Hole, named for John M. Fults (1851–1906), who once owned the farm in the creek's small valley to the right.

During high water the river isolates the Fults farmstead. Its owners during the 1950s, brothers Joe and John Perme, built a swinging footbridge here and parked their car across the bridge on the river's left bank. By the 1980s the farm was unoccupied and the Park Service took down the bridge after it became unsafe to cross.

23.7–23.8 Below Arrington Creek the river has moved against a bluff to the right. This is not shown on the topographic map, which is based on aerial photographs made in 1964.

23.9 **Moore Creek** enters the river from the left, discharging into a pool once known as "the swimming hole across from the Boxley store." Until the 1940s the store was located a short distance to the west, near the junction of Highways 21 and 43.

Just beyond Moore Creek and on the right, a small stream flows into the river. A short distance up this stream is—as U.S. government land surveyors noted in 1845—"a cave out of which runs a spring." Men from around Boxley once gathered in the mouth of the shallow cave for all-night poker parties.

For years the cave and 80 acres of steep, rough hillside above it were owned by a local resident, George Self, who had traded a horse for the land. In 1978, Self sold it to the Park Service for $24,000.

24.0 Here the Buffalo has abandoned a left-hand channel in favor of one on the right. Then it curves to the right, with several shoals.

24.2 As the river turns left to flow past a 20-foot bluff, red rock is visible along the bottom of the cliff. This is the red marker band of the St. Joe Limestone at the base of the Boone Formation, whose higher strata were seen in the 100-foot bluff near the beginning of this float. So here is evidence that the river is cutting downward in the sequence of flat-lying rock formations.

24.3–24.6 This pool stretches for more than a quarter mile. To some it is the Long Hole. To others, the Clyde Hole, for former landowner Clyde Villines. Or "the hole at the back of Clyde's field."

24.6–24.8 The river divides into two channels past an island. The left-hand channel does not show on the aerial photograph made in 1964 for topographic mapping.

25.0–25.2 A 60-foot bluff of Boone limestone overlooks the Cold Hole, fed by underwater springs. (Says old-timer Walter Williams: "Water's cold all the time. You can't hardly swim in it in the summertime.") Below an overhang of the bluff are calcite draperies.

Some call the Cold Hole the Clear Hole. Or Island Hole, because it lies next to the Island Field, which becomes an island during floods when overflow runs around the far side of the field.

25.4 Mill Creek enters from the left into the Mill Hole. (Bill Duty: "Old-timers called this hole the Blue Hole." Thus we count this as the first of ten Blue Holes at intervals along the Buffalo River.)

Mill Creek originates at the Boxley Spring, in the field above the head of Boxley's millpond. Downstream from Boxley's historic mill, Mill Creek is joined by **Whiteley Creek**, a much longer creek but in drought not having as much water as spring-fed Mill Creek.

25.7–25.8 Here are spills over ledges. Here, though exact locations are uncertain, are the Slickrock Hole, where bedrock can be seen in the river, and then the Hickory Hole, which was reported to be waist- to chest-deep.

25.9 Similarly, the Hez Hole is in this area but of uncertain location. The hole is named for Hezekiah "Pretty Hez" Villines, who lived in the nearest house, on Highway 43 opposite a well known landmark, the shed-roofed cobblestone building where Hez and his wife, Minnie, had a country store.

26.1 Below a right-hand bluff is the Bluff Hole or Grabbing Hole. (Walter Williams: "People used to grab suckers in there. Or you could drop a crawdad off there and catch them goggle-eyes.")

26.4 About where Highway 43 passes close above the river, the Plum Bush Hole once was. It is no more; it washed out.

26.6 The Bridge Hole—or Swinging Bridge Hole—had its own cable footbridge across the river until the big flood in May 1961 wrecked the span (a drawing, page 267, shows a similar bridge).

26.7 Just below the Bridge Hole, County Road 164 fords the river and allows an exit to the left, up the short steep hill to Highway 43. Floods wash out the ford, but it can be crossed at low water after the county's road grader operator fills in potholes.

26.8 Dry Creek enters from the right, a dry gully, and…

26.9 Running Creek then arrives from the right, flowing. Past the creek is what one old-timer calls "a flat-rock shoal hole of water."

27.0–27.3 The Clarkie Hole or Baptizing Hole extends past the mouth of **Clark Creek**, which comes from Lost Valley. The creek enters at a gully on the left, usually dry but often having a pile of gravel spilling into the Clarkie Hole.

The river now is almost 100 feet lower in elevation than at the Boxley bridge, and the smooth-faced right-hand bluff overlooking the Clarkie Hole is sandstone of the Everton Formation, which underlies the Boone Formation seen earlier in this river trip.

27.6 The river races down a chute over bedrock and passes the mouth of **Big Hollow**. After several more rapids and short pools it arrives at…

28.2–28.3 the Billy Beaver Hole, the last lengthy pool above the Ponca low-water bridge. William "Billy Beaver" Villines was the son of James "Beaver Jim" Villines; both father and son lived nearby. One more shoal, and the river reaches…

28.4 the **Ponca Low-Water Bridge**. Exit from the river just upstream from the left (west) end of the bridge.

Ponca was named after the Ponca City, Oklahoma, Mining Company acquired the town site about 1900. Estella Clemmer, who had come from Ponca City with her husband, suggested that the town the mining company laid out be named Ponca. The company sold building lots, and during World War I, as lead and zinc ore prices soared, Ponca prospered. When the boom faded at war's end, Ponca became a quiet, backcountry village.

Ponca Low-water Bridge to Kyles Landing

River miles 28.4 to 39.0. Distance 10.6 miles. Average gradient 12 feet per mile. Tumbling rapids, towering cliffs. Put-in at Ponca low-water bridge off Highway 43 near Highway 74 junction. Take-out at river access area at Kyles Landing, down a steep, unpaved three-mile mountain road from Highway 74 between Ponca and Jasper.

Of this section of the river, Harold and Margaret Hedges say in their *Buffalo River Canoeing Guide*:

> While the Buffalo is not technically a white water stream it can be rough and dangerous to novice paddlers in periods of high water.... [But] its rock strewn channel and twisty course make it one of the finest canoeing streams in the Midwest.... The river...in the right water, is an exciting, gunwale washing canoe ride.

Ponca Low-Water Bridge to Steel Creek, *2.6 miles.*

At the launch site there's parking space at the west end of the low-water bridge, but for day trips only. The area is subject to flooding and overnight trippers must leave cars at Ponca or elsewhere.

28.4 The **Ponca Bridge** has an informal gauge for floaters. Bands five inches deep are painted on a pier to indicate water level, thus:

• less than 10 inches of air space under the bridge's deck (yellow area) means the river is open to experienced floaters only;

• 10–30 inches (green area) means open to the less experienced, though below 25–27 inches you probably have to walk shoals. (Even with more water, the shoal just below the bridge can be bumpy.)

28.6–28.7 The first pool, at a 70-foot bluff that can be seen from the bridge, is known by some as the Big Bluff Hole, though neither bluff nor hole is very big. Local old-timer Walter Williams calls it the Blue Hole, a better name for its deep, calm blue-green water.

The bluff is of the Newton Sandstone, but above it is limestone, and water has carried dissolved calcite down onto the bluff face and left it as draperies—above-ground cave formations. Venus maidenhair fern grows only on such wet, limy surfaces and here its "fern falls" spill from crevices in the rock.

28.8–28.9 Some remember the Salmon Hole as the next fishing hole downstream from the Blue Hole, but its exact location is uncertain. Not so for the next pool…

29.1–29.3 the Clemmer Hole, a broad pool curving gradually to the left, with big trees leaning out from the banks. J. W. Clemmer (1860–1925) and his wife, Estella (1867–1940), had the farm along the left bank. Later J. E. Shroll, a newcomer from Ohio, acquired the farm, and the river pool became known as the Jess Shroll Hole.

29.3 In the early 1990s a major hazard for canoers appeared at the end of the Clemmer Hole. Apparently a flood pushed an eight-foot boulder from the right bank to midstream. There the rock squatted in the rapids, fast water piling onto it. Canoers attempting to pass on the left got swept close to the rock and swamped by the water spilling off; those trying to pass on the right got ambushed by other boulders. Ponca's float operators named this new peril Killer Rock. It remains so until another flood widens the channel.

29.4–29.7 Beyond Killer Rock rises the first of the Buffalo's high cliffs, 190-foot **Bee Bluff**, which once sheltered a colony of wild bees. Newton County historian Walter Lackey wrote that about 1850 a neighboring farmer first noticed bees flying into a cavity high up the cliff. For years people talked of robbing the hive, and how much honey it might contain.

Finally, in 1916, two young daredevils from Ponca built a long ladder and set it place. That night they climbed up to the hive and killed the bees with burning sulfur. The next morning they set a charge of dynamite and blasted open the cavity—and honey came streaming down the cliff.

Several hundred pounds, however, remained in the crevice. The boys cut the honeycomb with a long-handled knife and lowered bucket after bucket of honey and comb to a crowd of spectators below. When they finished and climbed down, they discovered the onlookers had made off with nearly all the honey.

29.5–29.6 The Bee Bluff Hole is at the base of the bluff, which here towers directly above the river. Next, just downstream, is (as old-timer Boyd Villines says) "a little flat hole of water," wide and shallow. Then shallow rapids into another pool…

29.9 at the upstream end of **Roark Bluff**, rising nearly 100 feet above water that gradually deepens from the gravel beach opposite the cliff—an attractive swimming hole close to Steel Creek's camping area. This is the Rushing Hole, whose name may have come from the sound of water at the exit shoal.

Not far beyond that shoal is Wrecking Rock, actually two or three large chunks, one of them 20 feet long, lying in fast-flowing water. Feared by canoers in the 1960s and 1970s, Wrecking Rock had by the 1990s been bypassed with a wider channel to the left.

30.2–30.3 The next pool is the Beech Hole, named for the large beech trees along the right bank. And next is the...

30.4–30.7 or **30.8–31.0** Hay Shed Hole, for a farm building that once stood somewhere nearby.

Roark Bluff overlooks all. From the Rushing Hole this massive cliff extends downriver, gaining height until it reaches to 220 feet above the water. Its lower part is made of alternating beds of sandstone and limestone; the upper 60 percent is a sheer, water-streaked wall, the Newton Sandstone. Roark is three-quarters of a mile long, the longest of the high cliffs along the upper Buffalo and one of the longest on the entire river (photos, front cover and page 54).

31.0 A quarter mile past the end of Roark Bluff is the **Steel Creek** boat landing, on the right (see *Steel Creek,* page 165).

Steel Creek to Kyles Landing, *8.0 miles.*

About 150 yards below Steel Creek's boat landing, Steel Creek comes in from the right (31.1). Beyond the creek, the Buffalo River is wholly within the Ponca Wilderness. (Up to this point, only the left side of the river has been in the wilderness area.)

Past the creek, another cliff rises above the river. Like Roark Bluff, here is a vertical wall of rock of the Everton Formation, with the lower half of limestone and sandstone, the upper half of the massive Newton Sandstone. But unlike Roark, above the vertical wall is a prominent wooded terrace, then many visible limestone cliffs and ledges of the Boone Formation among wooded or grassy terraces, with the highest rock seen about 530 feet above the river. This is a major bluff, mistakenly named Bee Bluff on the Geological Survey's topo map, uncertainly recalled as Horace Bluff—or Harvest Bluff—by a couple of old-timers, but apparently just no-name bluff.

Beyond the rock-studded, canoe-wrecking rapids where the river begins to pass beneath no-name bluff   *(Continued on page 165)*

A Sampling of
Plants and Animals LIFE

A flourishing community of animals and plants exists along the
Buffalo. There has been enough time for each species to find its
living space and its role in the community. For these Louisiana
waterthrushes, the preferred living space is in the woods close to
the river. Defying predators, waterthrushes nest on the ground.

Midnight snack for a screech owl, an unlucky mouse serves to illustrate a basic fact of life—that every living thing has its own assigned place. "Place" can mean a species' position in the food chain. Mice are one level up the chain from seeds or whatever else they eat, but one level lower than screech owls (mice are said to object to this last part). Place also can mean habitat, living space. Some habitat specialists, such as Ashe's juniper, are assigned to restricted spaces. Other species are more adaptable, tending to be generalists. One species, *Homo sapiens* (humans), is likely the most generalist of all— clever enough to be able to live almost anywhere.

Every living species, including the human species, has its position in the food chain, and its assigned living space.

Specialist plant. Ashe's juniper (opposite) has found its living space only where patches of soil lie next to carbonate rock. This multistemmed specimen grows beside limestone of the Boone Formation, on Peter Cave Bluff upriver from Tyler Bend.

Delightfully fragrant, feathery, inconspicuous flowers of the spring-blooming witch hazel (right) appear during the first warm days of February. This water-dependent species stays close to river and creek banks; another type of witch hazel can be found high on mountainsides.

Intensely blue, a male rainbow darter is wearing his spring outfit in mating season, when the Buffalo's ten species of darters become the most colorful fish in the river. But darters are tiny —this one is shown nearly its actual size.

All plants and animals need water to live. The river sustains many that require water continuously.

A lush "fern fall" of Venus maidenhair ferns (opposite) spills over ledges of carbonate rock near Love Hensley Bluff. This species grows only where it can be in contact with wet limestone or dolomite. (Another type of maidenhair fern, more a generalist plant, occurs at many places in moist woodlands.)

In the river at the bottom of this bluff is another hydric, or water-loving, plant—water willow. Along the Buffalo it grows in the shallows or at the lowest edges of gravel bars.

Springtime in the woods along the river means new discoveries—maybe a cucumber magnolia blooming in the sunshine, or an Ohio buckeye's flowers attended by a zebra swallowtail butterfly. With so many things happening after winter's dormancy, spring can be the favorite season of the year.

Spring brings other kinds of changes. Along a trail at Tyler Bend (opposite), corn salad has taken hold—hundreds of plants, thousands of tiny white flowers. A couple of years ago there were none. Corn salad likes disturbed ground, so it spread onto bare soil beside the trail. In a few years it may disappear, to be replaced by other species of plants.

Sparring for dominance, bull elk face off in a field near Ponca. Settlers by 1840 had killed off the Buffalo's native eastern elk, and game managers in the 1980s restocked with the Rocky Mountain subspecies. The herd increased so that a regulated hunt was begun in 1998 to keep the numbers within carrying capacity of their range. Thus the river's mix of plant and animal species keeps changing—in this case with human assistance.

We have removed species, and replaced them with others.

Expanding its range, the armadillo responded to human activity—clearing of land, removal of its predators. The amusing "possum on the half shell" arrived along the Buffalo River after 1960.

are fishing holes that do have valid, known names. The first one is…

31.2–31.3 Big Rock Hole, named for a giant 20-foot-long boulder resting near the right bank. Next, with a tale to tell, is…

31.4–31.8 the Bud Hole, named for "Bud" Clifton, a local fisherman. One day when Clifton was fishing in this wide, quiet pool, he caught a large, snakelike eel, which left him shaken. He got rid of the eel and resumed fishing—only to hook another eel. Clifton then became so agitated that his friends named the site of his encounters with snake-fishes the Bud Hole.

Today the only unsettling aspect of the wilderness Bud Hole is its view for two miles ahead to a big, bulky **microwave tower** (Southwestern Bell Telephone) and thin radio mast (National Park Service) atop the mountain and within the National River boundary. The microwave tower predates the park and would be costly to relocate. The radio mast is there because the Park Service needed one on

---

Steel Creek is named for George W. Steele (1819–1887), who with his wife, Nancy Karol (of the pioneer Arrington family), settled here about 1846. In the 1870s, Steele sold the farm to Williamson (or William?) Roark, for whom Roark Bluff is named. After Roark's time the land was worked by a number of owners and renters until it was purchased in the 1950s by a Kansas City mortgage banker, P. W. Yarborough.

During the 1950s and 1960s, when land prices were depressed, Yarborough bought acreage along the Buffalo, isolated farms vacated by people who sought a better living elsewhere. Eventually Yarborough had 1189 acres, including five miles of the river from near the Ponca bridge to past Big Bluff. Clearing land and erecting buildings, he developed an Arabian and quarter horse farm he named the Valley Y Ranch. In 1964 his daughter Sue Anna became the property's on-site manager.

Following P. W. Yarborough's death, Sue Yarborough in 1975 sold the corporately held ranch to the National Park Service for $835,000. It was one of the largest acquisitions among 1307 parcels of land assembled for the National River.

At the former ranch headquarters at Steel Creek, the Park Service then sold sheds, stables, a hay barn, and a 17,000-square-foot arena and sales pavilion (big as a supermarket and located close by the river) and they were removed. Other buildings were kept for housing and for the park ranger's office, storerooms, and horse stable. The original ranch gateway spans the Steel Creek entrance road at Highway 74.

an elevated, accessible site. Tower and mast are in an area off Highway 43 that was excluded from the Ponca Wilderness. Someday new technology may allow removal of these intrusions. For now, floaters can move along and put them out of sight.

31.9–32.3 On leaving the Bud Hole, the view ahead is to another cliff, 200 feet high, at the mouth of **Cliff Hollow**, from which comes Clifty Creek. Then in quick succession are the Upper Clifty Hole (31.9–32.0); Clifty Creek and the rock-guarded rapids known as Clifty Creek Shoals (32.1); and the Lower Clifty Hole (32.1–32.3). In a confusion of names, Upper Clifty also has been the Fowler Hole and Lower Clifty the John R. (Arrington) Hole, for persons who lived within this bend of the river at different times past. That, and old-timer Walter Williams knows Upper Clifty only as "mouth of Clifty." The 200-foot cliff, by the way, is the John R. Bluff.

32.3 About 300 yards downriver from Cliff Hollow, a spring flows off an eight-foot bluff into the river. About at this point the Buffalo River's oldest rock formation, the thin-bedded, yellowish-gray Powell Dolomite, comes into view for a foot or two above river level. The Powell is also to be found later in this trip.

Just beyond the spring, the Buffalo swings to the right and flows down shallow shoals between low banks. Here, in the 1960s, P. W. Yarborough, the landowner, had his bulldozer operator channelize the river, creating a broad open swale, a floodway. The bulldozing (photo, page 168) caused canoers to work even harder for National River legislation. Left alone, the denuded riverbanks had by the 1980s developed a thicket of seedling sycamore trees.

32.6–32.9 Around the bend to the left is another (Hay) Shed Hole. Straight ahead, **Big Bluff** comes into sight. Here is the only full-face view of the upper parts of Big Bluff (photo, page 6). From the Shed Hole, a prominent "groove," or line of shadowed recesses, is visible across the upper cliff. At the lower edge of that groove is the Goat Trail, where hikers walk across the face of the bluff, some 340 feet above the river. A few feet above the Goat Trail, and recognizable if one looks closely, is a layer or streak of red rock less than two feet thick whose color makes it a geologic marker band, as part of the St. Joe Limestone, the lowest member of the Boone Formation.

All of Big Bluff above the Goat Trail is Boone limestone and chert. Just below the Goat Trail are a few remnants of minor geologic formations, mostly hidden by vegetation. Below those, most of the rest of the bluff is Everton Formation, the upper part hidden behind the area covered with trees and shrubbery. Below the vegetation the Newton Sandstone forms a massive water-streaked wall about 110 feet high. Below the Newton, and mostly behind trees at the foot of the bluff, is "lower Everton" dolomite, sandstone, and limestone; and below that to river level, 20 or 30 feet of Powell Dolomite.

33.0–33.1 Just below the upstream end of Big Bluff is another Blue Hole, which outdoorsman Roy Wishon describes as "a little round hole, deep, right under the high bluff." Counting down the river from the first Blue Hole at Boxley, this is #3.

33.1–33.4 Past another shoal is the Big Bluff Hole, described by Boyd Villines as "the long hole under the Big Bluff." Here a gravel bar makes a good lunch spot and viewing site. From this place so close to Big Bluff, the lower cliff looms almost directly overhead. Above it and beyond, the upper cliff reaches to the sky.

Big Bluff has long been considered the tallest of the Buffalo River's cliffs, though its exact height is uncertain. The bluff was once estimated to be 525 feet high, but the Geological Survey's topo map shows it may be 560 feet. Actually, topographic maps indicate that three of the terraced bluffs along the lower Buffalo are about 590 feet high. Big Bluff, though, is more nearly a vertical cliff than those three downriver. So which is highest? Take your choice.

33.4 A quiet bay, or slough, straight ahead at the end of the Big Bluff Hole is the usual landing place for those wanting to climb to the Goat Trail. Climbers work their way up the steep hill around the end of the bluff, eventually finding a beaten path going farther up, then leveling off along a bench that narrows to become the ledge that is the Goat Trail (the trail is described on pages 327–328).

From Big Bluff Hole the river turns right and spills for 150 yards over bedrock ledges and into…

33.5–33.6 the Goat Rock Hole, then through 200 yards of shoals and into…

33.8–33.9 the Beech Hole, named for **Beech Creek**, which comes from its right-hand valley and flows into the pool's lower end.

The next pool is the Benton Smith Hole, past the mouth of…

34.2 Jackies Big Hollow, another right-hand valley, short and steep-sided, whose opening to the river is flanked by west-facing sandstone bluffs with pine trees that favor the dry, acidic soil along the top. The hollow is named for George W. "Jackie" Villines (1874–1931), who lived downriver opposite Jim Bluff. Villines was killed by falling from a cliff nearby when gathering wild onions.

Bulldozed. Canoers in 1965 discovered that the river a half mile upstream from Big Bluff had been converted to an open ditch. The owner of the horse ranch at Steel Creek had channelized the Buffalo. Canoers became more determined to protect the river.

34.4–34.6 The next lengthy pool, the Pear Tree Hole, provides for close-up views of the Buffalo's oldest rock, the Powell Dolomite, along the left bank. It appears first as two-inch layers in an eight-foot bluff rising from the river (34.4), then as five- or six-inch ledges just above water level (34.5). The rock is typically yellowish-gray.

From Pear Tree the river spills into another long pool…

34.7–35.0 Jim Bluff Hole. Straight ahead is **Jim Bluff**, about 110 feet in total height, overhanging a walkway along a ledge near river level. Jim Bluff's ledge walkway, overhanging cliff, and streak of red rock above the walkway (photo, page 55) are all remarkably similar to features along the Goat Trail on Big Bluff. That is because Jim Bluff is located within a *graben*, a depressed section of Earth's crust lying between two geologic faults (photos, page 18). The fault on the south side of the Jim Bluff graben is just beyond view at the upstream end of the bluff. At river level to the south of that fault is older rock: Everton Formation, Powell Dolomite. But at Jim Bluff the red rock is one clue that the bluff is of the younger St. Joe Limestone and overlying rock of the Boone Formation.

A flat rock standing on the walkway has the name JIM BLUFF in faded blue lettering, the work of Jim Little, who in the 1960s lived in an old school bus by the river near Sneeds Creek and painted this and other directional signs for canoers. The bluff was named not for Jim

Little, but for Jim Henderson, who lived nearby in an earlier time.

As it extends downriver, Jim Bluff dips (slopes, tilts) downward. A result of this downward tilt of rock strata is that the next bluff, on the right (at 35.2), is still younger rock of the Boone, still within the Jim Bluff graben. The appearance of this 30-foot cliff, rough and rubbly, is typical for thin beds of Boone limestone and chert.

Next, the river spills off to the left and into…

35.3–35.4 the Beaver Hole, now beyond the north fault line of the Jim Bluff graben and extending to the mouth of **Sneeds Creek**. Where the creek enters from the left, there's a trail junction with choices for side trips: Hemmed-in Hollow, the Goat Trail, Granny Henderson's house, Rocky Bottom, or points beyond.

From the Beaver Hole, the river goes rollicking down one of the longest, fastest rapids of the Buffalo—several hundred yards of open, racing water, swinging to the left, with standing waves, finally spilling into another geologic oddity…

35.6 the Suck Hole. Here, during drought, all the river's diminished flow goes underground (is sucked) from the deepest pool at the foot of the 30-foot cliff on the right. The cliff is Newton Sandstone, but apparently there is a cave passage in limestone or dolomite of the Everton Formation beneath the bluff. Through this passage the subterranean stream crosses the neck of **Horseshoe Bend**, then emerges from under another bluff on the other side. In dry times the Suck Hole is a small pool with the river trickling in, and instead of a deep rapids at the Suck Hole's surface exit, there is only bare rock.

35.7 But with enough water for canoeing those rapids, the next pool—the California Hole, below **California Point**—is more than six feet deep past the 25-foot bluff on whose face Jim Little once lettered HEMMED IN HOLLOW in red, with an arrow pointing downstream. (Jim waited till the California Hole went dry, then set his sign painter's ladder in the riverbed at the foot of the bluff.)

Beyond fast water passing low, open ledges on the right, the river enters a small pool with a gravelly shore on the left…

35.9 the landing for **Hemmed-in Hollow**.

Here at the mouth of the little creek that flows from Hemmed-in Hollow is the very heart of the Ozarks' deepest canyon, the gorge that extends from Ponca to Erbie. From here at 910 feet elevation to the mountaintop a mile to the northeast at 2310 feet, the elevation difference is 1400 feet. At seven other places along the river from Steel Creek to Erbie, the differences are between 1200 and 1300 feet over distances of even less than a mile. For deepness and steepness, these figures cannot be matched anywhere else in all the Midwest.

From the river landing it is 0.7 mile up Hemmed-in Hollow to the high waterfall at the end of its box canyon, a side trip that many river travelers take (see page 333 and *Hemmed-in Hollow,* page 336).

From Hemmed-in's river landing, the Buffalo executes a tricky S-turn before arriving at a short deep pool. Here is a…

36.0 Big Rock Hole, with three giant boulders on the left. The river exits this hole through a rock-studded slot, then soon passes…

36.2 Fishtrap Hollow, where somebody around 1900 corraled fish at the shoal, and arrives at…

36.2–36.3 the Clubhouse Hole. The low bluff on the left has rows of pits along its surface, where for some reason the sandstone lacked as much cementation as the surrounding rock and weathered out.

Atop the bluff's downstream end are a stone chimney and piers, the **Seamster Cabin Site** (see *Clubhouse,* opposite, and page 321).

36.4 Past the next shoal, the 30-foot bluff on the right contains a large plug of sandstone that filled a sinkhole in older rock (photo, page 172). A few feet downstream from the "fossil sinkhole" is the outlet of the underground passage across Horseshoe Bend from the Suck Hole at mile 35.5. Here, at the right bank, water emerges from beneath a ledge about three feet below the surface, making ripples.

About 50 feet beyond, an old road (part of the Old River Trail) comes down the hill on the right, providing a way to walk into Horseshoe Bend (see *Horseshoe Bend,* page 321). The river here runs down a shallow shoal leading into the next pool…

36.5–36.7 Dug Bank Hole, curving to the left and ending where the river spills noisily down over broken ledges to **Lick Ford**.

About 1955, when canoers from Kansas City first ran the upper Buffalo, their leaders stopped here at the head of the rapids and hung toilet paper on bushes to warn the followers of hazards just ahead. Many canoers came to know this place as T. P. Shoals.

Bill Villines, who once lived nearby, says that Lick Ford, at the lower end of the ledge shoal, was named for a salt spring on the north side of the river that attracted animals to a salt lick. The ford was a river crossing for the settlers' wagon road along the upper Buffalo.

36.7–37.0 T. P. Shoals empties into the Long Field Hole: long, straight, wide, shallow, open to the sun. The long field, now over-grown, lay along the right side. Halfway down the pool and on the left, a stream of clear water issues from **Bear Cave Hollow,** spilling over ledges, making pretty little cascades that people walk up the creek to see. (Somebody once called the stream Coors Creek, after the beer supposedly made from Rocky Mountain spring water.)

On the slope to the right of the creek's lowest cascade is a slab of sandstone having ripple marks. Geologist Jim Liles explains:

> This rock was made from shoreline or beach sand, rippled by gentle wave action, then softly buried by more sand…and eventually compressed into the Newton Sandstone Member of the Everton Formation now eroded to view—more than 400 million years after the seashore waves left their mark on the sands of the mid-Ordovician sea.

Straight ahead now, the Newton Sandstone is also seen as a high smooth-faced cliff, streaked with mineral stains and having a dense growth of dark green junipers along the top.

37.1–37.2 The bluff stands 180 feet above the next pool—the Jim Henderson Hole—and the pool's exit shoal, where the settlers' road crossed at Arbaugh Ford. The ford probably was named for Conrad "Coon" Arbaugh. About 1858, it is said, Arbaugh built a cabin where a spring flowed from below the high bluff a few yards beyond the far end of the ford. (The cabin washed away in the great flood of 1915 and nothing remains.)

37.2–37.6 Below Arbaugh Ford is the Clover Hole. This lengthy pool, once flanked by open fields, today is shaded by river birches and other large trees leaning out from the banks. Gradually the river bends to the left. In view ahead is a wooded mountainside.

Clubhouse. On a low bluff a half mile below Hemmed-in Hollow are stone piers and a chimney, remains of a cabin built in 1936 by a Fayetteville, Arkansas, lawyer, Bernal Seamster (1910–1961), and his friends. The log structure had two rooms with a hall between and an open porch at the edge of the bluff.

The cabin was far from an improved road. One of the friends told his wife, "It's almost like you have to swing in on a grapevine to get to it." Seamster's sister Margaret says the men rode "little jenny-mule things" down the mountain to the cabin.

Seamster and his friends swam in the river and fished off the porch. Says Bill Villines: "They called it a clubhouse…had bunk beds. There'd just be a bunch of boys and men come there and camp for weekends. I saw .22 hulls *piled up*, on the porch."

After a few years Seamster became tired of his isolated cabin and he sold it. Not long afterward it burned down.

"Fossil sinkhole." Erosion by the river has revealed a massive plug of sandstone that filled a sinkhole in older rock. Just to the left of the plug is the underwater outlet of the subterranean passage the river takes across Horseshoe Bend from the Suck Hole.

37.7–38.0 Next is the Pond Bluff Hole. The bluff, on the right, rises from the water—dark Everton limestone or dolomite and then a bulging face of the Newton Sandstone. Every crevice of the carbonate rock has its garden of wild hydrangeas and other attractive plants.

Toward the end of the pool the distant sound of rapids becomes an ever louder roar. First there is a brief shoal, and then…

38.1–38.2 the Buffalo River's premier rapids, Hell's Half Acre, also known as Gray Rock Shoals, three more or less distinct sets of ledges in about 500 feet of river—shallow rock to hang up on, big waves to be swamped by. With adequate water the skilled—or the lucky—make it through unscathed.

Indian Creek, coming from a major side canyon to the right, enters the river near the head of the shoals. The creek usually is dry (flowing underground), and its gully is hidden in the bushes. In any case, paddlers are in the rapids and too busy to notice Indian Creek.

At the end of Hell's Half Acre is, or was, another obstacle: **Gray Rock**, a five-foot ledge of Everton limestone jutting from the river's left bank. Until a flood in May 1991 widened the channel past Gray Rock, this was the river's best known disaster spot for canoers, where many, through ineptitude combined with fright, overturned on arrival (photo, page 436). Others would perch on the rock, shouting exactly the wrong advice to oncoming paddlers: "Go left! Go to the left!"

38.2–38.3 Just past Gray Rock the river becomes placid Gum Spring Hole, welcome relief from recent distress. While relaxing, one can examine the high bluff ahead, looking for the natural letter "A" cut into the rock about 20 feet below the top. Canoers who discovered this in 1965 informally named this cliff the "A" Bluff.

After Gum Spring Hole, the Buffalo bends left, right, and left, through several rapids and short pools (including one of uncertain location that old-timers call the Little Rock Hole), ending at...

38.8–39.0 the Jim Cecil Hole. There's a campground just beyond the trees along the right bank. The **Kyles Landing** take-out is ahead at the end of the pool. (Also see *Kyles Landing*, page 301.)

Kyles Landing to Ozark Campground

River miles 39.0 to 50.1. Distance 11.1 miles. Average gradient 9 feet per mile. Less traffic, gentler river than upstream. Put-in at Kyles Landing river access area, down a steep, unpaved three-mile road from Highway 74 between Jasper and Ponca. Take-out at beach at Ozark campground, 1.5 miles off Highway 7 north of Jasper.

Along this reach of the river, the Buffalo emerges from its canyon in the Boston Mountains to meander across a gentler landscape of the Springfield Plateau. Compared with that from Ponca to Kyles, this section of the river has little recreational float traffic. The water isn't so tumultuous, the scenery isn't as spectacular. Which is to say: The floating experience can be more relaxed and the river's beauty can be enjoyed on a more intimate scale.

Kyles Landing to Erbie Landing, *5.6 miles.*

The bluff overlooking the Kyles boat landing is more than 200 feet high. Its upper part is the massive Newton Sandstone, the same rock so prominently displayed in cliffs upriver. From here downstream, however, the sandstone unit dips rapidly to lower elevation, all the way down to river level, and becomes thinner and less recognizable.

39.1–39.2 Beyond the shoal at the landing is a short deep pool, long a favored swimming hole (though in 1979 a young man dived in, hit a submerged rock, and became paralyzed, with one outcome being that the Park Service put up DIVING IS DANGEROUS warning signs along roads to the river's swim areas). This pool is the Mud Cave Hole. The cave's opening is in the base of the bluff on the left.

39.2 Past Mud Cave the river turns sharply right, and overlooking the bend is a strange-looking cliff about 100 feet high and called the Castle. A ruined castle, perhaps, with broken battlements, sagging courses of stone, a deep split down its front wall. A geologist tells us the Castle is Newton sandstone that apparently settled into a void created by gradual solution—dissolving—of underlying Everton carbonate rock. Here the sandstone high above Kyles Landing has already dipped down to the river (photo, opposite).

39.2–39.7 The Buffalo passes through a shoal, a pool, and more shoals past **Bee Bluff**, an unobtrusive rock face behind trees along the left bank. Now a really high cliff looms ahead…

39.7–39.9 Buzzard Bluff, up to nearly 500 feet. The Newton Sandstone is present for about the first 30 feet above the river, then Everton Formation dolomite and sandstone for about 70 feet. The remainder of the cliff is Boone Formation limestone.

Except where the rock has streaks of rusty orange, where seepage water has deposited iron oxides, most of Buzzard Bluff is gray—drab, gloomy (photo, page 367). Probably that's because the cliff faces north and gets very little drying and bleaching by the sun.

At its downstream end Buzzard Bluff rises straight out of the water. High up the cliff, a thick slab of rock has separated from the wall behind, creating a needle's eye to the sky.

40.0–40.2 The next pool is known as the Bee Bluff Hole (though maps have Bee Bluff on the other side of the river's bend). Here, in the summertime, boys paddle canoes; this is the Boy Scouts' **Camp Orr**. Camp facilities are beyond sight on both sides of the river. Most are up the hill to the right (see *Camp Orr,* page 304).

40.3–40.6 Gar Hole Bluff, overlooking the Scouts' swim area, is more than 200 feet high. Gar Hole's geology is Everton Formation, including the Newton Sandstone, up to 100 feet above the river, and Boone Formation the rest of the way to the top.

Gar Hole Bluff is pale gray, buff, and white—noticeably lighter in color than Buzzard Bluff—probably because it faces south and gets lots of sun. High on the bluff, in the sunshine, are calcite stalactites —cave formations.

The pool below the bluff (40.3–40.4) is, of course, Gar Hole.

40.7–42.0 Over the next mile or more beyond Gar Hole, the river subtly changes. Shoals are frequent but become more open, easier to

At Kyles Landing. The far end of the bluff dips downward. Thus
the Newton Sandstone in the foreground is 200 feet above the
river, but at the bluff's other end is much closer to water level.
The dip probably resulted as underlying carbonate rock slowly
dissolved and the sandstone layer gradually settled into the void.

navigate. There are tree-shaded runs with solid ledge rock along the river bottom, and sometimes low bluffs decorated with plants in the crevices. Scenery seems to be smaller in scale. Pools are short and probably were not given names by local fishermen.

Past **Dry Creek** (mile 41.3) the hills begin to close in. All the way here from Ponca, the valley has been nonsymmetrical, one side of the river against a bluff or steep hillside, the other bank at the edge of an easier slope, often with space enough—in the past, at least—for a farm. But now, a mile and a half below Gar Hole Bluff…

42.0–42.2 the mountains come down to the river on *both* sides. There's no bottomland at all, just the river cutting through—and leaving the Boston Mountains at canyon's end. It's as if the Bostons wanted to put one last squeeze on the Buffalo before releasing the river to the lower country of the Springfield Plateau.

Here the river is at elevation 855 feet and midway between two high promontories or "gateposts" flanking the canyon's downstream end, 2060-foot **McFerrin Point** a mile to the northwest and 2150-foot **Mutton Point** a mile southeast.

42.3 The old settlers' road—now part of the Old River Trail— crosses the river and apparently marks the upper end of the Nixon Hole (42.3–42.5). Old-timers Robert and Ray Hickman, cousins who grew up at Erbie, recalled names of fishing holes here at the upriver end of their boyhood territory. The White Bluff Hole, or Rock Hole, was above the Nixon Hole, and the little Round Hole was downstream, but the Hickmans could not recall their exact locations.

42.6–42.8 Uncle Jim Farmer's Hole, though, was "behind Uncle Jim's field," says Ray Hickman. "It wasn't too big of a hole." Jim Farmer's place, shown on the Trails Illustrated map as the **Farmer farmstead**, is at the upstream end of the historic **Erbie** community.

43.1–43.3 Below the Farmer place the river bends to the right, past 100-foot **Goat Bluff**. The lovely deep-green pool at the foot of the bluff is the Goat Bluff Hole or Goat Hole, once a watering hole for a flock of goats. (Ray Hickman: "Jimmy Richardson had goats. He was real old, had a long white beard.") The bluff is Everton rock at its base, and Boone Formation above the three-foot-wide red streak of St. Joe Limestone at 12 to 20 feet above the river. At one point the red rock is covered with calcite flowstone, cave deposits in daylight. Like other bluffs of the Boone, Goat Bluff has interesting features across its face: step-backs, overhangs, alcoves, shallow caves. Ancient, twisted Ashe's junipers grow from narrow footholds.

43.4 Downstream from Goat Bluff the river divides and the left channel runs past a high erosion bank. In the mid-1990s the Park Service tried to stop the erosion by laying and pinning cedar trees along the river's edge, but here the bank was in direct line of floods that tore the trees loose and carried them away. Elsewhere along the river the Park Service has successfully used these cedar revetments to control bank erosion.

43.5–43.8 Then the river bends left into a broad, curving pool. In the 30-foot bluff along the right are shallow caves, several in succession at water level. Farther along, the bluff becomes higher, with a shelf halfway up that once anchored the cables for a footbridge across the river (43.7). This pool is the Swinging Bridge Hole, but was the Gar Hole before community volunteers built the bridge in the 1930s. The bridge by the 1980s was near total collapse and a safety hazard, so the Park Service removed it.

43.8 Just beyond the bridge site, a sizeable creek enters the river from the left—a creek of uncertain name. One early map calls it **Cecil Creek**, for the pioneer Cecil family who may have reached this area as early as 1827. Local old-timer Ray Hickman, however, says this is **Cove Creek**, the name of the larger stream that joins Cecil Creek about a mile up from the river.

And just beyond the creek is a **Ford**, Erbie Ford, a concrete slab across the river. The road here was once Main Street for the Erbie community (see *Erbie*, page 350). Floaters portage across either end of the slab to avoid hanging up on it or being swamped in the standing wave on its downstream side. (At high flow, it may be possible to float across at midstream.) From the ford the river spills into…

43.8–43.9 the Elm Hole—pronounced "Ellum"—named for elm trees along the bank. Along the right side is a landing by the road to the **Parker-Hickman farmstead** (photos, pages 263 and 308), a quarter-mile side trip to an 1840s log house and its outbuildings.

Beyond the Elm Hole are short pools, easy shoals, and then…

44.3–44.5 the Spring Hole, named for a spring, about 100 yards up the hill on the left side, whose outflow spills into the river here. Beyond the right side of the river at the Spring Hole is the Erbie campground. At the downstream end of the hole is…

44.5 Bucking Shoals, a steep ledge drop that can have big waves. The shoals empty into Little Bottom Hole at Erbie Landing (44.6), a boat ramp located at the downstream end of the campground. Here are a parking area, toilets, and a public telephone.

Erbie Landing to Ozark Campground, *5.5 miles.*

Downriver from the boat ramp the scenery is small-scale, but there's always something of interest: the occasional ledge shoal, the choice of channels at several places where the river splits around islands, the various shapes of rock in the bluffs. Most of the cliffs are of modest height—30, 40 feet—and are of limestone, dolomite, or sandstone of the Everton Formation. The beds of carbonate rock are from inches to a few feet thick, revealed where weathering has produced deep cuts along the bedding planes. The sandstone can have a pitted surface where weathering has removed pockets of less resistant material. The undersides of ledges projecting above the water can have bright, rippling reflections of sunlit ripples below.

Old-timers have little to say about rock formations but remember that even the riverside fields, as well as the holes of water, had names. Today the Erbie campground occupies two stream terraces, higher and lower, that were once the Upper Bottom and Lower Bottom. The hole of water at the boat ramp was named for a small field across the river there, the Little Bottom.

45.0–45.1 Old-timer Robert Hickman, who came from the south side of the river, recalls that below the Little Bottom Hole, and under an electric power line, was the Round Hole. His cousin Ray Hickman, from the north side, remembers that below the Little Bottom Hole is the Boat Hole, where the family had a boat for crossing to the grandparents on the south side. "The family kept the boat tied at the upper end of the Boat Hole," says Ray. "Right across the river was the Dripping Spring, an everlasting spring."

45.1–45.2 Ray Hickman says that next below the Boat Hole is the Joshul, or Joshulin, Hole, named for the noise made by the river as it slapped against the undercut bluff. Next is…

45.3 the deep blue-green Blue Hole, where the river bends sharply to the right and passes a 40-foot bluff. (Here's Blue Hole #4, counting Blue Holes downstream from the first one at Boxley.)

45.4–45.7 Below a long shoal over bedrock is the Redhorse Hole. "For redhorse fish that shoaled below the Blue Hole," says Ray Hickman. "A redhorse is a red sucker—a reddish color. In the spring the redhorse came up on the shoal to lay eggs—hundreds of them, for a day or two. People grabbed them. They would tie a weight on the line, with three straight hooks. And when the fish came schooling by, you yank them right out of the water."

Three species of redhorse suckers are found in the Buffalo. The black redhorse is the most abundant. Its flesh is tasty but very bony.

45.7 At the lower end of the Redhorse Hole, a bluff 125 feet high bends close to the left bank, its smooth, water-streaked upper face the most obvious show of the Newton Sandstone since Kyles Landing. Below and past the bluff are shoals, short pools…

46.0–46.3 and then Long Hole, with big rocks, tilted, along the right bank. Rising beyond Long Hole is…

46.4–46.7 a 200-foot bluff, the highest between Erbie and Ozark. Actually the bluff is two bluffs separated by a ravine, with the first one (at 46.5) having calcite draperies at one spot on its face and a fringe of dark-green Ashe's junipers along its top. The second bluff is more in view, and about midway up is the red marker band of the St. Joe Limestone, indicating that the upper half of the cliff is Boone Formation. Below would be the Everton Formation (and Everton is the only rock in the bluffs from here to Ozark).

46.6–46.9 The bluff overlooks the Bill Taylor Hole, a wide, placid body of water. A peaceful place named for a tormented, violent, ult-mately tragic individual. Bill Taylor lived up the hill to the right, and it is said his troubles began when others abused his property rights, firing guns into his field, probably trespassing too. Taylor became so obsessed about trespassers that he would draw a gun on anyone who even so much as stopped along the public road through his property. Everybody became afraid of him. One day, however, he shot and killed a man's dog, and the man shot and killed Bill Taylor.

46.9 After turning southeast and then south, the river now heads southwest, providing a long view to a distant mountain—Mutton Point. Floating around the Buffalo's bends, one tends to lose sense of direction. Even noting the position of the sun may not help.

47.3 The next bluff, on the right and reaching to 80 feet above the river, has features to excite the imagination: a shallow cave with a chairlike ledge inside under the ceiling arch, another cave like a key-hole, and then, nearly 40 feet above the water, a projecting ledge like a diving board. Then there are shoals, and another pool…

47.4–47.7 the Miss Hickman Spring Hole. (The spring, about 150 yards south of the Buffalo, enters the river through a sandbank.) Another old-timer says this is the Mine Hole, for the Big Jumbo Mine above the right bank. The mine had two tunnels, one below floodline and now filled with mud, the other caved in.

47.7 On the right is a 30-foot bluff easily remembered for its ledge that extends for about 80 feet along the face and projects to more

Landmark.
Like a front porch, an overhanging ledge juts from the face of Porch Bluff. When people gave names to features along the river, size did not count—uniqueness did.

than 12 feet over the water. This is Porch Bluff (photo, above) and the pool here is the Porch Bluff Hole.

A hundred feet past the bluff is the mouth of **Sawmill Hollow**, at massive tilted rocks, one of them five feet thick and 20 feet long.

47.9 On the left is a 20-foot erosion bank that, unlike the bank at mile 43.4 at Erbie, the Park Service was able to stabilize in the mid-1990s with cedar trees laid on the slope and pinned down.

48.0 The river turns right and into another Bucking Shoals, past ledge rock on the right. (At several places, rapids that kicked up waves were named Bucking Shoals.) Below the shoals is…

48.1–48.3 the Leypoldt Hole, so named since the 1960s, when Melvin Leypoldt was the landowner before the Park Service. Before Leypoldt it was the Taylor Hole, for landowner Ewing Taylor.

Here on the left is a wall of sandstone reaching from 10 to 20 feet above the water. For more than 100 yards it overhangs the river. One can float along below the stone ceiling, watching reflections of sun-lit ripples moving across it.

Below the overhang are patches of maidenhair fern on the wet rock; above it are gnarled Ashe's junipers hung with gray-green wisps of old-man's-beard. Higher up are more junipers, including red cedars, and exposed limestone for about 200 feet up the hill.

48.6 As the river begins to bend left, it may be possible to see a rail fence on top of the 40-foot bluff behind trees to the right. The fence is at an overlook at **Cedar Grove**, a picnic area. Forty yards downriver is the mouth of a ravine where people come down from

Cedar Grove to swim and fish. In earlier times there was a wagon road down the ravine and in late summer the diminished river flowed under the gravel here and this was known as the Dry Ford. The pool just downstream is the Dry Ford Hole. And just downriver from that is an alternate to Cedar Grove as a picnic site…

48.8 spacious open ledges along the left side of the river. Then, beyond shoals and shallow pools, is a large, deep pool…

49.3–49.5 the Hiner Hole, named for landowner Lessly Hiner (1910–1974), who operated a dairy on the farm within this bend of the river. "Before Les Hiner owned the farm," says local native Richard Holland, "it was owned by Silas Gibson and the hole was known then as the Gibson Hole." On the right, a 40-foot bluff of smooth, water-streaked sandstone rises from the water.

For another half mile the river follows a generally straight course.

50.1 Then it bends sharply right into Briar Bluff Hole, past 70-foot **Briar Bluff**, easily recognized by the deep alcove in its face. A gravelly beach on the right is the take-out point. From the beach a path leads up the slope to the **Ozark campground**.

Ozark Campground to Carver

River miles 50.1 to 63.2. Distance 13.1 miles. Average gradient 5 feet per mile. A larger, more gentle river with several distinctive bluffs. Put-in at beach below north end of Ozark campground, 1.5 miles off Highway 7 north of Jasper. Take-out at Carver boat landing off north end of Highway 123 bridge south of Hasty.

Ozark Campground to Pruitt Landing (Highway 7), *2.1 miles.*
The gravelly beach at Ozark campground borders Briar Bluff Hole facing 70-foot **Briar Bluff**. On the left just past the bluff…

50.2 is the mouth of a small creek, Tom Smith Branch. The name has historic interest but uncertain origin.

50.5 Near here in 1965, on Memorial Day weekend, a landowner

Ozark. The campground was probably once a cow pasture, and maybe before that time, a cornfield. Or it may have grown the farmer's cash crop, cotton. A private developer in the 1960s opened a camping area here (Ozark Kampgrounds), which in 1972 was purchased by the Park Service. The pavilion was then built of lumber salvaged from another building downriver.

felled trees across the river to stop canoers from continuing down-river to Pruitt. The incident, related to the controversy over whether or not to allow the government to acquire private land to create Buffalo National River, was widely publicized and encouraged canoers and others to press for National River legislation.

51.0 Here for about 200 yards the river flows as a long, sparkling riffle down a broad chute with trees forming an archway over the water, an unusual and pleasing interlude along the Buffalo. Ahead is a high hill. The river is approaching Highway 7 and traffic noise can be heard from near the top of the hill. The river turns left into…

51.1–51.2 Crane Bottom Hole. Did cranes—great blue herons, maybe, which local people sometimes call cranes—once nest in the tall trees of Crane Bottom along the left bank?

51.3–51.8 The next pool, extending to just above the Highway 7 bridge, is called the Upper Hole to distinguish it from the Swimming Hole, just downstream from the bridge.

51.7–51.8 Within view of the bridge, Upper Hole lies along 110-foot Pruitt Bluff. Earlier, this was Goat Bluff, named for goats seen on top of the cliff. Earlier still, it was Adair Bluff, for the family who lived here before the Civil War. Opposite the bluff is part of the historic Pruitt community site (see *Pruitt,* opposite), now having a picnic area, water hydrant, toilets, parking, and information station.

Geologically, Pruitt Bluff is Everton Formation. The lower one-third is limestone alternating with sandstone, and the upper two-thirds is the massively bedded Newton Sandstone. The sandstone beds are smooth, rounded, projecting. The limestone beds are thinner, having horizontal cracks along the bedding planes. (One layer between two of the nearest parallel cracks is a *bedding unit,* representing deposition in an ocean or on a beach when conditions remained the same through that period of time. Thus each unit records its own depositional environment. The climate then was quite warm, and limestones just like these are forming today in ocean water offshore in the Bahamas, also in lagoons. The lower limestones or sandstones in Pruitt Bluff formed in a lagoon or offshore situation. The Newton Sandstone, higher up the cliff, formed on a beach after the ocean had moved back.)

Gray or black coloration of the bluff comes from manganese oxide carried down onto the bluff face by seepage water that evaporated and left the mineral. The orange color where the bluff is wet may be organic, like a slime. (Orange on other bluffs can be iron oxide, like

Watermelons.
The Hammons family
feasts at the Pruitt store
in the summer of 1935.

Pruitt

In 1913 the first bridge across the Buffalo was opened just down-stream from the present Highway 7 crossing. Around 1920, with traffic increasing, Frank Hammons (1871–1958) built a general store, with living quarters, near the south end of the bridge. Soon he also opened a tourist camp and fishing resort on the property, and in 1925 a post office was established in the store with Hammons as postmaster. The post office was named for William Wilshire Pruitt (1843–1925), a neighborhood elder.

Hammons added gas pumps at the store, accommodations for swimmers, tourist cabins, and a dance pavilion. Shady Grove, as the place was called, became the center of a larger community, and eventually another developer built cabins at the north end of the bridge. Shady Grove was run by Hammons' stepdaughter Pearl Holland until the Park Service bought the property in 1973.

rust, brought down and deposited by surface water.) Buff or yellow can be the color of the rock, or it comes from clay left on the surface.

51.8 The steel bridge that carries Highway 7 across the river was built in 1931. To highway engineers the bridge is a through-truss span, meaning that traffic actually moves through its framework.

The 1931 bridge replaced a spindly steel bridge, one lane with a wood floor, that was located about 200 feet downstream. The earlier bridge, built in 1913, was the first one on the Buffalo River. Chunks of broken concrete on the right bank mark the site.

51.8–52.0 The Swimming Hole at Pruitt, just downstream from the highway bridge, has a 25-foot bluff with stone steps from the top to a ledge halfway down. Swimmers dive off the ledge. A safer way to get into the pool is from the beach along the right bank.

52.1–52.4 The next pool, the Big Rock Hole, is named for a rock that probably fell from the bluff that overlooks the river here. The cliff, about 250 feet high, has no firmly established name. It was once known as Hurd Bluff, for a family nearby; it also has been called Desmond Bluff by people at Pruitt, for a man who fell from the bluff and was badly injured (but survived).

About 90 feet up the cliff, the marker band of the St. Joe Limestone is visible as a five-foot-thick layer of red rock. So this bluff fits the geologic pattern of many of the bluffs upriver: Everton Formation for the lower part, Boone Formation for the upper. The Everton extends to about 75 feet above the river.

Hurd/Desmond Bluff also is said to have a colony of wild bees.

52.2 The Pruitt boat landing is opposite the bluff.

Pruitt Landing to Hasty Campsite, *6.8 miles.*

A short distance below the Pruitt landing is the mouth of Mill Creek on the left (52.4). And then a pool (52.4–52.6) that local old-timer Richard Holland calls "kind of a flat hole," meaning wide, shallow. Then comes Crow Ford (52.6), where the road from Jasper to Harrison crossed the river until the Pruitt bridge opened in 1913.

52.8–53.0 Beyond Crow Ford is a 30-foot bluff displaying the red marker band of the St. Joe Limestone. The red streak dips strongly downstream so that at the downriver end of the bluff it has declined to water level. Geologist T. C. Hopkins wrote in 1890 that the dip of strata here was "further hastened by two small faults."

This bluff ends at Lee Hollow, a ravine entering from the left, said to be where a local citizen once operated a whiskey still. The site of the still may yet be marked by rocks that supported the boiler.

53.1–53.2 Lee Hollow is at the upstream end of **Welch Bluff**, having a geologic fault—the most visible of any along the Buffalo—that runs straight up the cliff (photo, page 17). The downstream side is lifted nearly 100 feet, so that the St. Joe's marker band, evidenced by red blotches on the rock, is now about 80 feet above the river.

This south-facing cliff is of many colors: pale yellow or buff, blue-gray, rose, salmon, orange, dark brown, in wet areas nearly black. Lichen-draped junipers, stunted hardwoods, and fragrant gooseberry grow on its ledges. The rock has ledges and balconies, recesses and

Welch Bluff.
In this painting by Thomas Hart Benton, the overall scale and proportions of the bluff are true to reality while smaller elements are expressed as curvilinear forms. Such curving lines are a recognizable feature of Benton's landscapes. The geologic fault that splits the bluff is above the boat's right end.

projections, alcoves and overhangs. Barely 130 feet high, Welch Bluff is one of the most distinctive on the entire river. (Tom Benton's painting of Welch Bluff, reproduced above, is of course a free interpretation not showing the cliff's smaller features.)

Welch Bluff was named for a couple who lived and farmed in this bend of the river, Lawrence Welch (1836–1901) and his wife, Francis (1848–1920). The bluff overlooks a beautiful green pool named the Crow Hole for later residents Sam W. Crow (1880–1939) and his wife, Cinda (1882–1957). The Crows lived up the hill by the Welch Spring, in a three-room farmhouse with a long front porch.

53.7 The next bluff, a low one on the right, has a cascade of Venus maidenhair fern growing on its face where water noisily splashes into the river—a fern fall on Dripping Bluff. This pool (53.5–53.9) is Dripping Bluff Hole, of course.

The map published with geologist T. C. Hopkins' report of 1890 names several small tributaries along the river's left side:

54.2 Coots' Branch (in a later report it becomes Cook Branch), where Richard Holland recalls a Scaggs Hole on the river, named for Ben Scaggs, who lived on the county road a half mile up the branch;

55.0 Fish Trap Branch—by which, Hopkins tells us, somebody had his trap at a river shoal near the mouth of this spring branch; and

55.4 Boomer Mill Creek, today known as **Boomer Hollow**.

Along this reach of the river (54.0–55.5) the Buffalo maintains a broad, open channel, but with ledge shoals that challenge the canoer to find the one best way through, especially in low water. Bluffs are mostly back in the woods, hidden from the river. Cedars and pines stand on dry, south-facing hillsides. Earth banks by the river may be marked by beaver (or otter?) slides.

55.8 Slanting, or Sliding, Rock, a 15-by-30-foot piece lying tilted into the left side of the river, marks the approach to…

55.9 the confluence with the **Little Buffalo River**, entering from the right. Just beyond is a gravel bar, a good landing for a rest or lunch break—and for learning.

Looking up the Buffalo from this bar, there are rock cliffs close to the river on *both* sides—**Flatiron Bluff** on the left and a bluff on the right that the map puts at the north end of **Lost Hill**. These two bluffs were once connected, part of a ridge having the Little Buffalo on this side and the Buffalo on the far side, flowing beyond Lost Hill. Thousands of years ago the Buffalo broke through the ridge and joined the Little Buffalo. This is called "stream piracy," when one stream—here, the Little Buffalo—captures the flow of another.

The ancient channel of the Buffalo beyond Lost Hill is today a dry, open field; old-timers called it the Valley. (Today the Valley remains in private ownership, off-limits to hikers.)

The Little Buffalo is the Buffalo's largest tributary, draining a watershed of 128 square miles, about 10 percent of the total area of the Buffalo River's watershed, and contributing nearly 30 percent of the total flow of the Buffalo River just below the confluence. The Little Buffalo was once known as Hudson's Fork of the Buffalo, after a pioneer family who settled along the Little Buffalo above Jasper. The Buffalo River itself was Cecil's Fork, named for that family of early settlers in the Erbie area. The main stream has also been known as the Big Buffalo, in contrast to the Little Buffalo.

Lost Hill, between the river's present and former channels, stands in isolation from the surrounding hills, which may suggest how it got its name. However, old-timer J. V. Waters says, "The story is that two children got lost on the hill and they found them there."

55.9–56.3 The pool alongside Lost Hill is known as the Hurd Hole, for the family who lived here on the right-hand side of the river. The Hurd Hole is followed by…

56.4–56.5 the Chaffin Hole, for a family of early settlers on the left-hand side of the river at the south end of Lost Hill.

56.6–56.7 The next pool, past the mouth of tree-shaded, spring-fed **Wells Creek**, is the Wells Creek Hole. Next below the Wells Creek Hole is a stretch of river known as…

56.9 "mouth of Bear Cave," where Bear Cave Hollow enters from the right. (Longtime county resident Fred Bell recalls also that a pool near the mouth of Bear Cave was known as the Sawmill Hole.) The hollow's mouth is a gully spilling creek gravel into the river.

About 100 yards below Bear Cave is Alice's Rock, a ledge at the right bank named for Alice Waters Henderson (1863–1949). She had come here, to her parents' farm, to live with her children. In 1894 her husband had been murdered—shot while plowing his field—by a man who wanted the land the couple had homesteaded.

A family member recalled that the widow "worked very hard, had rough times. Sold cows for $1.50 and material [homespun cloth] for three cents a yard. She spun thread…made her own cloth…knit." For relaxation, and food, she came here and fished at Alice's Rock.

But around 1905 Alice married a man who lived near Erbie, and we presume her life improved. Certainly she lived a long time.

57.2 Not far below Alice's Rock, about 1900, John J. Waters built a fish trap, a V-contoured rock fence across the river at a shoal. John's family waded into the river and drove fish to a gap at the point of the V, and into a pen. Says great-grandson Gene Waters: "There were no game laws. All the fish were eaten, or fed to hogs."

57.8–57.9 Downriver on the right is Gray Bluff, named for its color but known also as Tom Waters Bluff. Thomas J. "Rawhide" Waters (1869–1948), a son of John J., lived at this turn of the river, and the pool here is Tom Waters Hole. High up in the 200-foot bluff is a small cave from which comes a waterfall after heavy rain.

58.4–58.8 Next below the Tom Waters Hole is the Tutter Hole, whose name is of unknown origin. It extends past the mouth of Sooky Branch (or Sookie—or Sukey—Hollow, 58.5), with another name of unknown background. The Tutter Hole appears to have no distinct shoal dividing it from the next pool…

58.8–59.2 the Riggs Hole (or Ward Phillips Hole, for the operator of a fishing camp here in the 1960s). Facing the Riggs Hole is a ter-raced, or stepped-back, cliff of impressive height, rising to 330 feet above the river, Riggs Bluff or **Chimney Rock Bluff**. The Chimney Rock itself is a small natural bridge about 100 feet above the river near the upstream end of the bluff. It can be seen from the river in the wintertime but is hidden by vegetation at other seasons.

Though the Everton Formation extends nearly 150 feet up this bluff, only seven feet of its Newton Sandstone—so prominent in cliffs upriver—is visible at the bluff's base.

59.0 Opposite Chimney Rock Bluff is a path up the right bank to the **Hasty campsite**, which has a mowed tent area and a toilet.

Hasty Campsite to Carver (Highway 123), *4.2 miles.*

The Hasty campsite, which is reached by road, can serve as a take-out or put-in site. Or, a quarter mile downstream, there is…

59.3 the **Hasty Low-Water Bridge** (Phillips Ford). Road traffic at the bridge makes the campsite preferable. If putting in at the bridge, launch into the channel at the east (left) end. If portaging across the bridge, launch into the same channel. Avoid the bridge's west end, where water drops into culverts underneath—dangerous!

The original bridge, of logs and planks, was built in the 1930s by the Civilian Conservation Corps (CCC). Later it was replaced with a concrete slab, which the county rebuilt in the 1990s.

The low-water bridge is just that. Even at normal flow the river washes over the concrete slab. The county road is a shortcut between Hasty and Jasper but is closed during high water.

In the first two miles below the bridge are three named pools…

59.7–60.0 the Baughman (BAUF-man) Hole,

60.6–60.9 the Haywood Brown Hole,

61.2–61.5 and the Brown (or Stillhouse) Hole. At the lower end of the Brown Hole the river passes **Stillhouse Hollow** with its flowing stream. Then, where the river bends to the right…

61.6–61.7 is a bluff about 240 feet high. In pale gray Boone limestone below its summit are caves. Says Gene Waters: "I call one of those caves Hell-and-Gone Cave because it's so inaccessible."

61.9–62.2 The next pool is known locally as Blue Hole. (Along the river downstream from Boxley, this is Blue Hole #5.) But it also has other names: Eddings Hole, Aunt Melinda Hole, John Eddings Cave Hole. Aunt Melinda was John Eddings' wife.

John Eddings Cave is in the hollow between two 200-foot bluffs that face the Blue Hole. It is reached by a path that goes a short distance up the hollow from the river to the cave's opening.

John Eddings had a farm opposite the cave, and old-timer J. V. Waters says: "I remember the bats circling over the house, thousands of them. My brother took a fishing pole…revised his swing…then killed them." That incident took place around 1920. Today the cave is fenced off from March 15 to October 15 to protect endangered gray bats when raising their young.

During the rest of the year the cave is open for exploration. John Eddings Cave is a long one—6400 feet—but a short distance inside, the main passage is blocked by a deep pool of cold water.

The Blue Hole is a fishing and swimming place for local people, who come down a dirt road to the left bank.

About a mile below the Blue Hole is…

63.1 Highway 123. The present bridge, opened in 1976, replaced a one-lane span dating from 1916 (photo, page 101). Before the first bridge there was a ferry. There has been a crossing here since the 1840s, when the wagon road was known as Cheatam's Turnpike.

About 400 feet downstream from the bridge is:

63.2 Carver, at the boat landing on the left. Up the bank are campsites, a water hydrant, and a toilet.

Carver to Woolum

River miles 63.2 to 78.6. Distance 15.4 miles. Average gradient 5 feet per mile. Tranquillity—and some big-waves rapids. Put-in at boat landing at campsites at Carver, off north end of Highway 123 bridge south of Hasty. Take-out on gravel bar at Woolum Ford, seven miles southwest of Highway 65 at St. Joe.

Carver to Mount Hersey, *6.8 miles.*

The Carver campsites are on what once was part of the Carver community center and family farm (see *Carver,* page 191). A spur road leads off the high bank to…

63.2 the boat landing on a gravel bar. The pool here is the Tin Carver Hole, for community leader Pembrooke Tinsley Carver. The upper part of the pool, beneath the 123 bridge, is also known as the Bridge Hole. Across the Carver Hole and just a little downstream is the mouth of the Buffalo's fifth-largest tributary, **Big Creek**, draining 82 square miles, about 6 percent of the river's watershed.

64.1 The 160-foot bluff on the left has the first large exposure of rock to be seen on this section of the river, and it is fairly typical of all bluffs here: Everything in sight is of the Everton Formation. About 13 feet of the Newton Sandstone is present, beginning seven feet above the river, but the massive Newton is disappearing from the Everton's layers of sandstone, limestone, and dolomite.

64.4 After passing through short pools and easy shoals below the Tin Carver Hole, the river here spills over bedrock shelves having shallow channels; without enough water it's easy to hang up. This is Slickrock (or Ledge or Broken Ledge) Shoal.

Below Slickrock Shoal, beyond shallow water and another shoal…

64.7–65.0 the Teener Hole, named for past local resident Teener Lane, bends to the left below a bluff. There on the left (64.9), the creek from **Hancock Hollow** arrives. (Geologist T. C. Hopkins back in 1890 called this stream Gum Tavern Branch.) The creek occasionally has pushed a pile of gravel into the river—a small example of how material has arrived to replenish the Buffalo's gravel bars.

65.1 At the lower end of the Teener Hole a long, shallow shoal is called the Wide Shoals. Beyond the Teener Hole the left bank is covered for a quarter mile or more with river cane (or pipe cane, switch cane, or giant cane). *Arundinaria gigantea* is of the grass family and related to bamboo. The Buffalo's earliest settlers found the bottomlands covered with canebrakes, which they plowed up and burned to clear fields for cultivation.

65.8–66.3 The next named pool is the Upper John Morris Hole, overlooked by a bluff rising to 180 feet from the left edge of the water. A short distance beyond is…

66.5 Lick Creek, coming in from the right. For a nice side trip, walk up this spring-fed stream. And on the river a short distance below Lick Creek, watch for a fern fall, a green spill of Venus maidenhair fern on a wet bluff to the right (66.6), at the next pool…

66.5–67.1 the Lower John Morris Hole, where gray, ancient rock outcrops—turrets and other shapes—stand high among the trees on the right. Lower John Morris is also known to local people as the Oscar Canady Hole, or the Andrew Wallian Hole for Andrew J. Wallian (1899–1959). Andrew's family name, by the way, is sometimes spelled Wallain or Wallin, and may be pronounced "Walden."

Below the Morris Hole there's one more ledge shoal, then…

67.4–67.8 the Britt Hole. There, 150-foot **Falls Bluff** is the most noteworthy cliff between Carver and Mount Hersey. Vines climb up and patches of tan or salmon color enliven its gray rock. Its rough, uneven face has setbacks and overhangs, and alcoves with calcite draperies. In wet weather a waterfall comes from a cave about 60 feet up the cliff, splashing and spraying where Venus maidenhair fern grows in cascades of lush greenery.

Junipers hung with gray-green lichen cling to the face of the cliff, and large mats of woodbine—Virginia creeper vines—cover the rock. In summer, prairie rose blooms along the river bank. Finally, at its downstream end, Falls Bluff becomes six separate buttresses of stone that stand out from the wooded hillside.

67.8–69.8 For two miles downriver from Falls Bluff, the Buffalo is what old-timer J. V. Waters calls "broken," with no deep pools, only shallow stretches and shoals. The riffle at the exit of the Britt

Carver family. The older girl has ribbons and the boy a lace collar, but Sarah Rosa wears an everyday dress and P. T. his work shoes. The time is about 1905. A simple backdrop suggests this portrait was made by a traveling photographer who just stopped by (and Rosy Carver only took time to dress the kids). P. T.'s wife was part Indian, maybe Cherokee. She was short and, in later years, plump. Relatives say Grandma Carver "kind of jiggled when she laughed."

Carver.

Here in the early decades of the twentieth century was the home of Pembrooke Tinsley Carver (1876–1936) and his wife, Sarah Rosa (1878–1959). P. T. and Rosy Carver had a store, and from 1913 until 1929, the Carver post office. They operated a grist-mill, sawmill, and blacksmith shop, and on their farm they raised cattle, hogs, sheep, goats, horses, and mules (and P. T. is said to have made a little whiskey now and then).

For family and guests, Rosy's dining table could accommodate at least twenty people. The Carvers themselves had ten children (which probably explains who helped with all those chores).

Hole (67.9) is long—maybe 800 feet. The next shoal (68.2) is on bedrock, with some patches of rock washed clean—bright greenish-white. At the next shoal (68.7) the river spills down ledges with standing waves—500 feet of fast water. Then the river slows down, passing a high broken cliff on the right, where at intervals gray battlements rise above the trees.

Then another disturbance of the waters, the Whirl. J. V Waters describes it as "a small place, right above the Mount Hersey Hole. A whirl is a whirlaround, a circle, a sharp change of direction of the current." Whether the Whirl can be seen there or not, the river spills down a shoal (69.7) and into…

69.8–70.0 the Mount Hersey Hole, leading to the **Mount Hersey** landing on the left, having a primitive campsite and a vault toilet.

Mount Hersey to Woolum, *8.6 miles*

The Mount Hersey boat landing is at the mouth of **Davis Creek**, the Buffalo's tenth-largest tributary, based on the area of its watershed. Or its *surface* watershed, for hydrologists have learned that Davis also gets water by underground channels from the watershed of Crooked Creek to the north. And Davis Creek in its lower section *loses* water through underground channels to Mitch Hill Spring, which flows into **Mill Branch** (photo, page 368), entering the river about 200 feet downstream from Davis Creek.

The vanished community of Mount Hersey was a short distance up the road from the boat landing (see *Mount Hersey,* opposite).

On the river, through the exit shoal from the Mount Hersey Hole and past the mouth of Mill Branch, the view ahead is to…

70.2–70.6 Copper Bluff, 200 feet high, with parts of its upper face having iron oxide stains—red-orange, the color of copper. Probably that's how the bluff got its name, but river guide Jack Hensley has a different story: "Charlie Rogers—he was a little old bitty dried-up man…. He thought he had a little mine up there. Yeah, Charlie, that's all he wanted to talk about, was his copper mine."

Copper Bluff also marks the beginning of a geologic "high" where the Buffalo's oldest, lowest rock formation, the Powell Dolomite, begins to appear above river level. At the bluff, contact between the Powell and the overlying Everton Formation is about 55 feet above river level—though not visible to the casual observer.

Just past Copper Bluff is excitement…

70.6 Patton Shoal, a long, fast ride, first to the right…then left…then right—rapids twisting down over ledges, past rocks, through haystack waves, more than 300 feet of tumbling water…and 600 feet more of fast flow…

70.7–71.4 into Patton Bottom Hole—past Patton Bottom, a farm site on the left. Patton Bottom Hole, three-quarters of a mile long, connects through a brief chute with…

71.5–72.1 Cave Creek Hole, half a mile long. These two pools are the longest almost unbroken stretch of calm water on this reach of the Buffalo. Parts of these holes are deep—just below Patton Shoal and above Cave Creek—but much more is shallow water. With the river wide and shallow (at 71.0), with gravel or rock bottom, Jack Hensley says: "I don't believe I ever caught a fish in here worth anything, in my life. There ain't a *hide* in this old place." (Hensley is saying there's nowhere for fish to hide.)

Toward the end of Cave Creek Hole…

72.0–72.1 Clair Bluff (or Cave Creek Bluff) rises above the trees

Mount Hersey. About 1827 a young couple from Tennessee, Mitchell and Nancy Hill, came to make a home near the mouth of Davis Creek—perhaps they were attracted by the big spring whose flow enters the river 200 feet downstream from the creek. The Hills were among the first white settlers along the Buffalo.

About 1850 someone built a gristmill powered by the outflow from the Mitch Hill Spring. In 1875 prospectors discovered zinc ore in the hills nearby and in 1877 a post office was established. For decades miners continued to look for zinc, but what they found was not in paying quantities and eventually they gave up.

Armon Mays recalls that before 1920, Mount Hersey consisted of five interrelated families, a one-room school that also housed the church, and several enterprises run by his parents, Frank and Dora Mays: store and post office, steam-powered sawmill and cotton gin, the water-powered gristmill, and a small farm.

Mount Hersey was isolated, off the beaten track. A rural mail carrier provided the only regular contact with the outside. There was no indoor plumbing, electricity, doctor, or telephone. People moved away to find better situations.

In 1919 the post office was closed. The community's population slowly dwindled to zero, and today all that's left is Mitch Hill Spring, old masonry piers beside Mill Branch (photo, page 368), a long abandoned house (built by his parents, Armon Mays says), and a primitive campsite and the boat landing.

to 170 feet, presenting a high unbroken face for nearly 200 yards. At the downstream end of the bluff and straight ahead is…

72.1 the mouth of **Cave Creek**. The creek enters the river through a lengthy inlet that can be followed to its end where the stream flows in. There, one can get out of the boat and explore. Behind the undergrowth just beyond the stream is a small cave—did it inspire the name for Cave Creek?

For a longer exploring trip: A very high bluff, 360 feet, stands beyond the brushy bottomland east of Cave Creek and more than a quarter mile south of the river. This landlocked bluff, which can be seen on topographic maps, apparently was created when Cave Creek (or the river?) flowed farther to the south. Cave Creek has changed course at its mouth even in recent times, now entering the river a quarter mile upstream from where it did a few decades ago.

At the entrance to Cave Creek's inlet, the river turns left…

72.2 and plunges down steep rapids with protruding rocks and standing waves—Cave Creek Shoal, helping to make up for what paddlers have had to endure in the previous mile of calm water.

These rapids can be upsetting. On an Ozark Society trip one time, two middle-aged ladies in a canoe loaded with camping gear "tumped" here and spilled. People quickly retrieved whatever was afloat, but other things had sunk. Men dived in and brought up item after item. Presently one of the divers asked: "What's missing now?"

"Really, you guys have all of it." The lady looked again at the pile. "No—we're still missing a camp chair."

Somebody dived again into the foot of the rapids. No luck. He dived still again—and came up holding a camp chair! Triumphantly, he held it high and waved it back and forth.

The lady looked perplexed and said, "That's not *my* chair."

72.2–72.5 Past the rapids, the Lower Cave Creek Hole extends downriver to a shoal. Then, on the left, there is a small exposure of Powell Dolomite, thin-bedded, yellowish-gray, as the river enters…

72.7–72.9 the Troy Kaylor Hole, named for a past resident on the north or left-hand side of the river. Now in sight ahead is…

73.3–73.4 John Reddell Bluff, another feature named for a long-time resident of the left bank. The bluff is about 175 feet high, and like many other south-facing cliffs displays colors on the brighter side of the palette—tan, buff, cream, orange—as well as shades of gray. And like many other bluffs it has large patches of dark green junipers. The cliff also has a "wavy" appearance, with curving pro-

Summer fun. Louisiana Boy Scouts play at Cave Creek Shoal.

jections. Scooped-out places have deposits of pale calcite flowstone.

72.9–73.6 John Reddell Hole extends past the bluff. Toward the lower end of this pool is John Reddell Spring (73.5), flowing from the base of an eight-foot bluff and spilling down among boulders to the river. At the pool's end, near an overhanging ledge 15 feet above the water, thin-bedded Powell Dolomite is exposed at river level.

73.6–73.9 The next pool, Cane Branch Hole, goes past the mouth of **Cane Branch**, on the left (73.7). And then an unnamed pool (74.0–74.2) ends at a chute having massive boulders, including an eight-foot specimen near midstream that river guide Jack Hensley calls the Rollover Rock. The big rocks lie in the river at…

74.1–74.5 Cane Bluff, which also overlooks the Snag Hole, just below the chute. Jack Hensley, however, says the shoal at the end of the Snag Hole has washed out. Thus the hole merges with…

74.6–74.9 Upper Akins Hole, a broad pool bending to the left and extending to near the mouth of **Jackson Hollow** (74.9). Upper Akins is followed by…

74.9–75.3 Lower Akins, more than 100 feet wide, with pine trees growing close to the water on the dry, south-facing hill on the left. Pines seldom are seen so close to the river.

A mild riffle (75.3) separates Lower Akins from…

75.4–75.8 Perk Spring Hole, which also is wide and quite long.

Perk Spring (75.5) is a small stream flowing from the base of an earth bank six feet above the right edge of the river. "Perk" Hale once farmed the strip of bottomland above the spring.

Across the river from Perk Spring is Ira Gentry Bluff, a 50-foot cliff mostly hidden behind trees. But some of the downstream end of this bluff (75.7–75.8) is visible, and its layers of rock are dipping or slanting downriver, plunging downward. Though it is not conspicuous, here is the beginning of a major change in the river's geology. The Everton Formation, which has been predominant in the Buffalo's cliffs for the last 50 miles, all the way downstream from Ponca, is now diving below river level. From here for nearly 20 miles downstream to Highway 65, all the bluffs will be of the Boone Formation, which overlies the Everton. Beyond Highway 65 the Everton will rise again, reappearing in riverside cliffs.

The cause of this "mid-Buffalo geologic low," which affects not only the Everton and Boone Formations but also any others above them, is not known. But many geologists believe that underlying deep-seated carbonate rock gradually dissolved away, causing overlying strata to subside—"dissolutional letdown," as one of them says.

The change becomes obvious at…

75.9 the next shoal, where the river hurries down a chute and over ledges, and where the widely known knife-edge cliff called **the Narrows** (locally, "the Nar's") comes into view. Here at the right bank are two ten-foot-diameter masses of fallen rock with a different look—thin-layered, rough-surfaced Boone limestone and chert, unlike anything seen upriver.

76.4–76.5 Along the Leafy Hole (named in the past for a bed of leaves on the bottom) the right-hand bluff is of the Boone's alternating layers of gray limestone and lighter colored chert. And the Narrows, all the way to its top edge—from 65 to nearly 100 feet above the river—is Boone limestone and chert (photo, page 369).

The Narrows, at river mile 76.5, is also at the Buffalo River's exact midpoint between its farthest source in the Boston Mountains and its eventual end at mile 153 where it flows into the White River.

76.7–76.9 Past the Narrows, the river curves to the left through the Bat House Hole, ending at **the Bat House (Skull Bluff)**. Local residents named this 80-foot cliff rising from the river the Bat House because it has a cave below water level. Probably only divers have seen the cave; Jack Hensley says the water is 14 feet deep.

The Ozark Society's founding president, Dr. Neil Compton, liked to give names to natural features. He saw the shallow cave openings just above river level (photo, page 57) as like the eye sockets of a skull, and he named the cliff Skull Bluff.

Thomas Hart Benton, the noted artist, created paintings of several features along this part of the river. One of them is of a fisherman's camp at the Bat House (see page 267).

Next below Bat House Hole is…

77.0–77.6 Roughedge Hole, past **Roughedge Ford** (77.1), then curving to the right past **Roughedge Hollow** (77.3). Says old-timer J. V. Waters: "At the mouth of Roughedge Hollow, about 1916, we stretched a wagon sheet over a pile of pawpaw limbs to sleep on. I fished with a cane pole and a live minnow."

77.3–77.5 Cash Bluff, on the left just past Roughedge Hollow, lies along the line of dipping rock strata seen upstream at Ira Gentry Bluff. The Everton Formation is already below river level here, but for the geologist, Cash Bluff has exposures of several other formations (in ascending order, St. Peter Sandstone, Plattin Limestone, and Fernvale Limestone) below the Boone Formation at the top.

Beyond Cash Bluff and a shoal, the river swings against…

77.7 a low cliff rising from the water on the left. This rocky promontory with its sloping profile also appears in one of Thomas Benton's Buffalo River paintings and is informally called Benton Bluff. Old-timer Leon Manes says there is a whirl (circling flow) at this bluff. Certainly the current runs *toward* the cliff.

77.7–77.8 Just beyond is deep water, another of the river's Blue Holes—#6 in the succession of Blue Holes that begins at Boxley.

A mere riffle appears to separate the Blue Hole from…

77.9–78.4 the next pool, the Boat Hole, or the Boat Landing as Leon Manes calls it. At the pool's downstream end, a family living in lower Richland Valley keeps a boat, for crossing the river when it is too high to ford at Woolum. On the left, the steep hillside has outcrops and low bluffs of Boone limestone and chert, with hardwoods growing along the river's edge and cedars higher up.

78.5 At the next shoal is **Woolum Ford**, with the take-out site on a wide gravel bar to the left. From there the road heads up the bank and past a vault toilet before continuing toward St. Joe.

Woolum, like Carver and Mount Hersey, was once a community center with its own store, cotton gin, stave mill…and earlier, after the Civil War, a saloon. All were gone before 1940.

Here at Woolum is the downstream limit of coverage of the Trails Illustrated *Buffalo National River, West Half* map and the beginning of coverage of the Trails Illustrated *East Half* map.

Woolum to Tyler Bend

River miles 78.6 to 93.8. Distance 15.2 miles. Average gradient 5 feet per mile. Rough-faced limestone and chert bluffs, and a river underground. Put-in on gravel bar at Woolum Ford, seven miles southwest of Highway 65 at St. Joe. Take-out at boat landing at Tyler Bend, three miles west of U.S. 65 at Silver Hill.

Woolum to Baker Ford, *10.9 miles.*

Like Carver and Mount Hersey, Woolum was a community (see *Woolum,* page 197), but is now only a point of access to the river.

78.6 The boat landing at Woolum Ford is at the river crossing for a low-standard road into Richland Valley. Across the river and just downstream is the mouth of **Richland Creek**, the Buffalo's third-largest tributary in terms of its 119-square-mile watershed, about 9 percent of the Buffalo River's drainage area.

78.7–79.1 Below the mouth of Richland is the Robertson Hole (not Robinson, as often pronounced). A published family history says the hole was named for Christopher Columbus "Lum" Robertson, a Buffalo River pioneer born in Tennessee in 1827. In 1867 Robertson drowned when trying to cross the river a short distance upstream and his body was recovered at the Robertson Hole.

At normal level the hole is nearly one-half mile long. During droughts it shrinks to one-tenth mile. The river trickles in but the pool's exit shoal goes entirely dry—and so does most of the riverbed for more than four miles. Like the Suck Hole on the upper river, the Robertson Hole drains into underground passages. The water reappears at White Springs at river mile 83.3.

79.1 Up the bank on the left is a primitive camping area at the edge of a large field. With wide-open skies and no house lights in view, this is the best place anywhere on the river for stargazing.

79.3 Beyond the Robertson Hole is (or was) the Wash Pot Hole or Well Hole, "a little round hole" at the left side of the river. Old-timer Leon Manes: "It'd be 20 feet deep." River guide Jack Hensley: "It ain't deep no more." Below the Pot Hole is…

79.3–79.5 the Honey Hole, ending at a ledge shoal.

79.6–80.2 The next pool is the Elm Root (or Willow Root or High Banks) Hole. "Ellum" Root is alongside the road from Woolum to St. Joe. At times the river here is entirely dry. At other times it has gone on a rampage, tearing at the left bank, threatening to take out the roadway. The Park Service placed limestone boulders along the bank in one area (79.9) to protect the road.

Downstream at the **High Bank** (80.1–80.2), the most actively eroding site anywhere along the river, the Park Service applied more extensive treatment (photo, page 131). During the 1990s the Buffalo here moved northward, completely bypassing **the Pouroff** (or Little Niagara or Horseshoe Rock), a ledge drop that had spilled many a canoe. Today the erosion area ends at…

80.5 Jamison Creek, close against…

80.5–80.8 Jamison Bluff on the left, the first high sheer cliff below Woolum. The bluff is named for the family of John Jameson, born in Virginia in 1784, who settled at the mouth of Jamison Creek in 1838—long before the river swung north and took away most of his bottomland. Jamison Bluff overlooks the Jamison Hole (80.5–80.9). ("Jameson" over the years has changed not only to the present spelling but also to Jamieson or Jimison.)

The bluff reaches to 170 feet above the river, its upper half bulging outward, weathered gray, its lower half more sheltered with areas of pale gray and orange on a cream-colored background. A dirt road on top passes an observation site, the Lookoff, at cliff's edge (80.7).

Past the ledge shoal at the exit from the Jamison Hole, the Jamison Bluff tapers down to a lower cliff alongside the river, and here…

81.1 are the Round Rocks. Lying in the river are two roundish masses of interbedded limestone and chert. A hundred yards downstream are two larger ones, 15 to 20 feet long and more than 10 feet through. The second pair are also known as the Twin Rocks. Lifelong fisherman Jack Hensley says the hole at the Twin Rocks doesn't ever go dry. River chronicler Fogle Clark says that the Buffalo may go underground from Round Rocks to White Springs even when water is on the surface upstream.

On this part of the river the Round Rocks are the first of several sets of big limestone and chert chunks that have fallen into the river from bluffs, then slowly weathered so their corners are rounded off. Other specimens lie ahead at Peter Cave and at Arnold Bluff.

Beyond the Round Rocks the river becomes shallow. **Point Peter Mountain** looms in the distance. Soon the river bends left, past…

81.7–82.0 Brewer Bluff (or Bend Bluff) and the Bend Hole, ending at **Bend Ford**, at the mouth of **Ben** (spelled without the *d*) **Branch**. In drought the Bend Hole, says Jack Hensley, "goes dry except just a pond, in the lower end—and that's over your head."

82.4 Below Bend Ford the river for a short distance flows over bedrock—slick rocks, the Rub Board Shoal or Wash Place Shoal. The place was known as the Wash Pot. Says old-timer Leon Manes: "People used to come to the river and wash, at the flat rocks."

It was here in 1965 that opponents of legislation to create Buffalo National River found a like-minded farmer who owned land on both sides of the Buffalo. Believing the landowner had the right to fence off the river, they strung barbed wire across to stop Memorial Day canoe racers coming downstream from Woolum. The canoers managed to get past the wires, the incident was reported in newspapers, and National River proponents pressed harder for legislation.

Beyond Rub Board Shoal, on the right, is the outlet of…

82.5 a quiet backwater, the Grandpaw Manes Slough, or Dave Slough, for local patriarch David C. Manes (1856–1947). Sloughs are the vestiges of old channels abandoned when the river changed course. Here the river once flowed along the base of **Dave Manes Bluff**, off to the right. (The bluff also is called the Dave Bluff, or Uncle Dave Manes Bluff, with "uncle" being a term of address for an elderly man. The name Manes is pronounced MAIN-ess.)

82.5–83.2 For three-quarters of a mile below the Dave Slough, much of the riverbed is solid rock that in drought is dry except for small pools. But nearing its next bend to the right, the river reappears. Here is a long pool…

83.2–83.8 the Margaret White Hole (or to some, Lonzo Hole or Gallion Hole). In the riverbed near the head of the pool are the White Springs (83.3), the exits for underground channels from the Round Rocks and the Robertson Hole. During drought the springs make visible ripples and boils on the surface of the pool here. At normal flow, canoers come down Rocky Shoal (83.1–83.2) and then pass over the springs without seeing anything.

The Margaret White Hole lies below 200-foot **Margaret White Bluff**, and this area is simply Margaret White to locals and others who come by back roads to fish, swim, camp, or picnic.

"Aunt" Margaret White may have been the widow of Wilson C. White, remembered for supporting her family on a farm nearby. She may have been a grass widow (one view is that Wilson simply abandoned her). Or Margaret may have been the widow of Christopher Columbus White, who may have been Wilson's half brother, and who in 1880 was shot in the back of the head, making *his* wife a widow. Wives of both Wilson and Columbus are known to have been named Margaret. In other particulars the record is clouded.

84.1–84.5 The next hole and bluff below Margaret White are called **Buzzard Roost**, for a congregation of turkey vultures. The bluff, which has a rough surface of limestone and chert about 100 feet high and 200 long, is known to some as Crabtree Bluff. The next hole beyond the Buzzard Roost is the Bill Crabtree Hole (84.6–84.7)—a short pool about 200 yards long, says Leon Manes.

84.8–85.3 The next lengthy pool extends past **Slay Branch**, which enters the river from the right at a camp and swimming site used by local people. The branch was probably named for Nathan Slay, born in North Carolina in 1809 and, by way of Georgia and Alabama, here at the Buffalo before 1850. The pool is the Slay Branch Hole, or to locals the "mouth of Slay Branch." Or the Will Goggin Hole, for a former owner of the farm opposite the branch. Or the Blue Hole—Blue Hole #7, counting down the river from Boxley.

85.1–85.3 Immediately downstream from Slay Branch is **Slay Branch Bluff** (or Blue Hole Bluff). Just beyond the bluff is…

85.3 Whisenant Hollow, on the right and a little distance back from the river. Also at some distance back, but visible beyond the trees and reaching to 260 feet above the river, is **Whisenant Bluff**, well recognized because its towering wall curves back into a deep recess, an alcove midway across its expanse of rock. The bluff face is sometimes called the Roman Nose (photo, page 202).

At Whisenant Hollow the river spills to the left over a shoal, and to the left is a steep bank of gravel, dumped into the river by flood waters sweeping across the point. Just beyond is…

85.4–85.5 Whisenant Hole. To the right is 20-acre Whisenant Bottom—sand and gravel, trees and brush all the way to the base of Whisenant Bluff. Old-timer E. G. Grinder says Whisenant Bottom was farmed until the river swept away the topsoil.

Farther along, the river bends close to the downstream extension of Whisenant Bluff, by this time barely 50 feet high, overlooking the Stovepipe Hole (85.7–85.8). The next, more recognizable pool…

85.8–86.1 is the Love Hensley Hole, between the Crabtree Bottom on the left bank and the old Love Hensley place on the right. ("Love" was Lovette Hensley; see *Side trip,* page 375.)

Whisenant Bluff. The cliff's profile, with a deep alcove midway along the face, has inspired some to call it the Roman Nose.

Leaving the Love Hensley Hole, the river splits into two channels. By the year 2000 the left channel was being bypassed in favor of the one on the right. From the new channel the river flows into...

86.4–86.8 the Sand Hole or Hangover Hole. The pool lies along the base of **Love Hensley Bluff**, a long palisade with interesting geology and scenery, rising as high as Whisenant Bluff but broken into separate, smaller exposures of rock. **The Hangover** (86.6) is a deeply undercut face of the bluff at river level. Higher up the bluff at the Hangover are hollowed-out areas, maidenhair fern falls, patches of woodbine. Downriver are half a dozen fins or buttresses of rock, 50 to near 100 feet high and extending 40 or 50 feet from the bluff behind them. These features—the scooped-out places, the fins or buttresses, the odd shapes—are unique to the limestone and chert Boone Formation (photo, page 204).

River guide Jack Hensley calls this part of the bluff (86.8–86.9) the Buzzards Roost, and the Sand Hole here merges into the Buzzard Roost Hole (86.8–87.0). Buzzard Roost Hole ends at a shoal, known to some as Cow Ford (87.0), and the river enters...

87.1–87.5 the Bolen Hole, named for a family who once farmed within the bend to the left. Toward the downstream end of this pool is the Bolen Bluff (87.4). The bluff stands only 15 feet above the river but is unusual. It is in layers a few inches thick and so deeply cut along the bedding planes that the limestone appears to have been loosely stacked. Bolen Bluff also has two small caves near the water.

The Bolen Hole empties through Slick Rock Shoal into…

87.6–87.9 Peter Cave Hole, where the river bends to the left below **Peter Cave Bluff**. Like Love Hensley Bluff, this bluff is a classic expression of geology of the Boone Formation. Here the palisade rises to nearly 250 feet above the river, with spires, fins, buttresses, and scooped-out areas, with light gray limestone interbedded with chert of contrasting gray or white, the thin strata of rock rising and dipping, curving up and then downward. Here too are six gigantic masses of rock fallen from the cliff and lying in the river; two of them are 35 feet through. (For artist Tom Benton's capture of the essence of Peter Cave Bluff, see page 266.)

The bluff is named for a Civil War saltpeter cave located high up and beyond sight near the downstream end of the cliff. Troops are said to have taken earth or bat guano from Peter Cave and processed it to obtain saltpeter (potassium nitrate) for making gunpowder. Today the 500-foot-deep cave is closed from March 15 to October 15 to protect endangered gray bats as they raise their young.

Around 1900, it is said, timber men installed a cable extending from the summit of Peter Cave Bluff to the river, then stapled newly hewn railroad crossties to the cable and sent them sliding down. At the river the ties were collected and then floated to market. The cable site at the top of the bluff is known as **the Tie Slide**.

Peter Cave Hole empties into Peter Cave Shoal, or Bucking Shoal, which in the 1960s had a long series of standing waves. Since that time the riverbed seems to have changed; the shoal is not as challenging. Below the shoal and past the **Rye Bottom** are…

88.2–88.4 Slick Rock Hole, on bedrock, and then…

88.5–88.9 Vile (or Vol?) Rock Hole, extending to the mouth of **Rocky Hollow**. The Vile Rock is (or was; its location is not known) a big rock lying along the left side of the river. In local knowledge the river at the downstream end of Vile Rock Hole and into the shoal at the mouth of the hollow is "mouth of Rocky Holler" (88.9).

89.0–89.1 Just beyond is another Blue Hole (#8, still counting Blue Holes downstream from the first one at Boxley). It lies at the

Strange shapes.
One canoer imagined this cliff near the downstream end of Love Hensley Bluff as a squirrel's head. Others have seen other forms. These rough surfaces and scooped-out places are typical of the Boone Formation of limestone and chert. All of the bluffs along the middle Buffalo from the Narrows to Highway 65 are Boone.

foot of **Blue Bluff**, 130 feet high, rising from and leaning over the river. The bluff's upper face has broad streaks of blue-gray (photo, page 56). We can wonder whether Blue Bluff got its name from the Blue Hole, or vice versa. Vernon Williams of St. Joe says the Blue Hole has also been called the John Hunter Rock Hole.

Toward its downstream end, Blue Bluff turns away from the river and continues behind trees along the bank. Here at the base of the bluff are calcite draperies and stalactites.

Past Blue Bluff and high above the trees on the left is…

89.2–89.4 Red Bluff, stained orange by iron oxide and having two large stone "heads" perched on its top. Opposite Red Bluff on the right is a high erosion bank (89.3–89.5) believed to have resulted from clearing vegetation up the river's edge so there were no tree roots to anchor the soil. Part of this cutbank has been stabilized with a revetment of cedar trees laid and pinned along the river's edge.

Red Bluff overlooks Baker Ford Hole (89.2–89.7) and…

89.5 Baker Ford, once a river crossing for a road, now a point of access to the river by way of an unpaved road from south of St. Joe.

Baker Ford to Tyler Bend, *4.3 miles.*

Baker Ford is about halfway around **Cash Bend**. In 1910 James Manville (Jim M.) Cash bought the farm here and his family name became attached to the bend, just as the next five bends of the river were named for the landowning Arnold, Turney, Tyler, Grinder, and Lane families. Timber men floating logs or crossties down the Buffalo may have given these names to the river's bends as a way to describe their progress downstream.

Below the Baker Ford Hole (89.2–89.7), the next pool is...

89.9–90.1 the Greenhaw Hole, with **Greenhaw Bluff** on the right. The bluff is 15 to 18 feet high—hardly impressive—with the red marker band of the St. Joe limestone halfway up the face. Also, lying in view atop the bluff (at 90.0) is a rock shaped like an oversized burial casket: **Coffin Rock**. (Thus a local youth, who had come here to fish, called this pool the Coffin Box Hole.)

Beyond the shoal at the end of the Greenhaw Hole is...

90.1–90.4 the Smart Hole, named for another local family. On the left is **Smart Bluff**, with rock outcrops to 50 feet above the water. The red marker band of the St. Joe, now four feet wide, can be seen about 12 feet above the river.

The Smart Hole ends at a shallow shoal known as the Greenhaw Ford (90.5) and soon the river bends left, through...

90.6–91.1 the Arnold Hole, past 140-foot **Arnold Bluff**, sometimes called McRaven Bluff for landowners here in the 1960s. Two 20-foot slabs of rock are propped against the base of the bluff, and several huge rounded masses lie in the water farther along.

Just beyond the bluff is the site of the Arnold Ferry, on the old St. Joe to Snowball road. The ferry was in use by the 1890s and was abandoned before the original Highway 65 bridge opened in 1929.

91.1 Here, too, the river divides—or formerly divided—around **Arnold Island**. Originally there was one channel, to the left; that's the way it is on a map made in 1910. The next map of the area, from 1939, shows two channels, left and right. But for decades the left-hand channel was the scenic route for canoers, while the right channel was more like an open ditch. By the year 2000, however, the river had blocked entry to the left channel with gravel—but in 2001 some gravel had washed out and canoers floated through. Meanwhile, the right channel (91.1–91.5) had become deep, shaded, attractive.

The island itself has changed. Today it is covered with brush, but Helen White of St. Joe recalls that in 1941 she picked cotton on Arnold Island, known by her family as the Sixteen-Acre Piece.

Just beyond the lower end of Arnold Island the river passes...

91.5 Goat Bluff, on the left, one of several Goat Bluffs along the

Buffalo River. Two local fishing guides, thinking Goat Bluff's cliff face resembles a movie screen, have called it Theater Bluff.

Just past Goat Bluff is **Shop Hollow** (91.6), possibly named for a blacksmith shop that once stood at its upper end—though old-timer Leon Manes says this is Mill Hollow, for a sawmill there.

91.7–91.9 Fishtrap Bluff, beyond Shop Hollow, indicates by its name that someone had a fish weir and trap in the river here. The bluff is bisected by a side valley, Coon Hollow (91.8), of which Jack Hensley says: "There's water flows there the year round."

From Arnold Island past Fishtrap Bluff there are several shoals and short pools. Eventually the river becomes calmer, wider…

92.2–92.6 the Turney Hole, also known as Scott Hole, John Scott Spring Hole, or simply "above the mouth of Calf Creek." On the left is Turney Bend, named for a family who came here before 1840. On the left also, great blue herons have nested in the tops of tall trees.

92.7 The river turns left at the mouth of **Calf Creek**, a fair-sized stream draining 48 square miles, about 4 percent of the Buffalo's watershed. Just past the creek, the river spills down Calf Creek Shoal and into another pool (92.9–93.1) known only as "below the mouth of Calf Creek." Overlooking all this is 270-foot **Collier Bluff**.

Past the next shoal, however, is a pool having names…

93.2–93.5 the Mill Creek Hole or—for the ninth time so far along the Buffalo—the Blue Hole. The deep, blue-green water near the mouth of Mill Creek is why many call this the Blue Hole.

Along to the left of Mill Creek Hole is low-lying ledge rock, and about halfway down the hole is a minor mystery, a short piece of steel beam wedged between ledges. Jack Hensley: "George and John Watts put it there. One of them rode a mule to Shady Grove, this side of St. Joe, to get the piece of iron." But no one seems to know why they jammed it into the rock alongside the river.

Jack Hensley says that Mill Creek Hole a few years ago was full of gar—"They just about took it over." Hensley calls the Buffalo's longnose gar "pecker-bills."

On the right above the mouth of Mill Creek is the little used upper landing (93.5) for Tyler Bend. Past the creek (93.6) and Mill Creek Shoal, and past the upstream end of 150-foot **Tyler Bluff** on the left, is the **Tyler Bend** boat landing (93.8) at a paved road to the right.

For river travelers arriving at Tyler Bend, this road leads to restrooms, a public phone (go up the road, take the first right), camping, showers, and a visitor center with information and exhibits.

Tyler Bend to Gilbert

River miles 93.8 to 99.2. Distance 5.4 miles. Average gradient 3 feet per mile. A short float but with a variety of scenic features. Put-in at boat landing at end of paved road to Tyler Bend off Highway 65. Take-out at Gilbert gravel bar, two blocks past Gilbert store.

Tyler Bend to Grinders Ferry (Highway 65), *1.4 miles.*

93.8 The river-access development at Tyler Bend—a loop drive along the gravel bar—is up against a river having a mind of its own. Every flood that tops the concrete curb along the road scours gravel and sand from the road and piles it elsewhere. Keeping the loop road open for traffic is an ongoing maintenance chore.

The access site faces **Tyler Bluff** (93.6–94.0), named for a mem-

Tyler Bend. The family of Baker Tyler settled in this vicinity about 1839 and farmed the north side of the river at the present Highway 65 bridge. Peter A. Tyler, a son of Baker, in the 1850s acquired land where Tyler Bend's visitor center and campground are today. Peter and his wife Eveline then farmed the land and brought up their eight children.

After the outbreak of the Civil War, Peter was forced against his will to join the Confederate army. Some months later he died of illness or was killed in battle east of the Mississippi River; there is no record of the circumstances. Peter's widow remained on the farm until her death in 1897. Old-timers called her place Eveline Tyler Bend.

After Eveline's death the property passed out of the family. Succeeding owners grew crops in the bottomland and, later, produced hay and pastured cattle there.

In the 1960s the U.S. Army Corps of Engineers proposed to build a dam at Tyler Bend to create a reservoir for flood control, electric power generation, and recreational use. The Corps' Gilbert Dam, as it was called, was at the center of the ten-year-long controversy over whether to dam the Buffalo or to have a national river. In 1972 the national river idea was enacted as law by Congress. Ironically, the very spot where the dam would have been built is now occupied by Tyler Bend's visitor center and campground, opened in 1991.

It also appears that had the dam been built, there would have been serious leakage through fractured Boone limestone of the ridges at each end of the structure, for similar problems have occurred in karst at Beaver Dam on the White River.

ber or members of the Tyler family, who lived here for generations. The upper two-thirds of the bluff is the typically rough-surfaced limestone and chert of the Boone Formation, deposited during the Mississippian Period. The lower one-third is rock that dates from the earlier Silurian Period. Another major rock formation, the Everton, from the still earlier Ordovician Period, is seen in most Buffalo River bluffs but here lies below the river and out of sight.

The oldest rock visible in Tyler Bluff is about 440 million years old, the youngest about 350 million years.

The gravel bar contains all the kinds of rock that exist upstream and uphill—after all, that's where the gravel came from. A random sample of 100 rocks from the bar should yield about 49 pieces of sandstone (tan or brown, well rounded, with tiny quartz crystals that sparkle in the sun), 49 of chert (many colors from white to black, having angular edges, texture varying from porous to very smooth like flint), and only two pieces of limestone (gray, having odd, rounded shapes, smooth).

Why so little limestone? It's because pieces of limestone are subject not only to abrasion as they roll and tumble down the river in floods, but also to solution, dissolving by dilute acid in the water. As floods carry chunks of limestone along, they disappear. Sandstone and chert, both much less soluble, survive.

Downstream from Tyler Bluff, the first lengthy pool is…

94.3–94.6 the Upper McMahan Hole, a long, broad, straight, calm stretch of water. Ahead are a hill and McMahan Bluff. On the left bank is Eveline Spring, named for Eveline Tyler, who lived at Tyler Bend before 1900. Past the next shoal the river turns sharply left…

94.7–95.0 against McMahan Bluff. Here (at 94.7) is a "whirl" when, at the right water level, the river hits the bluff and turns back. Along this bluff—and the old McMahan farm on the left—is Lower McMahan Hole, extending to the Highway 65 bridge.

About 100 yards upstream from the bridge, the bluff has a good site for learning geology. At water level (or a little below, if the river is running high) is a flat ledge of sandstone, Silurian, from about 400 million years ago (MYA). The ledge provides a landing spot.

Beginning about six feet above river level is 15–20 feet of thin-bedded St. Joe Limestone. The base of the St. Joe dates from about 360 MYA. A layer of sandstone a few inches thick below the St. Joe is basal Mississippian or possibly Devonian in age. Above the St. Joe, the remainder of the bluff is of the Boone Formation.

95.0 Highway 65 crosses the river on a bridge opened in 1990, replacing the original bridge that opened in 1929. At the new bridge, two pipes snake down the bluff into the river, carrying sensor lines for a water-level gage. Just beyond, in a ravine on the right, was the landing for **Grinders Ferry** that preceded the first bridge.

95.2 A short distance farther is a 20-foot cutbank on the left, one of more than a dozen along the river where removal of bank-side trees in the past encouraged erosion. Part of the bank has been stabilized with cedar trees laid and pinned along the river's edge. Downstream, an area hit more directly by floods continues to erode.

On the right, the gravel bar is a boat landing having a road to Highway 65 (see *Grinders Ferry,* page 210).

Grinders Ferry to Gilbert, *4.0 miles.*
The Grinders Ferry boat landing is near the upper end of…

95.3–95.5 the Swimming Hole or Grinder Hole, with 50-foot Swimming Hole Bluff (95.3) on the left. Canoers can float into the shallow cave at the base of the bluff, where, at the back, is greenish thin-layered Cason Shale (Ordovician); this is the only place to see the Cason at the river. The overhang's ceiling is pockmarked pinkish Brassfield Limestone (Silurian), which overlies the Cason. The Brassfield also is the "smooth" face extending about three-fourths of the way (38 feet) up the bluff. Above that, in ascending order, are the St. Clair Limestone (Silurian) the rest of the way up the bluff face, then a thin bed of Sylamore Sandstone (Silurian?), then slabby St. Joe Limestone (Mississippian). This area, from Tyler Bend to a few miles below Gilbert, is the only one along the Buffalo where these minor formations of Silurian age can be seen.

Beyond the Swimming Hole are shoals and short pools, with one of the holes having two large "round rocks," rounded masses of Boone chert lying in the river. Then the river moves alongside…

95.9–96.1 Shine Eye Bluff, where there's a ledge shoal (96.0), a steep drop with standing waves. Here in the early 1900s, says E. G. Grinder, men built a fish trap having logs angled across the river to guide fish into a corral from which they could not escape. Grinder believes that fish traps were present after 1910 but were gone by 1940. In this trap, Grinder says, the men caught fish going down the river after spawning in the spring.

Past this shoal is…

96.1–96.2 the Little Bluff Hole, or Shine Eye as people call this

Tie hackers face a traveling photographer at Grinders Ferry (today's Highway 65) about 1895. They have hauled wagon loads of their hand-hewn crossties onto the ferry. There the man in the dark suit—Bill Wallace, buyer for the Hobart-Lee Tie and Timber Company—has inspected each tie. Wallace accepted only the ones that were finished on four sides and of correct length, width, and thickness. Each tie he accepted he whacked with an iron branding hammer, and the tie was pushed off into the river.

Now some of the hackers stand on the boom, keeping the ties corraled until they can be assembled into a raft. Several men will float with the raft down the Buffalo, then down the White River to the railhead at Batesville, a water trip of 146 miles.

But the ties have been sold. For tie hackers, it's payday. (And for this photographer, it looks like a chance to sell pictures.)

Grinders Ferry. Samuel Grinder, born in Tennessee in 1818, is said to have come to this area before 1840 and to have begun operating a ferry here in 1853. With more certainty, family members Josh and George Grinder were providing ferry service in the 1870s. And in the 1920s Charlie and John Passmore operated a toll ferry (75 cents for automobiles) at the Grinders site. Ferry service ended when the first Highway 65 bridge opened in 1929.

place having a swimming area and gravel bar accessible by dirt road. How Shine Eye got that name is uncertain. One informant guesses that Shine Eye is a type of fish. Another says something in the water was shining at night. E. G. Grinder of St. Joe was told by his father that "a man named Shine Eye lived right there." But Ray Jordan at Gilbert says: "That crossing at Shine Eye seemed to be a treacherous place. A man rode a horse across the river there when the horse went down in quicksand. Either the man's head was out or his glasses were there, shining."

96.1 Like the Swimming Hole Bluff, Shine Eye's bluff displays Silurian rock formations. At the downstream end is a smooth sloping face of pinkish limestone, probably Brassfield, to 20 feet above the water. Above that are 35 feet of St. Clair Limestone and then 30 feet of Lafferty Limestone. Upstream, the bluff also includes a geologic feature known as an angular unconformity (photo, page 212).

Below Shine Eye, the next deep hole is…

96.3–96.7 the Lane Hole (or Lane Bend Hole), past **Lane Bluff** (or Lane Bend Bluff), a low cliff where rectangular rocks have tumbled into the river. The largest block, about ten by ten feet, is known as Square Rock. Farther downstream the bluff has pinkish Brassfield Limestone visible from five to ten feet above the river.

The Lane Hole ends at the undercut downstream end of Lane Bluff as the river moves swiftly toward the next pool…

96.8–97.2 Long Bottom Hole, bordering the **Long Bottom**, on the left. The hole ends at a shoal draining into…

97.3–97.5 the Spring Hole, which extends downstream from Long Bottom Spring, at the end of Long Bottom.

The river then goes through shoals and short pools past…

97.3–97.8 Long Bottom Bluff, intermittent exposures of rock. Red rock—the marker band of the St. Joe Limestone?—appears about 25 feet above the water at one point. On the skyline high above the bluff is a grove of pines: Pine Ridge.

Near the downstream end of Long Bottom Bluff and just beyond a rocky point that extends from the left bank is…

97.7 the Judge Moore Whirl. When the river is at the right stage, the point causes water to reverse direction and flow back along the downstream side of the rocks. The Moore Whirl or Judge Whirl is named for John Alexander Moore (1853–1929), who lived in a log house nearby and served two terms as county judge.

Just downstream from the whirl is Judge Moore Slough (97.8), a

Revelation. Geologist John McFarland demonstrates the idea of angular unconformity shown in the layered bluff across the river at Shine Eye. Upper layers within view are at a slight angle to the lower ones, indicating that the lower ones were formed, then uplifted, tilted, and planed off by erosion. Then the upper beds were formed, followed by more uplifting and tilting to put everything in its present position. All of this took millions of years.

quiet inlet extending downriver from the left bank. Both the slough and the rocky point at the whirl are visible on topographic maps.

The next pool, at the neck of Lane Bend, is called…

97.9–98.2 the Boat Hole. Says Jack Hensley: "They used to keep an old boat tied up at the lower end. People used to use it crossing the river to go to Gilbert—that Silver Hill bunch."

The Boat Hole also is known as the Log Hole, for logs in the river there. The logs may have been some that could not be moved downstream into the next pool…

98.3–98.6 the Boom Hole, where floating cedar logs probably filled the pool from bank to bank, kept from moving farther downstream by a heavy cable—the boom—stretched across the river. "Pond men" could walk a platform along the boom and raise a section of it to let trash pass through. Their main duty, though, was to keep pushing logs toward a steam-powered drag chain that pulled them from the river and toward the slat mill. These cedar logs had been cut upriver (see pages 97–98 and upper photo, page 99). Here at Gilbert they were reduced to seven-inch slats and shipped by railroad to a pencil factory. Ray Jordan: "The 1915 flood washed everything away—ruined the mill and probably washed out part of the railroad spur. Cedar slabs were washed far down the river."

98.6 At the downstream end of the Boom Hole, close to where a high-voltage power line goes overhead, the U.S. Army Corps of Engineers in the 1960s proposed to build a low dam—a re-regulation dam. The dam would have impounded water for a pumped-storage power generation unit at the proposed Gilbert Dam located upriver at Tyler Bend. During the day, when power demand would be at a maximum, a generator at Gilbert Dam would be running and its outflow would fill the pool extending downstream to the re-regulation dam. Late at night, when power demand would be low, the generator would be reversed to pump water from the re-regulation pool back into the Gilbert reservoir. Thus the pool level would have risen and fallen several feet each day.

Past the Boom Hole, the next pool is…

98.7–99.0 the Sand Hole, or Sand Bottom Hole, which actually has become part of the Gilbert Swimming Hole, as the shoal between the two pools has disappeared. The shoal would have been close to where **Dry Creek** enters from a gully on the left.

The Swimming Hole extends past…

99.2 the boat landing on the long gravel bar at **Gilbert**.

Gilbert to Maumee North

River miles 99.2 to 110.7. Distance 11.5 miles. Average gradient 3 feet per mile. A river in transition from pastoral midsection to more rugged country downstream. Put-in is at gravel bar at village of Gilbert. Take-out is at Maumee North landing, two miles southeast of Maumee at end of extension of County Road 86.

99.2 The put-in site is at the Gilbert Swimming Hole, about two blocks down the street past the general store (see *Gilbert,* page 214).

At the lower end of the Swimming Hole, the river bends left and spills over broad shallow ledges into the next pool…

99.4–99.9 the Spring Hole, named for the Gilbert Spring, whose spring branch reaches the river near the pool's upper end. Gilbert's Ray Jordan, in 1997: "It was always a deep hole at the Spring Hole [in the 1920s] when we were kids…a diving board. Now it's not over three feet deep…. We wore bathing suits down there. At the hole above Dry Creek, we skinny-dipped."

Past the next shoal is…

100.1–100.6 the Bear Creek Hole, or "mouth of Bear Creek," a swimming hole for people living up the ridge toward Marshall. On the left just below the creek are two flat rocks, each of them five feet across and standing a foot above river level, that serve as diving platforms—"swimming rocks," Jack Hensley says. He also says there

> *Gilbert* originated as a construction camp for the Missouri & North Arkansas Railroad and was named for Charles W. Gilbert, secretary-treasurer of the company building the M&NA. The railroad began service to the town site on December 1, 1902, and a post office was established in 1903. Gilbert became a shipping point for cotton, zinc ore, and timber products. In its heyday the town had a cedar slat mill, a stave mill, storage yards for stave bolts and railroad ties, cattle pens, a cotton gin, a gristmill and a flour mill, two hotels or boardinghouses, general stores, and a grocery store. Also a saloon—but it floated away on the great flood of August 1915.
>
> In 1920, families belonging to a millennialist religious group began to converge on Gilbert from Illinois and several other states, coming to this isolated place to establish a colony, the Incoming Kingdom Missionary Unit. Under the magnetic leadership of a preacher, John A. Battenfield, the newcomers soon built substantial homes, a church, a schoolhouse, and a stone building that was to house a print shop for a weekly four-page newspaper, *The Kingdom Harbinger*. In 1925, after a couple of Battenfield's prophesies failed to come to pass (the last one was that he could raise a person from the dead), he suffered what was termed a nervous breakdown and abruptly left Gilbert. The religious experiment was abandoned.
>
> By the 1930s the timber industry had played out and in 1946 the railroad shut down. Gilbert settled into a quiet existence as a village of well kept homes. Other than the coming of Buffalo National River, probably the most notable event during the rest of the twentieth century was the record flood of December 1982, whose waters almost reached the front steps of the Gilbert store.

once was a fish trap in the shoal at the end of the swimming hole.

100.4 Bear Creek is the Buffalo River's fourth largest tributary in terms of the area it drains, 84 square miles, about 6 percent of the river's watershed.

100.7–101.0 The next pool extends to the mouth of **Brush Creek**. Often this creek is dry in its lower reach, but apparently part of it flows underground to small springs at the river's edge about 200 feet upstream from the surface channel.

101.1 Just below Brush Creek are massive concrete **bridge piers** (photo, page 216; also see *May Never Arrive,* page 383). During the record flood of December 1982, water covered the tops of the piers.

At the right bank about 25 yards below the piers are more springs, probably underground flow from Brush Creek. Here also is…

101.1–101.2 the Mussel Hole, where around 1950, Jack Hensley says, "Women from Zack and all out that Peavine Ridge used to hunt for pearls. Mussels—big beds of them. Shallow, a humongous bed of gravel." (Also see *Pearl diver,* page 218.)

Beyond the Mussel Hole is…

101.3–101.8 the Sand Hole, curving to the left past 60-foot Sand Hole Bluff. The lower part of the cliff is of the Everton Formation. The upper part is St. Peter Sandstone, which will become increasingly prominent farther down the river.

From the Sand Hole's gravel bar a path leads up the bank to the end of a dirt road—an emergency exit from the river, also a way of access for local people, mostly, who come here to fish. Locals know this as "the old Carl Martin place," for the farmer who lived in this bend of the river. The National Park Service named it Plumfield, for thickets of wild plum trees here in the overgrown field.

101–102.3 The next pool, the Red Bluff Hole, curves sharply to the right and passes below 260-foot **Red Bluff** or Goat Bluff. The red color is actually pale orange, on the topmost face of the cliff.

That overhanging upper face of Red Bluff is of Boone limestone and chert, which form the entirety of many bluffs within the "mid-Buffalo geologic low" from the Narrows to Highway 65. Here, however, several rock formations older than the Boone are above ground and visible. The lowest cliff face of Red Bluff, with deeply scored, or incised, strata, is of the Everton Formation. Above, in ascending order, are the St. Peter Sandstone (the smooth 20-foot cliff); the Plattin, Fernvale, and St. Clair Limestones (exposed in minor cliffs between sloping terraces); and finally the Boone Formation, near the

Bridge piers of the Missouri & North Arkansas Railroad stand
tall, but were inundated by the record flood of December 1982.

top. Above the Boone, pine trees stand in silhouette against the sky.

The gravel bar at Red Bluff may be the highest of any along the
Buffalo. The river here makes a tight bend, and flood waters are swift
and powerful as they round the corner, able to push gravel 20 feet
above normal river level. In general, the tighter the curve, the more
substantial the gravel bar on the inside of that curve.

Past Red Bluff and then a series of shoals is…

102.7–103.1 the Wolf Hollow Hole—wide, curving to the left,
with high hills crowding the right bank. Just past Wolf Hollow on the
right (103.1) the river flows down Ezell Shoal and into…

103.3–103.9 the Upper Ezell Hole, extending past the mouth of
Ezell Hollow (103.4). The name Ezell comes from Isaiah Ezell, who
in 1859 became owner of 40 acres here along the left bank; his land
was called Ezell Bottoms (see *Isaiah Ezell,* opposite).

At the left bank of Upper Ezell is the Ezell Spring (104.5), and
soon beyond is an example of what geologists call "dip" of strata,
where layers of a low bluff slope down in an upstream direction.

Upper Ezell ends with a short, steep shoal that pours into…

104.0–104.8 Lower Ezell Hole, a wide pool open to the sun. On the right are broken bluffs. The geologic formations are the same as at Red Bluff, but these are hidden by vegetation. About halfway down the pool, dip is seen again, here in a 20-foot face of rock.

Lower Ezell empties down a shoal into a short pool at…

104.9 Tomahawk Creek, ranked as the Buffalo's ninth-largest tributary, draining 33 square miles. Approaching the mouth of Tomahawk, the river in the 1990s lost stability and cut deeply into its left bank, realigning its channel.

105.2 Past Tomahawk, the next bluff having exposed rock is situated within a *graben,* an area where Earth's crust has slipped or settled downward between two geologic faults. In this graben at **Wilson Point**, the Everton and St. Peter Formations, normally seen above river level, have disappeared below view and formations usually higher up are here just above the water line. Thus a massive, smooth, sloping exposure of St. Clair Limestone is visible for 20 feet above the river. Above that, a brownish-red layer of the St. Joe Limestone can be seen in an overhanging part of the bluff about 30 feet up.

105.3 Just beyond the graben's display of rock is a feature quite different, one of the Buffalo's most impressive fern falls, about ten feet wide and 25 feet high, a bright-green, bulging mass of Venus maidenhair fern on the wet bluff, reaching close to river's edge.

105.6 Beyond the fern fall, Low Gap Slough opens into the river from the left (this is visible on topographic maps). About 100 yards up the slough, Ebb and Flow Spring bubbles and trickles in a shady alcove; look for it about 50 yards beyond the two big rocks that stand ten feet high. "Ebb and flow" means that the spring alternates between little flow and increased flow, depending on whether its underground reservoir is drawn down or again refilled.

105.4–106.0 The lengthy pool past Low Gap Slough is known as the Wilson Hole. Old-timer E. G. Grinder calls it the **Low Gap**, for

Isaiah Ezell, born in Tennessee about 1816, was on the Buffalo River in 1841 and was said to have married a Cherokee Indian, earning him a nickname—Buck. His life story is not well known but he was reportedly a blacksmith, a ferry operator, and (so it was said) involved in counterfeiting. The record does show that he acquired 40 acres on the left bank of the river on July 1, 1859, for which he paid $50. He survived the Civil War but lost his property and was killed not long after.

the low point along the top of the ridge that overlooks the river here.

Midway down the pool, large rocks lie in the water. Jack Hensley says: "People used to do their washing here. Old Lady Wilson was washing, on the bar on the right, when the bluff caved off and all them big rocks come in the river."

The river now is outside the Wilson Point graben, so that older rock formations are exposed in the bluff on the left (105.7–105.9), including the St. Peter Sandstone about 100 feet above the water.

106.2–106.5 The next pool is the Davey Keeling Hole, past a long-ago bottomland farm on the left that is still known as the Davey Keeling place. Beyond the Keeling Hole the river begins 300 yards of riffle, down a chute floored with bedrock of a whitish color. Here in the past was another of the Buffalo River's fish traps.

The river calms as it flows into a still pool (106.9), curving gradually to the left. This pool—unnamed—continues past a narrow bottomland on the left, the Bee Bottom (107.1–107.5).

Pearl diver. Three miles below Gilbert, in the summer of 1910, two government biologists looking into the commercial value of the Buffalo's mussel beds came upon a professional pearl hunter. Charlie Cookson had been there nearly a week, first working over the shallows and now in water about five feet deep. Clutching a weighted sack for mussel shells, he drew himself underwater and searched for shells as long as he could hold his breath, then came to the surface, took another breath, and went under again. During the week he had collected about ten bushels of shells. He did not believe many were left.

Cookson opened the shells of all that he took. He told the biologists he averaged about $300 a year from collecting pearls.

Local farmers and their wives also looked for pearls during low water in summer, leaving piles of shells along the banks. At these places the biologists found very few living mussels in the river. The pearl seekers they met said the stocks of live mussels had always recovered by the next year.

Pearl hunting ran its course; it was not very renumerative and probably the supply of mussels became depleted. But Cookson continued to dive. He lived alone near the river, beneath an overhanging bluff that people eventually named Cooksun Rock.

One day fishermen came upon Cookson's partially decomposed body in the water, along with his sack of mussels. They carried the remains up the bank and buried them.

Ahead now is a very high bluff, to 380 feet above the river—stepped-back, or terraced, vertical faces of rock alternating with slopes having trees and grass. Here is the first bluff since Buzzard Bluff on the upper Buffalo to exceed 350 feet in height. It is the first of the high terraced bluffs that occur from here to the White River.

And this bluff seems not to have a name, except one bestowed in the 1970s by Searcy County historian James Johnston. He calls it Nitre Bluff, for a Civil War saltpeter works somewhere nearby.

The Buffalo bends sharply to the right to pass below the bluff. The water becomes deeper, blue-green: Blue Hole. Among the Blue Holes at intervals down the river from the first one at Boxley, this is the tenth and *final* Blue Hole (as far as we know).

The Blue Hole ends in a series of shoals past the mouth of **Rocky Creek** (107.8) and the river flows into…

108.0–108.5 Little Rocky Hole, past the mouth of **Little Rocky Creek** (108.3) and merging with…

108.5–108.7 Flat Hole, a shallow pool. Overlooking Flat Hole is a bluff as high as Nitre Bluff but having no name, probably because its rock faces are mostly hidden behind vegetation. And then…

108.7–109.3 over the next half mile is a series of shoals, some of them over bedrock, alongside **Cane Island**.

Ahead beyond Cane Island is…

109.5–109.8 another high bluff, reaching to 360 feet but having no name, overlooking the river at a left-hand bend. Closer, the bluff reveals its outcrops of gray rock, isolated exposures appearing as uneven, broken faces reaching to 150 feet above the water.

From here downstream the cliffs for several hundred feet above the river will usually be of the Everton Formation. Everton rock will be dark gray, blocky, broken, with intervening patches of junipers and slopes with grass. St. Peter Sandstone will often be present as a bulging, water-streaked layer of smoother rock above the Everton.

109.3–110.7 Compared with other parts of the river, the reach from Cane Island to Maumee North is not as well known by float guides and others who have provided the place names for this book. Old-timer Felix Clingings recalls a pool at Cane Island named the Caney Hole; its exact location is uncertain. Others say that the Perry Hole or Big Rock Hole (109.3–109.8) is followed by the Smith Hole or Spring Hole (109.9–110.3). There is another hole a short distance above the boat landing that may be known only as "a hole above Maumee" (110.4–110.5). And another old-timer, Joe Barnes, says the hole at the Maumee boat landing has been called the Jug Hole.

110.7 The location of **Maumee North**, the boat landing, is on the left where a dirt road loops down onto a low gravel bar.

Maumee North to Buffalo Point

River miles 110.7 to 122.1. Distance 11.4 miles. Average gradient 3 feet per mile. Placid pools, open shoals, impressive bluffs. Put-in at boat landing two miles southeast of Maumee, at end of extension of County Road 86. Take-out at boat landing at Buffalo Point.

Maumee North to Spring Creek, *5.3 miles.*

110.7 Because the landing here is approached from the north side of the river, the Park Service named it Maumee North to distinguish it from another landing, Maumee South, on the opposite shore a short distance downstream and approached by a road from the south. The name Maumee originated much earlier (see *Maumee,* below).

The Maumee North boat landing is near the upper end of the Boat Hole or Ferry Boat Hole (110.6–111.0), or as old-timer Joe Barnes calls it, the Jug Hole. The ferry crossing was at the downstream end (photo, page 101). The hole's exit shoal empties into…

111.1–111.2 a short pool at the mouth of **Maumee Hollow**. This pool empties into a much longer hole of water…

111.3–111.9 the Butler Hole, curving to the right, around the end of the long finger of land that extends to the **Maumee South** boat landing area (111.3). On the right is a road-accessible gravel bar, three-quarters of a mile long, around the bend. On the left is Maumee

> **Maumee** came into existence in 1907 when a mine developer arrived from Maumee, Ohio. During World War I, as the price of zinc went sky-high, investors built an ore mill in Maumee Hollow and opened mines. "There was a lot of activity," says one old-timer, "but not great profit." The ore was hauled by wagon along nearly ten miles of rough trails to the railroad at Gilbert.
>
> Toward the end of the war, prices collapsed and the mining boom was over. About 1950, speculators rebuilt the ore mill on the expectation that the price of zinc was going up, but it did not. Maumee remained as a community centered on a country store (or a vacant building, after the store closed) a mile north of the Buffalo at the head of Maumee Hollow.

Bluff, equally long, reaching 370 feet up from the river to near the top of **Schoolhouse Ridge**, with broken cliffs of gray rock, old junipers on high ledges, and Virginia creeper covering lower faces.

The Butler Hole was named for John Butler, a preacher who in the early 1900s owned and worked the farm within this bend of the river. A field that runs for more than a mile down the river here is still known as the Butler Field. Long before Butler, the first settler at this place was Thomas Massey, who arrived in 1838.

111.9–113.2 Beyond the Butler Hole, for more than a mile, shoals divide the river into several short unnamed pools, and there are no named features in view along the banks. Finally the river bends right, then left through shoals (112.9–113.0) and enters…

113.2–113.7 a long pool, the Stepp Hole or Stepp Eddy, named for a family who once farmed along the left bank. The Stepp Hole's exact extent is now questioned. Local fisherman Mike Cash says, "The Stepp Eddy was one big old hole. Now it's about three little holes." And while Stepp Eddy is not divided by shoals, river guide Leon Somerville calls the upper portion the Stump Hole, for stumps and snags along the left bank and in the river. Old-timer Deward Still, however, calls the lower end the Stump Hole or Stump Eddy.

113.7–115.0 From Stepp Eddy to near the mouth of **Spring Creek** the river after 1960 began to change course, and around 2000 was still abandoning older channels, erasing old gravel bars, forming new ones. The river settles down as it turns left into…

115.0–115.3 the Spring Creek Hole, past the mouth of Spring Creek (115.1) and **Spring Creek Bluff** (115.2; photo, page 142).

The bluff is barely 800 feet long at its base but reaches to 360 feet above the river, forming a high arch; some have called it Pyramid Bluff. Coming down the Buffalo, this is the first bluff to show a conspicuous layer of St. Peter Sandstone, a smooth, bulging layer of rock streaked with gray and tan, about 150 feet above the river. Below the St. Peter, the Everton Formation is all broken faces, overhangs, horizontal cracks. The Everton rock is in shades of gray (light, dark, bluish) and buff, with junipers growing wherever there's a foothold. Above the St. Peter are ledges of younger rock along with grassy slopes, junipers, and shrubs. Geologist T. C. Hopkins in 1890 reported that the red marker band of the St. Joe Limestone could be seen high on the bluff above the St. Peter.

Opposite Spring Creek Bluff is an extensive gravel bar. Behind the bar is an overgrown field, part of what local people still call the old

Tom Shipman place, though Shipman has been gone since the 1940s. The first settler here was Silas Rose, in 1838.

After the Spring Creek Hole, the next pool is…

115.3–115.8 the Slough Hole or Howard Marshall Hole, the latter name referring to the former owner of the bottomland on the right. At the beginning of the next pool is…

116.0 the Spring Creek boat landing on the right, with access to County Road 99 leading to Highway 14.

Spring Creek to Dillards Ferry (Highway 14), *4.6 miles.*

116.0 Though the landing reached from County Road 99 has only minimal facilities—a primitive campsite with mowed grass and a toilet—it allows for a short, easy float to Dillards Ferry or Buffalo Point. The put-in is at the upper end of a lengthy pool…

116.0–116.4 Sitton Eddy, named for the family of Joshua and Hanna Sitton (photos, opposite), whose farm once lay beyond the left bank. After the last of the Sittons moved away, the spelling of their place name gradually changed from Sitton to Sutton and, at times, Setten. The 360-foot bluff (116.1–116.5) overlooking Sitton Eddy has no formal name, though Sitton Eddy Bluff might be acceptable (but not "Setten Eddie Bluff," as it has appeared in print).

Sitton Eddy Bluff is the first really *long* bluff of the lower Buffalo having large areas of exposed rock. The sequence of formations is the same as in Spring Creek Bluff and in other cliffs downriver. Incised, layered Everton carbonate beds extend from the bluff's base to the St. Peter Sandstone. The St. Peter is obvious: smooth, bulging, with streaks of tan, brown, gray, and orange where water has carried minerals down onto its face. Above the St. Peter, formations are mostly hidden by vegetation, as far up as the St. Joe Limestone and the rest of the Boone Formation at the top of the ridge.

For a mile and a half beyond Sitton Eddy…

116.4–117.9 the river is divided by shoals into fairly short pools, only one of them known by a name, Jackpot Hole (117.2–117.3). The name comes from the Jackpot Mine, a zinc mine active between 1910 and 1920 at the foot of…

116.9–117.6 Jackpot Bluff, which overlooks the Jackpot Hole. Most of the bluff is behind vegetation. The St. Peter Sandstone is high and in view, first as three widely spaced outcrops and then as a cliff about 300 yards long. Some of it is stained rusty-orange with iron oxide, so at times Jackpot Bluff has been called Red Bluff.

Topographic maps show this bluff reaching 405 feet from river to top, making it the first one exceeding 400 feet to be encountered by river travelers on the lower Buffalo.

Half a mile beyond Jackpot Bluff is the upstream end of...

118.1–118.5 Stairstep Bluff or Pump Hole Bluff. It was named for a ladder or stairway down from the bluff to the river, where a pump was installed to provide water for the nearby Evening Star

Joshua and Hanna. In their Sunday best and gazing serenely at the camera, Joshua and Hanna Sitton offer no clue to their roles as farmers among millions who moved west during the nine-teenth century. Both were born in North Carolina in 1836 and lived in Georgia after 1855. They came to Arkansas about 1874 and with eight children settled on the Buffalo below Maumee. There another child was born, and after a son died in 1885, Josh and Hanna took in his widow and their two small boys.

The children grew up, married, and moved across the county, or to Oklahoma. After Joshua died in 1898, Hanna left the river farm to be near family and the property passed to others.

Today the only reminder of this family's decades of presence on the Buffalo is the name of a lengthy hole of water bordering the old home place. Often pronounced or spelled "Sutton" or "Setten," the pool is, correctly, Sitton Eddy.

Mine. The mine probably was abandoned by 1920 and pump, pipe, and stairway are long gone, their former locations unknown.

The bluff is first seen as broken ledges rising to about 80 feet above river level. Near its downstream end (118.4) a rock face about 40 feet high rises out of the water. Stairstep Bluff overlooks…

117.9–118.5 the Stairstep Hole or Pump Hole. From the Stairstep Hole the river passes down a shoal into…

118.7–118.8 the Water Creek Hole, known locally as "mouth of Water Creek," a brief stretch of quiet water where **Water Creek** enters from the left. The creek drains 36 square miles and is the eighth-largest tributary of the Buffalo River. Just beyond the creek are the noisy rapids of Water Creek Shoal.

From Water Creek the view downriver includes…

118.8–119.2 Kimball Bluff, 460 feet high, the highest cliff between Maumee and Buffalo Point—in fact the highest this side of Buzzard Bluff on the upper Buffalo. Kimball (sometimes spelled and pronounced with an *r*, Kimbrell) has two or three separated faces of incised layers of Everton rock to about 100 feet above the river. And then, far above at the top, a continuous wall of the St. Peter bends in and out with the bends of the ridge, a high rampart that is the most visible part of this bluff nearly a half mile long.

Kimball Bluff faces southwest, so its vegetation is adapted to dry sites. Stunted hardwoods and bushy junipers occupy the ledges and terraces of the Everton; pines as well as hardwoods and cedars stand on the highest slope, from the St. Peter to the skyline.

Between Water Creek Shoal and the next shoal downstream is a short pool, the (George) Cantrell Hole (between 118.8 and 118.9). Past the Cantrell Hole is…

118.9–119.2 another Pump Hole, beneath Kimball Bluff. At the hole's upstream end, Kimball Slough enters from the right. The slough is shown on topographic maps. It probably receives the flow of **Kimball Creek**, whose direct outlet to the river farther upstream near river mile 118.7 is blocked by a wide gravel bar.

Kimball Bluff also overlooks another right-bank strip of gravel, Griffin Bar (119.3–119.5), named for a landowner before the Park Service. Griffin did not own Griffin Bar, only a part of its access road a mile downstream at Highway 14. Fishermen probably started saying "Griffin" when crossing his land to get to the bar.

Next below the Pump Hole is…

119.4–119.9 Tie Chute Hole or Tie Hole, curving past…

119.4–120.4 Tie Chute Bluff or Tie Slide Bluff. Timber men around 1900 cleared the trees from an area down the face of the bluff and then slid or rolled railroad ties down the "chute," off the bluff and into the river, to be rafted to the White River and sold.

At 420 feet, Tie Chute Bluff is not quite as high as Kimball Bluff but it is longer, a mile from its beginning opposite the Griffin Bar to its end at **Saltpeter Hollow**. Like Kimball, Tie Chute has a prominent wall of the St. Peter Sandstone along its upper edge.

Next beyond the Tie Chute Hole is…

120.2–120.7 the Griffin Hole, which, unlike the Griffin Bar, was on the Griffin property. The hole extends past the downstream end of Tie Chute Bluff and under the **Highway 14** crossing.

120.6 Just upstream from the highway bridge is the boat landing at the site of the historic **Dillards Ferry** (photo, page 226).

Dillards Ferry to Buffalo Point, *1.5 miles.*

120.6 The landing at Highway 14 is just west of the bridge. East of the bridge, at the access road, are picnic sites and restrooms.

The Highway 14 bridge is 660 feet long, stands 60 feet above normal water level, and has been in service since 1958. It was designed to stand above maximum level of the impoundment behind Lone Rock Dam, to be built at a site 29 miles downriver. The dam was not built, of course, but on December 3, 1982, the bridge successfully withstood even deeper water as a record flood flowed through the guardrails along its roadway (photos, pages 32 and 228).

Just beyond the bridge the river bends to the right and then left, through shoals and into…

120.8–121.4 an unnamed pool, long and straight and shallow with a bottom of gravel or bedrock. The solid rock is eroded—or dissolved, since it is carbonate rock—with grooves or furrows in the direction of the current, and many rounded humps and bumps.

Partway down this pool (at 120.9) and hidden by hillside vegetation is a geologic fault. Rock formations on the downriver side of the fault are downthrown (depressed). Thus the St. Peter Sandstone, nearly 400 feet above the river at Tie Chute Bluff a mile back upstream, is close to river level at the bluff in view downstream.

121.6 At this same bluff the St. Peter lies from 30 to 60 feet above the water. Between the base of the sandstone and the underlying Everton Formation is an obvious line of contact—wavy, undulating—easily recognized elsewhere as well. Not as obvious are the

Dillards Ferry was established in 1928, when Highway 14 was opened from Yellville toward Marshall. Local entrepreneurs J. F. "Doc" Dillard and his sons Ira and Pate and son-in-law Whit Davenport built the original ferry to carry a wagon or an automobile across. In the late 1930s the younger Dillards replaced the boat with a two-car ferry, seen here about 1945. Pate and Ira operated the ferry until the Highway 14 bridge opened in 1958.

The boat was attached by cables to two trolleys running along a fixed cable that stretched across the river. By turning a windlass on the ferry's upstream side (behind the truck in this photo), the ferryman could lengthen or shorten the trolley cables, turning the boat to an angle upstream so the current would push it across. The ferry's operator collected a small toll.

Pate Dillard's son John remembers building this second boat. It was of pine instead of oak because pine floated better. That summer the ferry was built upside down on the riverbank; it seemed easier to do it that way. But then the boat had to be turned over and set afloat. Says John: "It was a *big, heavy* deal."

Pate's daughter Doretha Shipman remembers some people got their brakes overheated, coming down the long hill to the ferry. Unable to stop, they rolled onto the boat and off the other end into the water. In some dry years that wouldn't have mattered— the river became too low to float the ferry and it straddled the narrow stream and became a bridge.

bluff's formations above the St. Peter: Plattin Limestone, Fernvale Limestone, and the Boone Formation. They, too, occur elsewhere around Buffalo Point and can be seen along the area's hiking trails.

A short distance beyond the bluff is…

121.8 Skull Rock, jutting from the left bank, an angular block of the St. Peter Sandstone about 30 feet high. In its flat top are pits like the eye sockets of a skull. At the base of Skull Rock is an overhang with shallow caves at the back. And beginning at Skull Rock is…

121.8–122.2 the Rock Creek Hole, extending past **Rock Creek** (121.9), on the right, and past…

122.1 the **Buffalo Point** boat landing, on the left.

Buffalo Point to Rush Landing

River miles 122.1 to 129.5. Distance 7.4 miles. Average gradient 3 feet per mile. Big gravel bars; three bluffs more than 400 feet high; a river easy enough for novice paddlers. Put-in at Buffalo Point's boat landing. Take-out at landing at mouth of Rush Creek.

Buffalo Point has been a public recreation area since the 1930s (see page 408) and over the years has seen a number of destructive floods. The boat landing, located on a gravel bar within a sharp bend of the river, has been hit many times as high water has dumped gravel on the bar or taken it away. Anyone coming to this boat landing and swimming area year after year can probably see the changes.

The landing faces **Painted Bluff**, named for the colors of brown and gray on its water-streaked St. Peter Sandstone. The St. Peter, however, is only the upper half of the sheer wall that rises from the river. The lower half is dolomite of the Everton Formation, incised layers of rock very different from the St. Peter (photo, page 53).

Painted Bluff reaches to 320 feet higher than the river, but most of it above the 70-foot wall of Everton-St. Peter is behind vegetation. In winter the higher-up rock becomes more visible: a ledge of the upper St. Peter, a fairly prominent cliff of Plattin Limestone, then ledges of St. Joe Limestone and more of the Boone Formation.

This bluff also lies within a geologic "low," an area where the rock formations are lower in elevation than up the river or down. Here the base of the St. Peter Sandstone—that wavy line of contact with the Everton Formation—is about 40 feet above normal river level. Not far downstream it will be elevated to as high as 400 feet.

One more comment: Painted Bluff produces a good echo. Stand on the gravel bar and shout at it. The echo returns quickly because the distance across Rock Creek Hole to the bluff is short.

Rock Creek Hole ends at Hickory Creek Shoal, past the mouth of **Hickory Creek** (122.2) below the boat landing. The river passes…

122.2–122.9 Buffalo Point's camping area, extending along the bottomland behind the river's high bank, and then…

123.0–123.2 a 320-foot bluff on the left. Already the cliff of St. Peter Sandstone has been raised more than 250 feet from what it was at the boat landing. On top of that cliff near its left end (123.0) is a parapet wall at the overlook on Buffalo Point's Overlook Trail. On top of the ridge above the viewpoint is Buffalo Point's restaurant.

The cliff is opposite a bottomland on the right side of the river known as the Matlock place. W. N. Matlock's 120-acre farm was here around 1940. The Army Corps of Engineers, however, produced a map in 1940 on which the bottomland was labeled "Suggsfield Bend." Suggs was an earlier owner of the property.

A half mile down the river, **Panther Creek** arrives from the left

Sightseers stroll across the Highway 14 bridge during the record flood of December 3, 1982. Water spreads across the valley, and at its maximum will overflow the highway and almost reach the bridge's guardrails, 65 feet higher than the river at normal stage.

(123.5). Half a mile beyond the creek is a shoal when entering...

124.1–124.4 the Ingram Hole or Sours Eddy. This hole (at 124.2) happens to be the last resting place of the Highway 14 ferry after it was abandoned in 1958 when the highway bridge was opened. By 1965 the boat had washed this far downstream and had become a conversation piece, a decaying hulk lying against the left bank.

Ingram Hole extends past the narrow valley of **Ingram Creek**, on the right and named for local citizen John Ingram. The creek also has ties to another local landowner, Henry Sauer (whose misspelled name was given to Sours Eddy), who apparently lost money in a zinc mining venture here. Probably during the World War I zinc boom, he or others found evidence of ore along Ingram Creek; the diggings are called the Sauer prospects. So a processing mill was built.

The Sauer ore mill stood on the right-hand hillside about 150 yards from the mouth of Ingram Creek. Its massive foundations are still there, covered with moss and hidden behind river cane and grape-vines. In the late 1930s salvagers removed the mill's machinery and sold it for scrap. As if they expected to someday replace the machinery, they put the washers and nuts back on the foundations' anchor bolts. But there is no pile of waste rock at the mill site, no evidence that the mill ever processed a single ton of ore. Like many other zinc diggings in this area, it turned out to be wasted effort.

On the right past Ingram Creek is a high bluff. Atop the St. Peter Sandstone that caps the bluff, about 430 feet above the river and overlooking the Ingram Hole, is the **Devils Tea Table**, two massive toadstools of sandstone having less than a foot of space between their flaring tops. They stand about eight feet high, fantastic shapes called hoodoos, the last remnants of an eroded layer of rock.

The Tea Table sits at the upstream end of...

124.5–125.2 a long, curving bluff known as Ingram Bluff, appearing on maps as the extension of **Tea Table Ridge.** The stratum of St. Peter along the top is visible in places, mostly toward the bluff's downstream end. From the St. Peter down to the river are broken, discontinuous faces of Everton rock. Much is hidden by vegetation.

The Ingram Hole ends opposite Ingram Creek at Gooseneck Shoal or Ingram Creek Shoal (124.4), which pours into an unnamed pool (124.5–124.7). Next beyond that is...

124.8–125.3 the Toney Bend Hole, curving to the left beneath Ingram Bluff on the right and past the bottomland of **Toney Bend** on the left. Toney Bend is probably named for Lorenzo Toney, who owned land and farmed here around 1900. ("It was named for 'Uncle Buck' Toney," says old-timer Lee Davenport.) In 1917–18, about the time of the mining boom, Toney Bend had a post office, Helva, named possibly by Henry Sauer for his wife; he was postmaster.

Past the exit shoal from Toney Bend Hole and at the end of a 300-yard chute are…

125.6 three "swimming rocks," the Toney Rocks, eight- or ten-foot boulders in midstream, rising two or three feet above the water at normal stage, favorite perches for swimmers in the summertime.

Beyond and overlooking the Toney Rocks is Lorenzo Toney's most imposing monument…

125.6–126.0 430-foot **Toney Bluff**, first seen from more than a half mile upstream, now recognized for its massive squarish block of rock almost directly above the river, a stone fortress perhaps 100 feet wide and 150 high. Above that, the highest layer of rock seen from the river is the St. Peter Sandstone, rough and uneven with overhang areas colored tan and orange. All the rock from the river up to the St. Peter—nearly 400 feet—is of the Everton Formation, stepped back and broken up by terraces between cliffs. Even with the setbacks below it, the St. Peter requires much neck-bending to see.

Toney Bluff looks down on…

125.8–126.2 the Jones Hole, and across a spacious gravel bar to **Jones Bend**, where the family of J. J. Jones (1837–1898) farmed during the early twentieth century. Later someone subdivided part of the farm into six- and twelve-acre strips having river frontage. It was these small parcels—with several owners, no buildings—that the Park Service purchased in the 1970s for the National River.

Beyond Jones Bend the river begins to turn sharply to the left around **Bice Bend** or Horseshoe Bend, passing through a pool…

126.8–127.2 called the Bias Hole. Here the names become uncertain. "Bias" might be "Bice," a family who owned land near Rush around 1900, but as far as is known the Bice family had no connection to Bice Bend. And local-names expert Leon Somerville, Jr., says, "My neighbors have called this bend 'Bicey.'"

The bluff overlooking the Bias Hole seems to have no name, except perhaps Ludlow Bluff. Tax records show that from at least 1902 to 1932, James H. Ludlow owned 160 acres centered on a low point, now named **Ludlow Gap,** on the ridge above the bluff. His acreage included the downstream half of the bluff, but Ludlow was a homesteader obviously intent on acquiring level, productive land—if you could call it any such—along the top of that narrow rocky ridge.

This bluff of uncertain name, though, is 590 feet high—higher by 30 feet, if we can believe the topographic maps, than Big Bluff on the upper Buffalo, long considered the highest bluff on the river. This bluff in fact has legitimate claim to being not only the highest of any along the Buffalo, but the highest in the Ozarks, and highest in the entire Midwest (photos, pages 233 and 371).

One could question that. Ludlow Bluff here is terraced, stepped back; Big Bluff is more nearly vertical, having at one place a strip of continuous bare rock from base to top. Ludlow also has two 590-foot rivals downstream, Smith Bluff and Woodcock Bluff, but both of those are more stepped-back, less precipitous.

For all its height, this bluff has the same geologic components as lesser cliffs already described upstream. The Everton Formation makes a series of cliffs that alternate with steep grassy terraces from the river up to the St. Peter, which can be seen as a smooth, bulging, water-streaked layer up near the top. Above the St. Peter and to the left near the very top is a small outcrop of red St. Joe Limestone.

Ludlow Bluff also stands at the narrow neck of the river's **Seven-Mile Bend**. A half mile behind the bluff, but seven miles as the canoe travels, is the river at the far end of this bend. The bend's other name is the **Duck's Head**, for the shape of its outline on maps.

The gravel bar facing Ludlow Bluff, very wide and half a mile long, is at an unusually sharp turn of the river—Bice Bend—where high, swift waters move lots of material to sustain the bar.

At river's edge at the foot of the bluff is one named feature, Slant Rock or Driveway Rock (127.1; photo, page 234), sloping down to the water. Then, about 200 feet beyond Slant Rock, a buttress projecting from the bluff is pierced through—a natural arch. The archway is about 75 feet up the rocky slope from the river, and behind trees and bushes. The opening is about 15 feet wide and 20 high, and apparently it developed in an area of fractured Everton dolomite. The arch's ceiling has loose rock. Visitors must be cautious.

Beyond the Bias Hole is a short stretch of river having several shoals (127.2–127.6), and then…

127.6–128.1 the Bailey Hole, curving past a narrow strip of land sloping above the right bank that Joseph Mullins (or Mullin) acquired by homestead and managed to farm—thus the Mullin Place or Mullens Bend. Partway down the Bailey Hole, Mullens Spring can be heard (though usually not seen) in the woods about 50 feet above the left edge of the river. The spring, which may go dry in the summer, is at the upstream end of a 60-foot bluff.

A hundred feet beyond the spring is a rock face, 20 feet long by 6 feet high, rising from the river's edge. Below its overhang and about two feet above the water is a wavy pattern of thin layers, or laminations, of the rock. These developed when the rock was formed, as mounds of algae grew by stages to remain above the layers of limy mud being deposited on them (see *Stromatolites,* page 38).

Leaving the broad, placid Bailey Hole, the river turns to the right into a shoal, then to the left into…

128.1–128.4 Hat Chute, flowing swiftly down a narrow, deep channel. The chute goes on for more than a quarter mile, gradually widening to near a hundred feet, with the water slowing down, becoming still. Hat Chute was once called Dirst Shoals; Jesse Dirst around 1910 owned land astride the river here. As for Hat Chute's hat, its owner is unknown. Hat Chute opens into…

128.4–129.0 the Gage Hole, named for the Geological Survey's water-level gauge that once stood on the left (at 128.9) beside **Gage Bluff**. This pool is also called Red Cloud Eddy, for the long defunct Red Cloud Mine a short distance beyond the right bank.

Gage Hole farther along becomes very wide, about 200 feet across, and noticeably still. There's opportunity to drift and look at…

128.6–129.0 Gage Bluff, more than 300 feet high from the waterline to the topmost exposure of rock, the St. Peter's prominent cliff that is visible in several places beyond the trees. Below the St. Peter are ledges and broken faces of dark gray Everton rock, incised between the layers. Near river level, 60 feet of the bluff's gray Everton supports large patches of poison ivy and Virginia creeper, vines whose autumn leaves paint the bluff red.

Gage Hole empties into another wide, placid pool…

129.2–129.8 Rush Creek Hole, extending to and beyond the mouth of Rush Creek. Pulling in to shore at the creek, one may notice in warm weather that Rush Creek discharges cold water into the river. Most of its normal flow comes from springs.

129.5 Rush Landing is there at the mouth of Rush Creek.

> *Ludlow Bluff* (opposite), upstream from Rush, reaches to 590 feet above the river—about 30 feet higher than Big Bluff, long believed to be the Buffalo's tallest cliff. Ludlow thus has a claim as the highest bluff of the Buffalo, the Ozarks, and the Midwest.

Rush Landing to White River

River miles 129.5 to 153.0. Distance 23.5 miles. Average gradient 3 feet per mile. River through Lower Buffalo Wilderness; usually a two- or three-day trip. Put-in at landing at mouth of Rush Creek. Take-outs along White River at points described on pages 251–252.

Rush Landing to Mouth of Buffalo River, *23.5 miles.*

129.5 Rush Landing, at the mouth of Rush Creek, is often simply called Rush, though the center of the former community of Rush was more than a mile up the creek. The area around the landing did have several active zinc mines and, during the World War I mining boom, another community called New Town. (For more about Rush, see pages 93–96, 264, and 409–417.)

The landing is beside Rush Creek Hole (129.2–129.8), a broad, placid pool of water. But almost within hearing is…

129.8 the wildest rapids of the lower river, Clabber Creek Shoal. Where **Clabber Creek** enters from the left at the end of Rush Creek Hole, the shoal spills off to the right and then sharply to the left. The first hazard is getting swept into the right bank; immediately afterward the danger is being swamped in big haystack waves.

Below Clabber Creek Shoal is a short pool known as…

129.9–130.0 the Bluff Hole, because it is within a stone's throw of Clabber Creek Bluff on the left. This 140-foot cliff is dolomite of

Slant Rock.
Resting at an easy slope to the water by the foot of Ludlow Bluff, the rock is a handy platform for fishers and spectators.

the Everton Formation surmounted by the St. Peter Sandstone; the St. Peter has oddly rounded knobs on top. The formations dip (slope downward) in the downstream direction, so that the base of the St. Peter descends from about 120 feet above water level at the upstream end of the bluff to 80 feet at the downstream end.

Past another set of shoals or riffles is…

130.2–131.0 the Silver Hollow Hole, a lengthy pool that curves to the left past the mouth of **Silver Hollow** (130.4).

This reach of the river's left bank was also part of the historic road that wagon freighters traveled during the boom years at Rush, as they hauled zinc ore to the White River and returned with supplies for mines and the town. The old road trace can still be traveled on foot, but near the upper end of Silver Hollow Hole, floods deposit driftwood in the roadway (at 130.2). During the 1990s the drift pile was 6 feet high and 200 feet long, visible from the river. Old-timer Dale Laffoon, whose family once lived nearby, says that local residents used to burn the piled-up driftwood to clear the road.

Just beyond Silver Hollow, on the right, is…

130.5–130.7 Silver Hollow Bluff, 350 feet high. Its uppermost face is 40 feet of St. Peter Sandstone, a prominent wall ending with a flat-sided shape resembling a vase—a curious and distinguishing feature of this bluff. The base of the St. Peter is around 300 feet above the river, and below that are wooded terraces and dark gray rock exposures of the Everton Formation.

There's no shoal to mark the boundary between Silver Hollow Hole and the next pool downstream…

131.0–131.4 the Graveyard Hole, which extends past the mouth of **Cabin Creek** (131.1). The hole is named for the **Laffoon Cemetery** (or Cabin Creek Cemetery), located beside the old ore road beyond the left bank. Most of the graves (photo, page 236) belong to members of the Laffoon family, who farmed Laffoon Bottom along the right bank. The oldest recorded burial was in 1878; the most recent is said to have occurred in 1940. The Laffoons (whose family name was French) moved away from Laffoon Bottom about 1946.

Next beyond the Graveyard Hole is…

131.6–132.0 Cedar Creek Hole or Cedar Creek Eddy, which ends just past the mouth of **Cedar Creek**. On the left bank at the creek is a landing that provides an emergency exit from the river via a four-wheel-drive road connecting to County Road 662 going toward U.S. Highway 62/412. To allow vehicular access here, the landing and adjacent riverside are excluded from the Lower Buffalo Wilderness.

Opposite the mouth of the creek, Cedar Creek Shoal spills off, making plenty of noise. The river bends sharply to the right, past the mouth of **Boat Creek** (132.1, probably hidden behind a gravel bar), and around part of the old Laffoon farm, known as Laffoon Bend.

Below Cedar Creek Shoal is…

132.1–132.4 a stretch of calm water known as Boat Creek Hole or Table Rock Hole (132.2–132.3). Dale Laffoon says it contains "a whirl, two or three hundred feet long." The next fast water is at…

132.4–132.5 Dog Leg Chute (but called Blind Chute on an 1896 map by the Army Corps of Engineers). The chute discharges into…

132.6–132.8 the Sand Hole. Here we can note some changes in the river since the Corps of Engineers mapped the Buffalo in 1896.

"A tender mother and faithful friend" is the epitaph for Mary Armenda—the first wife of Thomas M. Laffoon— who died at age twenty-one when giving birth to her fourth child. Mary and the baby lie in the Laffoon Cemetery, now in the Lower Buffalo Wilderness area.

In a sense this last part of the river has always been a wilderness— rugged, isolated, thinly populated, far from schools or medical help. There also have been floods. More than once, this riverside graveyard has been underwater.

After 1900, people moved away. After 1950, hardly anyone lived here.

At the downstream end of the Sand Hole, for instance, the Corps called a passage on the east side of the river Dog Leg Chute. Later, to others, this was known as Mining Bucket Chute. By the 1990s the exit from the Sand Hole was an open passage on the west side.

With Mining Bucket Chute washed out, there's no definite upper boundary for the next named pool…

132.9–133.1 the Purnell Hole, which extends to…

133.2 Petitt Chute (Petits Chute on the 1896 map). Apparently the chute was named for Andrew J. Petitt (1846–1896). He and his wife, Lucindia (1854–1897), are buried at Laffoon Cemetery.

Petitt Chute empties into…

133.3–134.4 Lonely Hollow Hole (or Lonely Hole or "mouth of Lonely"). This pool becomes 150 feet wide, extending straight toward a high wooded ridge. As the pool then curves to the left, past the mouth of **Lonely Hollow** (134.0), the right bank is at the end of the river's seven-mile bend that began above Rush. On maps the river's meandering course around the bend suggests another name: **Duck's Head**. The duck faces right. The top of its head is at Rush and Clabber Creeks. The end of its bill is at Cedar and Boat Creeks.

From the beginning of the big bend at river mile 126.9 to its end at 133.9, the Buffalo loses about 25 feet of elevation, from 465 to 440 feet. In a survey made in 1910 the difference was calculated at 40 feet. The person heading the survey, W. N. Gladson, proposed that a half-mile tunnel be opened through the neck of the bend so that water could flow through and drop down to an electric generator. With better power sites elsewhere, nothing was done.

Next beyond the Lonely Hollow Hole is…

134.5–135.3 Cow House Eddy, a wide pool heading straight toward **Cow House Bluff** (134.7) or Cow House Rock or just Cow House. The bluff is only about 80 feet high but is a prominent landmark, visible from half a mile or more up the river. Its curving face bulges above the water; dark-green junipers grow on top; Virginia creeper hangs on the sides. There are overhangs, with calcite fluting. But no overhang appears large enough to shelter a cow.

Past the Cow House the river curves to the right, around…

135.0–136.0 **Brantley Bend**, once the home of James and Rhoda Brantley and their family. In 1903 Rhoda and James died within six days of each other, leaving three little boys to be raised by an older brother. The Brantley Cemetery, back in the woods to the right near river mile 135, has no inscribed markers, only slabs of rock that stand at the graves. Someone planted spirea—bridal wreath—and this white-flowering shrub has spread over the entire cemetery.

From Cow House Bluff to **Rough Hollow** (135.7) ancient ledges of dark gray Everton rock occur in isolated outcrops rising to 80 feet above the water. Much more rock is hidden behind foliage.

Cow House Eddy ends in…

135.3–135.5 a series of riffles that the Corps of Engineers map in 1896 labeled Roaring Rock Shoals. Below the shoals is…

135.5–136.3 Rough Hollow Hole, followed without an intervening shoal by…

136.3–136.5 the Avey hole, described by family member Leo Avey as "a short hole, just above Fishtrap, in the bend." The Avey Hole lies beneath a 470-foot bluff, wooded but also having an exposed cliff of the St. Peter Sandstone at the top.

The bluff stands across from **Horseshoe Bend**, the family farm where Leo Avey grew up. The Aveys moved away in 1943 and the farm then had a succession of owners, including one named Marsh and another named Parker. Leo Avey: "Marsh made moonshine. Parker did, too. I bet Parker made it right there in the house."

In 1972 Parker went to prison for manslaughter. The land passed to a subdivider who sold much of it in five-acre lots to out-of-state buyers. By the mid-1970s, when the National Park Service had funds to purchase Horseshoe Bend, there were 24 tracts having about 15 different owners, though no one had opened a passable road into the area or put up any new buildings.

Horseshoe Bend faces **Fishtrap Hollow**, whose creek empties into Fishtrap Slough, which opens to the river on the right at Fishtrap Shoal (136.6). Fishtrap Shoal is shown on the Corps of Engineers map of 1896, indicating that someone already had a diversion dam and corral there for catching fish.

Below Fishtrap Shoal is, of course…

136.6–137.0 Fishtrap Hole. Here on the right is a high ridge having three summits: **Warner Mountain** or Little Warner Mountain (136.5–137.2). Some call the steep side that faces the river Buzzard Bluff. A flat rock on the lower end of the ridge is the Tea Table.

The base of Warner Mountain is a cliff of dark gray Everton rock rising 80 to 100 feet above the water. Then a wooded slope goes up to the St. Peter Sandstone, whose upper edge is about 470 feet above the river. Thus the St. Peter on Warner Mountain lies at the same elevation as that atop the bluff on the other side of Fishtrap Hollow.

At the base of Warner Mountain and about 400 feet downstream from Fishtrap Shoal, a spring branch trickles into the river. Leo Avey recalls that in the 1920s a pipe was run down the slope from the spring to a hydraulic ram (a pump powered by the momentum of flowing water). From the ram a pipe was laid under the river and across a field as far as the water-powered ram would push a stream of water, to within 200 feet of the Avey house. The tiny, but constant, stream delivered by the ram was enough for household needs.

Floods repeatedly broke the pipe across the river. The Aveys made repairs but eventually abandoned the water system.

The next hole beyond Fishtrap is…

137.1–138.0 Smith Eddy, curving to the right below **Smith Ridge**. Apparently a farmer named Smith lived in the bend of the river opposite the ridge. He may have farmed along **Smith Bottom**. His surname also became attached to Smith Bluff, facing the river below the crest of Smith Ridge; archeologist M. R. Harrington called it Smith Bluff after visiting the area in 1922.

137.5–138.2 Smith Bluff is composed of isolated faces of rock—one of them rising directly from the river, others at intervals higher up, a couple of them more than 100 feet in height. There also are steep slopes with grass, junipers, and scrub hardwoods. High up, the St. Peter Sandstone is recognizable. Above the St. Peter is slabby rock whose topmost ledge is about 590 feet above the water, making this one of the highest bluffs of the Buffalo River.

138.1–138.9 Past Smith Bottom is a long stretch of shallow water (138.1–138.6), then what old-timer Everett Boyd calls "a little short hole of water" (138.7–138.9).

Then a lengthy shoal, and then more shallow water that finally deepens to become…

139.7–139.8 the Boom (or Boomer or Boone) Hole or Eddy. Says old-timer A. B. Marberry: "There was a timber chute into Boom Eddy. They cut cedar and skidded it off bluffs…assembled a raft." The Corps map of 1896 labeled the exit shoal of the Boom Hole as Boone Ford.

139.8–140.0 For about 300 yards below the Boom Hole, the bed of the river is solid carbonate rock, trenched and potholed, scalloped and finned by both abrasion and solution. Then the river reaches **Big Creek**, which has washed in gravel to cover the river bottom.

140.0 Big Creek is the Buffalo River's second-largest tributary in terms of drainage area, 124 square miles, about 9 percent of the river's watershed. Viewed from the river, Big Creek appears to have a broad valley with a low skyline except for one distant, conical hill. (That unnamed hill, a mile south of the river, is just east of **Log Wagon Gap**.) For several decades around 1900 lower Big Creek had a viable farming community (see *"Little Egypt,"* opposite).

The first swift water below the mouth of Big Creek is...

140.1   Rocky Shoal, which empties into a pool extending about 200 feet to...

140.2   Cold Spring Shoal, opposite the mouth of **Cold Spring Hollow**. From the shoal the river enters...

140.2–140.3   the Cold Spring Hole, along 50-foot **Killingsworth Bluff** on the right. Beyond the bluff and another shoal is...

140.4–140.8   the Killingsworth Hole, having a sizeable gravel bar on the right that appears to have been frequented, around 1960, by Arkansas governor Orval Faubus. While Faubus gained notoriety for his role in opposing school integration, he also stood for protecting the Buffalo River. Faubus canoed as an escape from political pressures and says that a gravel bar below Big Creek—probably this bar —was a favorite campsite. Because a big sycamore tree shaded the site, he and his camping friends called this spot the Sycamore Hotel.

From the upstream end of the bar, a path into the woods joins an old road to the **Cold Springs Schoolhouse**. On the quarter mile to the school, the road also passes the remains of a small log house, known as the old Bob Wynn place, above Killingsworth Bluff.

The schoolhouse was built in 1936, one of many one-room rural schools constructed with federal funding through the Depression-era Works Progress Administration (WPA), with local men employed to do the building. The school closed about 1946 after many neighborhood families moved away from this isolated area to find steady jobs and community services. In the 1980s the Cold Springs Schoolhouse was added to the National Register of Historic Places.

On the left and overlooking the Killingsworth Hole is a 100-foot bluff, much of it hidden by trees. Near the downstream end of the hole and a few yards above the water's edge, a cave goes about 75 feet into the bluff. Everett Boyd recalls that in the early 1930s, as a teenager watching out for his family's free-ranging cattle, he camped one winter in this cave.

The Killingsworth Hole empties into...

140.8–141.0   rocky Berry Rose Chute—Rose Berry Chute on the Corps of Engineers map of 1896. The chute probably was named for one of the Rose family, who lived nearby. Next past the chute is…

141.0–141.7 the Berry Rose Chute Hole, extending past **Sunny Hollow** (141.1) and the Sunny Fields (141.2–141.5) on the left. The hollow—wide, shallow, facing south—gets lots of sunshine.

Below the Berry Rose Chute Hole…

141.7–142.0 a long chute with riffles and then a "rock garden" shoal take the river to **Bear Branch**, on the left, and into a right-hand bend around what is still known as the Tom Rice place, though Tom Rice has been dead since 1907.

By one account, Rice captured two bear cubs in the hollow across from his farm and thus the hollow came to be Bear Branch or Bear Gulch. A family member says Rice and a bear-hunting friend "made torches…went into caves in the wintertime and killed bears."

Bear Branch also is reported to have been the site of a licensed whiskey still around 1900, and a post office as well. Old-timers Ruby Franks and her sister Ruth both say their father carried mail on horseback from Buffalo City to a post office in Bear Branch hollow. Postal records indicate that a post office existed here or nearby in the years 1902–1903. Its name was Jacfontan.

In the 1980s, Park Service employee Jim Liles hiked up the **Left Prong** of Bear Branch. About half a mile from the river he found a big shortleaf pine, later recorded as the third largest in Arkansas.

Below Bear Branch is…

142.2–142.5 Bear Branch Eddy or Bear Branch Hole, past…

142.0–142.5 **Woodcock Bluff** or Bear Bluff. At the bluff's upstream end is a tower of rock reaching to more than 100 feet above the river. Beyond and above the tower are sloping faces of rock, grassy terraces, many ledges, and trees and bushes. In winter with foliage gone, the sloping bluff looks like a vast broad flight of steps. At the top, the St. Peter Sandstone goes to 590 feet above water level,

"Little Egypt" was a nickname for the fertile farmlands along lower Big Creek. From 1896 to 1924 the community had a post office named Hepsey, and folks came from miles around to pick up mail and trade at the store. They brought corn to the water-powered gristmill and cotton to the steam-powered gin. Kids attended the district school and both youngsters and grownups played or watched baseball in a field by the creek.

Today Hepsey is a cemetery, hidden in the woods and long neglected, with graves marked only by slabs of native rock.

making this bluff one of the highest of any along the Buffalo River.

Bear Branch Eddy ends at rock-bottomed Woodcock Shoal, which the Corps 1896 map identified also as a ford. Beyond is…

142.7–143.7 Maple Eddy, past 490-foot **Caney Bluff** on the right. On the left was the farm of the pioneer Woodcock family, whose pre–Civil War log house long outlasted the family's presence and figured in local history (see *This old house,* opposite).

Maple Eddy ends at Middle Creek Shoal, at the mouth of…

142.7 Middle Creek, coming from a narrow valley on the right. Now within the Lower Buffalo/Leatherwood Wilderness area, lower Middle Creek was once on the direct route of travel between Allison on the White River and Yellville to the northwest. In the 1930s the federal Works Progress Administration built a graded road, with culverts, down the creek to the Buffalo, where a ferry was planned to carry travelers across, but the idea died.

Earlier, around 1920, timber men set up a stave mill near the mouth of Middle Creek. For a while, millworkers and their families lived there in shacks and tents. About that time a schoolhouse was built a quarter mile up the creek.

Farther up the creek and high on the hillside at a spring, an individual named Pete Hocott had a whiskey still. He is said to have delivered his product to Tulsa, Oklahoma, for sale. Hocott's distillery was just one of many in the back hollows of what is today's Leatherwood Wilderness. A local old-timer, Dumas Payne, says the area was once "the heart of moonshine country."

Middle Creek flows into Middle Creek Slough, a secondary channel of the Buffalo. The downstream end of the slough opens into…

143.8–144.1 rock-bottomed Raft Eddy, suggesting that timber was collected here for floating downriver. Raft Eddy ends at…

144.1–144.4 Greasy Shoal—30 yards of boulders, 200 yards of flat water, a drop over a ledge, 300 yards of rock-bottomed channel, and finally 50 yards of sloping ledge rock. Everett Boyd: "You can't hardly get a boat through there, for the ledges."

Short Creek, on the right at Greasy Shoal, has at times been called Greasy Creek, and on the right there's also Greasy Bottom (144.1–144.5), once known as the Greasy Field but now washed out and mostly gravel. A hill farther back on the right is Greasy Knob.

How did the name Greasy get started? With the shoal, perhaps, except that the river bottom here seems not to be slick rock.

Greasy Knob (near 144.4) stands more than 600 feet above river

Woodcock cabin, c.1920. Surely there were happy days for those who lived within these walls, but today the house is remembered for times of tragedy and fear.

This old house.

At a bottomland down the river from Big Creek, Henry and Deborah Woodcock built this cabin after moving from Tennessee. Henry had had eleven children by his first wife, and by 1848, when this log house took form, he and Deborah had a new baby. They were to have six (seven?) more, and the cabin—one or two rooms below, sleeping quarters above—was crowded.

In 1858 Henry opened a post office and named it Rock Fish. But Deborah died in 1864 (she was 39), the post office closed in 1866, and Henry died in 1867 (he was 62). Woodcock children may also have died at that time, in an epidemic. The family plot is said to have the graves of the parents and seven children.

Various owners and renters then lived here. All are anonymous but Ira and Ada Robinett, remembered for a day in December 1925 when a bedraggled teenage boy walked up, brandishing a pistol, and demanded food and lodging. Fearful, Ada and Ira prepared a supper. (Ira's brother Houston, however, slipped away.)

The Robinetts fed the youth and showed him a bed. He got in and went to sleep, and Ira and Ada remained in the house....

4:00 a.m. Scratching on the windowpane. Houston: "Get out." Outside, a sheriff's posse. Whispers.

A deputy went inside and—here accounts vary—grabbed the boy and pulled him out of bed. The gun was under his pillow.

The fourteen-year-old, a mental defective named Arnold Comer, had been on a four-day spree from Buffalo City, stealing money and guns and committing three murders. He went to prison, later to the state asylum.

A few years after Comer's capture the Woodcock house became abandoned. Sometime in the late 1930s it burned down.

level, with a layer of the St. Peter Sandstone visible at about 400 feet.

The next named feature along the river is…

144.5–145.4 Spencer Eddy, past **Spencer Bluff**. The bluff begins with a buttress of rock that juts from the hillside about 400 feet above the river. Then a giant's staircase of rock ascends the hill to the St. Peter Sandstone, here an overhanging 50-foot cliff stained with buff and orange. Where the cliff turns a corner, a huge flat boulder sits balanced on top, 450 feet up. More rock is exposed above the St. Peter cliff, so that Spencer Bluff is 510 feet high.

Spencer Eddy empties into rapids that the 1896 Corps map called Fox Bar Shoal. The shoal ends in…

145.4–145.7 Leatherwood Eddy, or Leatherwood Hole. Here on the right bank was once the house of John Morris, grandfather of James Corbett Morris. The grandson, deeply influenced by his family heritage and this hill country, is better known as Jimmy Driftwood, musician and composer of songs including "Tennessee Stud" and "The Battle of New Orleans."

Just beyond the old Morris farm…

145.7 Leatherwood Creek arrives on the right. The creek, named for the leatherwood shrub that grows in its moist bottomlands, in turn provided the name for the wilderness area that encompasses most of its watershed.

Leatherwood Eddy ends at…

145.8 Leatherwood Shoals—rock-studded rapids, then 200 yards of calm water, finally a steep 80-foot-long drop. The shoals end in…

145.9–146.0 Brewer Eddy at the foot of High Burr Bluff—which probably should be named Hy Brewer Bluff. Two local old-timers say "Burr" is a misspelling. Ruth Harrington Franks, born in 1921, says: "I heard talk of Hy Brewer. I heard my mom and dad talk of the Brewers a lot."

Everett Boyd, born in 1917, doesn't recall Brewer's first name, but adds: "High Brewer Bluff was named for a man who camped there. The family spent the winter under the bluff." Boyd also says that the pool below the bluff is Brewer Eddy.

Burr—or Brewer—Bluff is indeed high, topping out at 540 feet above the river. Thus it is one of the Buffalo's major cliffs, with many gray ledges, steep grassy terraces, and gray-green junipers wherever there's a foothold. At the summit is the St. Peter Sandstone, overhanging, with tan and orange coloring.

At the end of Brewer Eddy the river spills down a ledge shoal with rocks visible above and below the water surface, and flows into…

146.1–146.9 Foster Eddy, extending past **Foster Hollow**, then bending to the right past **Sheep Jump Bluff** and ending at **Sheep Jump Hollow**. Sheep Jump Bluff (146.6–146.8) reaches to 500 feet above the river but its rock faces are hidden by foliage, except for 80- to l00-foot exposures low on the hillside.

Sheep Jump Shoal (146.9), a rock ledge just below the mouth of Sheep Jump Hollow, is shown on the Corps of Engineers map of 1896. Old-timer Baxter Hurst: "Waves slapping on rock reminded someone of sheep jumping, so he named the shoal Sheep Jump."

Sheep Jump Shoal empties into…

147.0–147.2 Sheep Jump Eddy, without a shoal before…

147.2–147.7 Shields Eddy just downstream. On the left near the lower end of Shields Eddy is the Shields homesite, close to an outflow of water which became known as the Goodman Spring.

Rainbow Family. Described as a loosely organized back-to-nature religious group, the Rainbow Family of Living Light emerged from the counterculture of the 1960s. The Rainbows rejected the idea of having leaders, tended toward Native American beliefs and faith in the power of peace and love, and espoused kinship with the Earth. Each year around July 4 they held a gathering at some remote site on public land. In 1975 they congregated at an isolated spot on the lower Buffalo.

Today the exact location of the gathering is forgotten; it may have been at Spencer Bluff, between Middle and Leatherwood Creeks. The Park Service estimated there were up to 600 people —men, women, children—at the campsite at any one time. Afterward, some of the Rainbows stayed to clean up the area.

But the Rainbows were counterculture. Local people were outraged when seeing or hearing about their public nudity and use of drugs. Park rangers patrolled the gathering, partly to keep irate locals from attacking the "hippies." A sheriff wanted to mount a cavalry charge through the camp area but backed off when rangers told him small children and babies were there.

For the rangers it was a new experience. One later said he had been present during a nude wedding. "The bride was nude, the groom was nude, the preacher was nude," he reported. "I was the only one that had any clothes on. In fact, I felt a little awkward."

And what was the wedding like?

"I never saw so many chigger bites in my life."

147.7 At the end of the eddy **Brush Creek** enters the river from the right. Here at the mouth of Brush Creek is the birthplace of the person most knowledgeable about the Lower Buffalo/Leatherwood Wilderness country, Everett Eugene Boyd. It was he who provided many of the names of places downstream from Rush that are printed in this book and on the Trails Illustrated *East Half* map.

Shields Eddy exits through a shoal the Corps of Engineers in 1896 called O. Shield's Chute but which more recently has been known as Brush Creek Shoal. The shoal is wide, about 100 yards long, and bends to the right as the current becomes slower.

147.8–148.2 The river then flows arrow-straight, with a wide-open gravel bar on the right. The feeling here is of spaciousness, so different from the aspect of other parts of the Buffalo having over-hanging trees. Here, too, there's a long view ahead, three-quarters of a mile to a strangely shaped rock outcrop on the hill.…

But here also (at 148.0) is a different sort of rock, close up. Along the left bank is yellowish-gray Powell Dolomite in thin layers for a few feet above the water. The Powell is the Buffalo's oldest geologic formation, found only at scattered locations along the river.

148.2 Cow Creek enters from the left, flowing on bedrock. The river turns right, into Cow Creek Shoal, which the Corps in 1896 called Tinnan's Rock Shoals. The Buffalo then turns left into…

148.3–148.8 Bob Trimble Eddy, where it flows past five rock out-croppings fringed with junipers and known as **Trimble Bluff**, which the Corps in 1896 called Tinnan's Rock Bluffs.

148.5 The second of the five outcrops is the **Elephant Head**—the strangely shaped pile of rock seen from far upstream. Viewed from the river directly abreast, a column of rock becomes the elephant's trunk, a dark area above and to the right of the trunk is an eye, and expanses of rock spreading out behind could be ears. The outcrop stands about 210 feet above the river (photo, page 426).

148.8 Trimble Eddy and Trimble Bluff end at **Gosha Creek**—which around 1890 was called Trimble's Branch—and the river enters the rapids named Cow Rock Shoals on the Corps 1896 map.

In recent years there have been three shoals, spaced over 1000 feet (148.8–149.0). In reporting on a survey of the river in 1910, engineer W. N. Gladson called one of them Jumping Shoals.

Downstream from the shoals the river bends to the right, passing a bluff having a high face of rock, to 350 feet, set back from the water's edge. Here (at 149.4) is the site of the Corps of Engineers' proposed Lone Rock Dam, whose impoundment at maximum stage would have reached up the river to past Highway 65.

A short distance downstream from the dam site…

149.6–149.7 low rocky islands stand at a riffle that has been called Campbell Shoal, though Raymond Rasor, who grew up on the farm along the right bank, says that Campbell Shoal was about a half mile farther downstream and has become shallow, over gravel.

Below the Campbell Shoal is Rasor Eddy (149.7–150.6 or 150.2–150.6), named for Raymond Rasor's family, who lived for several decades on that right-bank farm. Rasor Eddy ends at…

150.6 Rasor Shoal, a brief spill over and between rocks at the mouth of **Stewart Creek**. Raymond Rasor knows this place as Birds Ford, a name used on the 1896 Corps of Engineers map. Rasor also says that when flood water is flowing over the spillway at Bull Shoals Dam on the White River, water from the White backs up the Buffalo to this shoal. Below Rasor Shoal/Birds Ford is…

150.7–151.3 the Hudson Hole, named for a family who came to this area before 1840. The hole curves to the left around **Hudson Bend**, past the last major cliff on the Buffalo…

150.9–151.9 called Grayface Bluff, reaching at its upstream end to 420 feet above the river. The bluff has exposed rock high up, overlooking a steep wooded slope down to the water. The high rock is Everton. Close to the water the Buffalo's oldest rock, the Powell Dolomite, may also be visible.

The Hudson Hole at its lower end arrives at obstacles…

151.3–151.5 three ledge shoals spaced over a quarter mile, probably qualifying as the river's longest "rock garden," annoying if not actually hazardous to boaters. But Hudson Hole can boast…

150.9–151.9 the Buffalo's longest gravel bar, a mile from end to end. The upstream end is a reasonably good campsite. The downstream part can overflow when water released through electric generators at Bull Shoals Dam backs up the Buffalo. From there to the White River the Buffalo's shoreline is then submerged.

In 1896 the Corps of Engineers identified a pool located a mile upstream from the White as…

151.8–152.2 Gin Eddy. Others have called it Big Eddy. There was a cotton gin on the south (left) bank. Before 1900, steamboat captains brought their wood-burning stern-wheelers up the Buffalo to the gin to load bales of cotton to go down the White to market. (Also see *River voyage,* page 248.) Past Gin Eddy is…

152.4 Crane Ford, the last shoal of the Buffalo, where the river divides around an island. Here, about 300 yards inland from the right bank, is the site of Winnerva, envisioned in 1891 by Kansas City capitalist Willard B. Winner as the southern terminus of his projected Springfield, Yellville & White River Railroad. In 1892, Winner began building his railroad but was stopped in early 1893 when a nation-wide recession cut off funding. Almost seven miles of roadbed had been graded, including a section at the base of **Stair Bluff**, which extends up the White from the mouth of the Buffalo.

Winnerva's only lasting structure was a frame building—two stories above a raised basement, having 12 rooms, kitchen, and dining room—intended to be a hotel. The Winnerva hotel's paying guests were travelers coming on foot or horseback and men building today's railroad along the White River. The hotel contained the only bathtub closer than Mountain Home. And from 1892 to 1911, a post office.

After 1908 the building became quarters for a farm family. Then it was abandoned. About 1960 the hotel was torn down for its lumber.

Not far beyond Crane Ford is the Buffalo's last tributary…

River voyage. Will T. Warner, captain of the White River steamboat *Dauntless,* was one to take chances, and in the spring of 1896 he was given one. Officials of Rush's Morning Star Mine (photo, page 414) contracted with him to bring his boat up the Buffalo to Rush Creek to learn whether the river could be navigated—if it could, Warner would be in line for shipping business. Warner was also to bring some machinery and passengers this first trip.

The 73-ton *Dauntless* drew only 12 inches when empty and 2 feet 6 inches when fully loaded, and the Buffalo was above average stage as Warner headed his boat up the river. But progress soon became very slow, with frequent stops as the crew chopped tree limbs to clear a way for the vessel's smokestacks.

And there were rapids the steamboat could not ascend under its own power. For these, the crew tied a line to a tree upriver and attached the other end to the capstan on the bow of the boat. Six or eight men then inserted poles in the capstan and turned it to reel in the line and pull the *Dauntless* up the shoals.

It took a day and a half to steam 23 miles from the White River to Rush Creek. Once there, the crew quickly unloaded the cargo and Captain Warner headed the *Dauntless* downstream.

No one else tried to take a steamboat up the Buffalo to Rush.

Tranquillity. Near Leatherwood Creek, a river becomes a mirror.

152.5 Moreland Creek, coming out of **Cook Hollow**, on the left. Stone abutments at the mouth of the creek supported a bridge. Local old-timer Garland Woods says that he broke down the bridge when hauling 100 bushels of corn across it in a 1939 Ford truck. The road followed the left bank of the Buffalo to the White River, where it followed W. B. Winner's railroad grade along the base of Stair Bluff, providing a quick way out of the lower Buffalo country.

But for circumstances, there might have been a railroad up the Buffalo instead of the White. When railroad surveyors coming up the White reached the mouth of the Buffalo in 1901, they were ordered to survey up the Buffalo to Boat Creek. The intention was to avoid a route up the White that would require tunneling. But the Buffalo's high bluffs stood in the way, and the railroad was built up the White to Cotter, then across the White and through a tunnel.

152.6–153.0 Below Moreland Creek is the Buffalo's last bluff, on the left and extending to the White River. Close to the White it shows its last face of rock, about 35 feet high. Ahead is Smith Island, a low sandbar island lying between the two channels of the White.

153.0 Mouth of Buffalo River. Here the Buffalo at normal stage is about 375 feet above sea level. At its farthest source it is about 2410 feet. The five highest points of its upper watershed—and of the entire Ozark region—are at elevations a little over 2560 feet.

White River Take-out Points.

For anyone entering the White River from the Buffalo, there are five possible sites for taking out boats, baggage, and people. Here are the two sites on the White located upstream from the mouth of the Buffalo:

• **White-Buffalo Resort**, 0.4 mile up the White River, has a private dock where the owner charges a small fee for landings. The resort may also be able to provide tow service up the White, for a fee. Their phone number is (870)425-8555. People canoeing the Buffalo have used cell phones to call for tow service.

• **Buffalo City public boat ramp**, 0.7 mile up the White and directly opposite the most imposing face of Stair Bluff, has a concrete ramp, parking area, and toilets, maintained by the Arkansas Game and Fish Commission. There is no charge for landing there.

If paddling up the White to the resort or the public ramp, stay near the left bank to avoid the main current, then cross to the landing. At low to medium flow it's possible, with extra effort, to paddle upstream. At high flow, when most or all of the generators have been discharging 31 miles upstream at Bull Shoals Dam, it's impossible to go up the White without a motor.

When do those generators run? It's impossible to predict. They are turned on to fill regional demands for peaking electric power, or to draw down Bull Shoals Lake to maintain storage capacity for flood control. In the summer the "power surge" passes Buffalo City from around midnight to 8:00 a.m. following afternoon and evening operation of all eight generators at the dam to satisfy power demand for air conditioning. But at any time, especially from fall through spring, the schedule can vary. When the power surge comes down the White from Bull Shoals, the river rises about nine feet at a rate of up to two feet per hour.

Power generation is controlled on a regional basis by the office of the Southwestern Power Administration in Springfield, Missouri. Further information about generation schedules at Bull Shoals Dam can be obtained from a recorded message about present conditions,

Stair Bluff overlooks the Buffalo-White confluence at the upper end of Smith Island. Here at low flow the combined rivers move to the right, this side of the people on the rock jetty. Gravel in the foreground of this photo taken in 2003 was brought here by Buffalo River floods during the previous year.

phone (870)324-4150. Or the Corps of Engineers' project office at Mountain Home, (870)425-2700, may be able to provide information. Or the power plant superintendent at Bull Shoals, (870)431-5391, extension 3021.

Anyone taking out at Buffalo City will be able to view Stair Bluff, the highest sheer bluff along the White River, a towering wall rising to 500 feet above the water's edge. Interestingly, Stair Bluff on the White is within the boundaries of Buffalo National River, under the jurisdiction of the National Park Service. That's because the bluff's backslope faces Cook Hollow, with Moreland Creek that drains to the Buffalo.

An earlier name for Stair Bluff was Stair Gap Bluff, apparently because there was a natural staircase up to a gap, or low point, in the summit of the bluff near its upstream end.

Here are the three take-out sites downstream from the Buffalo:

• **Cartney Landing**, 3.6 miles down the White, is a public boat ramp on the right-hand (south) side of the river. The boat ramp and parking area are within the Sylamore District of the Ozark National Forest and are administered by the U.S. Forest Service and the Arkansas Game and Fish Commission. There is no charge for using the landing. Access is via Baxter County Roads 72 and 114 off State Highway 341 (see Trails Illustrated map). County Road 114 fords a creek, so may be impassable in high water.

• **Shipps Landing,** 5.6 miles down the White, is a public boat ramp on the left-hand (north) side of the river. The boat ramp and parking area are maintained by the Game and Fish Commission. There is no charge for using the landing. Access is via the Shipps Ferry Road off State Highway 201.

• **Norfork**, 11.6 miles down the White, is a public landing on the left bank just beyond the mouth of the North Fork River. Parking space is limited; make local inquiry as to where to park. If generators are running at Norfork Dam, 4.8 miles up the North Fork from the White River, water discharge from the North Fork may cause difficulty in reaching the landing at Norfork. Access to Norfork is from north and south via State Highways 5, 201, and 341.

In the summertime, cold-water releases from Bull Shoals Dam can cause a layer of dense fog to form along the White River. At times the layer of fog lies so close to the water that a person standing up in a boat can look across the top of the fog bank.

Part 3

TRAILS

Flower identification on
the Buffalo River Trail
overlooking Calf Creek.

Cob Cave was a Native American campsite—to get there with food and possessions, Indians scrambled up the creek. Today in Lost Valley, visitors find the cave near the end of an easy trail.

Trails Overview

The hiking trails, paths, and routes described on the following pages total about 120 miles, and there's also a seven-mile auto or bicycle tour of historic sites in the Boxley Valley. The auto/bike tour and 80 miles of hiking opportunities are on the upper river. Except for the three-mile Round Top Mountain Trail a few miles to the south, all are shown on the *Buffalo National River, West Half* map published by Trails Illustrated. The remaining 40 miles of the 120 are along the middle and lower Buffalo and are shown on the *Buffalo National River, East Half* map by Trails Illustrated.

These mileage totals, by the way, do not include several miles of short, optional side trips that are described below at the various points from which they depart from the main trails.

The trails described include every one along the Buffalo that hikers use with any frequency. These include practically all the hiking trails and many of the trails also open for horseback riding. They include most of the trails in the Park Service's Ponca Wilderness (with 31 miles described) and the trail to Hawksbill Crag in the Forest Service's Upper Buffalo Wilderness.

Except for the Hawksbill trail, the two Upper Buffalo wilderness areas and the Lower Buffalo/Leatherwood Wilderness have no designated, maintained trails. These areas are intended for "a primitive and unconfined type of recreation," as stated in the 1964 Wilderness Act that governs their management. In keeping with that philosophy, the wilderness off-trail hiking is described only in general terms.

Hiking is best in cool or cold weather, when summer's heat is gone and bugs and snakes are dormant. Floating the river, however, is best in warm weather, which suggests that hiking and floating can provide good times along the Buffalo the year round.

All of the trails are accessible for day hikes. (Another choice is *Float-Hiking,* a combination of river and trail travel for a day or two; see page 144.) Several of the longer trails, and the wilderness areas too, are well suited for trips of a weekend or longer, with overnight stays in the undeveloped backcountry. The 37-mile Buffalo River Trail from Boxley to Pruitt can be backpacked with nights spent at developed campgrounds (Their water systems, however, are shut down during the cold months).

In the following trail descriptions, the distance is one-way unless noted that it is round-trip. Elevation gain is shown so that, with trail mileage, it can suggest how strenuous the hike will be. How long a hike may take depends on the hiker. Allowing for rest and lunch stops, the average person travels about one mile per hour. A fast hiker may average two or more miles per hour. Add up the trail mileage you want to hike, know or estimate your average speed, and you can then estimate the time you need to allow for your trip.

The trail write-ups cannot even as much as suggest everything you may see. Instead they describe a few recognizable features relating to geology, plant or animal life, human history, or in some cases park management. These topics, of course, are related to what is said in the first four chapters of this book. Sometimes there are also remarks about the difficulty of terrain or about hazards to safety, but we cannot describe every rough stretch of trail or every hazard. You must always exercise caution and common sense.

If your hike extends from one trail to a connecting trail, the description of the first trail will include how to key into the description of the second one—a feature especially useful in the Ponca Wilderness, where segments of trail are joined in a network. Landmarks that are named on the Trails Illustrated maps are named in **boldface** in this guide, to make it easier to visually connect what you read here to places on the maps. Using both guide and map, you should be able to navigate without having to depend on trail signs or blazes that may or may not exist.

There. Go and see. Learn. Enjoy.

Upper Buffalo Wilderness Areas
Ozark National Forest, 11,094 acres;
Buffalo National River, 2200 acres.

These two adjoining wilderness areas encompass or touch 14 miles of the Buffalo River and include 11 named tributary canyons. Access to the National Forest wilderness is from parking areas (marked **P** on the Trails Illustrated map) off Highway 21 south of Boxley and east of Fallsville and off County Road 5 south of Boxley, and from elsewhere if entry is possible without crossing private land. Access to the National River wilderness is from County Road 5 where it borders the wilderness area; from the trailhead on Highway 21 at the south end of the Boxley Valley; and from a high-clearance road from State Highway 21 to past the site of the Whiteley School.

The only developed trail in either wilderness area extends for about one and a half miles to Hawksbill Crag (Whitaker Point) from a Forest Service parking area on County Road 5 south of the Cave Mountain Church. The crag, an overhanging projection of the "middle Bloyd" sandstone rimrock cliff above the Buffalo's side canyon of **Whitaker Creek**, caught the attention of hikers on an Ozark Society outing, in December 1980. One of the group, Neil Compton, made a photograph of the feature and in 1982 published the picture in his book *The High Ozarks*. Indulging his penchant for naming natural features, he called this one the Hawksbill Crag.

In October 1981 photographer Matt Bradley again put the crag on film, and his photo was published in 1983 in a National Geographic Society book, *America's Hidden Corners*. Since that time many amateur and professional photographers have visited the crag. For each of them it's been easy to get an eye-catching picture of people perched on a rock ledge suspended over space.

The trail ends at the crag and visitors invariably take the same path back to their cars. Down in the canyons beyond the crag are opportunities for cross-country hikes, at times along old road traces. Some

At Adkins Creek. When the Buffalo River in the Upper Wilderness is running full, drop-offs here create crosscurrents that whitewater paddlers call the Mixmaster. For hikers on a foggy autumn day the rapids are more a scenic attraction.

of the roads are open; others are overgrown. At least a part of every hike has to be bushwhacking.

Settlers and loggers made the roads. A Forest Service researcher found that the first known pioneer in the area settled at the mouth of **Terrapin Branch** in 1848. Settlers eventually claimed every piece of river bottomland, every level bench, every ridge top (see *American odyssey*, below). They cleared and fenced gardens and cornfields, turned cattle and hogs into the woods to forage, and cut timber for cash income. Along the river they had a sawmill, a stave mill, and a water-powered gristmill.

And, as everywhere throughout the hills, their topsoil and timber dwindled at the same time the cash economy was taking over. Through the 1920s and 1930s especially, families sold their land to the Forest Service and moved away. The last known resident within today's wilderness, Sherman Reed, who lived at Terrapin Branch, left in 1948, exactly 100 years after the first pioneer had arrived.

Between 1938 and 1970 the Forest Service oversaw timber harvest

American odyssey. After they learned their son Alexander had been selected for a retaliatory killing in a feud between two other families, James and Lavina Dixon moved their family from southeastern Kentucky to Arkansas. Eventually several of the Dixons homesteaded at the Buffalo River headwaters. James and Lavina in 1898 acquired 160 acres overlooking the river; their daughter Sallie and her husband, Robert Logan, in 1901 got adjoining land on the hill above Adkins Creek. Both homesteads were on rocky, uneven ground. The Logans, with two girls and seven boys to feed, probably farmed the better ground on her parents' place, where about 40 acres were more nearly level.

James and Lavina both died in 1901; Robert and Sallie sold out and moved their family to southwest Arkansas. Her brother Alexander stayed; he'd been postmaster of nearby Fallsville.

The Logan family—Robert and Sallie's offspring—eventually became dispersed over the United States, their lives far removed from their childhood homestead at the edge of today's Upper Buffalo Wilderness. One grandson, Jess Logan, wound up with an aerospace firm in California. He would head the team to design the compact but complex package of instruments to go aboard the Viking I spacecraft to the planet Mars.

Viking landed on Mars in 1976, exactly 100 years after the Dixons fled from that feud in the backwoods of Kentucky.

The old home place. Along with others who lived within today's Upper Wilderness, the Sparks family in the 1930s sold their land to the Forest Service and moved away. By the 1970s their house near the river below Whitaker Creek was gradually returning to the earth.

here in small, scattered areas. In 1973 a tornado flattened trees across the National Forest wilderness area in a northeasterly direction from near **Turner Ward Knob**. Another severe windstorm in 2000 left a wide tangle of fallen trees along the river above Bowers Hollow.

Today, except perhaps for a few isolated patches of trees, all the forest is second- or third-growth. The Forest Service estimates it to consist of white oak–red oak–hickory, 96 percent; shortleaf pine, 3 percent; and cedar-hardwood the remaining 1 percent.

So, what's there to see? First, a maturing forest, with a few huge trees in rugged side canyons the loggers never reached. And the remains of homesteads, at times with standing chimneys of native sandstone. Waterfalls and cascades in wet weather, icicles and ice-falls in cold weather. Wildlife—small animals, deer, maybe bear. Umbrella magnolias, found only here at the Buffalo headwaters. And views off cliffs (Hawksbill is but one of them). And of course the river: swim holes, lunch spots, pools with giant rocks. Even in the fall when the river goes dry, it is interesting (photo, page 150).

All for a price—the stress and sweat to climb down into there and to then make the 600- to 900-foot climb back out. This wilderness is of a steep, rocky, rough sort of attractiveness.

But for those able to go, rewards are to be found.

Boxley Valley History Tour

A tour by auto or bicycle along Highways 21 and 43.

The seven-mile-long Boxley Valley Historic District, listed on the National Register of Historic Places, preserves evidence of more than 150 years of change in building styles and farming practices. Look here also for clues to the lives of the valley's interrelated families, people having surnames most often English or Scotch-Irish (Casey, Clark, Duty, McFerrin, Scroggins, Whiteley) but also French (Villines) and maybe Dutch (Edgmon or Edgemon). And a black mother and son (also named Villines), born in slavery.

Settlement along the valley began in the 1830s, and before 1850 the fertile bottomlands were taken. Population has remained fairly stable ever since. Houses along the tour route therefore date from around 1850 to past 1960, including examples of the Ozarks' five most prevalent vernacular (native) building styles:

• *Log cabins* that appear to be of the Midland type that originated near the East Coast in New Jersey, Delaware, and Pennsylvania in colonial times and then spread westward throughout the southern states to Missouri, Oklahoma, and Texas. Houses of this type have squared logs, in contrast to ones in the northern states having round logs. The smallest houses having one room with walls of logs are "single-pen." Houses with two adjoining rooms of logs are "double-pen," always with an outside door to each room. For pioneer families of parents, kids, and other kin living in two adjoining rooms, two outside doors allowed more privacy—and quicker escape from fire. Some double log houses have log-walled rooms separated by an open hall (breezeway; dogtrot) between them.

• *Double-pen houses* of frame construction. Their two rooms side by side with two outside front doors are a carry-over from the double log house. Ozark novelist Donald Harington calls these houses "duples." The basic duple is one story, just two rooms, what architectural historian Cyrus Sutherland calls "the absolute minimum of a family house." Duples also may be one and a half or two story and may have additions at the back.

• *I-houses*, named for their long, narrow floor plan, one room deep (although extra rooms often were added as ells or lean-tos at the back) with a symmetrical facade facing the road. I-houses having one room on each side of a central hall and often a porch across the front were influenced by (Continued on page 269)

Two Centuries
of Euro-Americans   **PEOPLE**

Rewarded for service,
Joseph Bernard Vallière
(right), commandant at
Arkansas Post, in 1793
received a Spanish land
grant having the Buffalo
River as one boundary.
Vallière's land was a vast
wilderness. Some of it
remains so, even today,
along the river in the
Lower Buffalo
Wilderness (below).

A pioneer's epitaph, "Born in Moore County, N.C.," suggests origins of many Buffalo River settlers. The first ones arrived in the 1820s from east of the Mississippi.

The valley of Richland Creek (below), stretching for miles southward from the Buffalo, attracted some of the first seekers of land. Richland's level bottoms were more extensive even than those along the river itself.

Oldest building along the Buffalo, the Parker-Hickman log house, was built in 1847–1849 by Alvin Parker and family members, who had come from North Carolina and Tennessee. Highly skilled craftsmen, they half-dovetailed the logs so snugly at the corners that a knife blade cannot be inserted between them.

In 1857 Alvin Parker moved on, to California. Subsequent owners of the house added lean-to rooms. The one on the left sheltered a neighborhood store. The house's last resident, bachelor Gradon Hickman, is seen in 1968 at home on the front porch with his dog.

During the Civil War
William Villines (left) was in the Union army; neighbors upriver were Confederates. Neither side remained in control and the country was prey to outlaws who robbed, murdered, and burned.

After the war the Buffalo country became a source of raw materials to be taken elsewhere: lead and zinc ore, timber, cotton. A World War I zinc boom brought miners (below) to Rush, on the lower river.

Resources were used up.
Lead and zinc, timber
and topsoil became
depleted and people
moved away. Those who
stayed had the freedom
of the hills but only a
bare living. But Ozarkers
are hardworking and able
to make do—as these
men did (above) when
they put together a boat
from junked auto hoods.

One widely known
survivor was Eva Barnes
(Granny) Henderson
(right). She lived alone
near the river at Sneeds
Creek until in her mid-
eighties, caring for her
farm animals.

Beauty remained, even as other natural resources along the river became exhausted. Outsiders began to become aware of the Buffalo and spend time here. One was the noted artist Thomas Hart Benton (left), who first visited the area in 1926.

In later life Benton came every year to float the river and explore the country. In 1968 his friend Charles Wilson photographed him, sketch pad in hand, on the Goat Trail at Big Bluff.

Thomas Benton's art is distinguished by strong colors and curving lines, evident in his 1968 rendition of the Bat House (Skull Bluff) near Woolum (above) and a 1973 painting of Peter Cave Bluff (left).

Benton sketched a swinging bridge (right) during his trip along the Buffalo in 1926. The scene probably is based on a bridge that spanned the river near Ponca.

Suspended in time, some places speak of bygone years. Their very appearance can stimulate thoughts about the past. Along the Buffalo, the Boxley Valley is such a place. Another is Richland Valley (above), still isolated, still agricultural, still much as we imagine it was soon after settlement in the nineteenth century.

high-style houses of the South and became dominant in the rural Southeast during the nineteenth century. Like the duple, the I-house came from the British folk tradition of being one room deep. All share Anglo-American and worldwide folk practices in houses: (a) "frontality," (b) symmetry of facade, and (c) add-ons.

• *Craftsman houses*, so named because they were designed, with personal touches, by craftsmen who built them. Craftsman houses in the Boxley Valley are offshoots of the bungalow (one story, with low-pitched roofs having wide overhangs and exposed rafter ends), which became widespread in the early 1900s and until the 1950s was the most popular style in the Ozarks. Whereas log houses and duples and I-houses have gables that face to the sides, craftsman houses usually have gables that face to front and back.

• *Ranch-style houses*, one story with low-pitched roofs, with a long facade facing the road. Roofs are hipped, or with gables facing to the sides. The style originated in the 1930s with several California architects whose designs were loosely based on Spanish Colonial houses in the Southwest. Ranch was the dominant style in the United States in the 1950s and 1960s.

Farm buildings also have changed. Older barns had corncribs, feed bins, and stalls for workhorses and mules, with large lofts above for storing loose hay. But plow animals disappeared in the 1940s, when the valley's fields of corn, wheat, and cotton gave way to cattle pastures and hayfields. While a number of older barns still stand, today's valley farmers also have buildings for motorized equipment and high-roofed sheds for storing large round bales of hay. Valley people have abandoned their smokehouses and chicken coops; their bacon, ham, and chicken come from the supermarket. Several families, however, still grow and home-can fruits and vegetables.

The following guide to historic sites along Highways 21 and 43 runs the length of the Boxley Valley. It includes places open to the public—parking turnouts, several historic buildings, and cemeteries. But most of the valley's homes, farm buildings, and fields are privately owned. Respect owners' rights. **View private property only from the highway.** And if you want to slow down or stop anywhere, *watch for traffic approaching from ahead or behind.*

This tour can be done from either end of the valley, south or north. The trip description goes from south to north, but each point of interest is located in terms of highway mileage from *both* ends of the valley. Thus the first place described is **0.0** miles from the south end and **6.8** miles from the north end. Mileage from the south end is given first, followed by a dash, then mileage from the north end. If you prefer to start at the north end, begin at **6.8—0.0** miles, first reading the last part of the text, and then move site by site in reverse. (The Trails Illustrated *West Half* map is needed for reference.)

For each site, the letter **R** beside its mileage figure means that the point of interest is to the right, and the letter **L** means to the left.

0.0L—6.8R South end of tour route, about 0.1 mile south of **Smith Creek**, where Highway 21, going south, begins to climb the mountain. Ruins of a stone fireplace and chimney can be seen from the highway. Pull off and park in the area beyond the chimney.

Here was the home (built c. 1900, burned 1990; photo, opposite) of John A. W. Whiteley, a grandson of the valley's first settlers, Samuel and Lucy Whiteley, who came about 1835. The Whiteleys were farmers and preachers. Samuel's son Isaac and Isaac's son John both pastored Boxley's Baptist church.

About 1912, John Whiteley was called to preach elsewhere and John Turner Edgmon (1875–1952) acquired this property. In the 1920s, Edgmon opened a country store and from then until 1954 he, his wife, Fannie (1880-1964), and their children ran the store, the local telephone exchange located in the house, and a 300-acre farm.

An Edgmon granddaughter remembers the store: nail kegs on the porch, convenient to sit on. Bags of feed and a barrel of kerosene in the lean-to room on the right. Inside the front door and on the wall to the left, pigeonholes for mail—an informal post office for isolated families farther up the valley. To the right, a chest filled with bottles of soda pop kept cold with blocks of ice from Harrison.

Along one wall, a glass-fronted candy case and three lidded bins for flour, sugar, and coffee beans. Wherever they could be set down, cartons of eggs brought in by neighbors to barter for sugar, salt, baking powder. In the middle of the room, a wood stove. At the back, shelves of shoes behind a counter with bolts of dress material.

Across the road was a gasoline-powered gristmill run by old Will Banard. And down Edgmon's lane were drive-through scales for weighing livestock, or for loaded wagons.

Today the store building is gone; it stood at the south side of the parking area. In the hillside facing the store site is a root cellar. Beyond the cellar, the lane goes along below the hill 0.1 mile to the

"Trigeminal" is the whimsical name Ozark novelist Donald
Harington gave three-doored houses like this. The idea of having
three front doors must have begun in two-pen log houses with a
breezeway, or center hall, that was later enclosed. John A. W.
Whiteley built this frame house at the south end of the Boxley
Valley about 1900. An arsonist destroyed it in 1990.

Whiteley-Edgmon spring, close to the original homesite of Samuel
and Lucy Whiteley. For them, the spring was an important reason for
choosing to locate here. Their log house may have been where John
T. Edgmon's barn (c. 1920) stands across the road from the spring.

From near the spring an old road goes up the hill about 200 yards
to the **Whiteley Cemetery,** having family graves—mostly of children—dating from the late nineteenth century.

The next described site is 0.8 mile north on Highway 21.

0.8L—6.0R   Across from unpaved **County Road 25** (Walker
Mountain Road), which arrives on the right, is a craftsman house in
the bungalow style (c. 1928; later additions) built by Marcius
Lafayette ("Fayett") and Josie Edgmon. Today Highway 21 passes
the back of the house though originally the road lay below the front.
To avoid floods it was moved uphill when paved in 1962.

1.2L—5.6R   Junction with **County Road 5** (Cave Mountain
Road) at the end of the Buffalo River bridge (Boxley bridge), also
dating from 1962. It replaced a one-lane steel bridge built in 1924.

Side trip: Go 0.5 mile up steep County Road 5 to parking spaces
on the left at a bulletin board. Walk across the road and up the path
80 yards to **Cave Mountain Cave** (Bat Cave; Saltpeter Cave). Here

in 1862 Confederates set up a "nitre works" to extract saltpeter (potassium nitrate), an ingredient of gunpowder, from nitrogen-rich bat guano and cave earth. In January 1863, Union cavalrymen arrived at dawn one morning, captured most of the workers, and destroyed the saltpeter works.

The fence at the cave's entrance was installed about 1980 to protect endangered gray and Indiana bats during the period from August 15 to May 15, when they hibernate in the cave.

End of side trip; return to Highway 21.

1.3L—5.5R Private drive to the house built in 1895 for Francis Marion (1855–1898) and Talitha Tennessee Edgmon (1853-1934), near the site of the cabin built by his parents when they settled here in the 1830s. This I-house with its long porches, ornamental railings, and tall stone chimneys, standing on an elevated site at the foot of Cave Mountain, is the valley's most imposing residence.

Marion Edgmon enjoyed his fine home only three years. In 1898, in an altercation with a would-be suitor of a daughter, he was accidentally shot and killed by his eighteen-year-old son Fayett.

Marion's widow, Talitha, lived out her life in the big house. From around 1900 to 1950 she and her sons Fayett and John T. owned and farmed most of the south end of the Boxley Valley. Today, however, the Edgmon name (though not the bloodline) is gone from Boxley.

1.7L—5.1R A ranch house (c. 1965) is one of the valley's examples of that style. Continue 0.3 mile north.

2.0L—4.8R *Side trip:* The side road leads to the **Boxley Baptist Church** (1951, with 1990s additions), its ranch-style parsonage (c. 1961), and the Boxley Community Building (1899). Until the 1950s the two-story community building housed an eight-grade school having one and sometimes two teachers. It also sheltered Boxley's church—whose beginnings go back to 1838—until the present church was built, and lodges of Masons and Odd Fellows. Today the building is used for community gatherings.

Next to the community building is the still active **Walnut Grove Cemetery**, whose earliest headstones date from the 1850s. One of the stones is a Confederate marker for Isaac J. Whiteley, who served in the Arkansas Volunteer Infantry and returned to the valley to become a Baptist minister. Four of Whiteley's brothers and three brothers-in-law served the Confederacy; four died in the war.

Within view up the private drive to the left of the church is the A. F. and Miranda Casey house, originally a one-pen log cabin built in

1875 to replace the family's home burned during the Civil War. In the 1890s the cabin became part of a larger house and in 1996 dormers were added to the rear wing. The house's nineteenth-century facade (facing to the right when seen from the church) has been preserved.

End of side trip; return to Highway 21.

2.2R—4.6L Two white-painted buildings (c. 1946) beside the highway were a cafe/store and the bungalow-style home of Arvel and Elsie Casey—he a distant relative of earlier Caseys in the valley. The building with the smokestack housed Casey's steam-powered sawmill. From the 1940s to 1976 the mill's whistle announced times to begin and stop work for the valley's largest employer.

Continue north 0.3 mile.

2.5—4.3 Highway 21/43 junction. Though Highway 21 in the Boxley Valley was paved in 1962, Highway 43 to the valley's north end was not hard-surfaced until 1980. Go straight through the junction and continue along the valley.

2.6L—4.2R The twin-dormered house (c. 1897, with later additions) was built by Joseph P. "Boxley Joe" and Belle Villines for their daughter Ora and son-in-law J. Frank Carlton.

2.7L—4.1R This two-story I-house surrounds a one-pen log cabin built in 1873, probably by Joseph P. Villines. Before 1900, Villines added to the cabin to create the I-house.

Prosperous farmers often added high-style elements to their I-houses. The sidelights and transom at the front door and the boxed columns of the front porches are details of this house that were borrowed from the nineteenth-century Greek Revival style. The jigsaw-cut, vase-shaped balusters supporting the porch railings are what architectural historians call "folk Victorian."

Joseph Villines operated a store just south of the house, and for years the Boxley post office was in the store, then in the house until the office closed in 1955. In 1911, Villines sold the house and store to Ben McFerrin, a schoolteacher and political figure who became lieutenant governor of Arkansas. The property passed to McFerrin's daughter Orphea and her husband, Fred Duty, and after Fred's death in 1944 she continued to live in the house. Orphea Duty played leading roles in the community and its church until not long before her death in 2002, a few weeks short of her 104th birthday.

2.8L—4.0R The unpainted barn with twin windows in the gable was built by Joe Villines about 1900. The barn once stabled draft horses used to haul logs to a steam sawmill located across the road.

3.3R—3.5L The spring-fed pond, filling up with sediment and becoming a wetland, once stored water to power Boxley's mill, out of sight beyond the pond. Directly across the pond is a barn.

3.4R—3.4L This bungalow-style house (c. 1940) was the home of Clyde Villines (1898–1985), last operator of the water-powered mill, and his wife, Nellie (1900–1992). Stone veneer like that on the house was popular in the 1930s. North of the house are three small cabins (c. 1948) that Clyde built to rent to fishermen—the valley's first accommodations for tourists.

Down the lane past the cabins is the Boxley mill (1870, with later modifications). For 80 years the mill was run by three generations of one family—Robert Villines, his son James, and James' son Clyde—until the mill closed about 1950. The building contains most of its original equipment for producing cornmeal and wheat flour. At one time there were also a cotton gin and a sawmill. Guided tours are conducted on a limited basis (see page 115 and sketch, page 116).

Just north of the turnoff to the mill, the highway crosses **Whiteley Creek**, named for valley pioneer Samuel Whiteley, who owned an earlier mill (built c. 1840) near the site of the present one. Whiteley was also the name of the community's first post office, located near here and established in 1851.

The Whiteley post office closed in 1866, but in 1883 it was reestablished and named for a man remembered as D. Boxley, a merchant from Springfield, Missouri. Boxley's first name may have been David but another source has it as William. He is said to have been a storekeeper, or maybe a freighter who hauled goods to local stores from Springfield, who moved to the valley about 1870. Apparently he never owned land here and disappeared without leaving any record—except his name for the community.

3.5L—3.3R Just north of Whiteley Creek, the "duple" house with two front doors and twin dormers was built in 1917 by James Larkin Villines, then operator of the Boxley mill. This house is the only survivor of at least three valley houses built between 1910 and 1920 by local artisans using this same general plan.

4.0L—2.8R The white house is a duple doubled in size, to four rooms in a square. Its pyramidal roof makes it a "pyramid house," a craftsman type popular in the South in the early 1900s. Once the home of Samuel and Lieu Duty, the house was built about 1913.

The barn across from the house was built about 1915. In the barn lot is a large iron kettle with a broken rim, one of seven such kettles broken by Union troops in 1863 during a raid on the Confederate saltpeter works up the valley at Cave Mountain Cave. After the war, farmers salvaged the kettles for various uses. This one served as a vat for scalding hogs to remove hair before butchering.

4.5L—2.3R The Frank and Jenny "Barsha" Scroggins house (c. 1932) with its porch swing is a bungalow having exposed (not boxed-in) rafter ends, typical of that style.

4.6L—2.2R A bungalow (1948; porch later enclosed) built by Audie and Delia Ramsey after he returned from military service in World War II. The large spring north of the house made this a favored site for pioneer settlement. Two of the original members of the Villines family who came to the valley about 1837, Virginia Jane with her husband William Keith and Hezekiah with his wife, Elizabeth, built their homes near this spring.

4.7R—2.1L A cobblestone building (c. 1922) having a single-pitch, or shed, roof was a store operated by Robert Hezekiah "Pretty Hez" and his wife, Minerva Mae "Minnie" Edgmon Villines until the 1950s. Across the highway is their craftsman-type home (1919; later additions). The house is a variation on the bungalow style, here with gables to the sides. Note that it has two front doors.

4.8L—2.0R On private property up the hill in the field, a stone monument surrounds and supports the broken grave marker of Vilissa Piety Villines (1816–1884). A black woman born a slave, "Aunt Pity" was the lifelong companion of valley pioneer Elizabeth Penn Villines. Piety's stone is the only one surviving of several that marked this family plot.

5.0L—1.8R The stone-veneered house was built about 1947 by Waymon and Norma Lee Villines after his return from World War II. He is a fifth-generation descendant of family patriarch Abraham Villines. Through another branch of the family she also is a fifth-generation descendant.

5.3L—1.5R Up a private driveway is the Joseph Samuel and Susan Clark Villines house (c. 1905, with 1970s additions), a one-story duple, or double-pen house, having two front doors. "Aunt Susie" Villines was a granddaughter of valley pioneer Abraham Clark, for whom Clark Creek, just to the north, is named.

5.7R—1.1L The roadside turnout near Clark Creek has two interpretive display panels installed by the National Park Service.

5.8L—1.0R Junction with road to **Lost Valley** trailhead.

Side trip: Go 0.2 mile up the Lost Valley road, and where the road turns left, turn to the right into a narrow lane. Here, within the edge of the woods to the left, is a spring—a water source for pioneers Isom and Sarah Davis, who built their home here before 1845.

Up the lane 0.1 mile is **Beechwoods Cemetery**. The church building is used for special services; it once also served as a schoolhouse. Today it is empty except for benches and a lectern or pulpit. The building (photo, opposite) dates from about 1918.

Beechwoods Cemetery has the oldest (1842) marked grave in the valley, for William Keith, who was the first husband of Virginia Villines Henson. William and Virginia were among the valley's earliest settlers. Here also is the grave of Martha Villines (1778-1862), second wife of Abraham, patriarch of the Buffalo River's Villines clan. Besides daughter Virginia Henson, Abraham's descendants here include, for one, grandson Hosea Villines (1853-1916), a great-grandfather of country music star Merle Haggard.

And here, resting beneath a small concrete marker inscribed N. TIM is Tim Villines (1849?–1921?), whose mother, Piety, was a black slave of the Villines family. Somewhere close to Tim are one of his white common-law wives and two of his children.

This cemetery, with public access but privately owned and still active, is one of the largest within Buffalo National River boundaries.

End of side trip; return to Highway 43.

6.4L—0.4R A barn located in the mouth of a hollow. Built about 1915 by Tom Chafin, the barn passed into the hands of Jess Shroll, an industrious newcomer from Ohio who put the barn on a concrete foundation and built a ground-level concrete silo (something new in this area) along the barn's north side.

Elk graze in the fields along this stretch of highway.

6.7R—0.1L Junction with gravel road marked RIVER ACCESS.

Side trip: Follow this road 0.2 mile to the Ponca **Low-Water Bridge**. Park at its near end, walk across it, and follow the old roadbed to the park-owned **Villines Farmstead**. A right fork leads to a barn that housed work animals and to a log corncrib. The left fork leads up the hill about 200 feet to the farmhouse and other buildings.

The uphill half of the two-pen log house, of heavy oak and walnut logs carefully joined at the corners, was probably built by pioneer James Black in 1854. A later owner, James Villines (1854–1948), bought the farm after marrying Sarah Arbaugh (1855–1932) in 1880. Villines added the downhill half of the house, a pen of cedar logs—poles, almost—that appears to have been put up in haste.

Jim and Sarah Villines had a typical Ozark farm of the early 1900s. In the log smokehouse that still stands uphill from the house, they cured hams and bacon. They kept a vegetable garden, developed a peach orchard, and raised wheat and corn, cattle and chickens and turkeys. Down the hill by Leatherwood Creek they installed a sorghum press and made molasses. (Jim's grandson Ross Villines would make molasses into the 1970s; see illustration, page 314.)

Jim, a jack of all trades, made a dugout canoe from a 14-foot ash log and ferried folks across the Buffalo when the river ran high. He

Beechwoods Church. Artists have recorded scenes along the Buffalo in a variety of ways. For this historic building near Ponca, photographer Dale Burris worked with infrared film.

Burris says infrared is not easy to master. The film must be kept refrigerated until use and the camera must be loaded and unloaded in total darkness. The film behaves so unpredictably that exposure involves guesswork.

The results can be a pleasant surprise. Infrared has recorded leaves and grass here as almost white and softened the details of the scene, giving it an almost dreamlike quality.

(Another infrared view by Dale Burris appears on page 308.)

pulled people's aching teeth, free of charge (but without anesthetic). He became best known, though, as a trapper—"Beaver Jim"—who eliminated the beaver from this part of the Buffalo.

In 1936, after the death of Sarah, Jim sold the farm. Other owners in the 1940s added the present lean-to kitchen, the concrete fruit cellar, the concrete privy, and concrete chinking between the house logs. They pasted newspapers to the insides of the house, not for decoration but for insulation. Fragments are still there.

Today this old-time farmstead lies close to two of the most significant causes of change in the valley. Stretched high above the house and barn are wires that since the late 1940s have brought electricity. Just beyond view are highways that since the late 1960s have provided paved connections to and from the outside world.

Back at the river, the one-lane concrete bridge was a major improvement over Beaver Jim's dugout canoe. Local men began building the bridge in 1941 with federal funding through the Works Progress Administration (WPA). They excavated, then completed some of the bridge piers—but World War II began and the WPA shut down. A county crew managed to complete the bridge by 1944. Today the low-water bridge is itself a relic from the past. It was superseded in 1983 by the high bridge in view downstream.

End of side trip; return to Highway 43.

6.8L—0.0 North end of the tour route, at a parking turnout 100 feet south of the intersection of Highways 43 and 74. A few yards above the turnout is the **Villines Cabin**, a log house probably built in 1853 by William Villines for his new bride, Rebecca Cecil.

The house eventually became a barn. Only the north half of the original two-pen structure still stands. Foundation stones of the other log pen are visible on the ground beyond. Stones that mark the south end of the two-pen house lie far enough from the south wall of the remaining portion to show that an open hall (dogtrot) existed between the two pens of logs.

The open-slatted structure south of the house was a corncrib. The small building at the parking area served as a granary and as a tack room for storing saddles and bridles.

In this log house William and Rebecca's children were born and grew up, including James "Beaver Jim" Villines, who developed the farm whose buildings stand across the Buffalo River. James Villines' son William ("Billy Beaver") and William's son Ross Villines lived on the property until the Park Service purchased it in 1978.

Lost Valley

2.3 miles round trip. 200 feet of elevation gain to Eden Falls, 100 more to Eden Falls Cave. Woodland wildflowers; natural bridge; caves; waterfalls; bluff shelter below 200-foot cliff. Trailhead at end of spur road off Highway 43 a mile south of Ponca .

Past parking space at the road's end, the Lost Valley trail begins at a wooden footbridge across Clark Creek. The bridge, built in 1998 by telephone company retirees working as volunteers, provides handicap access to a campsite and to the first quarter mile of the trail—and easier access for everyone else when the creek is running.

Lost Valley is a narrow canyon along a quarter mile of upper Clark Creek. In three miles from beginning to end, the creek falls 1200 feet, losing most of that elevation in its upper part. The sheer power of falling water has done much to carve the canyon. Another potent force has been solution, for Lost Valley lies within the Boone Formation, limestone more than 300 feet thick. Over the ages, acidic ground water has dissolved this carbonate rock, and geologists believe that solution created an immense cavity, or cave, that extended along the present course of Clark Creek. Eventually the cavity's roof became thin and collapsed—cave became canyon.

Today the work of solution continues. Clark Creek still flows through subterranean channels. While there is surface flow down the entire stream bed after heavy rains, in dry times long stretches of a much smaller creek run underground. Many other tributaries of the Buffalo have karst features like this, but none of the others are as accessible as Clark Creek at Lost Valley.

The creek's watershed is on the east side of a mountain, so that its east- and northeast-facing slopes are protected from afternoon sun. Here is a mesic (moderately moist) forest having shade-adapted lichens, mosses, and ferns, many woodland wildflowers, shrubs such as spicebush and wild hydrangea, and moisture-loving trees including pawpaw, beech, cucumber tree, American basswood, and yellow-wood. A botanist cataloging plants at Lost Valley identified more than 600 native species, not counting lower forms such as mosses.

In 1898 one of the local Clark family led three government surveyors up Clark Creek to a big rock shelter. In its dry interior they found tiny corncobs and named it Corn Cob Cave (or simply Cob Cave). In 1902 two local Sunday schools visited Cob Cave for sight-seeing, an all-day singing, and a basket dinner; this was probably the first large-scale visitation by recreation seekers.

In 1931 archeologists from the University of Arkansas excavated at Cob Cave, recovering things preserved by the dryness: corncobs, pieces of gourds, sunflower and other native seeds, and woven work and basketry. Apparently Native Americans used the rock shelter around AD 1000 as a winter campsite, open to the sun and protected from wind. In warm seasons they probably camped nearer the Buffalo to fish and to grow crops.

In 1945 Glenn Avantus "Bud" Green, tourism publicist for the State of Arkansas, heard about Cob Cave and came with a *National Geographic* photographer (photo, opposite). Deeply impressed with what he saw, Green named the scenic area Lost Valley and the first waterfall beyond Cob Cave, Eden Falls. As a publicist he then wrote and talked about Lost Valley as a place to see.

Lost Valley, however, was privately owned. Owners of the scenic area's west end in 1960 sold (for $500, reportedly) the timber on their 80-acre tract, and loggers bulldozed a haul road to within sight of Cob Cave and cut the large hardwoods. The cutting helped convince people that Lost Valley should be protected.

In 1966, Lost Valley's principal landowner sold her property, 200 acres extending from today's parking area to the downstream end of Cob Cave, to an agent of the State of Arkansas. Lost Valley became a state park, enlarged in 1967 when the state acquired the 80-acre tract containing the remainder of the scenic area.

In 1973 the state donated 280-acre Lost Valley State Park to the United States to be administered as part of Buffalo National River.

Most of the Lost Valley trail is on an old woods road up Clark Creek. The first quarter mile is practically level, and is handicap accessible. Along the trail are numbered 4-by-4-inch wood posts; the first one is on the right a short distance from the trailhead. The numbers are keyed to the following site descriptions.

1 Clark Creek In the creek bed behind the post, limestone lies in horizontal layers. Unless there has been recent heavy rainfall, the creek here will appear to be dry—but there will be water flowing underground, somewhere beneath you.

2 Plants slowing erosion After heavy rainfall Clark Creek can become a torrent, cutting into banks, washing away soil and rocks. Tree roots help to slow erosion. So do smaller plants, whose leaves

May 1945. *National Geographic* photographer Willard R. Culver directs his models—Harrison, Arkansas, high school students— to their places at Lost Valley's natural bridge. This photograph was made by Glenn A. Green, guide and bag-toter for Culver on a trip around Arkansas to get pictures for a *Geographic* article.

Green was employed by the state as a publicist for tourism. Much impressed by this nearly unknown natural area, he named it Lost Valley and advertised it to the outside world.

shield the bare earth and break the fall of raindrops. Trees along creeks often develop long, tangled roots reaching toward water.

Behind you here, and across the creek also, are flat areas called stream terraces, old flood plains where in past centuries Clark Creek deposited material washed down from upstream.

3 Ancient stream bed Like other creeks and rivers, Clark Creek has changed its course over time. Centuries ago the creek flowed below the high bank to the left of the trail. The dip in the trail you just passed over is the old creek bed. As you continue up the trail, look for where the creek first crossed over from the present channel.

Now the valley becomes narrower and more shaded. Christmas fern grows on slopes near the trail, and one of spring's earliest wildflowers, hepatica, appears on the forest floor.

4 Prehistoric life Fossils of marine animals and land plants can be found along this trail. In the rock lying before you are fragments of the round stems of crinoids (CRY-noids; photos, pages 38 and 55), the kind of fossil most often seen along the Buffalo River.

Soon the trail meets another trail coming down the hill from the left—the logging road made in 1960. Continue to the right, the more direct way to the scenic area. And note how the hillsides have closed in, so the valley floor is only wide enough for the creek and the trail.

5 The Jigsaw Blocks Across the creek are huge square-cut pieces of rock that, like pieces of a jigsaw puzzle, fit the notch in the cliff from which they fell. The largest piece is 28 feet long and up to 20 feet wide and 11 feet high. It weighs more than 300 tons.

Rocks everywhere here are covered with green mosses and pale-green lichens. Their acid secretions help to break down rock surfaces—a first step in changing rock to soil.

6 Natural bridge Clark Creek has carved a 50-foot-long tunnel through beds of the St. Joe Limestone, the lowest division of the Boone Formation. The St. Joe's distinctive red rock is here, nearly ten feet thick along the base of the bluff at the creek.

On the left as you face the pool below the natural bridge is a massive piece of layered limestone, the same kind of rock as in the bluff. Several species of mosses and small flowering plants grow on the surfaces and in the crevices of this rock, evidence that plants will take hold wherever they can.

In 0.8 mile from the parking area to the natural bridge, the trail gains 100 feet in elevation. In the next 0.2 mile to Cob Cave and Eden Falls it gains another 100 feet, mostly up flights of steps to bypass the natural bridge. (Originally people climbed through the bridge tunnel. That's still possible but the rocks are slippery.)

After climbing the steps around the bridge, note that a side path goes down to the creek bed at the upper end of the tunnel. The creek here is usually dry, and a spring in the bridge tunnel provides the water that spills from the tunnel's lower end.

About 25 yards up the creek bed from the tunnel's upper end is a small cave in the base of the bluff. Several yards inside is a flowing stream—Clark Creek on its way to the spring in the bridge tunnel.

The hiking trail continues up the creek and soon joins a wider path, the upper end of the 1960 logging road. (To the left, the old road is an alternate route for returning toward the trailhead.)

At the next intersection a trail straight ahead climbs steps toward Eden Falls Cave. Continue to the right, toward the yawning black opening under the limestone cliff that now towers high above (photo, page 254). In 80 yards, come to...

7 Cob Cave Here is a vast sheltered area below a solid rock ceiling. For an even better sense of this immense space under the cliff, leave the trail and climb the slope to the back of the cave, then onto the elevated shelf to the right. Here the cave's dimensions can be better comprehended: 150 feet from front to back, 50 feet from creek bed to ceiling, 260 feet from end to end. In view beyond the upstream end is 40-foot Eden Falls, looking quite small.

Clark Creek helped create Cob Cave by sweeping against the cliff and dislodging slabs of rock that it then carried away. And, as mentioned earlier, acidic water slowly dissolved the limestone, even so much that it apparently created an immense cavern whose roof eventually collapsed. As that ancient cavern was opened to daylight, and as limestone everywhere along the creek went into solution, the overlying sandstone broke up and fell, slid, or settled into the space where the limestone had been. Today along the Lost Valley trail, the canyon bottom is littered with boulders of the more resistant sandstone. The sandstone, too, is slowly disintegrating. The old angular, broken corners of the boulders have become rounded as weathering has proceeded over the centuries (see upper photo, page 59).

8 Eden Falls The surface channel of Clark Creek enters Lost Valley as a series of four steps, the lowest one being Eden Falls. Directly above Eden Falls is an eight- or ten-foot cascade and drop. Above that, and hidden by canyon walls, are a 40-foot fall and a sloping 80-foot fall; both of these falls are usually dry.

At Eden Falls the strata, or layers, of rock are wavy or curved, unlike the flat-lying layers in other parts of the cliff. This is evidence there may have been a geologic fault here, or at least flexing that could have opened cracks in the limestone, allowing water to enter and begin the process of creating a cavern.

From the end of the trail at Eden Falls, backtrack a few yards to follow a trail up rock steps toward Eden Falls Cave. This trail is steep, with many steps in 100 feet of elevation gain.

9 Eden Falls Cave The built trail ends at the mouth of the cave.

There, a stream of water runs out of the tunnel, down a waterfall hidden below, and into the surface channel of Clark Creek.

Using a flashlight, it's possible to walk and crawl 150 feet to a large room at the rear of the cave. Partway inside, a right-hand passage has a narrow walkway that bypasses part of the crawl space.

In the back room is a 30-foot waterfall that comes down from near the ceiling. In full flow, the waterfall fills the room with its roar, and with showers of cold spray.

Seeing this underground waterfall, or even viewing Eden Falls at Cob Cave, is a fitting climax to visiting Lost Valley.

Buffalo River Trail, Boxley to Pruitt

Boxley Trailhead to (and along) County Road 25

2.4 miles. 450 feet of elevation gain. Views of fields, forest, and valley. Trailhead off west side of Highway 21 about 0.1 mile south of Smith Creek bridge at south end of Boxley Valley.

Park in the open area beyond the chimney ruin that is visible from the highway. This home site originally belonged to the Whiteley family; later it became the John Turner Edgmon place (see page 270).

To get on the trail, walk across the highway into the driveway, around the gate, and down the drive. Cross **Smith Creek** (if the slab is wet, it can be slippery). Then go left, around the end of the field.

The creek was first named Austin Smith Creek for an in-law of the Whiteleys. When Smith settled here in 1841 he probably had to clear the bottomland of cane like that along the trail at the north edge of today's field. He may also have built the rock wall that runs beside the trail, using pieces of Boone limestone fallen from the cliff above.

In more recent times this farm became the Doy Edgmon place. Today the field and house are government-owned but under long-term lease to relatives of families who have lived in the Boxley Valley for generations. The trail, however, is outside the lease area.

The path bends uphill, becomes steep, and turns up a ridge to climb past outcrops of gray limestone of the Boone Formation. At about 1400 feet elevation the trail levels off. After crossing a stream bed, the path curves back and forth, going up easy slopes through open woods. Here the exposed rock is brown sandstone—the Batesville Sandstone, the next formation above the Boone.

At about 1600 feet elevation the trail joins an old logging road along a bench, first running northwest, then north. The road emerges from the woods into an overgrown field. From here, a temporary route marked occasionally with blazes—not a built trail—continues northward for over half a mile through the field. *NOTE: This temporary route through the field to County Road 25 will eventually be replaced by a trail to be located farther up the mountainside. At that time the information on this page will be revised.*

(The Trails Illustrated map shows two separate fields along this bench, based on forest cover as it was in 1964. Later a farmer cleared the woods between the two fields, creating one long field).

The bench is developed on the Fayetteville Shale—relatively soft, easily eroded, forming benches—occurring at about 1500 to 1600 feet elevation along the Boxley Valley. Within view across the valley is **Cave Mountain,** having a prominent midlevel bench that matches this one. Also in view on Cave Mountain is its cliff of "middle Bloyd" sandstone near the summit. Northward are other mountains having midlevel benches and summit bluffs. The open field along the bench also allows for views of Boxley farms, the Baptist church, and the two-story community building.

Beside the path and partly hidden in the brush about halfway along the field is a huge sandstone boulder, 20 feet wide and 40 long, a swaybacked rock, low at the middle and rising to peaks 15 feet high at each end. Somehow, over tens of millions of years, it survived the forces of erosion that pulverized and took away everything around it. Somehow, by slow degrees—by settling, sliding, creeping from a higher elevation—it reached its present resting place. Erosion is still at work, rounding off the corners of this rock, gradually reducing it to fragments as small as those taken away in the past.

During the 1990s this field was leased by the Park Service to a local resident who supplemented his income by raising cattle. After the man became employed elsewhere and gave up the lease, much of the pasture rapidly became overgrown, and may remain so.

Toward the north end of the field the path turns downhill, becomes an uneven track through tall grass, passes a stock pond, and soon reaches County Road 25. The way then is to the right, following the road 0.5 mile east to the next junction, where a path leaves County Road 25 to descend the mountainside toward Arrington Creek. About 100 yards beyond this last junction, there is trailhead parking, a couple of head-in spaces beside the road at an old rock wall.

County Road 25 to County Road 164

5.8 miles. 610 feet of elevation gain. Moist and dry woodlands; wildflowers; homestead sites. Trailhead on County Road 25 (Walker Mountain Road) about one mile up mountain from Highway 21.

The trail leaves County Road 25 just east of a wooded area (visible on the Trails Illustrated map) that extends about 0.1 mile along the downhill side of the road, between overgrown fields. About 100 yards east of the trail junction are parking spaces at an old rock wall.

From the road, a temporary path heads almost straight downhill for about 200 yards. This path replaces a graded trail that was located a short distance to the west. During a boundary survey, the trail was found to be on private property. The Park Service in 1979 had purchased a scenic easement on this property but no trail right-of-way. *NOTE: The temporary path will eventually be replaced by a graded trail at another location. At that time the information on this page will be revised.*

At its downhill end, the temporary path joins a standard graded trail. The trail, at about 1450 feet elevation, follows the lower edge of gentle slopes (the easily eroded Fayetteville Shale) and soon overlooks steep slopes (less easily eroded, cliff-forming rock). The views downhill are toward Arrington Creek; uphill, into open woodlands.

Eventually, after crossing three wet-weather stream channels and looking into a miniature gorge cut into the gray Boone limestone, the trail joins an old logging road, bulldozed about 1960 for access to timber down the hill. These loggers, with little formal education but keen instincts for finding a way through steep, rough country, opened this track down the only feasible route into this part of Arrington Creek. Thus the trail must follow the road.

Toward the bottom of the hill the trail turns to the left off the roadway to run along a moist north slope and across smooth, slippery outcrops of Boone limestone, then down to cross **Arrington Creek**. On the other side, the trail climbs about 30 yards to a stream terrace. Along this shaded flat area—and on other terraces down the creek, off-trail—are stands of beech trees and early wildflowers.

The trail now turns up a tributary, a ravine choked with sandstone boulders that have slowly descended from higher formations as the Boone limestone has gradually dissolved away. These boulders also exhibit how natural processes can change angular, broken rock to rounded, weathered rock (as in upper photo, page 59).

Across the gully's stream bed, the trail climbs the cherty hillside, zigzags up a Boone outcrop, and crosses another cherty slope to the edge of a side canyon of Arrington Creek—ahead is a drop-off.

But up to the right is a natural stairway! Up the canyon's edge is a series of limestone ledges, 24 steps toward the top of the Boone Formation (photo, page 288). Above the stairs the trail levels out, then steps up onto the Batesville Sandstone.

Beyond is a gradual climb, on a ridge facing south and having drought-tolerant vegetation: cedars, winged elm, farkleberry. Farther up on this dry and infertile southwest-facing hillside, the dominant trees are scrubby oaks and hickories. By easy stages the trail comes to an old road trace along the bench at elevation 1600.

Within the angle where the trail now joins the road, Thomas and Jessie Wisdom built a homestead cabin shortly after 1900. After the Wisdoms went to Oklahoma, another family named Downs lived here. All that's left are a few foundation rocks and maybe one or two rotting logs. Old-timer Walter Williams of Ponca remembers the house had two rooms, one of them a lean-to with a dirt floor.

Early in the spring, however, flowering shrubs create a corridor of white along the roadway just east of the trail intersection. They are spirea—bridal wreath—planted by a woman to lend a bit of cheer to her impoverished bench homestead.

The trail follows the bench road northward for 1.5 miles, staying between 1600 and 1700 feet in elevation. Here is a west-facing slope on clay and shale, with cutover woods. Several logging tracks lead off to the left, toward the lower side of this wide bench.

Beyond the Wisdom home site 0.8 mile, a spring flows from a limestone outcrop a few yards above the road: Manchester Spring, named for Omar Manchester, another homesteader. Manchester soon left. Walter Williams says he became a railroad engineer in Kansas.

Manchester Spring is a *conduit spring*, typical of those coming from limestone. It flows rather than seeps or drips as springs do in sandstone and shale. Probably it comes from the Pitkin Limestone, the formation just above the impermeable Fayetteville Shale that underlies the bench. The Pitkin is close to the top of the mountain, so that the spring drains less than one square mile and goes almost dry in summer and fall. By 2003 feral pigs had found Manchester Spring and made it a muddy wallow.

About 80 yards beyond and 100 yards downhill from the spring is the site of another homestead. Two woman teachers, it is said, came

Natural steps.
On limestone ledges,
the Buffalo River Trail
climbs up the brink of
a deep side canyon
of Arrington Creek.

here about 1970 and began to build a solar house. Like many other back-to-the-landers, they soon gave up and left, leaving an unfinished cabin, broken fruit jars, and a ruined Royal typewriter.

About 300 yards north of the spring is more evidence of the Omar Manchester homestead. From 25 yards above the road, a sturdy rock wall runs straight up the steep hillside. Why did anyone want to build this massive wall? Was it Omar's urge to fence his only possession, this piece of rock-strewn mountainside?

Beyond the spring 0.2 mile (at elevation 1687 as shown on the topographic map) is a campsite used by volunteers building trail nearby in the spring of 1993 and of 1994. Scattered through the woods are level spaces large enough for tents.

Past the volunteers' campsite the road bends eastward, beginning to cross a north slope. Here, with more moisture than on the west-facing slope, trees are noticeably larger, and different species of trees and new kinds of wildflowers make their appearances.

A half mile from the campsite, the trail turns off the bench road and heads down a logging track. Leaving the track a quarter mile down the hill, the path crosses and then overlooks a wet-weather creek with mossy boulders and a five-foot waterfall. Soon afterward the trail reaches an abandoned quarry.

Walter Williams remembers that a man named Warren opened the quarry about 1967 to obtain limestone to be cut, polished, and sold as ornamental building stone, a product resembling marble. The developer stripped away dirt and sandstone to reveal gray limestone, which he drilled and blasted apart. From the broken rock he produced some polished stone, but people did not buy and he gave up.

The trail crosses the quarry on a natural stone floor having two-inch-diameter drill holes. Pebbles embedded in the limestone indicate that here was the surface of contact between it and the brown sandstone that formed above it. Loose rocks lying on the floor contain cylindrical fragments of crinoid stems.

The trail climbs to the upper edge of the quarry, labeled **Quarry site and overlook** on the Trails Illustrated map. The view is down a side canyon to Boxley Valley bottomland originally settled in 1838 by a family named Murphy.

On the bench behind the quarry are scraps of rusty sheet metal—another homestead site. Walter Williams says that an uncle of his, Cleve Sparks, and his wife, Tilda, homesteaded here "just to get the land." Ironically, Tilda was a granddaughter of the pioneer Murphys who had acquired fertile land in the valley below.

Cleve and Tilda (or Tildy, as local people would pronounce her name) cleared and fenced a few acres for growing corn and sorghum cane. Their livestock foraged in the surrounding woods. Their kids walked down the mountain to Beechwoods School in the valley.

About 1920 the Sparks couple sold the place, loaded household goods and children into wagons, and moved a hundred miles south to Scott County, Arkansas, where their descendants still live.

Today a part of the home site lies under piles of dirt pushed up by the quarryman, but in the woods behind the dirt piles are clumps of spirea. Maybe the two wives, Tilda Sparks and Jessie Wisdom, shared cuttings of this easily propagated shrub. It grows in either sun or shade, in almost any kind of soil.

From the quarry the trail winds down the mountainside, very soon passing a linear pile of rocks that Cleve Sparks probably put there. Then past cliff-top junipers, limestone ledges, hardwood groves, and eventually into and out of three side hollows of the Buffalo where moist north slopes have many spring wildflowers.

Even on hillsides covered with Boone chert—so abundant at times that the trail is carved into its gravelly rubble—there are stands of Ozark trillium, an endemic wildflower considered to be a "special" species if not actually endangered. On this mountain are thousands of these plants, perhaps the largest single population to be found anywhere.

Actually the side hollows provide a variety of exposures—north, east, west—and thus have varying combinations of plant species. The cool shady slopes may shelter wild orchids, usually inconspicuous little plants. One alluvial flat near a stream has Dutchman's breeches. Cherty acidic soils have huckleberry and mountain azalea. Beech trees occur where there is enough moisture.

As the trail nears the bottom of the mountain, the views downhill through the woods are into pastures, and across the Buffalo to fields, buildings, and Highway 43. The farmland is privately owned, with the Park Service holding scenic easements.

Then as the trail begins to level off, it crosses a strip of this private land marked by signs at each boundary saying STAY ON TRAIL. Cattle follow a path along this corridor into a pasture visible on the right.

In another quarter mile are **Dry Creek** and **County Road 164**.

Side trip: For a short trip to a waterfall, take County Road 164 to the bottom of the hill, 0.1 mile below the trail crossing. Then walk along the edge of the field to the right and follow a road trace into the woods. About 100 yards off Road 164 is Pearly (or Pearlie) Falls, named for Pearl Villines, who lived up the hill in the early 1900s. The waterfall is on private land but people can go and see.

County Road 164 to Ponca Low-Water Bridge

3.2 miles. 530 feet of elevation gain. Limestone outcrops; views of Boxley Valley; trail-side sinkholes. Trailhead on County Road 164, 0.3 mile south of Buffalo River ford; see instructions below.

To reach the trailhead, either (a) follow a roundabout route and then drive three miles down the mountain on County Road 164 (Watson-Williams road), using the *Ponca* and *Murray* topographic maps or a Newton County road map for guidance; or (b) drive in from Highway 43 if the river is low enough so that it can be forded.

County Road 164 is narrow and steep, and when wet can be very slick. The river ford washes out during floods; normally it is useable only in the summer and fall. Use a high-clearance vehicle, preferably four-wheel drive. If the weather is moderate, consider parking at the turnout on Highway 43 south of Clark Creek, then wading the County Road 164 ford to get to the trail. (Leave the road gates at the river as you found them, whether open or closed.)

At the trailhead, where the trail crosses County Road 164, pull in and park on the old roadway that the trail follows.

Above the trail 200 feet from County Road 164 are foundation stones of the early 1900s home of Hezekiah and Pearl Villines. Hezekiah had a Villines cousin, also named Hezekiah, across the river. To distinguish between them (not because of their appearances) the cousin was "Pretty Hez" and the one here was "Ugly Hez."

Pearl's name was attached to Pearly Falls down the hill (see *Side trip*, page 290) and to Pearly Spring, on private land a short distance below the trail. The spring was the household water supply, and Hez rigged wires and pulleys to facilitate delivery. Pearl could crank a bucket down the wire, have it dip into the spring, and bring it back full, doing it all from the front porch.

Leaving the old roadbed just beyond the Hez home site, the trail runs for a quarter mile along a shady north-facing hillside, then descends into a strip of privately owned pasture along **Running Creek,** where STAY ON TRAIL signs mark the boundaries. Beyond the creek (either a wade or a rock-hop to get across) the trail ascends a low bluff. Here is one of the farthest upriver exposures of the Newton Sandstone, which becomes more than 100 feet thick a few miles down the Buffalo.

For the next half mile the trail climbs up a side valley. Soon after the climb begins, the St. Joe Limestone's layer of red rock can be seen down in the hollow to the left, in a low bluff at a six-foot waterfall. This red St. Joe rock is at the base of the Boone Formation. The Boone's gray limestone and broken chert then are present all the way up the hill, even after the trail levels off at about 1400 feet elevation.

By that time the path is along the rim of the Boxley Valley, soon passing through "rock city," 300 yards of limestone outcrops and ledges that overlook Highway 43, the Lost Valley entrance road, and white-painted Beechwoods Church and its cemetery.

The trail bends uphill, away from the valley rim and toward a wide bench above elevation 1500. Soon it goes past a shallow **sinkhole** about 40 feet across, then another sink about eight feet in diameter.

Loggers about 1960 opened haul roads along this bench. The trail reaches the end of one of these roads, a log-loading site where several discarded oak stave bolts remained into the 1990s (see related photo, page 99). From there the path is on logging tracks above **Big Hollow**, running along the lower edge of the bench, crossing small streams that all head down to steep drop-offs into the hollow.

Rock exposures along the trail are of the Fayetteville Shale that lies above the Boone limestone. Toward the north side of Big Hollow, blue-black shale appears in the footpath. Shale of this color was formed when sediments lacked oxygen to decompose all the organic matter, as in the still water of a swamp or lagoon. Exposed to air, blackish shale weathers to sticky reddish or yellowish clay.

Here also is poor soil, if any at all. But here is interesting vegetation, a dryland forest with post oak, hawthorn, and huckleberry.

Then the logging road/trail begins a three-quarter-mile downgrade to the Ponca bridge. Almost immediately there's a **sinkhole**, a pit 8 feet across and about 15 feet deep, to the left of the trail. Cavers who mapped this Leatherwood Sink Cave found that its single passage at the bottom extends about 40 feet under the hillside.

On both sides of trail here, several shallow funnel sinks are aligned with the open pit, evidence of collapse along a fracture of the underlying limestone. The surface rock, however, is sandstone, as revealed in the sides of the pit. Here, and elsewhere at this elevation just above the Boone Formation, the overlying porous Batesville Sandstone allowed acidic rainwater to enter cracks in the Boone limestone. Solution cavities developed along those cracks and the Batesville has settled or collapsed into the cavities.

A short distance downhill from the sinkholes, the trail crosses a level bench where limestone outcrops have odd shapes, the result of past immersion and dissolving by acidic water. The path then heads down the ridge between the river and **Leatherwood Creek**.

At one point there are views off the ridge, looking up the Boxley Valley, down to Highways 43 and 74 at the Buffalo River bridge, and up the Adds Creek side valley to Ponca. Then the trail becomes very steep, down a shaded east-facing hillside having large beech trees. Toward the bottom of the hill, the path crosses exposed red rock of the St. Joe Limestone—not obvious, but it can be seen—that signals the beginning of older geologic formations ahead.

Soon after that, the trail reaches the Ponca low-water bridge.

Ponca Low-Water Bridge to Steel Creek

1.8 miles. 280 feet of elevation gain. Views of river from low and high bluffs. Trailhead at east end of Ponca low-water bridge.

Trailhead parking is at the west end of the Ponca low-water bridge. To get on the trail, walk across the bridge and continue past the barrier across the old roadway 50 yards beyond the bridge. (The trail upriver also begins at the east end of the bridge.)

The trail passes under the Highway 74 bridge and into the woods. The next half mile, an easy walk with only minor ups and downs, is on the Newton Sandstone, sometimes bare rock, sometimes with a thin covering of soil and green moss with patches of pale-green lichens. At one point, rows of lichen-crusted rocks mark old fence lines, and on the right, a few rock piles in the woods suggest this gentle slope may have had a cleared field. If so, it was part of the early 1900s farm of Beaver Jim Villines (see pages 276–278).

Soon there is steeper, drier ground, acidic soil with patches of low-bush huckleberry and clumps of mountain azalea. The trail comes close to the edge of the sandstone bluff and overlooks the river about fifty feet below. Here are top-heavy, shallow-rooted cedars downed by strong winds. One fallen cedar pulled a slab of rock upright in its roots. With some of those roots in soil, the cedar stays alive.

The trail turns upslope onto a logging track, then turns off the road and into a moist, north-facing hollow. Christmas ferns grow here, and gray-barked beech trees are scattered across the lower slopes.

Crossing a watercourse on bedrock, the path begins a 200-yard hill climb. Here in March 1991 a windstorm toppled big beech trees. Their prostrate trunks have decayed on the hillside, leaving mounds of dirt and rocks that had clung to upturned roots. Blackberries and many seedling trees have filled openings where the big trees fell.

Leveling off, the path enters another north-facing ravine, then crosses two stream courses. In wet weather, twin waterfalls come off the 20-foot bluff, then off ledges uphill from the trail. In cold, wet January, these two creeks see no sun and become frozen cascades.

Above the trail, at the falls, the red layer of the St. Joe Limestone appears in the base of the cliff, and more red St. Joe rock will be seen in the next half mile along this high bench. This red rock signals not only presence of the St. Joe, but also of softer rock just downhill, eroded to form a shelf, or bench, suited for a trail. Such is the case here—and for the Goat Trail across Big Bluff, and for half a mile of

Upstream portal.
Passing between bluff and pillar at this highest point between Ponca and Steel Creek, the Buffalo River Trail is at the upper end of the river's canyon from Ponca to Erbie.

The path here is 300 feet above the river.

this Buffalo River Trail as it goes along a bench just below the red St. Joe across the river from Big Bluff.

Beyond the falls the path turns onto a drier, west-facing slope, without beech trees but with cedars. Here again are trees downed by the 1991 windstorm. Sun-loving greenbrier and green-barked rattan vines invaded open spaces among wind-splintered cedar trees.

One short stretch of trail is built on broken rock, Boone chert and a few flakes or slabs of red St. Joe, all fallen down here from points above. A low cliff of limestone becomes visible up the hill.

Downriver in the near distance is the high wall of **Bee Bluff**. Beyond that is the upstream end of **Roark Bluff**. To the left across the river, scattered cedars and a grove of pines provide contrasting color to the gray-brown of winter hardwoods on the mountainside.

The path climbs to the foot of the limestone cliff, then up several steps to a narrow gap between the cliff and a standing pillar of rock. Underfoot at these steps is a flush-cut cedar stump. That tree was probably cut about 1905, when loggers here were harvesting virgin cedar for lead pencils (pages 97–98; photo, page 99). Cedar heartwood is very resistant to rot, so the stump has stayed.

This passage between cliff and pillar (photo, above) provides a sort of symbolic upstream entry to the Buffalo River's canyon trail extending downriver to Erbie, where another cliff/pillar gap along the trail marks the canyon's downstream end (photo, page 306).

For 150 yards beyond the standing pillar, the trail goes along the foot of the cliff, with more red, shaly St. Joe in and beside the path.

Then it continues along a ledge that now lies high above Bee Bluff. Here are two species of trees found only on outcrops of limestone. One is Ashe's juniper, related to eastern red cedar but usually having several trunks and shrubby form, unlike single-stemmed red cedar.

The other limestone specialist is American smoke tree. Past the year 2003, at least, a smoke tree stood just below this trail where the path crosses a six-foot-long slab of red St. Joe Limestone. Smoke trees usually have several stems, both living and dead. There are oval leaves and feathery flower clusters like puffs of smoke.

The trail turns downhill. Views open up, downriver to Roark Bluff and upstream past Bee Bluff. Across the river is a long abandoned farm, the Clemmer place, its fields overtaken by cedars, hardwoods, and evergreen patches of switch cane.

Down the trail, a barrier warns hikers away from loose gravel near the cliff's edge and a plank provides a seat for taking in the view.

From here to the trailhead the path goes along, down, and below this bluff of Newton Sandstone. Down below the bluff, the path becomes easier as the slope tapers off, finally, to a sandy incline at the trailhead across the road from Steel Creek's campsites.

Steel Creek to Kyles Landing
8.4 miles. 1570 feet of elevation gain. Trail crosses Ponca Wilderness with high, panoramic views. Trailhead at marker post near restrooms across road from Steel Creek campsites.

The path first goes through a dense patch of switch cane, following a road trace. Leaving the roadway, the trail runs along the hillside in the woods, with a view through the trees and across the field to the sheer 100-foot wall of **Roark Bluff**. The cliff is more than 200 yards away but still produces an echo to a loud yell.

Rounded rocks lie along the trail. Thousands of years ago the Buffalo River deposited gravel and cobbles at this elevation, about 40 feet higher than the river's present course.

The trail soon enters an area cleared for pasture about 1960, when Steel Creek was part of an Arabian horse ranch. Since 1975, when the Park Service purchased the property, this hillside has been allowed to revert to forest through the gradual process of old-field succession.

Half a mile from the trailhead, the path crosses Steel Creek's entrance road. Forty yards beyond the road, the trail passes beneath what may be the Buffalo River's largest beech tree. When measured in 1999 this giant was three feet two and a half inches in diameter.

Soon the trail climbs, gaining 100 feet in elevation to bypass the buildings at the Steel Creek ranger station. The path dodges past big boulders, climbs, passes a low cliff of the Newton Sandstone—the same rock as in Roark Bluff across the river—then gradually descends toward **Steel Creek**. Here the hillside faces northeast, with a mesic (moderately moist) forest having beech trees and spicebush.

Past a wet-weather stream that spills down sandstone ledges, the trail reaches the moist, fertile bottomland along Steel Creek, a good place for seeing woodland wildflowers in early spring.

Then a rock-hop across the creek to a west-facing slope: drier, acidic soil, where sweet-smelling wild azaleas bloom in early May. (When crossing Steel Creek one also enters the Ponca Wilderness.) Beyond the creek the trail goes up steps cut into ledges of Newton Sandstone, passes cedars downed by a windstorm in March 1991, then swings to the left above a ravine having three noisy little water-falls—five feet, eight feet, five feet—hidden by trees. At the ravine overlook, low- and high-bush huckleberries grow on the acid soil.

The trail climbs, passes along a bench, and climbs a flight of steps to a higher slope. At the next stream course, water drips and slides down ledges. Venus maidenhair fern grows from a wet crevice in the carbonate rock a few yards above the trail.

Another unusual species that grows only on limestone, American smoke tree, is along the trail as it climbs beyond the stream. Smoke trees have oval leaves, scaly bark, and multiple stems. In May their feathery clusters of tiny pinkish flowers look like puffs of smoke.

The path levels off, turning across a broad bench where the 1991 windstorm knocked down cedars and oaks, opening sunny spaces soon filled with thickets of weeds and saplings. Leaving the bench, the path goes up a sloping ramp between a low bluff and a long "slump block" that separated from the bluff and crept down-slope. Here the red St. Joe Limestone makes its appearance. The St. Joe, at the base of the Boone Formation, means that the trail will be on the Boone's limestone and chert for hundreds of feet higher.

Boone chert—broken, gravelly—now appears on the trail. Another seasonal creek comes down on solid limestone. The trail steps up from the creek bed on limestone ledges. Beyond the creek a dry, open hillside faces southwest, with outcrops of gray limestone, patches of prairie grasses, sun-loving greenbrier, and smoke trees. Other trees, too—scrubby oaks, hickories, hackberry, ash, winged elm. Red cedar and shrubby Ashe's juniper. Here is poor ground, inaccessible. There is no timber to harvest and never has been. This is noncommercial forest…virgin forest.

Or it's a scrub forest invading a glade. Without occasional fires to kill the woody seedlings, trees are getting ahead of the prairie plants.

The trail becomes level, pleasant, uneventful—to the brink of a cliff, more than 300 feet above the river! Down to the left of this **overlook** are Steel Creek developments, Roark Bluff, and the river upstream. Straight ahead and downriver are another high bluff, wooded mountainsides, and distant ridges—the view on the front of Trails Illustrated's *Buffalo National River, West Half* map.

A few yards back from the cliff's edge, the trail continues uphill—up a flight of steps past spreading dark-green Ashe's junipers, then across and up a steep slope having limestone ledges and smoke trees along the path. Then up a winding stair that climbs an outcrop of rock. Finally the trail levels off.

Here are two odd pieces of limestone lying below the trail. One is all curves. The other, more oblong, suggests figures carved on a totem pole. Both were shaped eons ago by acidic water that dissolved the surrounding rock. Volunteers uncovered them when building this trail in 1987. One of the workers thought they looked like the creations of abstract sculptor Constantin Brancusi.

The path now crosses a steep open slope. The view is much the same as from the overlook back down the trail, but here the height is dizzying, nearly 500 feet above the Buffalo. And looking directly down on the river, one gets a better sense of the shape of its meanders carved deep into the Boston Mountains.

This highest overlook area is a glade that has developed on underlying limestone. Smoke trees occur frequently along the trail, along with native grasses, wildflowers, and other kinds of trees. Unless red cedar was cut here long ago, this can be called virgin forest.

Indeed, for a quarter mile beyond the glade the trail crosses a 40-acre block of land that no one thought worth acquiring from the public domain. On the west side of **Fisher Point** and extending from the river to the top of the ridge, at least half the 40 acres is isolated by vertical cliffs and the remainder is a scrub hardwood forest. After creation of Buffalo National River the tract was transferred from the federal Bureau of Land Management to the National Park Service.

At about the north edge of the 40-acre tract the trail starts downhill. Soon it passes a series of funnel-shaped holes. Some are natural sinks in the Boone limestone. Several with mounds of dirt beside them were made by prospectors for lead or zinc, probably during World War I, when prices for ore were high and nearby Ponca was the center of a mining boom. Ore often was found in sinks or crevices in the Boone, and the owner of this property must have hoped to strike it rich. He dug these holes but found nothing. The ore occurred instead along a line of geologic faults closer to Ponca.

As the trail approaches the end of its downgrade, a few rounded pebbles and cobbles can be found in the pathway. Are these remnants of a Buffalo River gravel bar from the distant past when the river flowed at this elevation of about 1350 feet, nearly 400 feet above its present level? We cannot be sure, for the evidence is too sparse.

Rounding the north end of Fisher Point ridge, the path descends to a bench at elevation 1300 feet. Here on a moist, northeast slope are big trees, limestone outcrops with moss and walking fern, and dense stands of beech saplings ("sons-of-beeches," a wit once declared).

Turning right to avoid the largest patch of young beeches, the trail passes below a huge tilted rock, 15 feet high and 30 feet wide, that has separated from the bluff behind it. Here again is the red layer of St. Joe Limestone, in the base of the tilted block and in broken pieces along the trail. And here as elsewhere, the red St. Joe lies just above softer rock that forms a bench, good for locating a trail.

Below this bench is a drop-off. Eventually the trail reaches an opening at the edge of the cliff, an **overlook**. This place has a clear view to **Big Bluff**, a half mile to the north. The 560-foot cliff looks small; it needs to have a canoe on the river below it, or hikers on the Goat Trail across it, to provide a sense of scale.

The Goat Trail appears to be at about the same elevation as this bench having the Buffalo River Trail. And, barely visible from here, is a red streak of St. Joe just above the Goat Trail, further proof that Mother Nature created places for trails just below that red rock.

Beyond the overlook the trail trends uphill for 200 feet, away from the river and onto a level "loading deck" where timber men about 1960 rolled logs onto a truck at the end of a bulldozed haul road. The road, now the trail, follows a bench a short distance to where the road headed straight down the nose of the ridge (with the loaded truck in compound-low gear and its driver riding the brake). Instead, the trail turns right to descend at an easier grade.

This brief downhill stretch ends at a spring-fed stream, where the trail finds another logging track down the branch, soon to turn onto the main-stem logging road up the west side of **Beech Creek.** For nearly half a mile the trail stays on the road, which follows a bench at about 1200 feet elevation and developed just above the massive Newton Sandstone. A few yards to the left of the trail the sandstone bluff drops off 50 feet or more. Farther along the trail the soil is sandy, acidic, with patches of huckleberry and scattered pine trees.

The trail turns off into the woods, closer to the edge of the bluff, where sandstone outcrops are decorated with gray-green lichens. Then down 37 steps through breaks in the cliff, and across the hillside to a four-way intersection with an old roadway, the Beech Creek horse trail, now 0.9 mile past the overlook to Big Bluff.

To the left, the horse trail follows the road trace down Beech Creek to the Buffalo and fords the river to intersect the Old River Trail. To the right, the Beech Creek horse trail is on woods roads to the top of Fisher Point ridge and along the ridge toward Low Gap, about three miles south. Straight ahead, the hiking trail follows a logging road 0.1 mile to Beech Creek, where the crossing is on bedrock at the head of a cascading waterfall—when Beech Creek is flowing. The creek is only two miles long and most often its stream bed is dry.

East of Beech Creek the trail climbs to about 1200 feet, to the bench above the Newton Sandstone along this side of the valley, and passes through a sandstone glade on a southwest slope. With decades of protection from fire, woody plants have encroached on this remnant of prairie. Even so, a botanist has called the assemblage of plants here "unique in the upper river area…probably the best example of a glade community found in the upper and middle sections of the riverway."

The trail continues through the woods. Where the path finally turns into a side hollow, it is fully a mile by trail, but barely a quarter mile straight back across Beech Creek to the trail's path at about the same elevation atop the sandstone cliff on the other side.

Crossing the stream bed in the side hollow, the trail begins a long and sometimes steep climb, passing from Newton Sandstone to Boone limestone and chert, finally to reach sandstone and the lower edge of the bench on the Fayetteville Shale at elevation 1600. Along the way are big hardwoods on north slopes. Farther up the trail are glimpses down into the depths of **Jackies Big Hollow**.

Still farther uphill at about 1750 feet is an intersection with an old road. To the right a path follows the bench along the west side of **Kilgore Mountain** (see page 316) to County Road 143 toward Low Gap. Turning to the left, the Buffalo River Trail follows the roadway 0.4 mile to a gap, or saddle, between higher slopes. To the right is a small, shallow pond probably bulldozed around 1960 as part of a waterholes-for-wildlife program. On the left 50 yards beyond the pond is an outcrop of flaky shale. Someone thought the shale was slate and named this spot **the Slatey Place**. The shale bed is surrounded by gnarled oaks no one considered worth cutting, so here is some virgin forest. That, and in summer this saddle can become a "wind gap" having a cooling breeze to fan the perspiring hiker.

The Slatey Place is a trail junction. This Buffalo River Trail, here open to hikers and horseback riders, has come in from the south and turns east. A trail to Horseshoe Bend heads north (see page 317).

For more than a mile the Buffalo River Trail continues along the bench east of the Slatey Place, staying at about 1700 feet, across the end of Kilgore Mountain. The shady, moist north slope has large, mature-looking hardwoods, expecially toward the east end of the bench, where grapevines hanging from the trees lend a jungle effect.

This trail along the bench was opened in the summers of 1984 and 1985 by high-school kids sponsored by the Student Conservation Association. In places they had heavy work—stepping stones, retaining walls. At one spot they installed a stone seat (with space underneath where snakes can hide).

At the east end of the bench the trail merges with a loggers' haul road. The timber cutters knew the terrain and so picked the only feasible route for taking logs off this corner of Kilgore Mountain. From the main-stem road along the bench, their spur road (now the trail) plunges down the hill, swings left and then right to continue down an extremely steep mountainside where the river can be seen more than 500 feet below. And so down to a cramped switchback.

Apparently the log truck driver would head into a level spot off the end of the switchback, then back his truck another 75 yards to a dead end where logs were loaded. Then go back, somehow squeezing around the switchback and heading up grades at times more than 20 percent, finally reaching the bench road toward Low Gap. When laying out these roads the loggers seemed to know the absolute most a loaded truck could do. Maximum grades were about 22 percent.

The hiking trail leaves the log-loading area and goes about 250 feet across the hillside to an intersection. The Buffalo River Trail turns down steps to the right, while a spur path goes straight ahead for ten yards to an **overlook** about 400 feet above the river. There a squat pillar of rock provides a seat for contemplating the view.

Only 0.2 mile farther down the mountain (and across two more old logging tracks) is another **overlook,** above **Indian Creek.** The view unfortunately does not include the creek's spectacular upper canyon, which is just around the bend to the right.

From this overlook the trail goes along the wooded hillside, then briefly on a logging road, then along and down a narrow spine of broken rock—Newton Sandstone—between Indian Creek and the Buffalo River. Then across Indian Creek, normally a dry bed of cobblestones, and quickly to two more intersections. The first is with a path up Indian Creek (see page 323). Near this junction the Buffalo River Trail leaves the Ponca Wilderness.

At the next fork a path goes downriver past **Gray Rock**, and the Buffalo River Trail heads uphill to the right, on an old farm road. About 500 feet up the hill is a clearing. On the right are the ruins of a barn and then red-flowering japonica (Japanese quince) shrubs that mark the site of the house, once the home for a family named Arbaugh. The trail here becomes level, crossing the hillside.

About 250 yards beyond the first japonica bushes, the trail passes just below another thicket of japonica. At this homesite, foundation stones are the remains of a little log house where Frank Villines (1885–1979) and his wife Frankie (1895–1970) lived for forty years (c. 1918–1958).

A few yards south of the Villines cabin was the dormitory living unit of Kyle's Boys Home, built in 1969 and removed in 1978 (see *Kyles Landing*, below). The Park Service sold the dorm building to a

Kyles Landing. Kyle Harris was the youngest son of a Baptist preacher at a church near Houston, Texas. During the 1960s the father, Reverend Floyd Harris, and his son dreamed of creating a home for boys from broken families, on land the elder Harris and friends owned here on the Buffalo River. In 1967, thirteen-year-old Kyle was killed in an accident, but in 1969, Floyd Harris opened Kyle's Boys Home with a dormitory housing 12 boys and two houseparents. Harris wanted to have facilities here for 500 boys but was unable to fund a larger program. In 1973 he sold the property to the Park Service. Apparently the sale agreement provided that this public use area be named for Kyle.

salvager. After it was removed the site's original slope was restored.

From the Villines cabin site it is a short walk downhill to a junction with a road trace, part of the Old River Trail (see page 322). To the left the road goes upriver. To the right, the Buffalo River Trail and Old River Trail share the roadway as it passes along the edge of an overgrown bottomland field. The Buffalo River is 200 yards north, beyond the field, but here in the road are river-rounded cobbles, evidence that the Buffalo was much closer thousands of years ago.

The trail passes another intersection where the Buffalo River Trail, headed downriver, goes to the right. Straight ahead, the road trace very soon reaches the trailhead parking area at Kyles Landing.

Kyles Landing to Parker-Hickman Farmstead

6.3 miles. 960 feet of elevation gain. Bluff-top views; side-canyon creeks; historic cemetery; wildlife pastures. Trailhead at left (west) end of Kyles Landing campground, at bulletin board.

From the trailhead parking area, a short connecting trail goes across **Bear Creek**—normally a dry wash—to intersect the Buffalo River Trail. At the intersection the trail downriver goes to the left.

For nearly half a mile the trail follows an old haul road that loggers about 1965 bulldozed up Bear Creek as far as they could go. A visitor at that time reported that "all large trees within sight of the road have been cut." Today the forest shows little evidence of that.

At first the valley along the trail is wide enough so that a farmer once may have attempted to clear the level ground, leaving several piles of rocks now surrounded by woods. Spicebush and leatherwood grow here, indicating the soil is moist and fertile.

Soon the valley becomes very narrow. On crossing Bear Creek once more, the trail heads up a west-facing hillside. The forest changes. Here are pine trees, huckleberry, and an occasional clump of azalea. There are many boulders that have come down from the cliff that soon looms uphill. Rocks and cliff are Newton Sandstone, the same as in the high bluff that faces the river at Kyles Landing.

The path climbs to the foot of the cliff, then up a flight of steps and into a narrow gap between the bluff and an outlying mass of rock. Then onto the top of the cliff, where for more than 100 yards it runs alongside pine trees and high-bush huckleberry. Here the views are attractive, especially when sunlight filters through the pine boughs.

Leaving the cliff, the trail climbs to a crossing of the Kyles access road at elevation 1300 feet, now more than 400 feet above the river. Beyond the crossing the trail continues to climb in order to pass above 490-foot **Buzzard Bluff**. From the road, the trail at first is on the Boone Formation's gray limestone and broken chert, but as it crosses above the summit of Buzzard Bluff, the path is on Batesville Sandstone and Fayetteville Shale that lie above the Boone.

Before leaving the top of Buzzard Bluff, the trail provides a view upriver to the cliffs at Kyles Landing. Then the path bends away from the river, crosses a stream bed, and heads downhill. Soon it enters private property, the Boy Scouts' **Camp Orr** (see page 304), whose boundary was marked with blue paint blazes. The trail crosses this boundary six times as it winds in and out of camp property.

Down this lengthy grade on a north-facing hillside, the trees were last cut before Camp Orr was established in 1955, and some of the largest hardwoods have been toppled by wind. Farther downhill the trail passes among outcrops of Boone limestone and the trees become smaller, with red cedars growing among the ledges.

Suddenly the trail turns right, into the steep-sided watershed of **Shop Creek** (at this turn a path goes left, down the hill into Camp Orr). Twenty yards beyond the right turn is a view into Shop Creek's canyon and to Mutton Point, nearly two miles to the east.

Along the moist, east-facing slope above Shop Creek are limestone ledges, patches of switch cane and greenbrier, and scrubby trees—a noncommercial forest, likely never logged. Approaching the creek, the trail is built on broken limestone, a talus slope below a cliff. Leaf-cup, a tall, rank-smelling plant with small white flowers, grows abundantly among the loose rocks along the trail.

Shop Creek at the trail crossing is usually dry; the stream is underground. This crossing is within the northeast corner of a 40-acre block of land too rugged and isolated for anyone to acquire from the public domain as a homestead. The view up the creek from the crossing is into the heart of this area—virgin forest.

As the trail goes down the east side of Shop Creek it passes many large boulders of sandstone. But the bluff across the creek is limestone, and so is a 25-foot cliff about 100 feet uphill from the trail. As in other side canyons of the upper Buffalo, the sandstone boulders are broken remnants from a much higher formation. Over millions of years they fell, rolled, slid, and crept down to present-day Shop Creek as the limestone below them dissolved away.

This slope along the east side of the creek has enough moisture and shade for plenty of moss and Christmas fern, for a colony of walking ferns on a big boulder beside the trail, and for tall trees among the boulders at the creek. Soon, however, the trail climbs to drier ground that receives more sun, with a more open woodland.

The path then crosses a ridge having pieces of sandstone both large and small, and sandy soil where the rock has disintegrated. Here too the sandstone originated much higher up, perhaps even from the cap rock, whose bluffs are in sight up the power line right-of-way that the trail crosses at the crest of the ridge.

Camp Orr, first opened in 1955, belongs to the Boy Scouts of America's Westark Area Council, in charge of Scouting activities in 19 counties of northwestern Arkansas. The camp is named for Raymond F. Orr, a Scout leader who played a major role in acquiring the land and raising money for initial development.

By the year 2000, Camp Orr staff and volunteer leaders were serving more than 1800 Scouts each summer, teaching merit-badge classes and camping skills. The camp's name had become Camp Orr Adventure Base, reflecting expansion of the program to include rappeling, backpacking, and overnight canoe trips. The camp's week-long sessions through June and July were attracting many Scout troops from outside the Westark Council and from states outside Arkansas.

In 1984 the Council and the National Park Service reached an agreement under which the Park Service purchased 375 acres of Camp Orr's outlying undeveloped land and scenic easements on the remaining 470 acres, including the area having developed facilities. Essentially, the Council can continue to serve youth with its Boy Scout camp, but the Park Service purchased rights to prevent other kinds of development of the property, such as for agriculture, residences, or tourism. The Park Service paid $522,000 for the land and the easements. The Council put the money in a trust fund whose income was to be used for camp-related projects.

The Scouts' property at Camp Orr is located on one or both sides of the Buffalo from near river mile 39.0 to 41.5. The river and a narrow strip on each side are federally owned, with Camp Orr having a special-use permit for organized swimming and boating. Because the camp is private property dedicated to use by the Scouts, there is no public access or camping except by permission of the Westark Council.

Past the power line and into the woods are more sandstone boulders, then limestone again at **Rock Bridge Creek**, where the stream has worn a trench in bedrock, a water slide from pothole to pothole. Beyond Rock Bridge are limestone ledges and rubbly chert. Soon the trail crosses the access road to the Boy Scouts' Camp Orr.

Toward **Dry Creek**, east of the Camp Orr road, the trail follows logging tracks; on the last downgrade to the creek it passes a bluff of the Newton Sandstone. Beyond the creek bed (usually dry, as the name indicates) the path approaches a 30-foot cliff where trickling water becomes glistening ice in winter. The trail then climbs onto the Boone Formation and is on rubbly Boone chert as it winds in and out of the river's side hollows. Beyond the Camp Orr road 1.1 miles, a short connecting trail goes downhill to the Old River Trail.

Near that connecting trail are traces of skid ways—straight gullies down the hill made by loggers when skidding (dragging) logs downhill to be loaded on a truck. Stumps and other debris from timber cutting have rotted away, but past year 2000 the forest here was young, a "pole farm" of small but tall trees on this part of the mountain.

The hillside becomes steep. A 15-foot bluff appears above the trail. The river lies almost directly 150 feet below. Then the path arrives at a climb up 31 steps, native rocks placed on a high-angle slope.

About 75 yards beyond is a lesser flight of steps, up past an outcrop of red St. Joe Limestone. Very soon the path is along the base of a 30-foot limestone cliff—the view is straight down to the river.

And then another set of steps, 14 this time, up through a narrow gap between the cliff and a pillar of rock (photo, page 306). This is the symbolic exit for the Buffalo River Trail's passage down the canyon from its upstream end near Ponca. From here the trail is on gentler terrain, though no less interesting.

Beyond the natural gateway, the path curves across cherty hillsides and comes to a graded dirt road. To the right, the road winds through the woods for 0.8 mile to the Parker-Hickman farmstead. The Buffalo River Trail follows the road to the left, and in 250 yards reaches one of the river's most historic graveyards, the privately owned **Cherry Grove Cemetery**. Graves include those of Nathaniel Villines (1816–1870), a member of the original Villines family that settled along the upper Buffalo, and Joseph Buchanan (1827–1864), who was killed during the Civil War. Members of the pioneer Cecil family are here also. A number of grave markers from those early times were made by local artisans. A few of these tombstones of the

Downstream portal.
At the eastern end of the Buffalo River's canyon through the Boston Mountains from Ponca to Erbie, this gap between cliff and pillar marks the edge of the Bostons at the Springfield Plateau.

softer red layer of the St. Joe Limestone have begun to break apart.

A hundred yards past the cemetery, the trail leaves the roadway and heads into a stand of cedars that have taken over an old field. For 300 yards across the field, cedars, other woody plants, and rank grass have competed for dominance. Beginning in the mid-1990s, the Park Service did prescribed burns in this area to thin out the encroaching cedars and encourage grass. One reason for burning is to maintain some of the historic appearance of the Erbie farming community. Another is that it provides a grazing area for elk.

The path enters the woods and goes along a hillside facing the river. Soon it passes a spring flowing from a pool, formerly enclosed by a wooden curb to make a rectangular basin for watering livestock. Venus maidenhair fern grows beside the pool.

After a brief detour into a side drainage known as White Oak Hollow, the trail again overlooks the Buffalo, passes for a moment under a low cliff, and arrives at a junction with a path to the left.

The path is short, ending on a ledge about 25 feet above the river. Embedded in the ledge are two heavy steel rods that once anchored the cables for a footbridge. Local old-timer Robert Hickman says it was built in the 1930s. Volunteers made holes in the rock with a hammer and hand drill, then drove the anchor rods into the holes. On the low bank across the river, workers erected two sturdy posts to support the bridge. Then they strung cables, built decking, and tied the deck to handrails. "It was a community project," says Hickman.

Families moved away and the swinging footbridge was not maintained. By the 1970s its floorboards had fallen away and the Park Service took down the cables to prevent accidents.

On that short spur path to the bridge site is a flight of seven steps. Beside the bottom step is a sloping rock having a bas-relief figure that appears to be a kneeling woman facing to the right with one arm outstretched behind her. Local people called it an Indian maiden, but the lady looks entirely too robust to be one of those stick figures of Native American rock art. Was this instead the work of some farm boy carving a likeness of his girlfriend?

From the spur path the main trail climbs to the top of the bluff and heads downriver at the edge of a hayfield. Rising beyond the field is the northern extension of Sherman Mountain, **Mutton Point**, 1200 feet higher in elevation than the trail and the last Boston Mountain ridge that flanks the upper Buffalo's canyon on the south.

Very soon the view across the river is into the mouth of **Cove Creek**. In sight only yards below the creek is a **ford** of the river; water spills noisily off the downstream side of the concrete roadway. As the trail continues along the edge of the hill, it intersects a spur path going down to the road that crosses the Buffalo at the ford.

Bending away from the river, the main trail goes past the hayfield. Here also, the Park Service removed encroaching cedars to maintain the historic farm clearing and provide pasturage for elk.

Finally the trail re-enters the woods and heads downhill to the dirt road that comes from the Cherry Grove Cemetery. At the road is the **Parker-Hickman farmstead** (photos, pages 263 and 308). A trailhead parking area is outside the front gate.

Parker-Hickman Farmstead to Erbie Trailhead

1.1 miles. 150 feet of elevation gain. Limestone glade; viewpoint; "rock city." Trailhead at Parker-Hickman farmstead parking area.

From the parking area the trail heads south along a tree-shaded lane following **Webb Branch** (Parker Branch). Soon the lane joins a traveled driveway that goes uphill to the right and outside the park; the trail continues straight ahead on the road. After crossing Webb Branch on a concrete slab, the trail leaves the road and heads through

Parker-Hickman cabin. This oldest known structure along the Buffalo was built between 1847 and 1849, apparently by brothers Alvin and Greenberry Parker, who had come from Tennessee. They were careful builders, cutting the chimney blocks to fit the dimensions of the stack, joining the cedar logs at the corners so snugly a knife blade cannot be inserted in the half-dovetailing.

The Parkers sold the farm in 1857; some of the family moved to California. Later owners added outbuildings that date from the late 1800s to the 1950s, and on one side of the cabin put a lean-to room that in the 1920s sheltered a country store. From 1912 to 1978 the house was occupied by the Hickman family.

The Park Service bought the property in 1982 and in 1984 stabilized the cabin and outbuildings. The cabin's chimney was taken down and rebuilt, log chinking was repaired, and deteriorated wood and stone were replaced with new material to match. A preservation worker who inspected the cedar joists under the floor declared they were "as sound as the day they were built."

In 1987 the 195-acre property was entered on the National Register of Historic Places as the Parker-Hickman Farm Historic District. Reminders of the past include the house, outbuildings, fence lines, livestock feeders, and road traces.

In this view of the house, the "snow" actually is green foliage, recorded as almost white by infrared film. (For another infrared scene by photographer Dale Burris, see page 277.)

a small glade, a dry sunny area with bare limestone and prickly pear.

After crossing another track that goes outside the park, the trail heads up a side drainage east of Webb Branch, an area of cedar trees, limestone ledges, and sparse, droughty soil. Farther up the hill, large amounts of rubbly chert litter the surface of the ground.

The path crosses the top of the ridge and continues along the north side, soon rising slightly to a high point. Here on the left is a flat rock about six by eight feet, a viewpoint. Straight down below is the entrance to the Erbie campground; beyond are the Buffalo River and mountains to the north. The most prominent peak looks like a mesa—flat-topped, cliff-ringed—but actually is **Newberry Point**, an arm of Gaither Mountain, which lies beyond. Gaither's entire summit area is relatively flat and connects along watershed divides to other summit areas to form the Boston Mountains plateau surface.

The viewpoint, though, is on the next-lower level from the Boston Mountains, the Springfield Plateau. Much of the Springfield, including almost this entire stretch of trail, is surfaced with limestone and chert of the Boone Formation. As the path begins to descend from the viewpoint, it winds among moss-cushioned ledges and free-standing outcrops of the Boone, a "city of rocks" on the hillside.

Leaving the big rocks behind, the trail continues downhill, swings to the left past a stream bed of sandstone—now below the Boone Formation—and soon crosses the Erbie road from Highway 7. Just beyond the road is a trail intersection. To the right the Buffalo River Trail continues downstream. To the left a spur trail goes 0.1 mile to the Erbie trailhead, just uphill from Erbie's boat landing.

(This section of the Buffalo River Trail is part of the South Erbie Loop in the list of day hikes on the Trails Illustrated *West Half* map. See that list for a brief description of the entire loop hike.)

Erbie Trailhead to Cedar Grove

4.3 miles. 340 feet of elevation gain. Sandstone glades; historic cemetery; river overlooks. Trailhead at Erbie boat landing.

The 0.1-mile spur trail from the trailhead parking area to the mainstem Buffalo River Trail is soon on top of sandstone bedrock having a thin cover of soil. Rain can quickly saturate the soil, and mosses thrive. Some of the Buffalo River Trail for the next half mile is also on sandstone having extensive beds of moss.

In this area are sandstone glades where soil overlying the rock is droughty, or there is no soil at all. Prickly pear cactus grows in these places, and other plants able to withstand dryness. The glade environment is different, interesting, and quite fragile, for the plants tend to be small and easily crushed underfoot.

Through this area the trail follows an old road. Then it leaves the road and heads through the woods to the edge of a hilltop. There's a view over the river to a cliff having a smooth face of the Newton Sandstone. On the hilltop to the right of the trail (at river mile 45.5) is the site of the Buffalo Basin Ranch. In the 1960s a couple from up North, Walt and Rose Gronwaldt, and their son and daughter-in-law acquired the land and built a guest lodge and cottages here. It was an attractive development but isolated, and open only from April to October, so the business was not profitable. The Park Service purchased the property and removed the buildings.

A short distance beyond, the trail enters an old road leading down the hill. Soon the trail heads off to the right while the road continues 0.1 mile toward the riverbank, a good place to take a break.

After leaving the road trace, the main trail curves up the hill and climbs to the top of the sandstone bluff. For 100 yards along the bluff it passes mounds of earth piled up by a bulldozer when the Gronwaldts, hoping to raise cattle, cleared land for a pasture. Since the 1960s the bulldozed area has undergone old-field plant succession. In the other direction, toward the river, is undisturbed nature: lichen-encrusted rock, and big hardwood trees below the cliff.

The path crosses a sandstone creek bed and turns left, passing low-bush huckleberry and then tall pines along a bluff overlooking the river. Soon, however, the trail moves away from the river, crossing a gentle slope and then an almost level area having high-bush huckleberry and cedars. Then along a road trace to another area bulldozed for pasture about 1960, where the trail at first is in a pine thicket, then passes openings with broomsedge, and finally closely spaced hardwoods. The young forest ends where the trail crosses windrows of debris the bulldozer pushed up at the edge of the cleared area. Bulldozed trees have rotted away; piles of dirt remain.

Beyond the dirt piles is an open stand of hardwoods, an attractive place made even more so because the trail overlooks a stream flowing over bedrock, the J. W. Hickman Spring Branch. After 150 yards the trail goes down the embankment and crosses the stream. Then the path heads uphill, following the trace of a road that appears on a map drawn in the late nineteenth century, a few decades after settlement.

Beside the trail at the top of the hill is a relic from the more recent past. A metal sheet having lines of nail holes across it was the bottom of an evaporating pan for making sorghum molasses at some time around 1950 (see illustration, page 314).

A few yards beyond is a spur path to the left, leading 50 yards to the nineteenth-century **Adair Cemetery** (see *The Adairs,* page 312).

Just beyond the cemetery path are remains of a farm: discarded pieces of equipment, the foundation of an outbuilding, the concrete walk to the house. Down the hill is a stock pond fed by a spring. Undoubtedly the spring and the fertile bottomland beyond caused the Adairs to settle here in the 1830s. The foundations and farm junk are from the mid-twentieth century, when the property belonged to one Bill Taylor, who probably was the maker of molasses.

From the Adair-Taylor place the trail heads down the road, leaves the road, and goes into an old field being taken over by oak and cedar, then into woods and across a steep hillside overlooking the Buffalo. At times now, the trail crosses the cleared right-of-way of a rural electric power line, which itself is part of the historic development of this region. The electric line has been here since about 1940, fully 30 years before the coming of Buffalo National River.

The trail swings away from the river, passes sandstone glades having cedar trees and prairie grass, and crosses a creek just above a cascading eight-foot waterfall. It then returns to a bluff above the river, passing a few foundation stones and a discarded bedspring. Here must have been a cabin in the woods for somebody long forgotten.

Eventually, after going down and then up, the trail descends into **Sawmill Hollow**, named for a sawmill that local people say was located a half mile up the creek. The trail crosses the creek within sight of a large culvert faced with stone, installed by the Park Service in the late 1980s when improving the Erbie road.

For some yards along the east side of Sawmill Hollow, its deep alluvial soil nourishes switch cane and big trees. Near the hollow's end at the river is a mysterious pit in the ground beside the trail. Six feet square and about eight feet deep with timber cribbing on the sides, it seems to have been intended for industrial use. But it is old enough that no one seems to know anything about it.

Soon the trail follows a road trace along the hillside, and to the left of the road are the remains of a stone fireplace, a sheet metal smokestack, and a sheet metal evaporating pan used for making sorghum molasses, like the pan beside the trail near the Adair Cemetery. The pan rested on a slight incline on top of the fireplace, and its baffles deflected sorghum juice from side to side as it flowed across the hot metal. Excess water in the juice was boiled off and the liquid remaining in the pan became thicker as it approached the bottom of the incline, where molasses was drawn off into containers (see illustration, page 314). Apparently this sorghum cooker, from around 1940, belonged to Ewing Taylor. He was a brother of Bill Taylor, on whose farm the other sorghum pan is seen near the Adair Cemetery.

The trail continues along the hillside, leaving the road trace,

The Adairs. In the late 1830s, it is said, John and Sarah Adair set out from Knoxville, Tennessee, and by raft, barge, and ox cart, with household goods and six children, journeyed down the Tennessee, Ohio, and Mississippi Rivers and thence overland to the Buffalo River. Locating by a large spring on the edge of an extensive bottomland, they became among the first settlers on the upper river. After the government surveyors marked section lines, John and Sarah acquired, in 1843 and 1845, 80 acres, and their son William, in 1853, 40 adjoining acres.

By the mid-1850s the Adairs had a large farm valued at $1000, a considerable sum in those times. The youngest of their nine children (three had been born in Arkansas) were still at home; the older ones were grown. Daughters Malinda and Barbara had both married and were both deceased (1845 and 1854) and at rest in a family plot on the farm. The oldest son, James, had his own farm downriver, and John, Jr., had moved to the county seat.

The Adairs had family ties to another of the neighborhood's pioneer clans, the Cecils. When John Cecil organized a company of Confederate soldiers, William Adair joined...and was killed in a Union surprise attack on the company's camp. During that same month—April 1864—James Adair was killed in a military action. John and Sarah had William buried in the family plot.

The younger Adairs by that time lived elsewhere, or departed soon after, scattering. James left children who would give rise to succeeding generations. One descendant, Dr. Charles Adair, a great-grandson, became superintendent of schools at the town of Harrison, twelve miles north of the original family farm.

John Adair's gravestone is inscribed "Rest for the weary," with a plow, mattock, shovel, hatchet, and a hand with the forefinger pointing toward heaven. He and his wife, Sarah, lie in comb (gable-roofed) graves in the cemetery at the old farm site.

approaching the top of a bluff near the Buffalo, then bending away from the river. It reaches a small creek, crosses on bedrock at the top of a three-foot cascade, and turns uphill. Soon afterward it passes over ground covered with moss, and beneath cedar trees, and arrives at the picnic site and river overlook at **Cedar Grove**.

Cedar Grove to Ozark Campground

1.7 miles. 150 feet of elevation gain. Wildflowers; views of river; creeks cascading over sandstone ledges. Trailhead at river overlook at Cedar Grove, on Erbie road two miles west of Highway 7.

From the overlook at Cedar Grove, the trail descends steps into a ravine. Near the bottom, a path to the left goes to the riverbank. The trail turns right, and about 200 feet up the ravine it crosses a stream. It doubles back toward the river, crosses an old roadway that once went to Dry Ford at the mouth of the ravine, and then heads down the river, going along the top of a sandstone bluff.

The trail soon crosses a creek—often dry, for its watershed is small—and continues along the hillside overlooking the Buffalo. Eventually the river moves off to the north and the trail gradually climbs to a saddle between two higher areas of a ridge. Here the sandstone boulders are almost covered with moss, which is probably sustained by moisture in the porous rock. Such moisture may move up by capillary action through the rock from the ground underneath, traveling in spaces between the sand grains.

Down the southeast slope of this ridge, the trail very soon is back on deeper soil, decomposed sandstone and organic matter, fertile and acidic enough for pine trees that grow here. The path turns left to follow a creek that flows over sandstone bedrock, with miniature waterfalls where the stream spills off ledges.

At the foot of a flight of rock steps the trail crosses the creek. (If the water is too deep here, retreat upstream to a wider but shallower crossing on the bedrock.) After the crossing the trail is along the edge of an alluvial bottomland having big sycamore and sweet gum trees, and springtime wildflowers on the hillside to the right.

The path then heads across a steep slope, where it looks into an overflow channel of the river. Finally it moves onto flatter ground, past a stand of leatherwood shrubs and into the upriver end of **Ozark campground**. (For some history of this place, see *Ozark,* page 181.)

Ozark Campground to Pruitt

2.6 miles. 250 feet of elevation gain. Woodland and glade habitats; evidence of human history; a river overlook; wildflowers. Trailhead on right at entrance to Ozark campground.

Leaving the campground, the trail goes up a hill, then levels off above a bluff facing the river. A quarter mile from the campground is a stone foundation (fireplace?) on the left, then a rock wall that extends about 60 yards along the trail. These, the relatively small trees here, and thickets of greenbrier at intervals for a while—these all say that this land once was cleared for farming.

Molasses making was once a cottage industry along the Buffalo. The process is shown in this lithograph by Thomas Hart Benton (based on Ross Villines' sorghum mill near Ponca, which Benton visited in 1968). The mule is hitched to a long pole attached to a shaft connected through gears to a pair of rollers. As the animal moves in a circle around the sorghum mill, the rollers turn and the man feeds sorghum canes between them, squeezing out sweet juice that runs into the barrel.

The woman has poured juice into a shallow pan over a wood fire. As moisture evaporates, she stirs the thickening sorghum molasses to keep it from overheating and burning.

Also along the trail are a few ancient cedar stumps covered with moss and gray-green lichens. Cedar heartwood is rot resistant; the stumps may remain from the widespread harvest of virgin cedar along the Buffalo for making pencils, about 1905 (see pages 97–98).

Another quarter mile and the trail enters an old road. Another half mile and the trail crosses a graded road that goes down the hill to a house used by temporary Park Service employees and volunteers. It is called the Ozark House because it is near Ozark campground.

Beyond the road 0.3 mile is a spring on the right, feeding a pond on the left below the trail. The earth dam to create the pond was probably built in the 1950s. Aquatic plants and animals have established themselves in and around the pond (these disappear during the winter but reappear with warm weather). Some plants could have spread downstream from the spring. Or seeds were carried up the spring branch, or from elsewhere.

Past the pond is an opening in the woods, a glade on sandstone where the trail passes through. Here are trees that are deep-rooted and tolerant of dryness—pignut hickory, redbud, southern red oak. Also plants that we easily associate with dry places—blackjack oak, prickly pear. And plants that suggest grasslands—little bluestem, prairie tea. Such places lend variety to a trail through the woods.

But even the woodlands have variety. Presently the trail follows an old road through open forest, mostly oaks, on a north slope. And for the observant, there are signs of past habitation: a concrete foundation 50 feet up the hill to the right, followed soon after by an old trash dump 40 feet downhill to the left. By this time the trail runs a short distance downhill from Highway 7, the way of access to any former home sites here. Sounds of traffic can now be heard.

About two miles from Ozark a spur path leads 50 feet down to the left, to an **overlook** on rock outcrops having a view up and down the Buffalo. Beyond the viewpoint the trail switchbacks down the hillside to be closer to the river. Then, as the trail continues along this steep slope with its view of the water, there is also a rich display of plant life, especially in the spring when wildflowers come into bloom. This is moist, sandy, but fertile soil, not only for the smaller plants such as bloodroot, dutchman's breeches, and celandine poppy, but also for shrubs including leatherwood and wild hydrangea.

The trail bends away from the river and continues through the woods and across footbridges spanning two gullies—deep ditches created by runoff from culverts on Highway 7.

A short distance beyond the second bridge, the trail reaches the picnic area at **Pruitt**. Now it goes by a clump of spirea, or bridal wreath, bushes having sprays of white flowers in the spring. They were planted long ago when this was someone's yard.

Past the picnic ground is the end of the trail at the parking area.

Ponca Wilderness Area

Kilgore Mountain Path

1.8 miles. 200 feet of elevation gain. Woods, old fields; a way into the wilderness from the south. Trailhead at end of County Road 143 (deep potholes, slick mud?) north from Highway 74 at Low Gap.

The trailhead is at the park boundary, where a locked gate blocks the road toward Fisher Point and boulders block a road trace heading to the right. Park so others can pass on the main road.

The trail follows the road trace to the right, passing around the head of **Beech Creek** and along a broad bench on the west slope of **Kilgore Mountain**. Like other wide benches at about 1600 to 1700 feet elevation along the upper Buffalo, this one developed on the easily eroded Fayetteville Shale. The topsoil is thin and poor but slopes are moderate. Parts of the bench were cleared for pastures, now reverting to forest with blackberry, greenbrier, cedars, winged elm, and other early-successional species in formerly open spaces.

A family lived here. The home site is marked by scraps of sheet metal, a dug well (capped by the Park Service to prevent anyone's falling in), and a thicket of red-flowering Japanese quince.

The path goes past two sizeable ponds, probably built in the 1950s as part of a federally supported farm program. Today they are filling with waterlilies and cattails. For a few years around 1990 the pond farther north had a colony of beavers. Apparently they reached this isolated body of water by traveling overland from a lodge on lower Beech Creek that beavers abandoned about that time. The beavers built a lodge, increased the height of the earth dam at the pond, cut every suitable tree within reach—including cedars—and then left.

Beyond the fields and the ponds is more than a half mile of woods. Here the terrain is uneven, with ridges, hummocks, swales, and shallow, wet-weather pools. Over millenia, underlying clay and shale have caused the ground to creep downhill, sagging or piling up. On other upper Buffalo slopes at about this elevation, unstable clay and shale have caused landslides—on Highway 43 north of Ponca and on Highway 21 west and south of Boxley.

The woods path joins an open roadway, and soon afterward it ends at the Buffalo River Trail above the head of Jackies Big Hollow. (To continue on the Buffalo River Trail, see page 300.)

Slatey Place to Horseshoe Bend

1.5 miles. 800 feet of elevation loss or gain. Connects Horseshoe Bend and Hemmed-in Hollow with the Buffalo River Trail.

This lightly traveled trail was envisioned and built as part of a route from Kyles Landing to Hemmed-in Hollow requiring only one river crossing, at the mouth of Hemmed-in. The trail also can be part of an 8.1-mile loop hike from Kyles to Hemmed-in: via the Buffalo River Trail from Kyles to the Slatey Place; then this trail and others to the high waterfall in Hemmed-in Hollow; then the Old River Trail (with four crossings of the river) back to Kyles. The loop hike is feasible only when the river is low enough to ford easily.

From the Buffalo River Trail at the Slatey Place (see page 300), this trail often crosses and sometimes follows an old road down the mountain to Horseshoe Bend. In places off the trail, the badly gullied road trace is on grades exceeding 30 percent. The trail is much less steep, descending in a series of switchbacks. The entire path, from top to bottom, was built during the summers of 1985 through 1988 by volunteers from the American Hiking Society and the Student Conservation Association.

As the path works its way down the mountain it passes through the normal sequence of geologic formations, beginning in sandstone and shale near the top. After several switchbacks down, a few limestone outcrops and much broken chert of the older, lower Boone Formation can be seen along the trail.

About halfway down the mountain the trail joins the old road and follows it along a bench; the grade is nearly flat. At the north end of the bench, where the trail turns down off the road, bits of broken glass and other trash are evidence of a homestead site. Out of sight a few hundred feet to the east are rock walls the homesteader built in his effort to wrest a living from the land.

This area also lies within the Jim Bluff *graben,* a strip of country between two fault lines where Earth's crust was depressed more than 300 feet (see page 18). Where the trail drops off the bench road, it is on sandstone and shale matching that at considerably higher elevation farther back up the trail.

As the path continues north and loses some elevation, the Boone Formation's limestone appears again. Then the trail crosses the fault line on the north side of the graben and is back in the normal sequence of formations. Soon it descends steps cut into a low bluff of Newton Sandstone and swings to the right past a viewpoint on a sandstone cliff about 200 feet higher than the river.

The view across the river includes the **Henderson house**, for many years the home of Eva (Granny) Henderson (photos, pages 265 and 329). Beyond the house is the valley of **Sneeds Creek**. On the mountain beyond the valley are a National Park Service radio mast and a Southwestern Bell Telephone **microwave tower**.

From the west-facing viewpoint with its twisted cedars, the trail moves onto a shady, north-facing hillside. Down the hill the slopes become gentler, on sandy soil. Here are both pine trees and hardwoods, but none very large, so this could have been a cleared field. The path crosses shallow gullies that run downslope—did they result from erosion of plowed ground?

At the bottom of the slope and on the right is a pine tree with a two-foot trunk. With massive, spreading limbs, it must have grown in a clearing. Probably it's the parent of many younger pines here.

Just beyond the big pine, the trail intersects the Old River Trail in Horseshoe Bend (see pages 319 and 321).

Old River Trail, Center Point Trail to Horseshoe Bend

0.7 mile. 70 feet of elevation gain. Provides connecting links to five other trails that converge on a small area near Hemmed-in Hollow.

The Old River Trail follows a road trace from the Ponca bridge downriver to Erbie. Most of it is used primarily by horseback riders. But any hiker in this area will probably walk at least one of the three parts of this short section of the Old River Trail, as follows:

• *Center Point Trail to mouth of Sneeds Creek, 0.3 mile*

This segment of the Old River Trail begins at, and provides a link to, the lower end of the Center Point Trail (see page 327), and it is linked to the Sneeds Creek Trail (see page 328). This segment begins downstream from **Jim Bluff**, stays by the river, and goes underwater during high floods. The trail nearer Jim Bluff is surfaced with river-rounded rocks. Here is an overflow channel of the Buffalo today—and part of an old gravel bar where the river deposited the rocks during past centuries.

Nearer Sneeds Creek the trail is on alluvial soil. Here between the trail and the river was the last Center Point School (see *Center Point School*, page 320). Close to Sneeds Creek the river since 1970 has eroded its bank, taking more than half of the road—now the trail—that once provided vehicular access to Horseshoe Bend.

At the mouth of **Sneeds Creek** is an intersection with the trail from Sneeds Creek to Hemmed-in Hollow (see page 333).

• *Mouth of Sneeds Creek to west side of Horseshoe Bend, 0.2 mile*

The trail crosses Sneeds Creek and goes over a low hill past the **Center Point School site**, a stone foundation in the woods on the left (see *Center Point School,* page 320). At one end of the foundation is a concrete floor where two kids scratched their names in the wet cement, probably in the 1920s. "Arbie" is the daughter of Frank and Eva (Granny) Henderson, who lived across Sneeds Creek, and "Hollie" (a boy) is Arbie's first cousin.

A side path leads up the slope past the foundation. In about 200 yards the path is on top of a bluff overlooking the river. In another 150 yards it is at the California Spring, which has a basin carved in bedrock. The spring provided water for the Center Point School.

About 150 yards beyond the school site, the main trail reaches the river at the Suck Hole—at low flow the river is "sucked" into a subterranean passage below the cliff that stands across the pool. At normal flow the river spills out of the pool at the ford. In drought the Suck Hole is almost a puddle, more than four feet below its normal level. The river trickles in. The surface outlet is dry.

About 100 yards beyond the river the Old River Trail reaches a junction with the trail from Horseshoe Bend to Hemmed-in Hollow (see page 332). The Old River Trail turns uphill to the right.

• *West side toward east side of Horseshoe Bend, 0.2 mile*

Soon after turning uphill the trail passes an expanse of bare rock, the top of the sandstone bluff overlooking the Suck Hole. Farther along, as the trail levels off, it is a onetime farm lane following an old fence line. A short distance farther and on the right is the trail from Horseshoe Bend to the Slatey Place (see page 318). The Old River Trail continues ahead to Kyles Landing (see page 321).

Center Point School was so named because its original site, across the river from Big Bluff, was at the center of its school district. A log schoolhouse was there from 1877 to around 1920, when it burned. A new school was then built near Sneeds Creek.

That building remained in use until one day, about 1937, when a pupil took off his clothes and paraded naked past everyone at school. The teacher made him dress and gave him a whipping. The next night he burned down the schoolhouse.

The school was rebuilt, but before it was to open he burned it down again. Or his brother did; both hated the teacher. "They's mean as snakes," says a woman who knew them. (One, or both, went to reform school and, it is said, became reformed.)

This last Center Point School stood beside the Buffalo above the mouth of Sneeds Creek. Its builders roofed it with hand-split shakes and later put sheet metal where the shakes were leaking. They added the most inexpensive, easily applied siding, brick-patterned asphalt that came in rolls.

Here, in 1959, the school was empty except for pupils' desks. After 1951 the remaining children were bused to Compton. On May 7, 1961, the building floated away on a cloudburst flood.

Old River Trail, Horseshoe Bend to Kyles Landing

1.9 miles. 100 feet of elevation gain. Exit of river's hidden passage; Lick Ford rapids; remains of farmstead. Most direct way from Kyles to Hemmed-in Hollow—but with five river crossings.

A high route from Kyles to Hemmed-in by way of the Slatey Place involves only one river crossing. Or, as a compromise, the high route can be combined with the low route along the Old River Trail to make an 8.1-mile loop hike from Kyles to the high waterfall in Hemmed-in Hollow with a total of six crossings.

This trail segment begins at the junction with the lower end of the trail from Horseshoe Bend to the Slatey Place (see page 318). About 50 yards past that junction, a path leads to the left into an old field having a barn, a house site, and an overlook atop a low bluff (see *Horseshoe Bend,* below). Within view up the river from the overlook is the **Seamster Cabin site** (see *Clubhouse*, page 171).

Horseshoe Bend once was home for Hosea and Harriet Villines. (He was a grandson of family patriarch Abraham Villines; see *Seed of Abraham*, page 105.) They had a daughter, Martha Frances Arizona Belle, born in 1876, who eventually became widely known as "Grandma Harp" (see *Hardscrabble*, page 338).

Later, the farm belonged to a family named Harper. Their house, standing in the open near the downriver end of Horseshoe Bend, once attracted a bolt of lightning that, it is said, zipped down the chimney, across the floor, out the door, and across the yard, where it blew a fence post out of the ground. It knocked a man out of bed and killed a hound dog lying on the floor.

In 1968, James Lochhead, a St. Louis businessman, and his wife, Ramona, bought the Harper place and built a house where the Harpers' had stood. In 1974 the Lochheads' house was struck by lightning and burned to the ground.

Past the year 2000 the Harper barn, with a loft added by the Lochheads, remained in place. It is a short distance off the Old River Trail, about 250 feet east of its junction with the trail from the Slatey Place. Near the barn is a small building of logs that the Lochheads used as a bathhouse. Some yards north of this structure is the site of the Lochheads' house, with a standing chimney and a concrete storm cellar.

The barn is on a 40-foot bluff having a view up the Buffalo. On top of a bluff beyond the river are stone piers and a chimney, remains of a weekend cabin (see *Clubhouse*, page 171).

Beyond the path to the barn, the trail soon heads down to the river. There, about 25 yards up the bank and below the foot of the bluff, is the outlet of the subterranean passage across Horseshoe Bend from the Suck Hole (see page 319). Water flows from under a ledge about three feet below the surface of the pool and makes ripples.

The trail crosses the river and follows the edge of a wooded bottomland to **Lick Ford**. Beyond the crossing at Lick Ford the path runs along the river past an overgrown field. This narrow strip of farmland known as the Long Field once provided part of a family's livelihood, but that family moved away generations ago.

The next river crossing was named Arbaugh Ford, probably for David Conrad Hennegar "Coon" Arbaugh, who is said to have built a cabin about 1858 on the riverbank just beyond the ford, where a spring flowed from below the bluff. The cabin washed away in the great flood of August 1915.

The bluff, 180 feet high and of the Newton Sandstone, apparently was never given a name. The pool below the bluff and just upstream from Arbaugh Ford is called the Jim Henderson Hole.

Beyond the ford the path skirts the edge of another overgrown field, this one more extensive and being invaded by switch cane. Then the path goes up a wooded rise and continues past still another field. This time, on the left, there is a decrepit building, the **Arbaugh house**. It was home for Arbaugh descendants, then became a barn. Its metal roof has protected it from total ruin and it remains as a man-made structure just inside the Ponca Wilderness. The Park Service refers to such features as "discovery sites."

In front of the house is a rusting hay rake. A photograph made about 1972 shows this area as an open field.

Past the house is one more river ford, narrow and fairly deep. In sight downriver is another cliff of the Newton Sandstone. Seeing a capital letter A naturally cut into its face about 20 feet below the top, canoers in 1965 informally named this cliff the "A" Bluff.

Beyond the ford, the next path to the right leads toward **Gray Rock**. Straight ahead the Old River Trail heads uphill—and here is a place to look for river-rounded rocks in the roadway. Rounded stones of this kind indicate that the river once was here, some 400 feet away from and 50 feet above today's river.

Soon the Old River Trail passes two closely spaced intersections with the Buffalo River Trail—first with the trail arriving from up the river, then with the trail departing to go downriver (see page 302).

The Old River Trail continues to follow the road trace straight ahead.

A hundred yards beyond that second intersection, the Old River Trail comes within view of the trailhead at Kyles Landing, with its bulletin board at the end of the campground.

Indian Creek
2 to 3 miles. 1100 feet of elevation gain or loss.

This trip on unimproved paths and cross-country routes involves climbing on steep inclines, huge boulders, and vertical cliffs. *NOTE: The trip is difficult and hazardous, and there have been many injuries from falls.* But Indian Creek can be an adventure for strong hikers who come properly prepared.

There are two trailheads: Kyles Landing for going up the creek, and an unmarked parking spot north of Highway 74 for hiking down the creek. The road to the latter trailhead, at the park boundary, is so badly gullied it is nearly impassable, and it crosses private property whose owner has the right to block access. The hike from Kyles up the creek into the canyon is longer but in climbing upward it is easier to pick safe footholds. Hikers who make it to the top of the canyon can get on the old logging track that circles the headwaters, and from there continue to the Buffalo River Trail back to Kyles.

Indian Creek, the Ozarks' most rugged canyon, was created in Boone Formation limestone, here with nearly four hundred feet of exposed rock. Geologists believe that the gorges of Indian Creek, Lost Valley, and lesser tributaries of the upper Buffalo have resulted from collapse of large caverns in the Boone. Indian Creek and Lost Valley are alike in many ways. Each has caves, subterranean stream passages, and a natural bridge spanning the surface watercourse.

The path going up Indian Creek leaves the Buffalo River Trail a half mile upriver from Kyles. At first the route is visible but eventually it becomes trackless, a scramble over increasingly large boulders in the creek. The going becomes ever more difficult, with no alternate route; canyon walls stand on both sides.

Then a 15-foot waterfall blocks the way. It used to be possible to climb about 25 feet up the bluff to the left and ease along a narrow ledge into the mouth of a cave, and then with a flashlight navigate the cave's short passage to a second entrance at the creek above the waterfall. The cave is known as Horseshoe Cave because of its curved, double-ended passage—or Arkansas Cave because the downstream entrance when viewed from inside resembles the shape of the state of Arkansas. Horseshoe Cave in wet weather has a waterfall pouring from the downstream entrance. But the cave is now off-limits year-round to protect endangered Indiana bats raising their young in the cave during the warm months and hibernating the remainder of the year. A sign at the cave warns people to stay out and there is a stiff penalty for any violation of the warning.

Thus the only way to get past the waterfall is to proceed in stages. The first one is to climb up the 25-foot vertical rock wall to the right. This should be undertaken only with help from an experienced rock climber. There is more than one possible route up the cliff and care should be taken to find the safest one.

Above the wall is an immense cavity under a higher cliff, and the next move is to scramble up its steeply sloping floor of dirt and loose rock to its back end, where there is a tunnel. The third move is to crawl through the tunnel to the canyon above the waterfall.

About 200 yards up the creek from the waterfall is a cliff having a high opening—the Needles Eye. When in flood, Indian Creek spills down through the Eye. At normal flow the creek runs underground. A short cave passage below and to the right of the Eye leads to a drop-off where the creek can be heard flowing in the darkness below.

To get past the Needles Eye, hikers scramble up a steep gully, go over the left buttress of the cliff, and inch their way down another gully on the upstream side. The gullies are badly eroded from decades of use by hikers. The bare clay is slippery when wet. The upstream gully is very steep and ends in a high, almost vertical cutbank above the creek bed. A secured rope about 150 feet long is needed here for inexperienced climbers.

Up the creek from the Needles Eye are more waterfalls, including a steep cascade about 50 feet high. Indian Creek's most notable features, however, are the Needles Eye and the subterranean passages that bypass the waterfall at Horseshoe Cave. That and the rugged, unspoiled beauty of the entire canyon.

At about 1600 feet elevation the creek is above the Boone limestone and at the lower edge of a bench developed by erosion of the Fayetteville Shale. The creek is filled with sandstone boulders that originated in a higher formation but shale should be visible in cutbanks. In this area a road trace crosses the creek. Loggers opened the road about 1965 and presently it is used as a horse trail.

The old logging track can be followed along the bench in either direction from the creek to intersect the Buffalo River Trail back to Kyles Landing at the foot of the mountain.

Center Point Trail

3.6 miles. 1240 feet of elevation loss or gain. Home sites; old fields returning to forest; access to Goat Trail. Trailhead on Highway 43 three miles north of Ponca and opposite County Road 10.

For the first mile from the trailhead, this former road is on a dry, south-facing hillside and on a nearly level grade. Then comes a steep hill, where the road loses 90 feet in elevation in 400 feet, a grade of over 20 percent—more than 20 feet in just 100 feet.

At the foot of this hill, called Parker Hill, is a home site on the left. William Parker and his family lived here in a small house beyond the still existing concrete walk to their front porch. Foundation stones, scattered rubbish, and beds of garlic gone wild also mark the house site. Up the hill are the remains of a log barn with a dirt-floored cellar underneath, and a concrete-block enclosure that must have been a reservoir near a spring. The Park Service had the house removed after buying the property in 1981.

For nearly a mile beyond the Parker place the roadway stays on the north side of the ridge, following benches or taking short downhill runs. In areas uphill from the road, small trees and underbrush indicate the land once was cleared and is reverting to forest. Downhill, though, are areas of mature woodland having so little undergrowth that one can see hundreds of feet down the mountain. Distant views are across the valley of Sneeds Creek.

Half a mile beyond Parker Hill is the home site of Frank Little, a retired electrician who kept 15 to 30 cats and was known as the Cat Man. Bill Bates, who came down the Center Point road one time in the 1970s, recalls "a cat here, two cats there. A garden with a hog-wire fence. A small house—a shack house, really. Cats everywhere" (photo, page 326). Little died in 1978 in a nursing home, at age 87.

From the trailhead to nearly a mile past Parker Hill the roadway is on sandstone and shale. But as it crosses a gully near elevation 1500, the rock changes from brown to gray, sandstone to limestone. Here is the Boone Formation, flat or rounded outcrops of limestone, some having crinoid fossils. Broken chert is scattered along the path.

The Cat Man.
Frank Little lived a mile and a half down the dirt road from Highway 43. Only two miles from the Buffalo, he paid the river little mind. Instead he cared for his many cats. Passersby noticed the cats were everywhere.

Today Little's modest dwelling is gone, his garden plot overgrown. His Center Point road is a trail into the heart of the Ponca Wilderness.

About this time also, the roadway emerges from the north slope to run along the top of the ridge, a drier place having small hardwood and cedar trees. Then to the left is another feature of the Boone, a funnel sinkhole about 30 feet across and ten feet deep.

Then a very large tree—chinkapin oak, three feet through—stands at the left edge of the road. Here too is a broad saddle with flat expanses of limestone, a pleasant place with open woods extending up the hill beyond. On the right, a wide path heads downhill to the Goat Trail across **Big Bluff** (see page 327).

For another 200 yards the roadway is along the north side of the wooded hill. Then it begins to pass an overgrown clearing. On the right, a low retaining wall marks another house site. A settler, probably a homesteader about 1900, built a log cabin here. A succession of families lived here until past the mid-1950s. After that, the vacant house rapidly went to ruin. The wood shingle roof leaked, the porch roof sagged and collapsed, the rock chimney fell apart, the roof fell in. Wood rotted away. Daffodils still bloom in what was the front yard. A pile of rocks lies where the chimney stood.

Somewhere close to the cabin site, the geologic fault at the south edge of the Jim Bluff *graben* (photos, page 18) crosses the road. Beyond the fault line the Boone limestone is replaced by sandstone of a formation that normally lies higher than the Boone. The sandstone appears in the roadbed. Occupants of the cabin gathered and stacked pieces of it for a wall along the right side of the road.

Farther along, the road goes downward through the rock formations within the graben, and brown sandstone is replaced again by gray limestone and rubbly chert of the Boone Formation. From here the Boone extends down the hill almost to river level.

The road enters a clearing and comes to an intersection with the Sneeds Creek Trail on the left (see page 328). About 100 yards to the left is the **Henderson house**, where Eva (Granny) Henderson lived for more than 60 years (photos, pages 265 and 329).

From the Sneeds Creek Trail the Center Point Trail goes 0.1 mile down a steep, rocky incline to end at the Old River Trail (see page 318) a short distance downriver from **Jim Bluff**.

The Goat Trail

1.0 mile round trip from Center Point Trail. 120 feet of elevation loss and gain. A ledge path across upper Big Bluff. Path begins at Center Point Trail 2.7 miles down the mountain from Highway 43.

From the Center Point Trail a well-beaten path leads downhill through the woods. The path becomes steep but soon levels off on a ledge. Here are old cedar stumps, maybe from trees cut for pencil stock in the early 1900s. In the bluff just to the left is red rock, the marker band of the St. Joe Limestone of the Boone Formation.

Until now the distant view has been blocked off by young cedars along the path, but suddenly the trees are gone and the view is panoramic, to mountains and bluffs up and down the Buffalo, to the river about 340 feet directly below, to the downstream end of Big Bluff with its vertical face of water-streaked sandstone.

Straight across the river is a small house with a metal roof. This is the site where Abraham Villines, patriarch of today's extended Villines family, settled in the 1830s (see *Seed of Abraham*, page 105). It also is the site of the first Center Point School, built in 1877 (see *Center Point School*, page 320). The present house was built by Harris and Gertrude Mohler around 1915. The last residents there were William "Bud" Arbaugh and his family, who put the aluminum roof on the house before they moved away in the 1950s. The next owner, P. W. Yarborough (see *Steel Creek,* page 165), let the house stay but cleared much of its hillside for a horse pasture, in the 1960s. The present woodland has developed since that time.

Farther along the path, a high, foot-thick buttress of the bluff extends onto the shelf. Around 1910, to make a safer way for children walking the ledge toward the Center Point School, parents broke a crawl hole through the base of the wall. Today's hikers detour past the buttress—but have to go close to the edge of the cliff.

Beyond the hole-in-the-wall, the ledge soon narrows to barely three feet, sheltered and dry, below an overhanging cliff. Around 1950, wandering goats from a nearby farmstead walked this path. Dried goat droppings, and their smell, remained for many years.

Along the trail the red band of the St. Joe Limestone stays in sight a few feet above the sandstone ledge that forms this narrowest part of the tread. The Boone Formation, including the St. Joe, makes up the entire cliff that now reaches 200 feet above the Goat Trail.

Beneath the overhang along the trail are shallow caves or alcoves. In one of them, mineral-bearing water has oozed from cracks in the limestone and left little mineral waterfalls of travertine spilling over ledges. In another alcove at the hole-in-the-wall is a large mound of pale gray travertine, a stalagmite in broad daylight.

Along the shelf are ancient cedars—Ashe's junipers, actually, which occur only on carbonate rock. Able to tolerate drought, these low-growing trees with twisted, multiple trunks are centuries old.

The spectacular part of the Goat Trail ends where the only choice for going ahead is to climb onto a four-foot-high ledge where the hand- and footholds have been worn slick by climbers. Past that ledge the path is behind a thicket of junipers. And soon it leaves the bluff, emerging onto flat ground on a ridge. People come to the Goat Trail from this direction after climbing up the hill from the river.

Sneeds Creek Trail

4.1 miles. 1190 feet of elevation gain or loss. Historic farmsteads; Rocky Bottom; mountain views. Trail can be part of a loop hike.

The trail follows an old road and is open to horseback riders. It can be entered from its upper end a mile south of Compton (taking the horse trail, not the hiking trail, from that trailhead). Or entered from its lower end where it meets the Center Point Trail. The following description goes from the lower end to the upper.

Within 100 yards from the Center Point Trail is the **Henderson house**, where Eva (Granny) Henderson lived until well into her 80s (photos, opposite and page 265). Outbuildings are in ruins but the

Granny Henderson

She was less than five feet tall, but wiry. She had done farm work all her life, milking goats, doctoring cows, feeding pigs and chickens. She lived on Sneeds Creek for more than 60 years without running water or central heat, electricity, or telephone. After her husband's death in 1959 she remained alone but cheerfully accepted her lot. "I'm too busy to be lonely," she said.

Eva Barnes Henderson, called Aunt Eva or Granny Henderson, kept going into her eighties, holding to a rhythm of daily chores, bringing buckets of water from the river to her cows, keeping up the woodpile for her stoves.

At age 86 and in failing health, she moved up the mountain to Compton, near family. She died the next year, in 1979.

house with its protective metal roof remains in good enough condition for safe entry, even to an upstairs room having walls papered in the 1920s with pages from an agricultural magazine. The house is basic, though it has decorative wood shingles in the gable ends. In 1998 when the porch floor was near collapse, a park ranger and volunteer helpers made repairs, but no further restoration is planned.

From Granny's farmstead the trail follows the roadway down a hill and across a bottomland to Sneeds Creek. At the creek crossing, a tilted sandstone ledge forms a natural dam, and a short distance beyond the crossing is a level expanse of sandstone along the creek called **Rocky Bottom**—though local people are apt to say it's simply the Flat Rock. In the 1960s one writer called it Big Rock and pronounced it "flat enough for billiards and large enough for football." It's not that flat, but the bare rock averages 100 feet in width and goes 400 feet along the creek (photo, opposite).

The sandstone here is probably of the upper Everton Formation. It lies just within the north edge of the Jim Bluff *graben* (see page 18), whose north-side fault line can be seen crossing a side drainage of Sneeds Creek where the side hollow arrives at Rocky Bottom.

Upstream from the Flat Rock, Sneeds Creek flows in a sandstone trench having a sizeable pothole, or natural bathtub. The 1960s writer said it was four feet wide, eight feet deep, and 20 feet long.

Less than half a mile farther up Sneeds Creek is another farm site having a dwelling called the **Evans-White house**, which stands across the creek and about 100 yards south of the trail. The house is in poor condition, but in the 1990s it was safe to enter and read the walls papered with newsprint and magazine pages from the 1930s. How did *National Geographic* with its pictures of South Africa get here to this isolated Ozark farmstead?

About 1919, George Evans built this house for his parents. Evans apparently also built the vaulted stone cellar just off the back porch and added decorative shingles to the gable ends, like those of the Henderson house. George's parents had come from Tennessee in the 1870s and Jim Evans, the father, was a miller and blacksmith, a man well known in the area. The Evans house, a substantial one for its time and place, was a neighborhood social center.

About 1940 the house became home for Ray and Arbie Villines and their family—Arbie being the daughter of Granny Henderson. Ray piped water into the house from a spring, and he and Arbie had cattle and hogs and made a living. But in May 1961 a cloudburst dumped ten inches of rain on the valley. Sneeds Creek took out their fences and washed their car a mile down the creek to the Buffalo River. (They found the car buried in mud and gravel and did not recover it.) The Villineses then moved out and were the last people to live in the house. The name Evans-White refers to the builder and to the owner from whom the Park Service bought the property.

Upstream from Evans-White, the road trace crosses overgrown clearings that once pastured cattle, goes past pieces of car and truck bodies so old they have acquired an antique flavor, and crosses

Sneeds Creek spills off Rocky Bottom, proclaimed by one writer to be "flat enough for billiards and large enough for football."

Sneeds Creek four times. In places the creek flows down sluiceways in sandstone bedrock, or spills off ledges as little waterfalls.

After the fourth creek crossing the trail continues a few hundred feet, crosses the **Middle Prong**, and begins a three-quarter-mile climb up the wooded mountainside. Sometimes the trail levels off for a brief stretch, but mostly it goes up (providing opportunities, of course, to stop at intervals to consider the details of this second-growth forest on west- and northwest-facing slopes).

Eventually the trail becomes level for a hundred yards or more, past a knoll that can be seen on the topo map at a section line. After another quarter mile with more climbing, the roadway is into old fields along the top of the ridge, with open views to distant ridges.

Soon another feature that can be found on the topo map comes into view on the left—a huge excavation, up to 30 feet deep and 100 feet across, the quarry that in the 1960s provided material for rebuilding and paving Highway 43. One can speculate on how many millions of years the quarry pit will remain as a landscape feature.

From the quarry uphill, the old roadway is wider to accommodate the trucks that hauled material to Highway 43. A quarter mile beyond the quarry there *was* another local landmark, Compton's community dump, along the hillside below the trail. The dump was from the 1960s, predating Buffalo National River. On four weekends in the late 1990s a Boy Scout troop came and picked up and bagged trash and loaded it on trucks to be taken to a landfill. It was the largest and most conspicuous trash dump within park boundaries.

Some yards beyond the former dump and 2.6 miles beyond the Evans-White house, the roadway passes the west end of the Bench Trail (see page 337), an old road that goes along the mountainside above Hemmed-in Hollow. Beyond that intersection 0.1 mile, the Sneeds Creek Trail angles off to the right, leaving the roadway. The trail climbs across the hillside, then crosses the nearly level top of the mountain. Beyond the roadway 0.6 mile, the trail arrives at the trailhead on the road a mile south of Compton.

Horseshoe Bend to Hemmed-in Hollow
0.9 mile. 200 feet of elevation gain. Geologic features; waterfalls. From the south, the most direct way to the high falls at Hemmed-in.

Beginning at the Old River Trail in Horseshoe Bend (see page 319), this trail follows a road trace close to the Buffalo and soon passes an extensive shelf of bedrock along the river. There, some yards to the left of the trail, is an odd circular depression in the rock, more than 50 feet across (photo, below). One geologist describes this feature as a "collapse structure," or sink, that originated at the time this Everton sandstone was deposited some 460 million years ago.

About 250 yards from the Old River Trail, the path is nearly oppo-

*A **collapse structure**, or sink, exhibits a circular pattern in layers of sandstone beside the river near Hemmed-in Hollow.*

site the mouth of Hemmed-in Hollow. On the right, up the high bank and in the woods, is a good campsite at a respectful distance from the river, with room for a latrine in the old field farther back.

The mouth of Hemmed-in is opposite the downstream end of the bedrock area, where the river enters a shoal. The river crossing is at the head of the rapids, to an area of cobbles and gravel where the creek from the hollow may be seen in the wet months. To the right, past the gravel area, a wide path follows the creek and soon crosses it. The rest of the way to the falls is up the left side of the creek.

Although hikers want to get to the waterfall, the bottom of the hollow along the trail is interesting, too. The path is on an east-facing hillside having a moist environment for beech trees, and for spring wildflowers. Just a few yards away, the sunny, west-facing slope across the creek does not have the beeches, nor as many wildflowers, nor trees as large as those on the east-facing slope.

Partway into the hollow, the trail follows an old road. Loggers were here in 1967, cutting what must have been virgin forest, inaccessible until roads were bulldozed up the hillside above the trail. There was, however, a wagon track into the hollow several decades earlier, for somewhere between the river and the high waterfall there was a cabin, home for a free spirit named O'Neill (photo, page 334).

The hollow becomes narrower. A trail from Sneeds Creek (see below) arrives from the left. The path now is on a steep hillside overlooking the creek and small waterfalls. Then it descends to the rocky bed of the creek. Very soon afterward it reaches a dead end below a curving cliff. Within the curve is the highest waterfall between the Appalachians and the Rockies (photo, page 336).

Sneeds Creek to Hemmed-in Hollow

1.5 miles. 340 feet of elevation gain. Glades; woodlands; sandstone bluffs. Connecting link (while avoiding river crossings) between Hemmed-in and trails approaching from the north and west.

At its south end this trail intersects the Old River Trail at the mouth of Sneeds Creek (see page 319). At its north end in Hemmed-in Hollow it intersects the trail from Horseshoe Bend to the hollow (see above). It also is joined by the lower end of the path into the hollow from the Compton trailhead (see page 337).

From the mouth of Sneeds Creek the trail soon crosses the creek

Free spirit.
William Patrick Henry O'Neill was, as his daughter said, "a romantic with lucid intervals." In old age, he lived in Hemmed-in Hollow—around 1917, surrounded by his books, tending his garden, occasionally visited by his family. After he left, his cabin burned, and today there is no sign of his former presence.

and then ascends a low bluff, with steps cut into the sandstone ledges. The path continues upward, through a cedar glade with areas of flat sandstone on a south slope, and on through the woods. Then up another bluff having 19 steps cut into ledges.

After that, the trail follows the top of the bluff. There are views through the trees toward the river. At one point there's a glade with prairie grasses. Eventually the trail reaches an intersection with the path that comes down from the Compton trailhead.

Beyond that intersection the trail descends through a break in the bluff and makes its way down an east-facing slope (but on the west side) of Hemmed-in Hollow. Here, with less afternoon sun, is more soil moisture. Trees are larger than they were along the trail above the bluff, and beech trees appear for the first time. In 1967, loggers bulldozed a haul road up this hillside. The trail crosses the road trace.

Near the bottom of the hollow the trail ends at the path coming up the creek from the river and from Horseshoe Bend. From this intersection it is 0.2 mile to the high waterfall (photo, page 336).

Compton Trailhead to Hemmed-in Hollow
1.8 miles. 1100 feet of elevation loss or gain. Steep path to rim of Hemmed-in. Landforms; geology; views into the hollow.

This plunge down the mountain is a strenuous hike, not even considering the climb back up. It is, however, the most direct overland route from an auto road to the high falls, 5.0 miles round trip. To reach the trailhead, take County Road 19 three-fourths of a mile south from the Compton telephone exchange building (which is at the crossroads a quarter mile south of the former Compton school at Highway 43). Then turn west and go about 100 yards to the trailhead.

The path down to the rim of Hemmed-in is strongly influenced by the makeup of the underlying rock formations. Beginning at the trailhead, the path is across the Boston Mountains summit plateau, which developed above the erosion-resistant "middle Bloyd" sandstone. Thus the trail is almost level, dipping at one point to cross the little headstream of Hemmed-in Hollow's high waterfall, then going on through an open woodland of scrub oak and hickory.

A third of a mile from the trailhead, the path reaches the edge of the mountaintop and heads steeply downward to a bench. After this, a series of quick descents leads from bench to bench—bluff-and-bench topography with high-angle slopes or sheer bluffs developed on resistant strata of sandstone, and shelves or benches on softer beds of shale. The shale and the sandstone bedrock are usually hidden under topsoil, brown-colored sandstone debris, and leaf litter.

The path runs a quarter mile along one bench and soon afterward goes down to cross the **Bench Trail** (see page 337), an old roadway. The crossing is 0.8 mile from the trailhead.

From the crossing the path continues down bluffs and benches for more than a quarter mile. At around 1700 feet elevation it reaches the top of the Boone Formation, whose gray limestone first appears in a trail-side gully. Now the path heads downhill at a steep angle into a maze of Boone outcrops. There are short level stretches but many steps and drops off ledges, sharp turns around boulders, and abrupt slides down past low bluffs. One compensation: Through the trees are glimpses of a sheer cliff across Hemmed-in Hollow, and of the river farther off to the right, and the mountains beyond.

The path levels off, rounds a few bends, and is at an **overlook** on top of the cliff of Hemmed-in Hollow. Here, at about 1300 feet, the path is below the Boone Formation and on the Newton Sandstone of a lower formation, the Everton. The path has reached the southwest end of the high wall that describes a big horseshoe around Hemmed-in. Across the gorge is the southeast end of the cliff. Nearly half a mile back to the left, in the far curve of the horseshoe, below two ravines that angle down the mountainside and then merge above the cliff, is Hemmed-in's high waterfall. To be seen easily, the water

The high falls.
The waterfall at the head of Hemmed-in Hollow often swings from side to side in the breeze (those who get too close get drenched).

A measured 204 feet, Hemmed-in Falls is the highest waterfall between the Appalachians and the Rockies. In this view from the east rim of the hollow, the height is more easily visualized after finding the hiker in the opening in the woods near the bottom of the photograph.

With a steep watershed of less than half a square mile, the falls are at their best just after a heavy rain. In fair weather the pour-off becomes a shower. In drought, only scattered droplets come down, sparkling in the sunshine.

Hemmed-in Hollow is more than a waterfall. Close to the high falls, Venus maidenhair fern spills down a wet slope. Above the "fern fall" is a scooped-out area in the cliff with calcite draperies and stalactites where water has oozed out, evaporated, and left its limy deposits. In the creek bed is jewelweed, or touch-me-not (if touched, its mature seed capsules pop open, scattering seeds).

The creek is on the Powell Dolomite, which extends upward to the high ledge path behind the falls; here the Powell is uplifted more than 150 feet higher than anywhere else along the Buffalo. Above the Powell is carbonate rock of the Everton Formation. The top of the waterfall is on the Everton's Newton Sandstone.

needs to be flowing amply, and in sunlight. It comes from a deep notch in the rim of the cliff.

From the overlook the path heads to the right, down a steep incline close to the top of the bluff, then on a lesser grade. One eventful mile below the Bench Trail, the path arrives at an intersection with the trail to Hemmed-in Hollow from Sneeds Creek (see page 334), which heads to the left toward the high waterfall (photo, opposite).

Bench Trail

4.3 miles. 140 feet of elevation gain west to east; 300 feet of elevation gain east to west. Homestead sites; cliffs; "slump blocks."

At its west end the Bench Trail intersects the Sneeds Creek Trail (see page 332). At its east end it joins County Road 19 —the Compton-to-Erbie road—0.7 mile east of the park boundary and about 4 miles southeast of the Compton telephone exchange.

From its west end at the Sneeds Creek Trail, the Bench Trail zig-zags down the hill, then levels out and crosses the path from the Compton trailhead to Hemmed-in Hollow (see page 335). About 250 yards beyond that crossing, the trail looks down to the **Flowers Cabin**. The log building is at the upper end of a 97-acre tract extending to the bottom of Hemmed-in Hollow. The land had belonged to William O'Neill (who once lived in the hollow; photo, page 334), then to Myrtle D. Flowers. Her son Lloyd V. Flowers inherited the acreage and built this 14-by-18-foot cabin about 1935.

Lloyd Flowers lived here a while in the 1950s, but in 1956 returned to California, leaving the vacant house open to the elements. In 1975 a tenant replaced the cabin's wood shingle roof with a metal one. That year the Park Service purchased the property from Flowers. The cabin and plantings in its yard remain as a park "discovery site."

One-fourth mile beyond the cabin, the old road dips into a gully having three-foot sandstone boulders in the watercourse—the main stream down the mountainside to the high waterfall in Hemmed-in Hollow. In the quarter mile from here to the head of the falls, the stream loses 600 feet in elevation.

This bench, of course, is much less steep because it is developed on shale, probably the Fayetteville Shale, which erodes to flatter surfaces. Interestingly, the bench here is about 200 feet higher in elevation than it is at the east end of the Bench Trail. That is because the

Hemmed-in Hollow area is a geologic "high" where rock formations are elevated, compared with their positions in the surrounding area.

A quarter mile farther along the trail and a short distance up-slope, a rock wall parallels the roadway. Soon there are other signs of a homestead. An area of tree saplings indicates a former clearing. On the left are remains of a stone foundation—a barn?—with a stone wall beyond. Then a giant boulder on the left has man-made piles of rock on the far side. Farther left are more foundation rocks and what may have been a cellar hole.

Beyond is a grassy area, an old field. About 200 feet farther, as the trail bends downhill, is a dense stand of sericea lespedeza having tall, tough stems. Sericea is an alien plant that aggressively colonizes disturbed sites, often crowding out native plant species. It was brought to the United States from Japan in the 1890s. While the homestead existed for some years shortly after 1900, sericea lespedeza probably arrived when a landowner about 1950 planted it for pasture.

For more than half a mile beyond the homestead site there are no distinguishing features. The mountainside faces southwest, receiving the afternoon sun: Here is a dry woodland, rocky, infertile, probably never cleared by any homesteader. Eventually, when landmarks appear, they are "slump blocks," massive pieces of rock that broke off the bluff up the hill and gradually crept down to rest here beside the trail. The largest, just to the left, stands 12 feet high.

Hardscrabble. Between 1902 and 1905, on what has been described as "the Erbie bench between Compton and the Buffalo River," John and 'Zona Harp tried to scratch out a living. Not long after their first child, a daughter named Flossie May, was born there, the Harps gave up and moved to Oklahoma.

Flossie grew up, married a carpenter named Jim Haggard, and they moved on to California, Okies escaping the 1930s Dust Bowl. In 1937, at Bakersfield, a son, Merle, was born.

Merle grew up, became a rakehell, and landed in San Quentin Prison. Paroled in 1960, he got into music, and in 1965 a song of his hit *Billboard*'s Top Ten. Up to the 1990s he recorded more than 600 songs, about 250 of them his own compositions. Merle Haggard became billed as a country music superstar.

One of Haggard's songs was about his Grandma Harp. Until she married John Bohannan Harp, her name was Martha Frances Arizona Belle (or 'Zona, or 'Zon') Villines. She grew up on a farm beside the Buffalo River (see *Horseshoe Bend,* page 321).

A half mile beyond the slump blocks, the trail veers off the old road trace to find a way into and out of a large gully, the drainage for **Cecil Hollow**. The hollow extends half a mile down the mountain to the river at Kyles Landing, 900 feet lower in elevation. The Bench Trail, with hardly anything more rugged than detours around muddy spots, simply does not compare with the steep terrain downhill.

A hundred yards beyond Cecil Hollow, a beaten path goes up an old road trace to the left—the path that Boy Scouts take every summer from Camp Orr to a pine tree on top of the cap-rock bluff. Scouts hiking up to their Antenna Pine play king-of-the-mountain, taking down the flag hung on the tree by the preceding troop and putting up their own. (And like good Scouts, they return the preceding troop's flag to that troop, with due ceremony.) From Camp Orr across the river it's more than a 1200-foot climb in a mile and a half to the pine, which of course doesn't faze the Boy Scouts.

The path to the pine is not obvious, but about 200 yards beyond is a distinctive landmark on the right: an outcropping rock, bare and rounded-off and nearly 20 feet across, a good place to rest or eat lunch. The Boy Scouts know it as Fifty-Two Rock because errant Scouts once painted their troop number 52 on the outcrop. The number is gone but the name persists.

At a drainage swale 200 yards farther along, the Scouts' path from Camp Orr—the route for their scramble toward the pine tree—goes to the right. The Bench Trail stays on the old road bending to the left.

More than a quarter mile beyond the path from Camp Orr is the next distinguishing feature, a steep climb of 200 yards as the old roadway leaves the bench and gets up close to the cap-rock cliff. Then, as the trail levels off briefly, it crosses an obvious, large drainage channel. The gully is at the head of **Clemmons Hollow**, which suggests the road's builders routed it up here on the hillside to avoid having to cross a much larger gully down below.

In the next 200 yards are more steep upgrades and several more drainage channels. And here not far below the cap-rock bluff are several champion-size slump blocks. The grand champion, lying like a dead whale below the trail, is up to 20 feet high, 60 feet wide, and 100 feet long. Trees grow on top. The rock is splitting in two.

These blocks of the "middle Bloyd" sandstone cap rock have crept downhill from the bluff, riding on the underlying shale. The shale expands when wet and shrinks when it dries out. Rocks resting on shale attain lower positions, then, when the shale dries.

In some parts of this largest slump block are cross beds, layers of rock inclined at an angle to layers above and below. This "middle Bloyd" sandstone is crossbedded because the sand was deposited by shifting currents of a river at its delta, near the river's mouth.

The trail descends to the bench. Here, along the last mile of the Bench Trail, was the homestead of Elijah Lamb. He filed his claim for the land in 1909, received his patent for 160 acres along the bench in 1917, and died in 1926. His family left the place about 1939. Elijah's son Ernest says, "We had a few acres cleared up, and we farmed. We had a few cattle and hogs, both. And we worked in the timber. I helped cut stave bolts for barrel staves."

Ernest Lamb left the family's homestead in 1929. He says that when he visited the old home place about 1973, he found nothing but the rock walls along the north and west property lines.

The Bench Trail arrives at a power line whose cleared right-of-way opens a view down the mountain toward the Buffalo River. The right-of-way is also at the east boundary of the Ponca Wilderness.

Fifty yards beyond the power line clearing, the Bench Trail ends at County Road 19, the road from Compton to Erbie.

Cecil Cove/Erbie

Hideout Hollow

2.0 miles round trip. 400 feet of elevation gain. Views from rimrock cliff into box canyon with waterfall. Trailhead on County Road 19, the Compton-to-Erbie road, about three miles southeast of Compton.

Hideout Hollow, a side canyon of Cecil Cove (the valley of Cecil Creek), was named by Park Service employee Jim Liles because draft evaders once hid in the cove (see *The Slacker Gang,* opposite).

While the small, steep hollow seems a likely hiding place, with certainty it was the site in the late 1930s for a goat cheese factory owned by Ben F. Battenfield. Ben's brother John had been leader of the 1920s religious colony downriver at Gilbert, and sometime after the religious experiment ended, Ben moved here, acquired land, and began making goat cheese at Hideout Hollow. In 1965 Compton storekeeper Lex Burge recalled that Battenfield made three grades of cheese. "The best grade was buried in the ground about six weeks," said Burge. "Very dark. Didn't look fit to eat."

From the trailhead parking area the Hideout path first heads down through the woods to cross an intermittent stream. It then goes up a small tributary valley, running close to the park boundary, which is marked occasionally by survey monuments. Tall hardwood trees grow along the watercourses, but on the flat summit that the trail

The Slacker Gang. When the United States entered World War I in 1917, nine young men from Cecil Cove and around Compton refused to report for military duty after receiving draft notices. They collected rifles and ammunition and retreated into hiding places in the cove. Soon they were known as slackers, or the Slacker Gang.

Relatives and friends had pressured the nine to resist the draft. Old-timers told them that men had "hid out" during the Civil War, joining neither side. Others asserted there was no reason for American men to fight in foreign lands. Some of their socialist neighbors—in those days, socialism had many followers in the American heartland—said the war was benefiting only the rich. A local religious leader declared that since the Bible said, "Thou shalt not kill," the boys should not be taking the lives of others, even in war. The draft resisters themselves perceived the draft as unfair, passing over sons of prominent citizens but taking boys from the hills.

The slackers dropped out of sight, but 36 of their supporters signed a compact to defend them with armed rebellion if necessary. A number of local people did not back the draft resisters and freely expressed their opinions, but knew they risked their lives if they ventured into Cecil Cove. The sheriff, the U.S. marshals, the army—all wanted to corral the slackers, but on giving it thought all realized that armed confrontation could result in much bloodshed on both sides.

Months passed. The resisters began to relent. Two of them came out and reported for military duty. The sheriff was invited to come alone to the cove and talk to the holdouts. He had an offer from the War Department: The resisters would not be charged with desertion. With that, the slackers quietly gave up.

All of them went into the army. All eventually got honorable discharges. But they had "laid out" in Cecil Cove for almost the entire duration of the war, 1917 and 1918, while other men went overseas and into battle. In later years none of the resisters wanted to talk about avoiding service. As older men, some even enlisted for military duty at the beginning of World War II.

crosses, trees are little more than 30 feet high. There is no evidence of timber harvest—could these scrub trees be virgin forest?

Turning to the left, the path goes downhill and enters a stand of pines that continues down to the rim of Hideout Hollow. The path emerges atop a 75-foot cliff, facing a similar one on the far side of the canyon. Across the hollow a huge piece of the cliff has split off and moved downhill. This "slump block" looks as big as a ten-room house. On top of it grow several good-sized pine trees.

The track goes left and stays near the edge of the bluff. Soon it passes what appears to be a stone alcove or enclosure for a spring that has gone dry. Here also are rocks placed on the ground so that they suggest the outline of a long vanished building.

The cliff-top path continues, crossing bare rock and passing beds of moss where the rock is wet. Down below the cliff, other big slump blocks lie among the trees. The canyon is narrowing, with the cliff curving around the head of it like a horseshoe.

At the head of the horseshoe's curve is a small creek, and it drops off the cliff as a 50-foot waterfall. The stream must vanish in late summer when its watershed—only about 120 acres—dries up. But in the wet seasons it comes down toward the cliff in a series of miniature falls and shimmering cascades, then slips down the sloping bedrock and over the edge. Local people would call this a pour-off.

There is no safe, direct way into the hollow below the cliff, but when trees are bare everything below the rim is within view. Under the bluff near the waterfall are ruined stone walls of Battenfield's cheese works. Somehow, Ben must have climbed down—but how did he get all that goat's milk down there?

Barely 200 feet upstream from the waterfall is the National River's boundary. The bluff beyond the falls goes outside the park, continuing as part of the "middle Bloyd" sandstone rimrock cliff around Cecil Cove. With the park boundary so close on two sides, the path back to the trailhead must be the same as the path coming in.

McFerrin Point
0.9 mile round trip. 40 feet of elevation gain. Geology; views.

This unimproved path through the woods begins at the first switchback of County Road 19—the road from Compton to Erbie—as it starts to descend the mountain about 3.5 miles southeast of Compton and 0.4 mile east of the National River's boundary. There are one or two parking spaces where the power line crosses the road a few yards west of the switchback. (There's also a view down the cleared right-of-way to the Buffalo at Camp Orr.)

The path begins where a drainage swale leaves the road at the uphill side of the hairpin turn. From there the path goes eastward along a bench below the cap-rock bluff. The way may be blocked by fallen trees and often the path dodges past boulders that have fallen from the bluff. This is "middle Bloyd" sandstone, breaking into pieces, slowly creeping downhill, gradually weathering away.

The "middle Bloyd" originated as sands deposited by a river at its delta. Usually the currents laid the sand in horizontal layers but at times crosscurrents piled sand on inclines, and these angled, cross-bedded layers are occasionally visible here in the bluff.

Farther along, the continuous bluff becomes separate blocks that stand along the ridge (photo, page 58). And soon there is an open ledge overlooking the Buffalo River. A mile and a half to the south-east is **Mutton Point**, standing at about the same elevation as this overlook on McFerrin Point. Mutton and McFerrin Points flank the Buffalo River like gateposts where the river emerges from its canyon in the Boston Mountains.

Along the Buffalo downstream are clearings around Erbie and the curving roads of Erbie's campground. Along the horizon to the left of Mutton Point are other ridges that form the sinuous northern escarpment of the Boston Mountains: Sherman Mountain, then Judea Mountain and Lick Mountain. Then Point Peter, its sudden drop-off twenty miles distant but in plain view against the sky. Beyond Point Peter is at least one more ridge, pale blue.

Those are views to the south and southeast. Better views to the northeast and north are another 100 yards along the narrowing ridge. *NOTE: This rocky path becomes barely eight feet wide, with uneven footing and with drops of nearly 100 feet on each side. This is no place for those afraid of heights or inclined toward horseplay.*

The view from near the end of McFerrin Point includes flat-topped Boat Mountain, ten miles away, with Pinnacle, Sulphur, and Pilot Mountains surrounding Boat. To the left of Pilot Mountain, and only four miles northeast of here, is the eastern end of Gaither Mountain at Cone Point. To the left of Cone Point is **Newberry Point**, much closer and directly across Cecil Cove. Newberry has a prominent "middle Bloyd" cliff matching the one here at McFerrin Point.

Farther to the left is **Queen Point**, with some exposed cliff, and still farther left are the headwaters hollows of **Cecil Creek**. Finally there are the cliffs along the west side of Cecil Cove.

Like the bluff along the path to McFerrin Point, this viewpoint is coming apart. A massive piece of the end of this narrow fin of rock has already split off. It leans noticeably to the south. *It will fall.*

The fastest way back to the car is the way you came.

Cecil Cove Loop
6.7 miles. 760 feet of elevation gain. Old fields, stone fences, house sites, and cemetery of vanished community. Cave; geologic formations. Trailhead at road junction just north of Erbie church.

Cecil Cove, the valley of Cecil Creek, had little land that could be cultivated, but settlers came in the early 1900s, homesteaded or purchased its public-domain acreage, and established a community of more than a dozen families. Like other Ozark hill people of that time, they cleared small plots for gardens or field crops and turned cattle and hogs loose to fend for themselves in the surrounding woods. For cash they cut timber for the local sawmill and stave mill. For other needs they had general stores and post offices at Compton and Erbie, a Methodist church at Erbie, and a Baptist church two miles up Cecil Creek in the heart of Cecil Cove.

For several decades the community held together, even to the point of sheltering several local men who resisted the draft and "laid out" in the cove during World War I (see *The Slacker Gang,* page 341). During the 1920s and 1930s, however, timber and topsoil became used up and people moved out. The last family left in 1944.

From the trailhead parking area, the Cecil Cove Trail goes downhill to a beaver pond on the outflow from the **Van Dyke Spring**. Beyond the stream at the beaver dam, the trail crosses the largest field—about 250 yards long—to be seen along its course. By the year 2002 this field was becoming overgrown and the Park Service conducted a prescribed burn here, reducing fuel for wildfire and keeping the field open for wildlife, especially the elk that graze here.

According to records in the courthouse and the abstractor's office at Jasper, this area is within the first homestead in the cove, patented by Samuel Cecil in 1892. Except for about 30 acres closest to Cecil Creek, the 160-acre homestead was rocky hillside land.

The next homestead up the trail, acquired by John Neighbors in 1909, had even less farmland. About 15 acres might have been cultivated, in a small area where the trail approaches the first crossing of Cecil Creek and then in a narrow strip along the creek between the first and second trail crossings. (The first crossing, from the left to the right side of the creek, is a mile from the trailhead. The second, from right to left, is one-third of a mile past the first crossing.)

The next homestead up the creek, patented by Wade Sturgill in 1917, included strips of bottomland immediately before and after the third trail crossing of Cecil Creek. At year 2000, Sturgill's field just past the third crossing had not become completely overgrown. His rock wall, 50 yards long, still stood along the left side of the trail.

Just beyond Sturgill's homestead is the fourth trail crossing of the creek, right bank to left, two miles from the trailhead and now on land purchased—not homesteaded—by Hardy Willis in 1912. Willis bought his land in accordance with an act passed by Congress in 1820 that provided for sale of public land for $1.25 an acre. So we presume that Hardy Willis paid $200 for his 160 acres. Willis may have cleared some of the bottomland just above the fourth crossing but more likely he cultivated a larger piece farther up the creek. He, like the homesteaders, had only a few acres suited for cultivation.

A short distance beyond the fourth crossing and at 2.2 miles from the trailhead, a side trail goes to the right. At the junction, and squarely astride today's trail, was once the community's Baptist church. A few feet of rock wall on the left side and a stone pier (two rocks, one on top of the other) on the right are all that remains.

Side trip: The trail to the right at first runs along a hillside overlooking Cecil Creek, which has cut its channel into solid limestone, with scooped-out potholes, or "bathtubs." Then, 200 yards upstream from the junction, the trail is past the hillside and runs along an elevated terrace. In the woods on the left is a level area; volunteer trail workers camped here in 1989. Beyond the campsite are places to explore: rock piles of Hardy Willis' farm site, **Broadwater Hollow** with its little waterfalls, and the creek up **Bartlett Cove**.

The main loop trail stays on the road trace and enters a side hollow. About 100 yards from the trail junction it bends back to the right to climb the hill. At that point a spur path goes ahead into the woods. In 100 yards the path reaches a bluff at the head of the side hollow. In the bottom of the bluff is the low dark entrance to the Baptist church's summer quarters, **Mud Cave** (photo, page 346).

Within is a large room. Its floor slopes steeply down from the entrance, so that at the room's rear wall the floor is more than 30 feet below the ceiling. Except for stubby stalactites here and there, the cave has no decoration. From the right rear of this entrance room, a passage runs back about 600 feet, with mud enough to inspire the name for this cave. But the front room is dry. And in the summertime, cool. On hot Sundays the Baptists came here for services.

From the junction with the Mud Cave path, the main trail climbs steeply, swinging back up the ridge and around above the head of the Mud Cave hollow, then ascending more gradually from one bench toward a higher one. There it enters another homestead tract. William J. (Joe) Jones came to these 160 acres in 1907.

A half mile beyond Mud Cave the trail is at the **Jones Cemetery**, where William Jones' gravestone states that he died in 1914. Thus his homestead patent awarded in 1917 went to his heirs.

Surely the Cecil Cove families shared happy experiences, but this cemetery records the tragedies. Joe Jones' wife Lillie, 20 years younger than he, died in 1910 at age 33 after having four or five children. (Lillie was Joe's second wife. Apparently his first wife also died young, after having several children.) And here lie the wife of K. R. Jones, dead at age 38; Rutha, the wife of Wade Sturgill, dead at 42; and Hattie, the wife of J. F. Sturgill, dead when not quite 18. Among 20 identified graves, 10 are of infants or children. The oldest person of the 20 was Joe Jones; he died at age 56.

Mud Cave. When summer's heat became oppressive, Cecil Cove's Free Will Baptist Church met here in the "front room."

The earliest dated burial is Lillie's in 1910, three years after the Jones family came here. The latest occurred in 1933, eleven years before the last family moved out of Cecil Cove.

Two-tenths of a mile beyond the Jones Cemetery and about 15 yards past the ruins of a log barn within view on the right, a spur path to the right goes about 40 yards to the remains of the foundation and chimney of the Jones house. A surviving photograph shows a one-and-a-half-story log building with a center hall, or breezeway; this must have been the largest house of any in the cove. After Joe Jones' death a son lived here. Later the last occupants moved out. About 1960 the vacant building was sold to a developer, who dismantled the log structure and moved it to Bull Shoals, Arkansas. He renamed it the Martin House and re-erected it as an exhibit at Mountain Village 1890, a tourist attraction.

The next homestead, for which William F. Faddis received a patent in 1907, is located where spring water flows across the trail two-tenths of a mile beyond the Jones home site. The most visible, enduring evidence of settlement is the rock wall, four feet high, that begins at the spring branch and extends about 100 yards into the woods. About 60 yards back along the trail from the branch and up the hillside, the remains of a barn may still be seen. Another 40 yards back and about 50 feet uphill is Buffalo National River's largest walnut tree, over three feet in diameter.

This homestead eventually was owned by the family of Arthur Keeton. The Keetons were the last to live in the cove. They moved to the mountaintop near Compton in 1944.

A Keeton daughter, Faye Scroggins, remembers walking the two miles from here to Erbie to attend school. She took a shortcut path down the mountain, passing the Sturgill house. Two elderly Sturgill women in long dresses often invited Faye in for fresh-baked cookies. That occurred around 1940.

Side trip: Three-tenths of a mile beyond the Keetons' spring branch, the trail crosses a ravine watercourse having big boulders. Up this ravine eight-tenths of a mile—a steep bushwhack—is the head of Hideout Hollow, having a 50-foot waterfall and the stone walls of a 1930s goat cheese factory (see pages 340 and 342). There is no safe, direct way to go farther than the foot of the waterfall, so the easiest way out is to return down the ravine.

From the Keeton spring branch it is a mile to the next home site, which allows time to observe the forest on this east- and northeast-facing mountainside. With adequate moisture here, the hickories and oaks are sometimes of impressive size, two feet in diameter. The understory vegetation also has benefited from increased moisture.

The next house site is marked by the remains of a log barn, about 10 by 30 feet, on the left and next to an automobile-sized rock. The house once stood across the trail and about 50 feet up-slope. Foundation rocks (and in the 1990s, rotting sill logs) indicate it was small, about 16 by 18 feet. Unlike many other cabin sites, this lacks the pile of rocks that archeologists would call a chimney fall. There is only a discarded sheet metal collar from where a stovepipe went through the roof. A few yards from the house site, spring water trickles among mossy rocks.

Like Hardy Willis back there on Cecil Creek, Jake Franks here bought his government land in 1912, $200 for 160 acres. Franks did not stay very long; the place was home to two more families, Swayze and Jackson, within the 20-odd years before everyone left.

After the Franks place and one more ravine drainage having big boulders, the trail is on a moist north slope supporting a healthy variety of trees and shrubs. Here in April are thickets of Ohio buckeye with clusters of cream-colored flowers, and clumps of the endemic Ozark spiderwort with its white blossoms. Here too is wineberry, a raspberry native to Asia that has escaped from cultivation.

By degrees the trail has gained elevation to this highest section, above 1500 feet. At one point, where gray limestone extends across the roadway for six feet or so, an unseen spring noisily splashing below the trail indicates the presence of the Pitkin Limestone. In Cecil Cove, at about 1500 feet elevation, this limestone formation is the source of flowing springs.

Farther around the hill, on an east-facing slope, the trail runs along the top of a cliff, very likely of the Pitkin Limestone, for it is hard rock that tends to stand as vertical walls. It also is what old-time geologists called petroliferous limestone. When freshly broken it smells like crude oil.

From the Franks place the trail crosses two more homesteads—Noah Sisco's, 1918, and John Richardson's, 1908—whose house sites are somewhere off the trail. Richardson's land extended almost to the junction of the trail with County Road 19, the road to Erbie from Compton. At the county road this Cecil Cove loop hike continues to the left, downhill.

Side trip: Down County Road 19, 0.2 mile from its junction with the Cecil Cove Trail, the **Farmer Trail** provides an alternate way to the trailhead. That trail, however, is badly washed out as it heads straight down the mountain to the **Farmer farmstead** (see page 351). From the farmstead the side trip is on trails to the top of **Goat Bluff**, then to the county road 0.1 mile from the trailhead (those trails are described on pages 351 and 352). The hike past the farmstead is 0.8 mile longer than going down County Road 19.

Beyond its junction with the Farmer Trail, the county road crosses the last Cecil Cove homestead to be carved out of the public domain, 120 acres patented by James Arnold in 1926. Along the road, Arnold's land extends from elevation 1400 feet down to 1250 feet, across a wide, gently sloping bench. But all of it is dry, infertile, hardscrabble. Arnold got here last—and got the leavings.

Arnold's wide bench is developed on the Fayetteville Shale, which weathers to sticky clay. In wet weather the county road here becomes extremely slick, deeply rutted, at times impassable.

Below the Fayetteville shale and at about 1200 feet elevation is the Batesville Sandstone. Soon after that, the Boone Formation extends down the hill to the trailhead. At about the time the Batesville shows up, a funnel sinkhole 100 feet in diameter can be seen in the woods on the right. At the bottom of the wide, shallow funnel is a vertical pit into the Boone, about 15 feet deep and with a small passage extending horizontally maybe 20 feet from the bottom.

Beyond the sinkhole, as the road heads downward through the Boone Formation, the surroundings continue to be hardscrabble, with limestone ledges, chert rubble, stunted hardwoods, and many cedars lining the last half mile of the county road to the trailhead.

Erbie Loop

1.7 miles. 180 feet of elevation gain. Country church; historic farm buildings; views from Goat Bluff; possible side trip to early 1900s farm. Trailhead at road intersection 250 feet north of Erbie church.

The road junction north of the Erbie church was at the center of the Erbie community (see *Erbie*, page 350) and this hike reaches some of the outlying area. The first 0.4 mile is down the road past the church to the **Jones farmstead**, at the white house on the right. There the path turns to the right, in front of the house.

The farmstead, with its 30-acre field extending to the river, belonged to Joseph Buchanan, who was killed while a Union recruiting officer during the Civil War. After Buchanan the farm had a succession of owners, one of them being Rulus Jones. In 1922 Jones employed Arch Holloway, a carpenter from Harrison, to design and build this house. Although the house has manufactured components—lumber, roofing, windows—it retains one feature that originated in two-pen log houses: two front doors.

Down the lane in view past the house is Buffalo National River's largest barn, 50 by 50 feet, framed of oak timbers, completed by Rulus Jones in 1913. The barn has features that in its day were essential, including animal stalls, tack room, corncrib, center and side halls for access to the interior and for storing farm equipment, and a cavernous hayloft upstairs under the sheet metal roof.

The lane continues along the north edge of the 30-acre field, an area favored by deer and elk. The road trace ends at a grassy terrace between the river and the downstream end of **Goat Bluff**. Local old-timer Ray Hickman says this small level space is "Old Erbie," the site of the community's first post office.

In the 1960s a group of outdoorsmen purchased one acre here as a campsite and recorded ownership in the name of "Jasper in June, Inc." (Did the owners rendezvous at the nearest town, Jasper, each June before coming here to camp?) In 1980 the National Park

Erbie became identified as a community when a post office was established in 1915 to serve this neighborhood on both sides of the Buffalo River. Named for the daughter of former county sheriff Bill Green, the post office was first at "Old Erbie," beside the river at the downstream end of Goat Bluff. Later it was moved to the crossroads near the Erbie church and remained there, in a country store, until it closed in 1957.

The church still stands. Old-timers think the building dates from 1896. The church was first established by Nathaniel Villines (1816–1870), a Methodist preacher who settled here in the 1840s. (Villines was one of the original members of the largest extended family of any on the Buffalo: see *Seed of Abraham*, page 105.) Even into the 1950s the church building had the name VILLINES CHAPEL painted above the front door.

The Park Service, recognizing the historic significance of several sites in the former Erbie community, designates them as the Erbie Historic Zone. These include the church and the J. W. Farmer, Rulus Jones, and Parker-Hickman farmsteads.

Service purchased the acre and park employees call it Jasper-in-June.

From the old campsite, a long, breathtaking flight of 90 rock steps goes up past incised layers of limestone to the top of Goat Bluff. In view beside the steps about halfway up is a four-foot layer of reddish rock, the marker band of the St. Joe Limestone at the base of the Boone Formation. The rest of the bluff, to about 100 feet above the river, is Boone.

The path along the top of Goat Bluff meanders among and over limestone ledges, past gnarly trees living next to rock, past viewpoints looking down on the blue-green river and across to distant hills. The trail reaches a pair of intersections—a horse trail going to the right, then the hiking trail to the right—and here is the best of the overlooks. Flat ledges provide standing and sitting space. Ancient Ashe's junipers at the edge of the cliff provide frames for views. Down to the left is Rulus Jones' big field. Off to the right are the house and barn and fields of the **Farmer farmstead**, and beyond the Farmer place are river bluffs and the high knob of **Mutton Point**.

Side trip: From the trail intersections at the overlook, it is about 0.5 mile to the J. W. Farmer place, the Farmer farmstead. The trail continues along the top of Goat Bluff, then descends 50 natural ledge steps in about 500 feet of trail from the bluff's upriver end. From there it goes through woods past one of the Farmer fields. Then it joins the old settlers' road (Old River Trail) for the last 250 feet to the farmhouse, passing the Farmer spring, where remains of the log springhouse may still be seen below the left side of the path.

The J. W. Farmer house was built about 1904, and the one-room cabin near the house about 1913. The farm also included a smokehouse, a feed house, a privy, and a sizeable barn. The barn dates from about 1900. Local old-timer Robert Hickman says the barn's log walls were from the abandoned Cherry Grove schoolhouse.

The farm passed from J. W. Farmer to his son J. T., and from J. T. to another family member, W. Ross Farmer, before the Park Service purchased the property in 1977. The Park Service in the 1980s stabilized the buildings, replacing porch posts and part of the barn roof. But someone had stripped windows and siding from the house, and the place is isolated; the former access road is impassable. So the Park Service calls the farmstead, including its rubbish, "a walk-in interpretive discovery site." Perhaps the interpretive story here is about a lonely hill farm (but having electricity and telephone) that was home for a family through several generations.

The Erbie loop hike continues from the trail intersections at the viewpoint on Goat Bluff. The trail leading from the bluff into an old field goes to Erbie's horse camp. The trail leading into the woods is the hiking path toward the Erbie trailhead.

Much of the hiking trail is on, or in sight of, Boone limestone ledges, a hardscrabble landscape. Somebody did own the land, however, for there are old fences, and about 100 yards of rock wall the owner built with slabs of limestone. Why did anyone go to the trouble of building a wall? Was it to clear loose rock off a field?

Eventually the trail reaches County Road 19, the road to Erbie from Compton. About 0.1 mile down the road, the Erbie loop hike ends at the trailhead.

Pruitt and Vicinity

Mill Creek Trail

2.2 miles round trip. 100 feet of elevation gain. Log cabin; historic cemetery; views of spring-fed Mill Creek. Trailhead at east end of river access area at Pruitt, one-half mile off Highway 7.

This is an easy hike, but in summertime the trail has tall grass, ticks, and chiggers, so it's best to hike in other seasons.

From the trailhead the path first passes through a bottomland grove of box elder trees, then moves to the west bank of **Mill Creek**. Just below the trail are the creek's clear-water pools and riffles. Along this part of the trail in the spring are many wildflowers: crested iris, blue phlox, wild geranium, trillium, and white blooms hanging in clusters from bladdernut bushes.

Farther along, the trail merges into a road trace that once was the driveway to a house. Traces of the building and its fences remain in the woods. Japanese honeysuckle, ground ivy, and periwinkle—all of them alien, aggressive vines—cover the ground, along with day lilies, jonquils, and garlic. Where the trail passes under a power line, the cleared right-of-way has been taken over by opportunistic sun-loving plants, including blackberry.

At County Road 213, 0.6 mile from the trailhead, the path turns to the right, crosses Mill Creek on the low-water bridge, and turns right again to continue through the woods. Soon the trail crests a rise and passes by a **log cabin**. Thrifty Ozarkers who built this house in the

1930s used logs they salvaged from a cabin that stood nearby. The original cabin was probably built by Sion Lafayette Shaddox and his wife, Rebecca, after they and their four small children journeyed in a wagon from Georgia to Arkansas about 1860 to settle on 40 acres along Mill Creek. Here Sion and Rebecca raised eight children.

From the cabin the trail descends into a wooded hollow and comes to an intersection. The left fork crosses one end of an old field, enters the woods, and comes to another intersection. The spur trail on the left goes up the hill to the **Shaddox Cemetery**, a community grave-yard still privately owned and receiving burials. Here are the graves of Sion and Rebecca Shaddox and his parents, Ezekiel and Tillitha. A double gravestone marks the resting place of two brothers mur-dered during the Civil War. Many other stones have designs and inscriptions that give us information about local history.

From the lower end of the cemetery spur path, the trail to the left passes along the foot of the hill, staying in the woods by the edge of an old field. Spring wildflowers bloom on this hillside. At dawn or dusk, deer or elk may be seen in the field.

The trail rounds the downstream end of the field and returns up the east bank of Mill Creek. At one point the creek can be waded across at low water, shortcutting by half a mile the return walk across the low-water bridge and down the west bank to the trailhead. The trail up the east bank continues to the intersection near the log cabin, completing a loop east of the creek. From that intersection the way back to the trailhead follows the trail coming in, crossing the bridge and returning along the west bank of Mill Creek.

Koen Interpretive Trail

0.4 mile round trip. 30 feet of elevation gain. Handicap-accessible trail with trees and other plants labeled with their names. Trailhead is off the Erbie road 0.4 mile west of Highway 7.

The Koen Trail makes a loop with two shortcut trails across it, through second-growth forest on land that once was cleared for farm-ing. Today this area is part of the 720-acre **Henry Koen Experimental Forest**, which in 1950 became an outlying unit of the Ozark National Forest. U.S. Forest Service research people have undertaken projects here to learn how to best manage an Ozark for-est for yields of trees, wildlife, clean water, and other values.

From the trailhead with its shaded picnic area, the Interpretive Trail is a pleasant, easy walk on nearly level terrain. Probably the main interest here is the 25 species of native trees, along with a few native shrubs and vines, all having signs identifying the species.

Also there are five non-natives along the trail. Forest Service employees planted four eastern tree species (pitch pine, Virginia pine, white pine, and tulip poplar) and one southern tree (loblolly pine) in 1950. At 50 years of age, the white pine and tulip poplar were 20 inches in diameter with straight trunks 80 feet tall. The loblolly pine was 24 inches in diameter and 80 feet tall.

And there is one other tall plant, silver plume grass, with stalks that can become ten feet high, near the beginning of the trail.

This trail was built almost entirely by local volunteers.

Ponds Trail at Cedar Grove

0.4 mile round trip. 20 feet of elevation gain. Handicap-accessible trail; woodlands; views of ponds. Trailhead at Cedar Grove parking area on Erbie road two miles west of Highway 7.

This loop trail begins across the road from the Cedar Grove parking area. The loop begins and ends on the south side of the road, with the beginning being the wide, handicap-accessible left fork to South Pond. The handicap trail is 200 yards long and ends at a wooden platform with seating at the edge of the pond.

About ten yards back from the viewing platform, the path to North Pond heads into the woods on the left. It climbs and curves around a low ridge for 200 yards to the shore of North Pond. Then the path doubles back for 200 yards to the road at the parking area.

An aerial photograph made about 1940 shows that most of the land crossed by the Ponds Trail was a cleared field. The ground here is sandy—the end result of weathering and breakdown of Newton Sandstone—and is free of rock. This gently sloping hillside may have been plowed and planted in corn, or possibly cotton. The soil lost fertility, the whole economy changed, and farming ceased. The open field was invaded by grass and annual weeds, then perennial weeds, shrubs, and trees. Old-field succession is now well along, with the site having a forest of hardwoods and cedars.

The half-acre ponds were created around 1960 by building earth dams across small tributaries of the Buffalo River.

Round Top Mountain Trail

About 3 miles. 410 feet of elevation gain for entire trail. Geology; woodlands; wildflowers; views of Buffalo River valley. Trailhead off Highway 7 south of Jasper 2.4 miles, at Round Top Trail signboard.

The Round Mountain Trail is five miles south of the Buffalo River, so it is not on the Trails Illustrated map.

The trail offers an excellent overview of the results of 300 million years of erosion of the Ozarks (photo, page 60; text, pages 19–20). It also allows a much closer look at a "middle Bloyd" cliff of Boston Mountains cap rock than can be had from any trail along the river.

The paths consist mainly of a lower loop circling the mountaintop below the "middle Bloyd" sandstone cap-rock cliff and an upper loop around the summit above the cliff. Each loop has its own attractions. The lower one has a forest of tall hardwoods, with some trees having species identification tags. There are close-up views of the cap-rock cliff, which in places shows crossbedding of the layers of sandstone (photo, below). There also are impressively large pieces of rock that have split off the cliff and rolled, slid, or crept downhill. In the woods on the moist east side of the mountain are springtime wildflowers, including two endemic species, Ozark spiderwort and Moore's del-

Shifting currents at a river's delta deposited sand in horizontal beds, but also inclined beds in a foot-thick layer halfway up this view of "middle Bloyd" sandstone. Geologists call this cross-bedding. The cliff stands beside the Round Top Mountain Trail.

phinium. The spiderwort occurs only in the southwestern Ozarks of Missouri, Arkansas, and Oklahoma. The delphinium has been found only in this county and three adjoining counties.

Beside the lower trail is a memorial plaque where a B-25 bomber crashed into the mountain in 1948, killing the five servicemen on the plane. One of the bomber's two engines can be seen at the trailhead.

The upper loop above the cliff is on drier, less fertile ground having an isolated, inaccessible tract of noncommercial scrub forest. Here are post oaks, for example, barely 30 feet high but likely to be as much as 300 years old because of their slow growth. A side path off the north end of the upper loop leads to an overlook having the view across and beyond the Buffalo River, and to the east for 16 miles along the Boston Mountains escarpment to Point Peter.

The trail can be taken any time weather allows. Spring is best for seeing wildflowers, late fall to early spring for viewing the impressive cliff that rises to 75 feet above the lower loop.

The trail was built by the nonprofit Newton County Resource Council after the major landowner, William Stiritz, donated his acreage to the Council in 1997. It is named the Ray Crouse Trail for the retired Forest Service employee who oversaw its construction.

Middle River Trails, Richland Valley to Gilbert

Path to Point Peter
2.6 miles round trip. 340 feet of elevation gain. Mountaintop woods; homestead site; panoramic view from Point Peter. Trailhead at McCutchen Gap on County Road 12 west of Snowball 2.7 miles.

Point Peter, where Point Peter Mountain drops off sharply near its north end, is one of the most prominent features of the northern escarpment of the Boston Mountains, a landmark recognizable even from Highway 43 near Compton, 25 miles to the west. Point Peter can be a side hike during an auto trip to Richland Valley.

At **McCutchen Gap** are a couple of parking spaces that don't block emergency access to the Park Service gate across the road heading up the hill. The path follows that road, beginning with an upgrade for one-third mile. East of the road, to the right, are charred logs and tree trunks, and maybe a scarcity of undergrowth, the effects of wildfire here that occurred in 2000.

After the road levels off, an odd structure comes into view 50 feet to the left. It is an enclosure about 16 by 18 feet, having a massive stone wall about four feet high and three feet thick. There is one gap or opening on the south side. The purpose of this structure is unknown, though it may have been part of a makeshift dwelling for a homesteader. In the woods beyond the enclosure are piles of rock, evidence that someone was clearing the ground.

About 50 feet beyond the enclosure, the road forks. The more visible, right-hand fork provides access to a National Park Service radio repeater and antenna. The faint track to the left heads north toward Point Peter. The left fork is overgrown and badly infested with ticks; it is best to wait and hike this path in late fall or during the winter.

Side trip: For a good view to the east, take the right fork past the radio repeater and follow the power line right-of-way down the hill to the top of the "middle Bloyd" sandstone bluff about 0.3 mile east of the forks and a short distance south of **Rollins Point**. Within view from the bluff are buildings at Snowball and a wide swath of country farther east, to and beyond Marshall. To the northeast the view reaches past the Buffalo River. The slope above the bluff has an attractive stand of small pine trees and low-bush huckleberry.

The other fork, the path toward Point Peter, is not maintained and is often blocked by fallen trees; it is visible mainly because horseback riders use it. Their track soon goes past a rock wall extending a short distance to the left, to the west edge of the mountaintop. The wall is on land for which George Rollins received a homestead patent in 1924. Rollins may have stacked these rocks to keep his livestock from venturing farther along the mountain.

The path continues onto another homestead, acquired by W. R. Jones in 1905 and including the rest of the summit area to Point Peter. Along the way now are glimpses of isolated Richland Valley to the west and closer views of the open woods along this dry, infertile ridge at the north edge of the Boston Mountains.

Eventually the horse path becomes even fainter, though it may be followed some distance north of the **Point Peter** survey point (elevation 2011 on topographic maps). The final part of this hike is downhill, northeast of the survey point, off-trail to the top of the "middle Bloyd" cliff, where the view opens up.

From that perch on top of the cliff, the scene below and beyond is gigantic. Two miles below are the Buffalo River...Jamison Bluff...White Bluff. Farther away are other landmarks. Fifteen miles to the northwest are flat-topped Boat Mountain and its sister peaks, isolated outliers of the Boston Mountains. To the north and northeast at a great distance is the level horizon of the Springfield Plateau.

Using binoculars, one can find and recognize many more things, making the viewing more fun. But land features in view are mostly too far away, too small for making photographs.

The most direct way back to the trailhead is along the same path.

Ozark Highlands Trail, Richland Valley

4.0 miles. 80 feet of elevation gain. Backcountry road; scenic views to Point Peter Mountain. The Narrows; historic cemeteries.

The trailhead for the north end of Richland Valley is at the Buffalo River ford at Woolum. For the south end of the valley trail, the trailhead is at the Richland Creek ford west of Snowball. The two fords can be crossed with a high-clearance vehicle when the water is low, but most of the year it's necessary to leave the vehicle and wade. The Ozark Highlands Trail enters the Richland Valley road about 0.2 mile north of the Richland Creek ford.

Side trip: Going south, the Highlands Trail crosses a clearing (a house site) for about 100 yards, then enters the woods to follow an old road onto the Gene Rush/Buffalo River Wildlife Management Area. From there it goes along Horn Mountain onto the Ozark National Forest—isolated country, good habitat for black bear.

Going north, the Highlands Trail follows the valley road to the river, passing the sites of more than a dozen homes—the vanished Point Peter community that once had a school and a post office. Even in the late 1930s the houses and school were there. After 1940, people moved away, until very few lived in Richland Valley.

The post office, which closed in 1943, was established in 1848; Richland was one of the first areas along the Buffalo to be settled. During the Civil War the valley's extensive croplands attracted both Union and Confederate troops seeking food. Richland also was a convenient corridor: Confederates from the Arkansas River came down the valley on their way to raid in Missouri. Several military engagements took place along Richland, though today their locations are not known. On Christmas Day, 1863, Confederates attacked a Union scouting party. On May 3, 1864, Confederates fell upon and destroyed a Union wagon train; 38 soldiers were killed.

For many years after the war, Richland had its community, but the valley was isolated and subsistence farming gave way to a cash-based consumer economy. People left. One descendant of valley pioneers, Ernest Lee (Ern) Cash (1884–1968), stayed put and gradually acquired farmlands until he owned most of lower Richland Valley.

Ern Cash's land passed to his son Lunceford (Lunce), whose ownership of the valley extended to past year 2000. Lunce's son Fon became on-site manager of the family's cattle operation, and Fon and his family became the only inhabitants of the lower valley, with a home in **George Hale Hollow** west of the valley road.

The Park Service owns an easement requiring that the Cash farmland be used so as to maintain the historic pastoral landscape (photo, page 268). Other evidence of the old times is about gone. By the year 2002 there were a few weathered barns, and the stone pillars of a barn that once housed a mule- or horse-powered cotton gin.

About a mile north of George Hale Hollow the road passes the base of **the Narrows**, where the bareness and polish of the Boone limestone ledges above the roadside show that many have climbed them. The top of this steep incline is about 65 feet above the road and is at the lower end of the Narrows. From there the Narrows—a thin spine of rock—rises to a height of nearly 100 feet. People walk along the crest, then start scrambling up from ledge to ledge as the spine beomes higher and thinner (photo, page 369).

Richland Valley spreads below one side of the Narrows, and the Buffalo River flows against the other. Richland Creek once swept against the base of the Narrows on the landward side, but then it moved eastward to its present alignment. The Buffalo may continue to erode its side of the spine, and someday (but not in our lifetimes) may break through to join Richland Creek and abandon its present longer course from the Narrows down to Woolum.

Beyond the Narrows, the last mile of the valley road crosses park land and (unlike the Cash farmlands) the public has access. Here, where the road swings to the east a half mile above the Woolum ford, a lane leads off to the west past the **Hamilton Cemetery**, a family plot having a plank fence installed by the Park Service. Atop the hill a quarter mile south of the Hamilton is the **Narrows Cemetery**, somewhat larger. For many years neither cemetery was maintained because descendants had moved away from the neighborhood.

A few yards before the road reaches the Woolum ford, the trail turns off into a grove of trees toward a crossing of Richland Creek.

Buffalo River Trail, Richland Creek to Dave Manes Bluff

4.0 miles. 760 feet of elevation gain. Woodlands; geologic sites; early 1900s homestead remains; 1970s back-to-the-land cabin. Trailhead on Richland Valley road 100 feet south of Woolum ford.

Leaving the Richland Valley road, the trail winds among box elder and Osage orange trees to the west bank of Richland Creek about 75 yards above its confluence with the Buffalo. Normally the creek here is wide and shallow, on a bed of cobbles. The east bank is at the edge of an overgrown field known as the Island Field because at times it is isolated by high water when the river floods.

The trail crosses the field, marked by wood posts with white blazes. The posts may be hidden by weeds that overran the field after 1990, when cattle were removed. But directly across, the trail continues from the bottom of the hill, angling upward and climbing a long flight of steps with risers of treated wood.

Above the stairway the path doubles back along the hillside, a moist north slope with big oak trees. Then it turns back up the spine of a ridge having a different kind of forest. A virgin, never-cut stand of scrub hardwoods and cedars grows on patches of dry soil between limestone ledges. This was land considered worthless and never claimed by any homesteader, a 40-acre tract that remained in the public domain until transferred to the National River.

About 300 yards after starting up the ridge, the trail leaves the public-domain tract as the ledges disappear, the trees become larger, and a 1960s logging road arrives from farther uphill. The path follows the road trace up the ridge. Soon it goes to the right, off the road, and passes a sink on the left, then three more on the right, all of them shallow and funnel-shaped. These sinkholes developed in the Boone Formation, which the trail has crossed when coming up this hill. Now, however, the path is on a level bench with pieces of tan or brown sandstone lying about—the Batesville Sandstone, the next geologic formation above the gray limestone of the Boone.

Here also is a young forest. One or two big post oaks in these woods have large, spreading crowns, indicating they grew in the open. Maybe a homesteader cleared this land but saved these oaks.

At a three-way junction 1.2 miles from the trailhead, the path turns left to follow an old road across the north end of **Point Peter Mountain**. Climbing from an open post-oak woodland, the trail must be on the Fayetteville Shale that lies above the Batesville

Sandstone, but the badly gullied road is littered with rectangular blocks of sandstone from a formation still higher. Upward from the Fayetteville are many strata of sandstones and shales, not easy to identify as to their places in the geologic column.

Eventually the roadway levels off and a lengthy rock wall appears on the right—and its builder even backfilled behind the wall to make a level terrace. Then along the left is a rock fence, a linear pile running beside the road for nearly 400 feet (photo, page 362). Off in the woods is a cabin site—a chimney fall and bits of broken glass.

The record is sketchy, but Elgan Hall in December 1902 obtained his final receipt for a homestead on this land, and in March 1903 sold 120 acres—including the area now having the walls—to a young couple, Jesse and Margaret Welborn, for $300. Hall probably built the cabin, which was a requirement for obtaining a homestead patent.

Jesse Welborn was alive and paying taxes on the land in 1914, but was dead by 1924, when in his 40s. The Welborns must have had little to show for hard labor but acres of rocky ground.

Beyond the walls the trail heads downhill. Here again the washed-

Exodus. Big families, cheap land. Through the 1800s and past 1900 the rush to populate the rural United States continued. But then the reverse took place, an exodus from the country to towns and cities—first from land too poor to provide a decent living.

In New England, for example, Robert Frost in his poem "The Birthplace" describes a mountainside farm much like the Buffalo River's bench homesteads: cleared ground, rock walls, a family with many children. Within one generation, however, the farm was abandoned and was being reclaimed by the forest.

Writing about growing up in Montana, Ivan Doig describes homesteads in the high foothills of the northern Rockies:

> The homestead sites...in almost all cases turned out to be not the seed acres of yeoman farms.... They turned out to be landing sites, quarters to hold people until they were able to scramble away to somewhere else. Quarters, it could be said, that did for that region of rural America what the tenements of immigrant ghettoes did for city America.

The rural population of the United States, and of the Buffalo River's watershed, peaked about 1910. After that, the exodus got underway, as families fled impoverished farmsteads where they had subsisted while considering how to better themselves.

Rock fence.
With plenty of material lying around, a bench homesteader on Point Peter Mountain busily gathered and piled rock. Was this to be a barrier to wandering livestock?

Today, it appears the homesteader's hard work on infertile soil yielded little or no benefit.

out roadway is an obstacle course with chunks of sandstone and, in wet weather, streams of runoff and areas of mud.

The downgrade becomes gentler. In the road are the remains of a Dodge convertible, circa 1960, left there by a visitor to this bench. Beyond the car, the trail enters an old clearing. A little farther on the left are daffodils and periwinkle, yard plants of a long-ago home site.

And ahead, some yards off the trail, is the ruin of a house: concrete block walls and the remains of a roof. This was to have been an "environmentally correct" home, built by a back-to-the-lander about the time the Park Service began to acquire land for the National River. The owner here sold to the Park Service in 1980, reserving the right to salvage the steel beams supporting his sod-covered roof. He removed the beams and the roof collapsed.

Side trip: A **homestead site**, Buffalo National River's most revealing artifact of the back-to-the-land movement, is located at the end of a path going 0.1 mile south from the concrete-block house. There in the woods overlooking a small pond is a one-room cabin built by the back-to-the-lander and his girlfriend soon after they arrived in Arkansas from Ohio in 1971. They built its stone walls using instructions in a bible of the back-to-the-land movement, *Living the Good Life,* by Helen and Scott Nearing. Windows came from a salvage yard, ceiling beams from an abandoned log house. The cabin later became featured in a magazine (photo, page 364).

From the concrete-block house the trail follows the old road down the steep hill to **Ben Branch**, then down the branch to an intersection. The road trace to the left goes to the river at **Bend Ford**. The trail follows the road to the right, but instead of staying on the road as it heads up the right-hand side of a hollow, the trail goes a few yards farther and becomes a path up the left side.

The path climbs from moist woods that harbor many spring wildflowers to drier woods on a south-facing hillside. Before long the trail swings to the left, levels off, bends to the right, and is on the upriver end of **Dave Manes Bluff** at a short path to an **overlook**. Below lies the river. Beyond are broad hayfields and distant **Jamison Bluff** upriver, **Margaret White Bluff** downstream.

Going along the edge of Manes Bluff, the trail arrives at a side path to the right. A few yards up the slope is a parking turnout beside a dirt road, the first vehicular access to the trail this side of Woolum.

Buffalo River Trail, Dave Manes Bluff to the Tie Slide

4.7 miles. 660 feet of elevation gain. Varied forest habitats; river overlooks; nineteenth-century cemetery; side trips. Trailhead at parking turnout at west end of dirt road along Dave Manes Bluff.

From the parking space a short path goes to the trail, which heads downriver in open woods just below the road. After 200 yards there is a side path down to the left. Meandering past rocky outcrops, the path reaches a fin of limestone projecting fifty feet out from the bluff, a knife-edge more than 100 feet above the treetops below.

The view is panoramic. Beyond the river to the left is a large hayfield. Along the skyline farther left is **Point Peter Mountain**. A mile downriver to the right is **Margaret White Bluff**, its high vertical wall colored gray and buff with patches of orange.

The river's bend past Manes Bluff is a part of the Buffalo that goes underground during the dry months, July through October. Before fall rains come, the river below this viewpoint consists of isolated pools separated by stretches of bleached gravel and bedrock. The Buffalo's much diminished flow passes under the neck of the bend, emerging as White Springs in a pool this side of White Bluff.

Along the main trail not far beyond the overlook, one can begin to read the rocks. To the left is an outcrop of Boone limestone having deep vertical incisions; the cutting was done by acidic water, by solu-

OUR $300 STONE HOUSE IN SNOWBALL, ARKANSAS

TOM, MARCIA, EDWIN & MICHAEL

64

Back to the land.
He and his girlfriend came to the Buffalo in 1971. Like other young migrants from cities to rural areas at that time, they sought escape from a complex, fast-paced, rapidly changing world.

With stone from old fences, sand and gravel from the river, salvaged doors and windows and beams, and little cash but much labor, they built a cabin. Then they and two friends wrote up the experience and sold the story to a back-to-the-landers' magazine that paid them $200.

tion. Along the trail are lichen-crusted rocks in piles; the piling was done long ago by someone clearing the field on the right.

Then the trail reaches the corner of the field, turns away from the river, and is in a grove of maples—whose fall leaves lend a golden glow overhead—and soon the path reaches a road. Now the way is to the left, through a stand of oaks and hickories. After 0.3 mile there is a junction and the trail swings to the right onto another road.

Side trip: The road straight ahead from the junction goes downhill to hayfields and a gravel bar with campsites opposite Margaret White Bluff. It is joined at the hayfields by a farm road leading back to the main trail 0.4 mile east of the woods junction.

The main trail goes east, down the hill to the farm road, then turns right and heads south. On the left is an overgrown field. Soon the trail leaves the road and crosses a corner of the old field with its cedars and honey locusts. About 100 yards off the road, the trail is at the **Slay Cemetery.** Until the cemetery was cleared and fenced in the 1990s, its grave markers were hidden in a thicket of switch cane. Now in view, the stones date from 1872 to 1905, the period when local population probably peaked. *(Continued on page 373)*

National River and Wilderness Areas **PARK**

From beginning to end, this river and its special places have been saved for you to find, to explore, to know, and to enjoy.

Upper Buffalo Wilderness, Ozark National Forest

Boxley Valley pastures and hayfield

Cemetery, Boxley Valley

Changes of scene are part of the river's charm. The wooded, rugged Upper Wilderness opens into the Boxley Valley, a place of quiet beauty. The valley's houses, barns, fields, cemeteries, and more—these tell us of a local history that reaches back to before the Civil War.

Again there is dramatic change when the river flows from the Boxley Valley and the mountains close in. For fourteen miles downstream is the Ozarks' deepest gorge, having cliffs to more than 500 feet high.

Buzzard Bluff, below Kyles Landing

Another change of scene takes place when the river emerges from its canyon in the Boston Mountains. Towering cliffs are left behind. The scenery now is smaller in scale, more close at hand. The river is gentler; rapids are milder. There's time now to look at the shapes of rocks, the plants growing on bluffs, the spring-fed tributary creeks. As it turns out, these too are captivating.

Mill Branch, Mount Hersey

Passing its midpoint, halfway between beginning and end, the Buffalo enters a wider valley. Beyond bank-side trees and within the river's bends are broad hayfields. At the outside of each bend, though, is a sheer cliff, and each has its own distinctive form. The knife-edge Narrows, Whisenant Bluff with its curving alcove, Peter Cave Bluff with its pinnacles—these are here, and much more also. The river never ceases to entertain.

The Narrows, looking upriver

On Pine Ridge, near Gilbert

For miles downstream, past Tyler Bend and Grinders Ferry and past the village of Gilbert, the more open course of the middle Buffalo continues. Then by degrees the valley becomes narrower, the bluffs higher, with steep terraces between faces of rock.

Beyond Dillards Ferry and Buffalo Point, the river comes to the Lower Buffalo Wilderness—and cliffs to nearly 600 feet high. From upper-river canyon and headwaters wilderness, the Buffalo here again is in a canyon, and in a wilderness.

Ludlow Bluff, Lower Buffalo Wilderness

Suspended cliff-top boulder, Leatherwood Wilderness, Ozark National Forest

At river's end are two adjoining wilderness areas, Lower Buffalo and Leatherwood. Together they offer many places to explore, countless small surprises, escape from stress and care…here, in these hills, a wide and spacious, forever precious freedom.

One of the graves is of Delpha Manes, the first wife of David C. Manes, for whom Manes Bluff is named. Delpha had nine children, in all but one instance spaced two years apart, the first when she was 19, the last at 35. Delpha died in 1902, when 40 years old. David Manes not only outlived Delpha but also a second wife, Margaret, who died at age 50. Dave Manes died in 1947 at 91, having outlived five of his nine children. Old-timers remember him as a small man but strong, industrious, frugal, generous—a good provider.

From the cemetery the path crosses a muddy track that leads to a campsite by the river. Then the trail goes across Slay Branch—bone-dry much of the year—and up a few yards to follow the left edge of a stream terrace, looking down on a lower terrace.

The trail enters a side hollow of Slay Branch to follow narrow ter-races. (Here's an April flower garden with the park's best display of wild geraniums.) The path crosses the creek several times, then climbs steeply up an old logging road. Loose chert on the roadbed is a reminder that the trail is on the ever present Boone Formation.

Then off the road into the woods, with big oaks here, up the right side of a ravine. The path swings right, then left, around the head of the ravine. At the next right turn, and through the tops of trees down the bluff, there are impressive views—at least when the leaves are off. First the view is up the Buffalo, with the river coming straight toward…disappearing under the bluff directly below the trail. Then, 20 yards farther around the trail's bend, the river appears from below the bluff and moves away.

As the trail continues through the woods along **Slay Branch Bluff**, there are other glimpses of White Bluff up the river. Now the path is getting closer to **Whisenant Bluff** downriver, with its two tall faces of rock separated by a curving alcove.

The path heads away from the river and into **Whisenant Hollow**, going down an east-facing hillside, moist enough for dense under-growth and clumps of Christmas fern. Across the hollow on the west-facing buttress of Whisenant Bluff is a thicket of junipers hung with gray-green wisps of old-man's-beard.

Across the trickling stream at the bottom of the hollow, the trail climbs up a drier, west-facing hillside, with ledges and pieces of gray Boone limestone and a litter of rubbly chert. Higher up are pine trees where the limestone has dissolved away, leaving acidic soil.

Again at a summit where the trail bends sharply right, the scene opens up, for Whisenant Bluff stands 260 feet above the river. Pine trees here add a special flavor; they are not encountered that often. The trail passes around the bluff's deep, curving alcove, its rock wall in view just below. Through the pines are glimpses of White Bluff up the river. Much farther in the distance and to the left, 16 miles to the northwest and peeking above ridges along the horizon, is one of the region's major landmarks, flat-topped Boat Mountain.

A short distance down the hill, a path leads 20 yards off-trail to an **overlook** at the bluff's edge. Below is a grand sweep of blue-green river, curving from left to right, coming toward, then below, then away from the overlook, with a long hayfield within the bend. On the brink of the cliff, bushy green junipers frame the scene. Along the near edge, stems of prairie grass wave in the breeze.

The farmland within the river's bend once belonged to Captain Harry Love, who during the Civil War commanded this county's only company of Confederates. Union troops raided the farm more than once but never captured Love. Ever since that war, local people with Confederate forebears have usually been Democrats (and Union sympathizers, Republicans). So it seems fitting that eventually this farm passed to one Will Goggin, known as this county's Democratic boss. The Park Service purchased the land from Goggin in 1975.

Back at the edge of the woods are green mosses and gray-green lichens. Pines are sparse now; instead there's a mix of large and small hardwoods. The forest will keep changing.

Down the trail is another overlook, but the view is partly blocked by vegetation. Farther downhill, past a north-facing slope having tall hardwoods, the trail is on top of a ridge—cedars and outcropping limestone, almost an open glade, so different from the forest only a hundred yards back. Then the path gets beyond the limestone and the cedars, is in another stand of hardwoods, swings left as it continues downhill, and arrives at a cliff's edge with another view.

This time the side path leads onto a point of rock that extends about 40 feet toward Whisenant Bluff, straight ahead. Whisenant's rough gray surface has one patch of orange, near the top.

For a short distance beyond the viewpoint the trail passes along a west-facing slope facing the river, with pines and huckleberry. The path arrives at a saddle and turns away from the river, down a hollow, a little dry valley created as limestone dissolved along a fracture line and chert and soil settled into the void. After heavy rainfall there is some surface flow down the channel to the right of the trail.

Turning left into a larger hollow, the trail is on an east slope with a mesic (moderately moist) forest quite unlike the stand of pines 150 yards back. Crossing the stream bed at the bottom of the hollow, the path goes up a logging road—very steep—onto another hillside facing west. Pine trees are here again, including some big ones.

The trail bends to the right (where a path to the left goes toward a potential campsite in the woods) and starts across a gentle north slope. Pines disappear and once more there are hardwoods. Here, in the spring, patches of wild iris are in bloom. The trail then crosses another dirt road that goes into another bend of the Buffalo.

Side trip: The road leads to broad fields and points along the river. The area—and its high bluff—are called Love Hensley, for Lovette Hensley (1877–1957), who with his wife, Mary Susan (1889–1979), owned a 594-acre farm here. Hensley served as county sheriff and tax collector (he signed tax receipts "Love Hensley") and was part-owner of a mercantile store. Susie Hensley sold the farm to the Park Service in 1975 and today the fields are leased for producing hay.

Past the road, the trail goes along the south edge of the Hensley bottomlands, through a young forest on acreage once cleared. Except for a few big oaks the Hensleys may have left for shade or squirrels, the trees are small. Japanese honeysuckle and multiflora rose grow along the path; both species are evidence of human presence.

The path swings left to follow a shallow side valley. Here in the woods are many round rocks two to six inches across, not gray limestone of the Boone Formation hereabouts, but gray-brown sandstone from a higher geologic formation, brought here by the river ages ago, remaining as evidence of an ancient gravel bar. The round rocks continue in view after the trail swings to the right, following a road trace at the foot of a hillside. Apparently the river once flowed along this side of the present bottomland.

To the left of the trail, brush and saplings indicate the area was once a field. Then, just to the left, two shallow drainages feed into the abrupt head, or beginning, of a steep-sided gully 8 feet deep and 20 feet wide—a good example now of headward erosion.

We suppose the big ditch originated in a road that followed the fence still seen on the far side of the gully. Rainwater ran down the road, washing away its soft alluvial soil. The road was regraded but more soil washed away. This was repeated until the roadway became entrenched, impossible to maintain, and the road was moved to the base of the hill. Following this later road, the trail passes the gully for more than 100 yards. Then the gully bends away and the trail runs along a wire fence, and finally a rock fence. Off to the left beyond the fence is more old field, with occasional weedy openings and the rest of it having young trees…which, in time, will change.

The bottomland ends at a wide gravelly wash, the course of a meandering wet-weather creek. At the far edge of the wash, the trail heads up the steep left side of a ravine, climbing steadily among trees larger than those of the old field in the bottomland. Here along the trail are a couple of tall cedars more than a foot through.

As the path swings up to the left across a narrow bench, all the tread is surfaced with chert rubble, and more broken chert is scattered through the woods. The trail bends right and continues to climb, now on the side of the ridge facing the river. Soon in view is **Peter Cave Bluff**—towers and pinnacles spaced along the hillside, with one or two larger flat walls, one or two scooped-out surfaces, and patches of dark green juniper growing in places between the exposures of gray rock. All these features are typical of bluffs developed in the Boone Formation (illustration, page 266).

The trail crosses the top of the ridge to its south slope, then goes through a small glade opening with greenbrier and outcrops of limestone. Then into the woods again, where sizeable post oaks, red oaks, and hickories grow in a saddle, or dip, where soil is deeper. Then back along the north side of the ridge, poorer ground with mossy ledges, chinkapin oaks, and cedars.

Then downhill a few yards to another saddle, where a dirt road bends close to the edge of Peter Cave Bluff: the Tie Slide.

Buffalo River Trail, Tie Slide to Collier Trailhead

4.0 miles. 440 feet of elevation gain. Backcountry road; historic cemeteries; overlooks of river and Calf Creek. Trailhead is on dirt road at Tie Slide on top of upstream end of Peter Cave Bluff.

Around 1900, "tie hackers" using broadaxes hewed crossties from white oak logs and brought them to the top of Peter Cave Bluff. Here, it is said, each tie was stapled to a cable that stretched down to the river, then pushed off to slide down the cable. At the river the ties were collected to be rafted downstream and sold. Thus this place came to be known as **the Tie Slide**.

The Buffalo River Trail follows the dirt road eastward from the Tie Slide for 3.3 miles, to past Calf Creek. Almost immediately the road starts climbing, then heads up a steep incline having limestone outcrops too high for low-clearance cars. Beyond the top of the hill the road continues along the up-and-down ridge above Peter Cave Bluff.

Four-tenths of a mile beyond the Tie Slide is a 100-foot-long path from the road to an **overlook** on one of Peter Cave Bluff's limestone pinnacles. The path begins at parking turnouts on both sides of the road (on the right, one car, parallel; on the left, one car, head-in). From the overlook the view downriver includes orange-stained **Red Bluff,** with two massive stone "heads" on top. The view upriver extends to Point Peter Mountain, four miles away. Part of this view, framed with an ancient, twisted Ashe's juniper, is featured on the front of Trails Illustrated's *Buffalo National River, East Half* map.

Beyond the overlook, the road winds along a ridge for more than a mile past second-growth hardwoods. Unless wanting to stop and identify plant species, one will probably want to keep moving. At one point a gated road to the left leads into **Cash Bend,** having fields and the remains of long abandoned farm buildings.

Eventually the road descends to bottomland in **Arnold Bend** and another road to the left leads 0.4 mile to the **Arnold Cemetery.**

Side trip: Graves in the Arnold Cemetery date from the nineteenth century until well into the twentieth. Here is the grave of William Arnold (1822-1898), the earliest Arnold of Arnold Bend. He married into the Dean family, who may have settled here as early as 1834. Arnolds acquired most of the land in the bend by the late 1880s. At that time men were rafting timber down the Buffalo, and they may have named Arnold Bend—and several more of the river's bends— to keep tabs on how far they had come with their rafts.

Two late nineteenth-century graves of children have six-sided coffins of solid stone placed on top. These cenotaphs, or false tombs, probably made by local artisans, are on nineteenth-century graves of adults as well as children at cemeteries in the middle Buffalo area, elsewhere in Arkansas, and reportedly in Missouri and Tennessee. Their exact meaning or symbolism is unknown. They may have been only a tradition or trend of fashion spread by word of mouth.

Past the turnoff to the Arnold Cemetery, the road passes old fields and then enters a woods where the **Old Arnold Cemetery** lies within a board fence. The graveyard was established before the Civil War. There are a few inscribed stones. Some of the plain ones of native rock are said to mark the graves of slaves.

About 200 yards past the cemetery is a small house with board-

and-batten siding, built about 1880 and the home of John Arnold. Two-tenths of a mile farther is a house that John's son Luther built about 1915. Both houses have been long vacant and the Luther Arnold house has lost its front porch. The Park Service stabilized the buildings and left them as "discovery sites."

Beyond the houses the road overlooks a bend of **Calf Creek**, then rounds a turn and goes down to the creek. Calf Creek here is a 100-foot-wide bed of gravel for much of the year, or shallow flow over the gravel. After heavy rainfall the creek can loosen the gravel and create washouts. People who then try to drive across get stuck.

From Calf Creek the road curves across a bottomland hayfield and into a side valley. Up a rise about 25 yards beyond the edge of the field, the trail turns left, off the road, to begin a gentle 0.6-mile ascent. In that distance the forest changes several times. From big hardwoods on the moist, northwest-facing slope at the foot of the hill, the trees become progressively smaller, on drier ground. Hardwoods are replaced by large cedars, then by smaller cedars and Ashe's junipers on the upper part of the hill where limestone crops out. Then, toward the top, cedars are replaced by stunted hardwoods and by grassy openings with a view to Calf Creek and Point Peter Mountain (photo, page 253; description at *Side trip*, page 385).

At the top of the ridge is the Collier homestead **historic site** with its log house, smokehouse, and barn (see *Collier homestead*, page 386). At the log house the **River View Trail** (see page 385) goes to the left and the Buffalo River Trail turns right, along a broad path, handicap-accessible. In 100 feet another path, the **Return Trail** (see page 388), also goes to the left. The Buffalo River Trail continues 0.1 mile through an old field to the Collier trailhead parking area.

Buffalo River Trail, Collier Trailhead to Gilbert

5.9 miles. 430 feet of elevation gain. Bottomlands and ridges; cabin sites; views of river. Trailhead at Collier homestead parking area off Tyler Bend road, 1.3 miles west of U.S. Highway 65.

From the trailhead, the trail passes among big oaks and younger growth, crosses the park entrance road, and loses some elevation in the woods north of the road. Then it remains at about the same level for the next mile, running mostly through a hardwood forest on north-facing slopes. The geology also has uniformity—all Boone

Formation with no large outcrops of rock, only a mantle of rubbly chert under the forest's leaf litter and on the trail tread.

Soon there is a junction with the **Spring Hollow Trail**, going to the left (see pages 389–390) and 0.6 mile farther, a meeting with the **Buck Ridge Trail**, also going left (see page 390). Beyond the Buck Ridge Trail the path turns north to follow a road trace along a drier, west-facing hillside having a different array of plant species. Here are open patches of grass, and goldenrod, false aloe, greenbrier, fragrant sumac, and post oaks. Along the trail are outcrops of limestone where solution has created rounded openings in the rock.

The trail crosses a saddle and runs down an east-facing slope, and again the species are ones requiring more moisture. Then, past the **Rock Wall Trail** going to the left (see pages 391–392), the path begins down a rocky south slope and the woods again are dry, with cedars, scrub hardwoods, and small openings with grass.

Near the bottom of the hill is a wider clearing, a 100-foot right-of-way under long spans of power lines (161,000 volts, serving communities along Highway 65). The clearing has both woodland and sun-loving plants: ferns and stump sprouts, sumac and blackberry. And clumps of silver plume grass with stems to eight feet high.

On re-entering the woods, the path is in a shady, moist ravine with large trees and a stream flowing (or in drought, trickling) on bedrock. The place is also impacted by humans, for here are patches of Japanese honeysuckle and the remains of a wellhead pump house for a dwelling that once stood somewhere uphill.

There is traffic noise. Now the trail emerges from the woods onto a sloping highway cut. Sericea lespedeza was planted here to control erosion, and if not mowed it hides the trail, which runs along the cut slope to the Buffalo River bridge on **Highway 65**.

The pedestrian walkway across the bridge, 990 feet long, allows a look at the rough, bulging wall of Boone limestone and chert in McMahan Bluff just upriver. Across the bridge, the trail goes down a ramp from the highway shoulder, then doubles back to pass under the bridge and along the bottomland—an area subject to flooding, so that the path may be blocked by driftwood. Farther on, the trail goes across a gated lane to a hayfield, then heads up-slope into lowland woods, part of an old home place now growing up in old-field species such as honey locust. Patches of garlic, another plant associated with human habitation, have spread under the trees.

After crossing a gully, climbing a hill, and entering a field, the trail reaches a graded dirt road, now 0.4 mile past the lane to the hayfield.

Side trip: This road goes 0.6 mile east, ending on a high bank above a gravel bar opposite **Shine Eye Bluff**, an undeveloped picnic and swim area known both to canoers and to local people.

Across the Shine Eye road the trail heads uphill through a grassy area and into the woods, where it follows a roadway up the ridge. Toward the top of the hill, land was cleared in the 1960s for pasture. Bulldozed piles of rocks remain to the left of the road.

At the top of the hill, 0.6 mile past the Shine Eye road, the trail turns right, leaving the roadway. After crossing the level hilltop, it goes down to join another road, passing from acidic soil that nurtures hardwoods to a limestone area that favors cedars. This road continues along a ridge, soon going down to a saddle, where it crosses another old road trace. The path to the right leads into **Long Bottom**. The trail ahead climbs a hill—Boone chert is here in the eroded roadbed—and then it passes the foundation of a house.

Some of the history of this place comes from Loucille Baker and Ray Jordan of Gilbert. The cottage was built in the 1930s by two elderly women schoolteachers from Missouri, who also planted an orchard. Later a man named Wright from Houston, Texas, bought the property, but by 1970 the house was vacant and in poor condition. It was torn down after Wright sold it to the Park Service in 1973.

A hundred yards beyond the house site the trail veers off the road to run on the side of the hill, overlooking the river. Along this 0.3-mile section of trail are large pine trees—the most attractive stretch of woods between Tyler Bend and Gilbert, with its view of the river and beyond into the broad fields of **Lane Bend**. This hill is known locally as Pine Ridge (photo, page 370).

The trail reaches another saddle, where a woods road comes up from Highway 333. Here, around 1925 or 1930, Jack Francis and his wife, from Kansas City, established a year-round resort they named Back o' Beyond. They put up two log buildings for guests and constructed a stairway of pine logs down the bluff to the river. The business fell victim to the 1930s Depression and the vacant buildings were torn down or—more likely—burned. The foundation of the larger cabin (photo, opposite) is today a rectangular outline under a blanket of honeysuckle, on the right as the trail reaches the saddle.

From Back o' Beyond, the trail takes the road up to the downriver crest of Pine Ridge. The road along the top is soon a dividing line between the stand of pine trees on the drier, west slope and one of

Back o' Beyond, a resort on Pine Ridge, near Gilbert, fell victim
to the 1930s Depression. Here, around 1940, the main building
stands unused and empty (note the sagging front step).

hardwoods on the moister east side. Again there's a view through the
pines to the river, the fields of Lane Bend, and green hills and blue-
green mountains beyond. Another delight along Pine Ridge about the
first of May is the sight and intoxicating spicy-sweet smell of mountain azaleas in bloom (photo, page 5). Like the pines, these flowering shrubs grow only on acidic soil, provided here because the Boone
limestone has been removed by solution.

Down the hill at the end of Pine Ridge, the trail leaves the road and
continues its descent along the hillside. At first the ground is littered
with rough chunks of broken chert, but as the trail reaches a lower
elevation, there are rounded pieces of sandstone—scattered remnants
of river gravel and cobbles left thousands of years ago, before the
Buffalo cut down and moved sidewise to its present channel.

The trail this side of Pine Ridge also has spring wildflowers: trout
lily, rue anemone, bloodroot, and especially May apple. These disappear when the path goes into a former clearing now thick with bri-
ars, Japanese honeysuckle, and young trees.

Then into the open, under a power line (161,000 volts, belonging
to the government's Southwestern Power Administration and linking
generators at Bull Shoals and Norfork Dams on the White River with
communities in the Arkansas Valley to the south). Beyond, the path
is a grassy track toward the west bank of **Dry Creek**.

Normally the creek is dry, but it's several feet deep when floods back up from the river. The west bank may be undercut by high water, washing away the last few feet of trail above the creek bed.

Dry Creek's east bank is about 15 feet high, steep, and of alluvial soil that becomes slick when wet. The trail goes along this high bank, then climbs it to an extensive stream terrace. Following the edge of the terrace, the path first overlooks Dry Creek, then the Buffalo River while passing through thickets of switch cane, old-field scrub, and Japanese honeysuckle. Finally it emerges onto the road that comes down from the village toward the Gilbert gravel bar.

M&NA Railroad Grade

1.8 miles. 40 feet of elevation gain. Nearly level; views of river; geologic formations. Trailhead about one block from Gilbert store on road to river; parking in village or on Gilbert gravel bar.

From the road at the trailhead, a path goes about 100 feet east to the wide, level grade of the railroad. In another 100 feet, and ten yards to the right, are concrete piers on which stood the railroad's water tank for filling the reservoirs of steam locomotives. About 75 feet beyond the piers a steep path leads down the high embankment to Gilbert Spring, from which water was pumped up to the tank. About 200 feet beyond the turnoff to the path is a view off the rail-road grade to the spring branch as it flows toward the Buffalo River.

Interestingly, Gilbert Spring receives most of its water from Dry Creek northwest of Gilbert, where all the creek's normal flow sinks into its stream bed. Hydrologists dye-traced the underground stream and found it takes ten hours to travel 1.2 miles to the spring.

Half a mile along the grade below Gilbert, the builders of this rail-road encountered problems. With the primitive equipment available in 1902, they had to dig and blast away as much as 25 feet of bedrock—tedious, costly work that seemed to foretell the eventual doom of the M&NA (see *May Never Arrive,* opposite). This was rugged, sparsely populated country that stalled construction and would always stifle passenger and freight business.

In 1949, the year the railroad was abandoned and dismantled, geologists came here to examine this railroad cut. They knew that rock formations exposed on the surface along the Buffalo turn down-ward at the southern edge of the Ozarks, probably dipping far below

May Never Arrive. That's what M&NA stood for, said folks who talked about the Missouri & North Arkansas Railroad. At that time, about 1910, its rails extended for 359 miles, from southwestern Missouri to the Mississippi River. Soon to become bankrupt, the M&NA was not meeting schedules.

The M&NA was revived, and stayed barely alive for another 35 years. Its tracks were poorly designed, built, and maintained; its territory in the hills produced too little revenue; its absentee owners and managers were incompetent. Finally, in 1946, management shut down the line. In 1949 salvagers removed tracks and the Buffalo River bridge.

One day in 1906 when the train halted a mile below Gilbert, a passenger got off and recorded this scene.

the surface of the Arkansas Valley, where people were searching for oil and gas. To better know what might exist down deep, they came to the Buffalo to see what lay in view.

At this railroad cut they identified the Plattin Limestone, fine-grained and 75 feet thick. Above the Plattin they found the Fernvale Limestone, coarse-grained and 25 feet in depth. Farther up to the top of the hill were, in ascending order, exposures of Cason Shale, the Brassfield, Lafferty, and St. Clair Limestones, and the Boone Formation. The rock seen in the railroad cut is the Plattin Limestone.

Nearly a mile beyond Gilbert the roadbed is interrupted by a deep gully, where a bridge is gone. A path goes into the gully and back up the other side, and along the grade there's soon another 25-foot cut in solid rock. On the opposite side of the roadbed the ground drops off some 40 feet to the river. In the record flood of December 1982, however, the river was on this roadbed. Along the railroad grade past the village at Gilbert it reached a depth of eight or ten feet.

About 300 yards beyond the deep gully is a view across the river to the mouth of Bear Creek, one of the Buffalo's larger tributaries, originating in the Boston Mountains 20 miles to the south. Just beyond the creek is an open field, and from there a dirt road heads up the hill and out toward Marshall. Local people drive down to the field, coming to fish or swim—or to party at night.

After the view to Bear Creek the old grade is on gentler terrain with cuts and fills but no serious bedrock. Soon the roadbed bends away from the river. Soon afterward, where a road trace goes to the left off the grade, the railroad bed turns back toward the Buffalo.

Side trip: The road trace to the left goes through the woods to a graded dirt road that continues to a parking area near the Buffalo at river mile 101.7 (and 0.8 mile from the beginning of this side trip at the railroad grade). From the parking area a short path leads down the bank onto a gravel bar opposite a 60-foot bluff. Local people call this place the Sand Hole, and the overgrown farm site within this river bend is the old Carl Martin place. Park employees noticed the thickets of wild plum and named it Plumfield.

At the road trace toward Plumfield, the railroad grade begins a right-hand bend, and in the next 250 yards it turns directly toward the river on an elevated causeway, or fill. Then the grade suddenly ends. Ahead are massive concrete piers of the vanished Buffalo River bridge. Big sycamore trees now stand in line with the piers.

Near the end of the railroad fill, one can scramble down to the bottomland and walk out onto the wide gravel bar to view the piers from below (photo, page 216). The piers are spaced 150 feet apart. They are about 35 feet high. They were totally submerged during the great flood of December 1982.

> **Tyler Bend Visitor Center.** On a hill overlooking a Buffalo River bottomland, Park Service architects and exhibit designers placed this facility to provide you with close-up looks at nature and history along the river. A small museum has rocks and fossils, plants and animals, and Native American and pioneer artifacts to see (in some cases, even to touch). Here also are movies for viewing, Park Service interpreters for answering questions, books and maps for purchase, a wildflower garden for learning more of the native species, and a viewing deck for a relaxing interlude.

Tyler Bend

The ridges and hollows south of Tyler Bend's visitor center and camping areas have five trails: River View, Return, Spring Hollow, Buck Ridge, and Rock Wall. All five intersect the Buffalo River Trail and these trails can be combined for loop hikes of varying length.

River View Trail
1.5 miles. 180 feet of elevation gain or loss. Handicap-accessible trail to river overlook. Log buildings; wildflowers; limestone glade.

The trailhead at the upper end of the trail is at the parking area for the Collier homestead, off Tyler Bend's entrance road 1.3 miles west of U.S. 65. (At the lower end it is at the Tyler Bend Visitor Center, opposite the parking space reserved for the handicapped.)

From the upper trailhead a handicap-accessible trail (which also is part of the Buffalo River Trail) leads 0.1 mile to the homestead. The land here is in old-field succession, reverting to forest. By the year 2000 this cleared land was overtaken by blackberry and, especially, sumac. Trees had taken hold, including wild plum, winged elm, persimmon, cedar, and honey locust with its many long thorns.

Soon (just past an intersection with the **Return Trail**, which goes to the right) a log house is in view ahead. This house and its outbuildings and grounds are the Collier family homestead, now a designated **historic site** (see *Collier homestead*, page 386).

Side trip: Out the side gate at the Collier house, across the roadway, and 200 feet down the Buffalo River Trail is an area of open woods and glades with a view to Calf Creek and to Point Peter Mountain (photo, page 253). The woods are hickory and post oak with low-bush huckleberry and mountain azalea. In the sunny, west-facing glade openings a botanist found big and little bluestem, both of them grasses of the prairies. Here too are blazing star, pale-purple coneflower, goat's rue, two kinds of goldenrod, orange puccoon, prairie mimosa, stiff-haired sunflower, and prickly pear cactus. Blackjack oak and winged elm also are here on this dry site with its limestone, gravelly chert rubble, and orange clay.

The River View Trail continues past the log house and then the site of the Collier family's kitchen garden (where Sod grew his prize-winning Kentucky Wonder pole beans) and cornfield. Beyond the remaining outbuilding the path goes through an old field becoming a woodland as it is overtaken by sumac, cedars, and black walnut trees.

The trail continues through second-growth woods to the top of **Collier Bluff**, where a viewing platform stands about 270 feet above the river. The Buffalo, here a wide river, comes slowly toward the base of the bluff, moving out of sight directly below the platform. To the left is **Calf Creek**, flowing toward the river. Beyond the creek are the fields of **Arnold Bend**. Beyond the bend—and two and a half miles due west—is **Red Bluff**, beside the Buffalo.

Collier homestead. Solomon David "Sod" and Ida Mae Collier came to the Buffalo River from Kentucky and in 1931 applied for 40 acres of the public domain. The Colliers and several of their seven children cleared land, built a house, and lived there for five years, meeting requirements for a homestead patent. The Colliers' patent in 1937 was one of the last in the region to be granted under the Homestead Act of 1862.

On this small ridge-top farm with no plumbing or electricity, the Colliers managed a living. They raised cattle and hogs and had a vegetable garden and apple and peach trees. Sod hunted and fished and earned a little cash as a fishing guide and as a sheriff's deputy. Ida Mae grew medicinal herbs and used them for home remedies. She also was an avid flower gardener and filled the yard with hollyhocks and iris.

In 1961, with the children grown and gone, Sod and Ida Mae sold the homestead. Sod, at least, had thrived on the farm and would live to be 100 years old. One of his daughters, however, says that she "would just as soon forget the good old days."

When the Park Service bought the property in 1977, the land had become part of a cattle farm and the buildings were lost in undergrowth. Park employees made repairs to stabilize the buildings and reconstructed the house porch. Volunteers have helped to restore plantings and build the fence of hand-split palings that replicates the one the Colliers had around the yard.

In the log house the two rooms to the right were the kitchen and living area. The interior room at the center was a pantry for home-canned fruits and vegetables to carry the family through long winters. The large room off the left end of the porch was a bedroom—"filled with beds," a Collier son recalls.

Outside the right corner is a cistern for rainwater piped from the house roof. The log building in the front yard is a smokehouse, and in the yard are a few plants descended from ones in Ida Mae's herb and flower gardens.

The handicap trail ends at the overlook but a hiking trail continues down the ridge—steep, descending as much as 25 feet in 100 feet of travel. Soon the trail levels off at a junction with the lower end of the **Return Trail**, going back to the right (see page 388).

The River View Trail keeps straight ahead, now on gray limestone or gravelly chert along the top of the bluff. Mosses survive on thin patches of soil. Multi-trunked Ashe's junipers stand with wisps of lichen—old-man's-beard—hanging from their branches.

This stretch of trail lies near the center of a 43-acre block of land that never left the public domain. In 1905 an individual named Elijah Peoples filed a homestead claim on this acreage and an adjoining 40 acres to the south, but Peoples failed to perfect his claim. There are, however, several old cedar stumps along the trail. Somebody felt no guilt about taking cedars from public land.

A hundred yards from the junction with the Return Trail is an overlook, atop a sheer cliff about 140 feet above the river. The view is past Calf Creek Shoal to the fields of Arnold Bend.

From the overlook the trail heads back down into a hollow. At the bottom is a trickling stream, moist ground, and wild hydrangea. The path beyond the stream is in a dense stand of leaf-cup three to four feet tall; the plant's bruised leaves have a strong, unpleasant smell.

Down the hollow the path is along a west-facing hillside, drier now, with low-bush huckleberry. The trail enters a side hollow, goes across its stream channel, and turns back across a sunny, southwest-facing slope with exposed rock, a limestone glade (photo, page 388). Here a botanist has found plants that tolerate dryness or like the sun: cliff-brake fern, poverty grass, little bluestem, calamint, goat's rue, prairie tea, asters, goldenrods, stiff-haired sunflower, and prickly pear cactus. And shrubs and small trees: low-bush huckleberry, farkleberry, dwarf hackberry, and three kinds of sumac. And larger trees that withstand drought: red cedar, post oak, winged elm.

The glade is small and the trail continues in woods on the west-facing hillside. Soon it is at the mouth of the hollow and near the river, crossing a gully on a footbridge, and in the woods along the base of a hill that looks out on a hayfield. In the spring this part of the trail at the edge of the bottomland is Buffalo National River's best wildflower walk. In late spring and through the summer there are fewer flowers, though some new species come into bloom.

The path bends into and across a short side hollow, then very soon climbs to the parking area at the Tyler Bend Visitor Center.

Limestone glade.
Only a few yards from a
moist woodland, prickly
pear cactus shows up in
a dry opening. This
southwest-facing hillside
along the River View
Trail at Tyler Bend has
attracted many plants that
like sunshine and can
withstand drought.

Return Trail
0.4 mile. 100 feet of elevation gain or loss. A mesic woodland.

This trail provides an easier way of return for hikers who have gone from the Collier homestead to Collier Bluff's lower overlooks, for it bypasses the River View Trail's steep climb back to the highest overlook (see pages 386–387). The Return Trail also offers a change of scenery. The trail's easy grade is along an east-facing slope with a mesic (moderately moist) woodland having ferns and wildflowers, buckeye and dogwood, and a stand of white oaks.

There's much poison ivy along (but not in) the trail. The vines will invade disturbed ground, and here they may have spread after free-ranging hogs rooted up the forest floor. In later years with suppression of wildfire, a buildup of leaf litter could have protected the vines as they grew along the ground. Thus it is likely that humans' treatment of the land encouraged the abundance of poison ivy.

Nearing the upper end of the Return Trail, the woods become more open, with grasses and white clover along the path. Here again is a young forest replacing former pasture, on this hillside below the Collier house.

About 100 feet in front of the log house, the trail ends at the River View Trail (see page 385).

Spring Hollow Trail

0.9 mile. 240 feet of elevation gain or loss. Moist and dry woodlands. Trailhead at parking area next to campground pay station.

The Spring Hollow Trail begins at the top of the steps at the left rear corner of the parking area. From the steps the trail goes to the right, into the woods and up a narrow valley.

Just to the left is the stream course, normally a bed of dry gravel at the bottom of a gully about ten feet deep. This steep-sided ditch has been cut into a deep layer of soil and gravelly chert deposited there over a long time. The gully probably formed in a much shorter time. One cloudburst flood may have done most of it, though no one today knows exactly what happened. We can wonder, though, whether the erosion was helped along by human activity or whether it got underway without outside help.

A surer sign of human tinkering: Japanese honeysuckle along the trail. People once planted this Asian vine as a ground cover, or for its pretty, sweet-smelling yellow-and-white flowers. Birds ate its berries and spread its seeds. The vines overwhelm native plants but do provide food for deer and for fruit-eating birds.

The hillside above the trail was subjected to a prescribed burn about 1998 to remove accumulated forest debris and improve wildlife habitat. For some years after any woods fire, there is noticeably less undergrowth. For a longer time, charred areas remain on fallen trees and on the lower trunks of standing ones.

Beyond the trailhead 0.4 mile, the path meets the lower end of the Buck Ridge Trail, which goes straight ahead (see pages 390–391). The Spring Hollow Trail heads to the right, up a side hollow.

The deep gully's watercourse was dry gravel; the side hollow's creek bed often is bedrock with a visible amount of water, a spring-fed stream that inspired the name for this trail. The woods are shadier, the air more humid, the vegetation more dense. Among the plants at the forest floor are wild ginger and jack-in-the-pulpit. A few feet uphill on acidic soil are wild azaleas. Poison ivy is here too, and some Japanese honeysuckle all the way to the last crossing of the creek, where the path heads uphill into a different kind of forest.

As the trail climbs, then swings to the right, the woods become drier, more open, with less low-growing vegetation. Toward the top of this uphill stretch of trail, prescribed burns were done about 1998 and again in 2004, part of a program throughout Buffalo National

River to remove forest debris that could feed devastating wildfires.

These woods toward the upper end of the Spring Hollow Trail are within an 80-acre homestead patented by one Jasper Reeves in 1904. Reeves presumably lived on this homestead long enough to "prove up" his claim; the west half has some level ground for a cabin. But there's no evidence he intended to make this land his life's home. Like many others who obtained homesteads on these dry ridges and then disappeared, Reeves probably soon sold his land and moved on.

Past a left turn, the last climb up a ridge is a short ascent to the junction with the Buffalo River Trail (see page 379).

Buck Ridge Trail
0.8 mile. 320 feet of elevation gain or loss. Interesting woodlands.

From the Buffalo River Trail, much of the higher part of the Buck Ridge Trail cuts across a portion of a homestead granted by the government to John Peoples in 1903. Property records show that Peoples sold his homestead that same year to W. H. Bruner, suggesting that homesteading here was actually land speculation. The trail across the Peoples homestead also passes through poor, dry woodlands—but interesting because of their contrast with other woods at Tyler Bend. Here are new kinds of plants. Here too, we can imagine, are stands of trees so scrawny they had no money value and were never cut.

Beginning at the Buffalo River Trail 0.9 mile east of the Collier trailhead, the Buck Ridge Trail goes up and over a low rise, following an old road trace. On top of the hill is a sunnier, drier environment, attractive to huckleberry, post oaks, and cedars, with openings having grass, greenbrier, and fragrant sumac. But down the long grade off the hill's shadier north side, taller trees indicate increased moisture.

Then comes a low area along the ridge, with little openings in the woods having more sun. Hog peanut grows here, and winged elm. On the upgrade beyond the saddle, bare limestone appears on the trail, and alongside are stunted hickories, post oaks, blackjack oaks. And thorny gum bumelia or chittim-wood, a shrubby tree. And farkleberry and cockspur hawthorn. All worthless, virgin forest.

Up and over another low rise and past another slight dip, or saddle, the trail moves onto the west side of a hill. Here, post oak is the dominant species. The small trees are closely spaced, a dryland post oak forest with some blackjack oak and dogwood. There is no poison ivy. If free-ranging hogs rooting in the forest once triggered a woodland invasion of poison ivy here at Tyler Bend, those hogs must have kept off this poor, dry ground.

The trail begins the final downhill grade. Trees become taller. Post oaks thin out, and now there are other kinds of oaks, and hickories. But one more post oak is the largest yet, a 28-inch-diameter specimen that stands beside, and leans away from, the trail.

Now the woods are open, with huckleberry and mountain azalea that like the acidic soil of this cherty hillside. The trail comes to the edge of a ravine, swings down and back to the left, and continues downhill onto damp ground. May apple appears, and a patch of Japanese honeysuckle. The path reaches the valley bottom, crosses a stream gully, and is at the Spring Hollow Trail (see page 389).

Rock Wall Trail

0.9 mile. 180 feet of elevation gain or loss. Long rock wall; limestone glade. Trailhead at parking area next to camping pay station.

The trail begins at the top of the steps at the left rear corner of the parking area. From the steps the trail goes to the left across mowed grass to the near side of the campground road. It then follows the road shoulder across the stone-walled bridge and turns to the right onto the strip of mowed grass toward the woods.

In the woods the path goes along the base of a northeast-facing hillside where in the spring there are many wildflowers. These are moist, rich, dense woods having buckeye, pawpaw, and spicebush, with stinging nettle knee high and wild grapevines hanging from overhead. To the left beyond the trees is a hayfield, land that has been farmed since settlement before the Civil War.

Here, too, is evidence of the settlers' toil, the rock wall that suggested the name for this trail. We can believe that a pioneer farmer, maybe with a couple of teenage sons, gathered the pieces of gray limestone from the field or the adjacent hillside, piled them on a mule-drawn sled, and brought them here and built this wall. The wall's purpose was to keep pigs or cows out of the cotton, corn, or sorghum. In those times the animals were turned loose to fend for themselves in the woods.

Today the wall remains beside the trail—piled and stacked and tumbled pieces of gray stone, whitened in places by lichen or green with patches of moss, sometimes entirely blanketed by moss. One rock the farmer and his boys laid on top is four to six inches thick, two feet wide, and more than three feet long. And more than 400 pounds heavy. Obviously they accepted a challenge to lift it up there.

The wall, a couple of steps to the left of the trail, goes on…and on…and on. Toward the far end it becomes higher, to four feet, and thicker. At last, nearly 1200 feet from where it began, the wall turns away and disappears into the woods past the end of the field.

Here the trail goes the other way, up a side valley. The creek bed is filled with broken limestone; this could have been a source for rock to build the long wall. Soon the path crosses the creek, where in summer there's a dense stand of leaf-cup, plants three feet tall whose bruised leaves have a rank smell. The path proceeds on a steep grade up the hillside, rising as much as 20 feet in 100 feet of trail, until it comes to a switchback at the edge of an opening in the forest, a glade with broken limestone and sun-loving plants.

This limestone glade on a west-facing slope is worthless if one thinks only about its dollar value, but it adds variety to the trail experience, a place with sunlight in the woods. Also it has interesting drought-adapted plants. A visiting botanist identified poverty-grass, calamint, prairie dock, prairie mimosa, asters, Missouri coneflower, greenbrier, fragrant sumac, chittim-wood, and redbud growing here.

From the glade the trail turns back to the left and continues uphill across a slope mantled with rubbly Boone chert, with lichen-crusted chert boulders beside the path and broken chert covering much of its tread. In the first 100 yards beyond the glade are scrub hardwoods and rattan vines, indicating dryness. After that the trees become taller, and serviceberry appears, and Christmas ferns—subtle changes as the slope faces more to the northwest.

Eight feet to the left of the trail is a 20-inch-diameter oak that fell in 2002, tipping up a root-pan nearly nine feet across, creating a hole or pit in the ground. As the roots decay, the dirt attached to them will make a mound next to the hole—thus pit-and-mound, or pit-and-pile.

The trail bends to the right and trees become smaller (drought? logging?). Soon the path levels off, into a wide saddle where fragrant sumac (with leaves resembling poison ivy) grows alongside. Past the saddle and down an east slope, there again are subtle changes in the makeup of the forest toward species that need more moisture.

Soon the trail is at the Buffalo River Trail (see page 379).

Buffalo Point

Campground and Forest Trails Loop

1.7 miles. 290 feet of elevation gain. Geologic formations; differing forest habitats; historic road traces; sinkhole. Trailhead in camp area at information station (building with public telephone).

The Campground Trail begins with stone steps up into the woods behind the information station. From the steps the path continues up past moss- and lichen-covered boulders—the St. Peter Sandstone in the process of breaking down from massive bedrock to sandy topsoil. Soon it arrives at a flight of stone-and-mortar steps installed by workers of the Civilian Conservation Corps (CCC) when they built the trail around 1940 (see *Buffalo Point*, page 408).

Above these steps the trail emerges from the woods onto bare rock, the top of a cliff of the St. Peter Sandstone. Cedars, blackjack oaks, and farkleberry survive here in pockets of soil. A little farther along the trail and off to the right is a sandstone glade with lichens on the rock and patches of moss or grass on thin soil. For much of the year this glade is bone dry—tough going for its plant life.

As the path continues up the broad hillside beyond the bluff, the forest is at first mostly cedar, then mostly hardwoods. Then the trail is on top of a ridge that runs east to west. To the left of the trail the south-facing slope has drought tolerant cedars and a few pines. Off to the right, the north slope has a more mesic (moderately moist) forest of hardwoods with few if any cedars or pines.

Soon the path levels off, crossing a bench, or flat area, having many cedars, and small openings with grass and one or two prickly pear cactuses. And then, about 25 feet to the left where the trail crosses bare rock, there's an inconspicuous rock pile, pieces of gray limestone that appear to have been brought here from somewhere else. Did the CCC trail workers bring them? Or did a homesteader, sometime earlier? Ten- and twelve-inch cedars stand on the rock pile. Did these cedars and others on this bench take over a homesteader's clearing? We can only speculate. There is no written record.

The trail climbs the south side of the ridge, then levels off and comes alongside a smooth, sloping rock face about three feet high by eight long. The face is dull brick-red and speckled with little white crinoid disks: the red layer of the St. Joe Limestone, the geologic marker band near the bottom of the Boone Formation. Uphill from the trail are broken gray ledges of Boone limestone. Out of sight below the trail are each of the older formations. Underfoot here, gravelly Boone chert covers the trail tread.

Passsing other examples of the red St. Joe, the path moves onto the west end of the hill and down to a saddle and a trail intersection. The loop hike continues on the **Forest Trail**, going to the left.

Side trip: The Campground Trail continues straight ahead, on the old roadway 0.2 mile to a junction with the Overlook Trail (see page 396). Along this section of the Campground Trail the forest changes from cedars in the sunny saddle area to hardwoods (and a few pines, surprisingly) as the trail climbs the shady side of the next hill.

The Forest Trail follows an old road trace a short distance, then bends to the right into the woods, very soon crossing limestone outcrops and next a stretch of mossy or lichened limestone boulders and ledges. This is probably the Plattin Limestone, a formation that lies between the St. Peter Sandstone and the St. Joe Limestone.

The woods in this rocky, infertile place are mostly cedar. But suddenly the trail is past both limestone and cedars, as the path swings to the right and into a small valley with enough fertility for big hardwood trees. Turning left and crossing a stream course, the trail climbs to the paved road that goes down toward the campground.

Across the road and up the hillside, the path crosses a utility right-of-way, a sunny clearing where vegetation grows rapidly. Farther uphill the trail tread becomes almost entirely Boone chert, and then the trail is at another junction. A short distance to the right are group campsites, and a pavilion built by the CCC. To the left the Forest Trail follows an old roadway through open woods.

Here is another east-west ridge with a few pines along the top and on the south slope to the right, but none on the north side to the left. Also, the top of this ridge is nicely rounded off, typical of hills that have developed on the Boone Formation (see upper photo, page 28). As for the Boone's limestone, none is in sight here; it has weathered away, leaving insoluble Boone chert littering the surface.

In 2002 this ridge was burned off to get rid of decades of build-up of forest debris; blackened logs and tree trunks are evidence of the fire. To the left are several shallow pits with accompanying mounds of earth where the roots of fallen trees have decayed and disappeared. Several large wind-thrown hardwoods, with roots hanging onto dirt and rock pulled out of the ground, provide direct evidence of how these woodland pit-and-pile combinations originate.

Cedars reappear, and to the right is a rail fence around a deep hole, a limestone sink, Forest Trail Pit. Though the fence says STAY OUT! there's a beaten path beyond the barrier to the edge of the sinkhole. Trespassers may be disappointed. The pit is about 40 feet deep with side passages about 100 feet long, but there are no cave formations.

The trail has been going gradually downhill, following the old woods road. Past the sink it suddenly begins a steep plunge, going down more than 20 feet in l00 feet of trail. Did some farmer in the bottomland have to bring his loaded wagon up this grade?

Below the steep, but short, hill is a gentler south slope taken over by pines, cedars, and a dense ground cover of poison ivy. All suggest that this part of the hill was subjected to human influences. The farmer may have cleared the ground or his free-ranging hogs may have rooted it up, preparing a seedbed for these trees and vines.

Another trail junction. Straight ahead is loop "A" of the campground. The Forest Trail goes to the left, detouring through the woods around the campsites and descending to another junction, just above the road near the parking area for the boat landing. At this last junction, the path goes to the left, along and above the left side of the road, following it to the forks of the roads at the stop signs.

From there one must cross the left fork, then follow the middle fork about 100 yards to the trailhead at the information station.

Campground and Overlook Trails Loop

1.2 miles. 180 feet of elevation gain. "Solution valleys"; sandstone glade; wildflowers; a high overlook. Trailhead on road to Buffalo Point's restaurant, at head-in parking and picnic tables on right.

When one faces away from the road at the trailhead, the beginning of the trail goes to the right. The path is wide, on a nearly level grade along the hillside below several housekeeping cabins built by the Civilian Conservation Corps (CCC) around 1940. This trail was built about that time also, probably laid out by a National Park Service landscape architect assigned to work with the CCC to help develop Buffalo River State Park (see *Buffalo Point*, page 408).

Though these oak-pine woods are attractive—especially when the dogwoods are in bloom—this part of the hike can seem uneventful. There are, however, things that can be overlooked at first. The slope above the trail is littered with broken chert, for this hill was created on the Boone Formation of limestone and chert. Here the limestone has weathered away, and for several thousand years acidic hardwood leaves and pine needles have fallen to the ground, creating acidic soil. Huckleberry, which likes acidic soil, grows along the trail.

Another, larger feature of the Boone Formation appears as the trail gradually bends around the head end of a sizeable hollow. Below the trail, the wooded slope is curving, forming a wide, shallow bowl, or amphitheater. Here is the head of a "solution valley" created by solution, or dissolving, of Boone limestone (see page 27), first along a fracture line in the rock, then over a widening area centered on the fracture. As acidic ground water gradually carried away the dissolved limestone, overlying chert and soil settled into the void.

The path now crosses the ridge on the south side of the hollow and reaches an old roadway. To the right, the road leads uphill toward Buffalo Point's ranger station. The Campground Trail turns left.

The roadway, or trail, runs down the top of the ridge, a straight, open avenue beneath oaks and tall pines. There are more pines along this section of trail than any other at Buffalo Point—and a scarcity of poison ivy, so abundant elsewhere. Poison ivy tends to invade areas that have been disturbed, torn up by logging or perhaps in the past by the rooting of free-ranging hogs. Did this dry ridge escape both the tree fellers and the topsoil pushers?

The top of this pine ridge also is gently rounded off, left and right, which is typical for hills developed on the Boone Formation (upper photo, page 28). But now the trail reaches a saddle, or low point, on the ridge where a higher hill looms ahead, and the trail goes down the left side of the hill. Below to the left is another broad bowl-like head of a hollow developed in the Boone. The trail here is also on a northeast-facing hillside apparently having more moisture, for evergreen Christmas ferns are present on the slope above the trail. Drought-adapted pines are absent except for one or two trees.

Soon there is a junction with the **Overlook Trail**, to the left.

Side trip: The Campground Trail continues straight ahead on the old roadway 0.2 mile to a junction with the Forest Trail. From there the Campground Trail continues to the campground (see page 394).

Along the Overlook Trail, just past the junction, huge mossy rocks come into view downhill, and what appears to be a drop-off, a cliff. A little farther along, people have beaten a short side path ("social trail," in Park Service parlance) down the slope to look off the edge. Below a 30-foot sheer drop are moss-carpeted, automobile-sized masses of rock that have split off the cliff. Farther down are more big rocks that have rolled or slid toward the bottom of the ravine.

Detouring around fallen cedars that are attached at the roots and still alive, the path crosses a watercourse. Beyond that, and 20 feet below the trail, is a noticeable funnel-like depression about six feet deep. How did it get there? It may have developed when the ground sank into a gap or fissure in the sandstone that lies not far below—the sandstone that is visible in the bluff just downhill.

Now the path crosses a second watercourse, this one worn into bare sandstone. The Trails Illustrated map shows that this stream comes from the solution valley whose head end lies below the Campground Trail near the beginning of this hike. Up there, the landscape developed on Boone Formation limestone and chert, which can be hundreds of feet thick. Here, the trail is below the Boone and is crossing the St. Peter Sandstone, visible in this stream bed. A massive, solid layer of the St. Peter forms the cliff just downstream from the trail.

Beyond the watercourse the path continues on bedrock into an open area. Now the hillside faces south, open to the sun, and this is a sandstone glade along the top of the bluff (photos, page 398). Here are mosses, dryland ferns, and prairie grasses on wet or dry patches of soil; gray-green lichens on rock surfaces; scrubby cedars and post oaks along the glade's upper margin. And many wildflowers. Most of the mid-May flowers, for example, seem to have catchy names: spiderwort, sandwort, widow's cross, larkspur, beardtongue, sensitive brier, fleabane, goat's rue. Later, and earlier, other kinds bloom.

Stretches of bare sandstone are littered with gravelly Boone chert washed down from above. A protruding outcrop of rock has been sculpted into little whalebacks and domes. Then the trail passes below projecting ledges. There, about seven feet above the ground, a foot-high stratum displays layers of rock within it that are tilted, askew to the flat-lying strata above and below. Here is a suggestion of what geologists call crossbedding, where wind or water piled the original sand at an angle instead of depositing it in horizontal beds.

Next to the path here are club moss, reindeer lichen, prickly pears. And sandwort, a diminutive glade plant with stems like thin wires, tiny leaves, and white five-petaled flowers a quarter-inch across.

Another social trail goes 50 feet to the cliff's edge. The view is into the tops of tall trees, onto the tops of small trees. When all are in leaf, the ground is hidden somewhere more than 40 feet below.

Sandstone glade.
Where the Overlook Trail at Buffalo Point goes along the top of a cliff of the St. Peter Sandstone, a special environment has been created. A thin layer of soil on bedrock can be saturated after rain but powder dry in summer. Mosses and lichens thrive here in the spring but go dormant during drought. Prairie grasses grow, and surprisingly, many wild-flowers.

Many of the sun-loving, drought-adapted plants of this sandstone glade are easily overlooked except when in bloom. One such small plant, usually less than eight inches tall, puts out flowers crowded along branches at the tops of the stems. The white or pink blooms then demand notice. The branches form stars or crosses, giving the plant its name: widow's cross.

The path crosses sloping bedrock. Soon there are steps up, then steps leading down to a cliff **overlook** above the treetops.

More than 300 vertical feet below is the river and a big gravel bar. Down to the right is Buffalo Point's campground. On the hillside across the river is a prominent exposure of the St. Peter Sandstone—smooth, bulging, with a grassy glade above it, at the same elevation as this overlook. Beyond, to the horizon, are hills and hollows.

This overlook cliff, more than 50 feet high, has a stone wall along the edge as a safety measure. The CCC workers built it, but instead of using sandstone from here, they brought in blocks of limestone, probably carting them down the hill in wheelbarrows. Also they hauled down cement, sand, and water, and a heavy wood or metal mixing pan or a gasoline-powered concrete mixer for making mortar.

The trail goes up the hill those CCC men had to navigate. From the overlook the path heads into a stand of pines and hardwoods, trees that stand barely 40 feet high among sandstone boulders and ledges of the upper St. Peter. These woods harbor a few wildflowers; at the middle of May they include coreopsis, milkweed, and phlox. They cannot match the varied floral display in the glade, whose strip of open bedrock can be seen down below.

Farther uphill the trees become taller, past 50 feet, in open oak-pine woods. Still farther along, the trees are still taller, more prosperous—though hardly as interesting as the stunted ones downhill on the drier, less fertile border of the glade.

The path levels off for an easy ascent. This is a CCC-built trail. It crosses a small gully on a causeway having mortared stone walls.

Soon the path is at the trailhead where this hike began.

Indian Rockhouse and Return Trails Loop

3.5 miles. 460 feet of elevation gain. Rock formations, shelters, and sculptures; disappearing creek and resurgence spring; prehistoric Indian site; historic zinc diggings. Trailhead on road to Buffalo Point's restaurant, at head-in parking and picnic tables on right.

Across the paved road from the trailhead parking area, the trail follows an old roadway down the hill toward Panther Creek. But after heavy rainfall, Panther Creek can submerge the trail crossings. Avoid the creek at those times by taking the Return Trail, a path to the left about 20 feet beyond the road crossing at the parking area.

The trail on the roadway down the hill soon bends sharply to the right and continues down a hollow. This narrow valley is part of a *karst*, or sinkhole, landscape developed on limestone of the Boone and Plattin formations. In this "dry valley" there is no stream course on the surface. Rainfall disappears into underground waterways.

Soon the trail passes two "karst windows," openings to these subterranean passages. Down a short path to the right is the first one, a collapsed cave in the Plattin Limestone. The boulders at the mouth of the cave are typical Plattin—dense, fine-grained gray rock.

Farther down the hollow the trail leaves the old road and then skirts around the second karst opening, a big sinkhole about 20 feet deep and 50 feet across. Here, soil and rock have collapsed into a cavity created as acidic ground water slowly dissolved the underlying Plattin Limestone and carried it away. Below rock ledges on one side of the sink is a small crevice; when visible in the wintertime it appears to be a cave. Cool air (56–57 degrees F) issues from the hole, so this feature is named the Sinkhole Icebox. At times fog rises from the hole as its cool air meets warmer outside air.

Beyond the Icebox the trail and much of the hillside are surfaced with broken chert that originally was part of the Boone Formation, which overlies the Plattin. Some of this gravelly rock may have washed down from the Boone higher uphill. Most of it is residue left in place after Boone limestone dissolved away where the trail is now.

Past a few outcrops of the gray Plattin, the path enters a thicket of cedars. Soon it is on solid rock—brown rock now, the St. Peter Sandstone, which at Buffalo Point is the next formation below the Plattin. Now, by steps off ledges, the trail descends a St. Peter bluff—and here is a new geologic term, for the ledges "dip," meaning slope or slant, in this case downward in the direction of the trail.

Here to the left is a pit in solid rock, like a big dug well about four feet across. It is filled with rubble to about eight feet below the surface. And in sight about 50 feet downhill is a sinkhole, a shallow funnel several feet deep, indicating there's a limestone formation below the St. Peter Sandstone. The "well" in the sandstone is probably related to dissolving of the underlying limestone or of limy material in the sandstone. The dissolving must have taken place long ago—millions of years ago—when the water table was at this elevation, before Panther Creek had cut its valley to its present depth.

After descending the St. Peter ledges, the trail heads left, to a waterfall coming off the bluff. This splashing 20-foot fall is just downhill from the lower end of the hollow that the trail follows from the parking area. Water from this karst valley has emerged at a spring above the waterfall—where the underground stream down the valley reaches the top of the St. Peter Sandstone. Unlike the Boone and Plattin limestones above it, the St. Peter has no water passages, so the water flows along the top of the St. Peter to the surface.

Apparently the spring has only the small valley above it for a watershed, as the waterfall ceases to flow during drought.

The lowest five feet of the cliff here is not the St. Peter Sandstone but a thin-bedded limestone of the uppermost part of the next geologic unit below the St. Peter, the Everton Formation. The wavy, undulating Everton-St. Peter "contact" here is the most easily recognized boundary of any between the Buffalo River's rock formations and is seen at many places along the lower river (photo, page 53).

The wavy line of contact continues along the cliff beyond the waterfall. Thin, platy layers of Everton are visible in the first six feet above the trail. Smooth, massive St. Peter, with many rounded bulges, makes up the rest of the cliff.

Down the hillside, the trail passes an open cut that runs about 50 feet into the hill, to a low-ceiling tunnel that goes about 40 feet to a dead end. So also ended the hopes of this prospector who was looking for zinc ore. Others had searched the same geologic horizon, in the upper Everton not far below the St. Peter, and found riches in zinc at Rush, only three miles to the north. This prospect hole probably dates from around 1916, during the mining boom at Rush.

Two hundred feet down the hill from the tunnel, the trail bottoms out and turns left, up **Panther Creek**. Usually the creek is dry; any water flows underneath. At times the path runs in the edge of the creek bed and is littered with debris left by floods.

About 150 feet up the hill is the St. Peter bluff. Pieces have broken off and rolled or slid down, and these sandstone boulders, now weather-rounded and mossy, crowd the trail. Sand, an end product of weathering, is underfoot along the path. And in the creek is rock of all sizes, sand to boulders, a mixture of sandstone, limestone, and chert that floods have carried here from all places upstream.

The hillside above the trail is north-facing, shady, moist, with maidenhair fern, Christmas fern, and early spring wildflowers such as hepatica and bloodroot, which bloom in sunshine before the trees come into leaf. Here along the creek are wild hydrangea and fragrant spring-blooming witch hazel. And ironwood—sometimes called "muscle tree" for the ripples and bulges of its smooth grayish bark.

Eventually the St. Peter bluff dips downward, closer to the trail. The path also climbs away from the creek, and a short side path leads to an opening at the base of the bluff: a shelter cave. The room under the bluff is about 70 feet long, up to 10 feet high, and 40 feet back to the rear wall. Through its roof at one end is a big circular hole to day-light. Moss and ferns grow on its walls and on the pile of breakdown rocks lying below. On the cave's ceiling are stubby pendants of cal-cite, the beginnings of stalactites.

This shelter cave is the result of solution—dissolving of limestone by acidic ground water. Here the uppermost layers of the Everton once formed a dome, up into the base of the St. Peter. The dome dis-solved away and the St. Peter Sandstone is now the shelter's roof.

A short distance beyond the shelter the trail comes to what was a low-standard road. About 1960 the managers of Buffalo River State Park opened the road to let people drive to the Indian Rockhouse. It was also to serve as a hiking trail. The road had washouts and soon was closed to cars, and part of it was bypassed in favor of routing hikers down the hill to see the waterfall and the shelter cave.

Entering the road where asphalt pavement was laid to stop ero-sion, the trail goes down to the right, crosses a narrow stream course, and arrives at an intersection where a path to the left goes up the slope and connects to the Return Trail. Those wanting a shorter hike back to the parking area can take the path and the Return Trail instead of going on to the rockhouse. That makes a loop hike of 2.3 miles instead of 3.5 miles by way of the rockhouse.

Continuing toward the rockhouse, the old road crosses Panther Creek and climbs up onto the St. Peter Sandstone, here a low, south-facing bluff along the creek. This drier, sunny place has pine trees, and beside the path is prairie dock, with huge heart-shaped leaves.

Farther along on the left is a short path across Panther Creek to the Return Trail. (This path is not shown on the Trails Illustrated map.) Then the road itself goes back across the creek, on bedrock. At this crossing the Return Trail heads back to the left from the creek bank as the Rockhouse Trail continues up the old road to the right.

The roadway climbs (passing a few scattered pieces of Plattin limestone on the way) to a point about 40 feet higher than Panther Creek. The road descends over bare ledges of St. Peter sandstone and very soon crosses Panther Creek. The creek is probably dry, but from ahead there may come the muffled sound of running water.

And ahead in the woods is an immense dark opening, and water is flowing somewhere inside…the **Indian Rockhouse**.

The rockhouse is a shelter cave much bigger than the one visited a while ago. Along the Buffalo River—and in all the Ozarks of Arkansas—only Cob Cave in Lost Valley is larger. The entrance to the rockhouse is 270 feet wide (photo, page 404). Its main room is up to 100 feet deep and its ceiling averages 30 feet high, with a maximum height of 50 feet. Its total area under roof is about four-tenths of an acre. And just like the shelter visited earlier, the rockhouse has a skylight at its right end, a lens-shaped hole through its roof.

Here again, as in the smaller shelter, a mound of Everton limestone was dissolved to create a chamber below the St. Peter Sandstone. As in the other shelter, the hole through the roof was probably created as acidic water attacked a carbonate-rich "plug" in the St. Peter.

Slabs of sandstone two and three feet thick lie on the floor; these have fallen from the ceiling. But the pieces of rock stacked and piled at the shelter's left end are thin-bedded limestone of the Everton Formation from below the Everton-St. Peter contact where the wall meets the ceiling.

The room's back wall is covered with ribs of calcite like the pipes of an organ. These are cave draperies that formed when water entered along a fracture in the ceiling. The water brought dissolved limestone from the Plattin or Boone Formations above the St. Peter Sandstone, possibly also from limy material that had cemented the sand grains of the St. Peter. As the water evaporated, the calcite deposits were left behind on the wall, also as nodules and stalactites on the ceiling. And on a large slab of sandstone fallen from the ceiling is a cluster of joined stalagmites like fingers pointing upward. The longest finger is about eight inches in diameter and four feet high—which means it took a *long* time to reach that size. (Which means the slab of rock underneath it did not fall recently, either.)

Except in drought there is the sound of running water. At the left rear wall a cave goes back about 300 feet, with a room where water emerges from a hole in the floor. The water flows out of the cave, down a gully along the side wall of the rockhouse, and into another hole. Normally the creek is 15 feet below the shelter floor. After heavy rains it backs up and fills the gully.

Seventy-five feet outside that end of the rockhouse, paths lead to Indian Rockhouse Sink, 40 to 50 feet across. At the bottom are big boulders covered with moss and ferns living in moist air issuing from

Indian Rockhouse. A 270-foot-wide opening, facing south, admitted winter sun to Native Americans living in this shelter.

crevices. From under the rocks comes the sound of flowing water.

Seventy-five feet beyond the sink and near the trail approaching the rockhouse is another pit about eight feet across and six feet deep, the result of more recent collapse into the stream passage.

Local people first called this shelter the Panther Creek Rockhouse. It became Indian Rockhouse after archeologists learned it had been home for Native Americans. The rockhouse was well situated, with its flowing stream and its entrance that faced south toward the winter sun. In 1934 archeologists recovered several types of dart points, other chipped stone tools, and bone tools, mussel shells, animal bone and hide, fragments of cordage and basketry, and shell-tempered potsherds. There were also charred corncobs, acorns, hickory nuts, and pieces of cane. Burials also were present. A sample of the plant material that was carbon dated indicates the rockhouse was inhabited around AD 1350.

Except for the burials and a few unbroken tools and dart points, wasn't everything just trash? To the Indians, it was. To the archeologists, material such as this has been the only means for piecing together an account of the Indians' gradually changing lifeways (see pages 77–87). Artifacts from this site are in the study and display collections of the Arkansas Archeological Survey at Fayetteville.

From the rockhouse back to the trailhead, the way is along the old road coming in, over the rise and down to the bedrock creek crossing where the Return Trail begins, 0.2 mile from the shelter cave. But there's also a parallel route (not shown on the Trails Illustrated map) beginning about 300 feet back up the trail from the rockhouse. About 100 feet beyond the channel of Panther Creek, a path goes left, off the roadway. This path stays closer to the creek.

About 150 feet along the path is an intersection. To the left is a spur path toward Bat Cave—a steep, punishing climb up and then down, half a mile over the next ridge. The cave is a large tunnel having no formations and running 700 feet straight back to a dead end at a rockslide. Bat Cave developed as Everton limestone dissolved along a fracture line immediately below the St. Peter Sandstone.

In 1942 a newspaper writer described Bat Cave:

> So many bats it would take days to count them—some in single groups, hanging from rough projections on the walls, others hanging by hundreds and thousands in great festoons from the roof. There are…many more during the drab, cold winter than in the summer.

Today most of the bats are gone, their numbers greatly reduced as human activities have adversely affected them. Today two endangered species of bats—Indiana and Ozark big-eared—hibernate in Bat Cave, and the cave is closed from August 15 to May 15 to protect them. If hibernating bats are disturbed so that they take flight, they lose body fat needed for survival through the winter.

From the Bat Cave junction, the trail continues through an area of sandstone outcrops and acidic soil; here are huckleberry bushes, a few pine trees, and wild azaleas. The path crosses two forks of Panther Creek, then follows an old road down the creek. The road trace goes back across the creek and soon disappears as the hillside crowds close to the stream bed. Then the way is along ledges at the creek's edge for another 100 feet to the road crossing at the beginning of the Return Trail.

The Return Trail soon crosses a gully on a bridge, and soon afterward enters the edge of the creek bed, here an area of sculptured St. Peter bedrock. Panther Creek's surface flow—which usually is much less than the creek in the rockhouse—runs along a narrow groove in the sandstone. Rocks washed down the groove have rolled, turned, scraped, and chipped, forming small potholes, and then larger ones at the foot of a plunge. At high flow, water sluices down the channel, twisting and spilling from one pothole to the next. In drought, when the creek stops flowing, even the larger pools dry up, revealing odd, rounded dams of sandstone across the channel. One of these curving walls looks like a twisted, foot-thick tree root.

Across the creek and 20 feet beyond the present channel are two deep cylindrical potholes in the bedrock. These were made long ago when the creek ran at a higher elevation and flowed over them.

Farther along the Return Trail, a short side path goes down to Pebble Spring, set in a 20-foot-deep pit near the edge of Panther Creek. The spring's outlet is at the foot of a low bluff of the St. Peter Sandstone and is from 6 to 12 feet deep. Usually the spring is dry, but after heavy rainfall it comes to life. Chert pebbles dance and tumble in the current at its outlet, and just downstream its flow can be several feet wide and a foot deep. Pebble Spring is a *resurgence,* a rising, for water that went underground at the rockhouse.

Beyond Pebble Spring, the Return Trail looks down on Panther Creek as it follows a joint pattern in the St. Peter, widening into potholes and creating rounded, scalloped sculpture and deep plunge pools in the rock. After a big rain the creek here becomes a torrent of water swiftly racing down this little canyon below the trail.

Soon the trail turns right, into a side valley. To the left is the short path to the Rockhouse Trail near the blacktop section of old road.

Quickly the Return Trail moves close to the little creek that comes down the side valley. Here too the stream bed is in the St. Peter Sandstone. A few yards off-trail is a pothole called the Natural Bathtub. The creek drops into this plunge pool as a foot-high waterfall, then moves around it in a circular fashion, carrying pebbles that have worn a basin seven feet across. The stream leaves the pool in a straight channel along a joint in the sandstone.

The trail ascends natural steps on ledges and enters a sandstone glade. Soil is spread thinly over rock, and a southern exposure allows plenty of sun. Here are moss, reindeer lichen, prairie grasses, wildflowers, greenbrier, and yucca. Part of the trail is on bedrock.

After re-entering the woods the trail crosses the creek. Just upstream is another little waterfall, a three-foot cascade. Its plunge basin—which could be called a giant pothole—has water even in drought and supports a living community of insect larvae, water striders, and minnow-sized fish. The pool is the creation of flood waters that have scoured the basin below the falls and pushed sand and gravel to make a dam on the downstream side.

Up a flight of steps, the trail passes above the pool and continues along the creek. During the wet months this stream comes splashing musically down its course. During dry times there's no music, only a creek bed with chunks and blocky boulders of the gray Plattin Limestone, some of which have fallen from low bluffs up the hill across the creek. Farther along, the creek's bottom is Plattin bedrock.

Presently the trail begins to climb the hillside, steeply at first, eventually leveling off past small pieces and outcrops of Plattin, finally ascending a winding flight of steps all made of Plattin rock. By this time the rocky, open, west-facing hillside has a new kind of forest. The good-sized hardwoods down below have been replaced by smaller trees—cedar, redbud, wild plum.

Very soon the path is at another set of built steps. This time they are of reddish rock of the St. Joe Limestone, waste material from a quarry located a hundred feet to the left at the top of the steps.

This CCC Quarry was the source of stone for the original buildings and retaining walls of Buffalo River State Park (see *Buffalo Point*, page 408). Along its uphill side is a 20-foot vertical headwall of rock. Solution of the wall's St. Joe carbonate rock has made deep incisions along horizontal bedding planes and enlarged vertical fractures to as much as two feet wide. Weathering turned the exposed rock dark gray. Farther along, in areas that were quarried, the rock is dull red and has uniform one-and-a-half-inch grooves. CCC workers made the grooves when drilling holes for dynamite to split off pieces of rock that were then shaped into building stones.

Where the path enters the quarry, part of the exposed rock floor is the gray Plattin Limestone, here at its contact with the St. Joe, and dipping below the St. Joe as the path goes ahead. Farther on, the more extensive floor of the St. Joe Limestone is etched in short wavy grooves and knobs by solution. There are a few long straight cracks; these are joints. One joint crosses the path at the first exposure of the St. Joe pavement and another appears about 15 feet farther.

Freshly broken St. Joe limestone here is brick-red. The color comes from iron oxide. Many pieces of the red rock have little white disks in them, segments of crinoid stems, to about one-fourth inch in diameter. Geologists thus describe the St. Joe as "crinoidal" limestone. Indeed, it was formed about 350 million years ago during the Mississippian Period, which has been called the Age of Crinoids, for these creatures were extremely abundant in shallow Mississippian seas (photos, pages 38 and 55).

Near the far end of the quarry is a two-and-a-half-foot boulder of

Buffalo Point was originally Buffalo River State Park, initially developed by the Civilian Conservation Corps (CCC). After arriving in May 1938 and establishing a camp, CCC enrollees first built the road that provides access to Buffalo Point from Highway 14. They opened a sawmill and a quarry (above) that provided material with which they built roadside retaining walls, a four-unit lodge (near the restaurant, and now used for Park Service summer employees), a picnic pavilion (at the group camping area), and six housekeeping cabins. To serve these facilities the CCC also installed water and sewer systems.

The CCC was a Depression-era work program for men from 18 to 24 years old. In return for their labor the men received job training, room and board, and $30 per month—of which $20 was to be sent home to their families. The army administered the CCC camps, and architects and landscape architects from the National Park Service provided designs and technical assistance.

The CCC program closed at the beginning of World War II. Around 1960, when funds became available, the state built eight more housekeeping units (four double cabins), a restaurant, and a ranger station, and developed the campground. In 1973 the State of Arkansas donated the state park to the National Park Service to become part of Buffalo National River. Since 1973 the Park Service has made major improvements at the campground and in wastewater treatment.

In 1988 the CCC-built structures at Buffalo Point were placed on the National Register of Historic Places. Together they constitute the Buffalo River State Park Historic District.

light gray Boone chert that must have fallen from the hill above. The boulder is breaking into small angular pieces.

As the Return Trail continues uphill from the quarry, it passes through a dry area having plants adapted to drought: prairie dock, ground plum, orange puccoon. Smoke tree, which grows only in the presence of limestone, is here also.

This part of the trail follows a road that the CCC built for access to the quarry. Going up the roadway, the first rock outcrops are reddish St. Joe limestone. Then, 50 feet farther, there's a three-by-ten-foot outcrop of dense, fine-grained gray rock—but the next outcrops farther uphill are, again, red St. Joe. Apparently the gray rock is Plattin limestone, which should be below the St. Joe. Here the Plattin seems to have been uplifted as part of a *horst*, a raised rock mass between two faults. Or, if not Plattin, the gray rock may be Boone limestone from above the red St. Joe, but part of a *graben*, an area of the earth's crust that has subsided between two faults. The whole answer awaits exact identification of the gray limestone.

The trail continues into hardwood-pine forest, with pine trees becoming more abundant farther uphill, until the path reaches a grassy opening just below the blacktopped park road. Across this clearing, the path enters the woods about 50 feet down-slope from the pavement and runs just below the road. On this north-facing slope, the pines have been replaced by hardwoods.

After a short distance, the Return Trail intersects the Rockhouse Trail across the blacktopped road from the trailhead parking area.

Rush

Rush Landing Road
The road to the Rush boat landing and toward Clabber Creek runs parallel and close to trails at Rush. Thus the road serves as access to trailheads by car and, at times after hiking a trail, as a way to return to a trailhead on foot. Whether driving or walking, there are things along the road to see and learn about.

Walking the road is better in the cold months, when auto traffic to the boat landing has abated (cold weather also is much better for hiking, of course). Road walking at any time requires watching for cars.

Blacktopped County Road 635 from Highway 14 reaches the end of pavement at the National River boundary. The unpaved road then goes down **Star Hill** (named for the nearby Morning Star Mine), a steep, winding grade. At the bottom it arrives in **Rush** as it turns right to pass several long vacant houses, built about 1899 during the first of two mining booms. Then it passes the shell of a store building that also was the Rush post office. After the store and post office closed in the 1950s and people vacated the houses, this collection of buildings became known as the Rush ghost town.

A short distance farther, and just beyond the low-water slab, or ford, across Rush Creek, are ruins related to the Morning Star Mine (photo, page 414) and trailhead parking for the Morning Star Loop (described below) and the Mines Trail (see facing page).

About 0.4 mile beyond the trailhead, and above a stone retaining wall on the left, are walls of the Hicks store, which dates from Rush's second mining boom during World War I. When the store was built in 1916 it was an imposing structure two stories high. By the 1960s there were only the stone outer walls of the lower floor, and the landowner built a house within those walls. In December 1982, when a park ranger and his family were living there, the Buffalo River's greatest recorded flood backed water up Rush Creek. The house was a mile from the river. Water inside was four feet deep.

Other remains of the mining era are beyond sight of the road. The buildings, mine diggings, mill foundations, road traces, and other artifacts of that era lie within the 1200-acre Rush Historic District, entered in 1987 on the National Register of Historic Places. (Boom times at Rush are described on pages 93–96.)

Morning Star Loop

0.3 mile. 60 feet of elevation gain. Silver ore smelter; blacksmith shop and remains of ore mill for Morning Star Mine. Trailhead at parking area 0.1 mile east of low-water slab across Rush Creek.

From the parking area the trail goes to the left past the interpretive exhibit, then to an open hillside having a blocky stone structure, the oldest building at Rush, an ore smelter dating from 1886.

The first assay of ore from the Morning Star Mine erroneously reported not only zinc carbonate but also silver worth $8 per ton of ore. The mine's owners had the smelter built to recover silver, but while the smelter's first run produced a rainbow of colorful zinc oxide fumes at the stack, silver failed to appear in the molds at the bottom of the furnace. A few years later, under different owners, the Morning Star was developed as a zinc mine and became famous.

Past the smelter the trail goes across the slope to a road trace and follows the roadway a short distance uphill to the Morning Star's blacksmith shop, built in 1925. Just beyond the shop are ruins of a collapsed warehouse. Across the roadway are foundations marking the outlines of the mining company's office and store.

The trail turns right, across the hill. Soon it passes an intersection with the Mines Trail (see below), which heads up the hill on the left. Just beyond the junction are the remains of the Morning Star ore concentrating mill—heavy piers of concrete that was mixed by hand. The mill was first built in 1898. It was remodeled in 1911 and again during World War I (photo, page 414).

Ore was conveyed to the mill by gravity from mines farther up the hill. The ore and attached rock were crushed and then separated. The waste rock, called tailings, was spilled outside the mill and down the hill. In the form of fine gravel it also is called chat. From the mill site the trail meanders down a large spill of chat to the parking area.

Mines Trail

2.2 miles. 380 feet of elevation gain. Sites of six historic mines; tram road between mines; views of valley. Trailhead at parking area 0.1 mile east of low-water slab across Rush Creek.

The Mines Trail begins at an intersection on the upper side of the Morning Star Loop (see above). From the intersection the trail goes up an old roadway for 200 yards. About halfway up this steep grade, the west end of the Rush Mountain path (see *Alternate route,* page 416) joins the Mines Trail on the left.

After climbing 200 yards the trail proceeds along what was called the "mine level" because all the mines are at the same elevation (about 200 feet above the valley floor) in the Everton Formation on **Rush Mountain**. At the mine level the trail follows a tram road nearly 2000 feet long, where ore cars were rolled along rails from mine portals to the head of the conveyor to the Morning Star mill.

The first mine, the Morning Star, was the most productive one in northern Arkansas, famous for large masses of "free ore" having no waste material (see *Jumbo,* page 412). The mine was essentially a huge open cut—400 feet long, 100 feet wide, and up to 50 feet

Jumbo was P. T. Barnum's famous circus elephant—and thus the name for this elephantine mass of pure zinc carbonate from the Morning Star Mine at Rush. The mine's owners saw Jumbo as worth its weight in publicity. They got its 12,750 pounds hoisted onto a wagon and hauled behind 16 oxen to a barge on which it was floated down the White River to be put on a railroad car. Jumbo then traveled to the 1893 World's Fair in Chicago.

Jumbo won a medal at the fair and attracted new investors to the Morning Star Mine. Now somewhat slimmed down (freight handlers and souvenir hunters had broken off pieces), Jumbo was retired to Chicago's Field Museum of Natural History. Here we see it on exhibit about 1900.

Zinc carbonate, or smithsonite, of which Jumbo was a prize-winning specimen, constituted about 80 percent of the ore recovered in the Rush mining district, and most of the zinc ore from the Ponca district. Zinc carbonate is around 40 percent metallic zinc. Sphalerite, or zinc sulfide, runs around 60 percent zinc but was found only in limited quantities. Zinc silicate, about 40 percent zinc, also occurred in small quantities.

One writer has estimated that from 1882 to 1962, the entire period of mining at Rush, around 26,000 tons of ore concentrates were recovered from mines in the two-square-mile Rush district.

deep—above the trail, with openings in a few places onto the trail.

There also were short tunnels; one is visible about 50 yards past the beginning of the tram road. *This tunnel, and all the others at Rush, are not to be entered*, and many are fenced off. In 1984 safety inspectors visited all the tunnels and found deep pits, water-filled pits, large loose ceiling rocks, and signs of recent cave-ins.

At several places along the mine-level path are stromatolites, wavy or humpy sets of laminations, or thin layers, in Everton dolomite, the result of sediment accumulating on colonies of algae. They appear in rocks of a retaining wall about 50 feet beyond the tunnel, and the most obvious ones are in a ledge a few feet above the trail and about 100 feet beyond the tunnel (photo, page 38).

About 125 feet beyond the tunnel, a side path goes out on top of a tall pile of waste rock from the mines, providing an open view of the wooded valley of **Rush Creek**. At the beginning of the path are concrete piers. Here, or nearby, was the upper end of the conveyor that carried ore to the Morning Star mill (photo, page 414).

Miners with primitive hand tools built this tram road along the steep, rocky flank of Rush Mountain, clearing away the trees and brush, stacking waste rock from the mines to build retaining walls, hauling rock and dirt and shoveling it for fill behind the walls. Today the tram road is a quiet place. In sunlit areas along this dry, southwest slope, prairie grasses bend in the breeze.

The next tunnel, about 200 yards from the beginning of the tram road, is the Ben Carney Mine. Its 600-foot passage is caved in.

Lying beside the trail about 300 yards beyond the Ben Carney is a true relic of the mines, a sheet metal box riveted to a strap-iron frame, an ore car without its wheels. In its day a horse or mule pulled it along narrow-gauge tracks on this tram road, taking ore from a mine to the head of the conveyor to the Morning Star mill. There the mule driver opened the flap-gate at the end of the car and dropped the ore onto the conveyor. Then back to the mine for another load.

About 150 yards beyond the ore car is the portal of the Capps Mine. The opening has not only its chain-link fence but also is blocked with angle-iron bars for protection of endangered species of bats inhabiting the tunnel. The Capps opened in August 1915 and after 1917 was worked by the Morning Star Mining Company. From 1915 to 1917 it produced 1200 tons of ore concentrates. From 1917 to 1928, when it finally closed, it yielded only 140 tons.

The Capps Mine is at the east end of the mine-level tramway. From there the trail goes along the steep hillside, then across a pile of mine waste at the top of a precipitous drop of hundreds of feet to the Rush Landing road. Just past the waste pile is another tunnel, the McIntosh Mine, fenced and barred like the Capps Mine because its underground workings were connected to those of the Capps.

Unlike the Capps, the McIntosh was not a big producer. In the years 1915 and 1916 the McIntosh yielded only 417 tons of zinc ore concentrates. Prices were high at that time, so even those 417 tons may have paid for the 100-tons-per-day concentrating mill that owner J. C. Shepherd built at the foot of the hill below the mine.

A short distance beyond the McIntosh tunnel and ten yards to the right of the path, a level landing on top of a high retaining wall may have been the loading platform for the elevated conveyor taking ore to Shepherd's concentrating mill. Just beyond that and a few feet up the slope from the main trail is another artifact, an eye bolt driven into the ground, perhaps an anchor for a cable that braced the conveyor's wooden framework. A few feet above the eye bolt is a four-foot ledge having stromatolites.

From that point the trail is on an old road trace going down to the valley floor. At times the roadbed is aligned with the "dip" of a two-

Morning Star mill. By 1916, after expansions, the ore concentrating mill for the Morning Star Mine was going full blast.

foot ledge along the left side. About 400 yards beyond the McIntosh tunnel the trail leaves the road trace, going off to the left. (The old road continues another 80 yards to the Rush Landing road.)

No longer on a road trace, the trail is a narrow path crossing a series of low ridges and shallow swales, then going along rock outcrops and then across easy slopes. After more than 500 yards of this, it begins to climb steeply, soon arriving at a rocky glade on top of a bluff that looks down about 150 feet to the Rush Landing road. In sight beyond that is the side road crossing Rush Creek on a low-water slab as it heads toward the camping area.

From the overlook the trail heads downhill, soon passing between a funnel depression to the left and an open cut down the hill to the right. A few yards farther is a waste pile up the hill. Within another 100 yards the path is on a pile of chat (fine gravel), at an intersection.

The right fork goes about 80 yards to the parking area for **Rush Landing**, a good point of access to, or exit from, this trail. The left fork is the trail, which continues 0.6 mile to the Monte Cristo Mine.

At the intersection, and for a short distance toward the Monte Cristo, the trail is surfaced with chat from the mill that processed ore from the White Eagle Mine. Foundations of the mill are within sight about 150 feet down the slope. The mine, which opened in the 1880s, was near the mouth of Rush Creek and had a vertical shaft that went to 40 feet below water level of the nearby Buffalo River. The workings had to be pumped to keep them from filling with water. The shaft has been filled in to avoid accidents.

The mill was rebuilt in 1958 when investors thought the market for zinc ore would improve, but it was abandoned when the market stayed flat. The Park Service later removed the mill.

From the White Eagle toward **Clabber Creek** an easy, graded trail crosses a hillside having many boulders and broken ledges—dark gray rock, sometimes jagged, a good sample of the Rush Mountain terrain that miners had to deal with. Where the trail bends away from the river near the mouth of Clabber Creek, a side path goes downhill toward what appears to be an overlook. The view off a 60-foot bluff is through the treetops toward the river. In wintertime the noisy Clabber Creek shoal may be seen as well as heard.

Heading away from the river, the trail goes along an east-facing slope that is free of rock, with a thriving forest of white oak, sweet gum, maple, and other kinds of trees. Photographs from around 1916 show that this slope was clear-cut to supply wood for the mines, and for the crowd of miners and their families here during World War I.

The trail passes what must have been a mine prospect, a circular pit about 8 feet deep by 20 feet across. Then it goes downhill, soon reaching the former roadway to the Monte Cristo Mine. The old road overlooks Clabber Creek and gradually climbs along the top of a bluff that reaches to 100 feet above the stream. By this time the roadway runs below a 60-foot cliff of dark gray dolomite. Here beside the path is a heavy steel tank, meant to receive air from a compressor close by; the compressed air would have been piped into the Monte Cristo for rock drills. The equipment, probably secondhand, was brought here around 1960 for reopening the mine.

The Monte Cristo Mine, just beyond, has two openings behind angle-iron bars and chain-link fencing to protect endangered species of bats inhabiting the tunnels (also to protect people, for there are sudden drop-offs, deep pits inside). The mine first opened in the early 1900s and was a good producer during World War I. At that time owner J. C. Shepherd installed an aerial tramway to deliver ore from the Monte Cristo to a concentrating mill across Clabber Creek.

The Monte Cristo is at the end of the Mines Trail. One can follow the same path back to the trailhead or return on the old road that joins the auto road back to the parking areas at Rush Landing and the Morning Star Mine.

Alternate route: Another way to return from the Monte Cristo to the Morning Star is a path across the top of **Rush Mountain**. The path is 1.4 miles long and often is steep. It does, however, provide a different view of the area's rock formations and forest types.

To walk the Rush Mountain path, first continue on the roadway for about 250 yards beyond the Monte Cristo tunnels. The path heads uphill at a sign saying (in 2002), END OF MAINTAINED TRAIL.

Volunteers occasionally remove fallen trees from the path, but otherwise it is primitive, not a constructed trail. From the roadway it goes up—sometimes straight up—an east-facing slope. Here is a mesic (moderately moist) hardwood forest and very little rock except a residue of broken chert from the Boone Formation. Partway up the mountain, the path climbs through a gap in a 15-foot bluff of the St. Peter Sandstone, then goes along a level bench past a survey monument marking a corner of the National River boundary.

The path climbs up to and along the top of the ridge, now among trees more tolerant of drought. Then it turns down the west side of the mountain, and the first ledge below the summit has a four-foot layer of red St. Joe limestone, near the base of the Boone Formation.

Farther down—straight down, potentially hazardous—are many ledges of limestone or dolomite, without any St. Peter sandstone in view as on the east side of the mountain. This southwest slope gets the full force of the sun, and the scrub hardwoods and Ashe's juniper have to live with drought. The change in vegetation from the east to the west side of the mountain is obvious, even dramatic.

The path ends at the old roadway from the Morning Star Loop up to the mine level. About 80 yards down the hill, the old road meets the loop trail, which in both directions leads to the trailhead parking.

Lower Buffalo and Leatherwood Wilderness Areas

Buffalo National River, 22,500 acres;
Ozark National Forest, 16,956 acres.

The Lower Buffalo Wilderness extends for 29 miles along the Buffalo River to its confluence with the White River. (The river itself is excluded from the wilderness area because of the traditional use of outboard motors, now limited to ten horsepower, on fishing boats.) Much of the wilderness lies within the 21-mile "big bend" of the river between Cedar Creek and the White.

The Leatherwood Wilderness includes most of the watersheds of Brush, Leatherwood, Short, and Middle Creeks (with most of the remainder of these watersheds being within Buffalo National River).

Access to the Lower Buffalo is from the Buffalo River, from the White River at Buffalo City, and from several county roads to the wilderness boundary (with parking at principal access points marked **P** on the Trails Illustrated map). Elsewhere the north, south, and west boundaries of the Lower Buffalo Wilderness abut private land, so that entry in these areas can be only with the owner's permission.

Access to the Leatherwood is from the Buffalo River (and then by crossing the strip of National River east of the Buffalo); or from Highway 341 along the east boundary; or Brush Creek Road at the north boundary; or Rand Road at the south and southwest boundaries. Several parking areas (marked **P** on the Trails Illustrated map) are along the roads. Entry also can be at other points along these roads where not on private land.

There are no designated, maintained trails in either wilderness area. Topographic maps of the Lower Buffalo show primitive tracks along the principal ridges. These were roads that were improved by Marion County in the 1960s to provide access to river farms (and, probably, to potential subdivisions). The roads still exist as wide tracks along the ridges, though all are overgrown as they approach their lower ends at the river. There are many other old road traces that follow ridges or hollows to dead ends. In one instance, though, old roads make a 10.5-mile loop: along Cook Hollow and Cow Creek, with access from the trailhead in Hathaway Hollow.

The Leatherwood Wilderness also has many road traces; nearly every ridge and every hollow has one. Until designation of the wilderness area, several roads on the Leatherwood were kept open by the Forest Service, and the roadbeds are obvious today. None of these roads that appeared on earlier topographic maps are shown on the Trails Illustrated map. The citizens' advisory committee for the Leatherwood wanted to encourage route finding and cross-country travel on the wilderness rather than channeling people along trails, with most of the trails being on old roadways.

Settlers took land along the river before the Civil War and continued homesteading the ridges and hollows until after 1900. Miners dug for zinc in the Lower Buffalo area, though without significant profit. Timber people operated sawmills and stave mills. People in the Leatherwood–Push Mountain area made whiskey; one native old-timer describes it as "the heart of moonshine country." By the 1970s, however, practically everyone had moved out. Especially in the 1930s Depression, when federal funds were available for public works, the Forest Service encouraged the exodus, buying homesteads and allowing the land to revert to forest.

Today the combined wilderness areas offer space to roam. There are lowlands along creeks, high vistas from tops of bluffs, remains of old mines and homesteads, and wildlife including turkey, deer, fox, bobcat, and possibly cougar. The forest is second- or third-growth but is gradually progressing toward old growth, toward its appearance when the first settlers came.

The Lower Buffalo and Leatherwood have no spectacular destinations comparable to Hawksbill Crag or Hemmed-in Hollow, but there are countless opportunities to see and appreciate smaller things— even a lichen- and moss-covered boulder suspended for centuries atop a bluff (photo, page 372). We can reacquaint ourselves with the rhythms of the natural world. These experiences have value.

They will have greater value in times to come.

*Outcomes:
things that
follow as
results or
consequences.*

OUTCOMES

One outcome
of devoted effort—
a clean, beautiful river
for today and tomorrow.

420

Temporary refuge from a changing world, Gradon Hickman's front porch at the Parker-Hickman cabin was a holdover from an earlier time. This was 1968. Within a few years Gradon was gone and his log house was empty. The cabin would be protected as a reminder of our heritage, even as changes happening all around us would continue at a fast pace, becoming ever faster.

CONCLUSION

This river's future will be influenced by its past. And considering the past, we discover that change keeps coming on faster. Geologic change, the creation of the Ozarks, proceeded during hundreds of millions of years. Biologic change, the development of today's forms of plants and animals, took less time but still some tens of millions. Fundamental change for the Buffalo's prehistoric Native Americans took much less time, around ten thousand years.

Then came the European Americans. The first ones who arrived in the Buffalo River neighborhood around 1800 "lived off the woods" by means not even as advanced as the Natives', except that the Euros had firearms. From that point, however, the river's people and the rest of us have seen sweeping, staggering changes in agriculture, manufacturing, communications, everything—*in two hundred years.*

For the first century the river's increasing human population lived by exploiting deposits of lead and zinc, stands of cedar and hard-woods, acres of fertile soil and free-range forage. Each activity peaked for a while, then subsided as its natural resource played out and as subsistence farming gave way to a cash-dependent economy dominated by manufactured goods from elsewhere. Around 1900 in response to these changes, people began to leave the area to better themselves. Others remained in the Ozark hills, but they had to be hard-working and ingenious—tough, really—to make a living.

About 1960 the Buffalo's population leveled off at half of what it had been fifty years earlier. Cattle had replaced row crops; outsiders moved in as local youngsters moved out. Another natural resource–based industry, tourism, bore the promise of permanence. Timbering might also remain for the long term.

Cattle, timber, tourism—each has its ups and downs influenced by market forces. Beyond the market, the question is sustainability of the basic resources: soil and water for cattle, a continuing supply of trees for the timber industry, water of the quantity and quality required for river recreation.

Our main focus here, of course, is the health of the Buffalo River, which depends on what happens in the river's watershed. From the 1960s to 2000, for instance, more roads were built, more timber was cut, and much land was cleared for pasture or subdivided for home sites. From these and other developments the river can suffer inputs of nitrates, phosphates, bacteria, sediment, and other pollutants.

How can we help protect the river?

First, we must know the Buffalo River very well, and know the watershed's geography and trends in development. While it can be fun to explore the river and its hinterlands, field trips aren't enough; there's homework to do. We must keep up with news, read reports, study each aspect of each problem that arises.

Second, we must be involved with organized groups working to protect the river (several are listed on page 425). We must become active, not just paying our annual dues but also contributing our time.

Third, we must be aware of larger problems that can affect both the river and all of us. The Buffalo River is only one part of our environment. No less than for every other living species, our existence depends totally on clean air, clean water, and healthy soil. And unlike other species, we depend on Earth's gifts of timber, minerals, and energy. Along the Buffalo and everywhere else, the human economy depends on the natural economy.

We must be aware that environmental concerns—indeed, *all* concerns—are linked to how many people inhabit this Earth, and how much each person needs or wants of Earth's limited natural wealth. To sustain at least a minimum state of satisfaction for everyone requires a balance involving just three basic elements: population, resources, and consumption. If, for example, the natural resources are not there to sustain satisfaction, either population or consumption—or both—must give way.

Today the world is small enough that our efforts to better balance those three basic elements must reach beyond national borders and even the continents. The task is exceedingly large and complex. But each of us is involved, like it or not. Success or failure, either way, affects our well-being.

Talking about universal human needs may seem unrelated to protecting the Buffalo River. But whatever we do to improve the balance between population, resources, and consumption, either locally or over a larger area, also counts toward sustaining places such as the Buffalo River that contribute to our happiness.

Change keeps happening faster. For better or worse, big changes will arrive in our lifetimes, affecting how we live.

Think about that. And act to solve problems.

Further Reading

Here we list resources for further reading or research about the Buffalo River's geology, biology, history, and park management. First are those having publications for sale (and, on request, price lists). Following are names, addresses, phone numbers, websites, and descriptions of subject matter:

• Arkansas Archeological Survey, 2475 N. Hatch Ave., Fayetteville, AR 72704-5590; (479)575-3556; www.uark.edu/campus-resources/archinfo Prehistoric and historic Native Americans in Arkansas.

• Arkansas Geological Commission, 3815 W. Roosevelt Rd., Little Rock, AR 72204; (501)296-1877. Technical reports, USGS topographic maps.

• Bookstores. Field guides such as those of the Audubon or Peterson series, and other books on the "Nature" or "Regional" shelves (or by special order, with titles and prices found in the store's *Books in Print* catalog).

• Eastern National, c/o Buffalo National River, 402 N. Walnut, Harrison, AR 72601. Private nonprofit organization offering items related to natural and human history of the National River.

• Missouri Department of Conservation, P.O. Box 180, Jefferson City, MO 65102-0180. Natural history books, videos, and audio recordings, often relating to Arkansas. (For example, their *Fishes of Missouri* includes all the Buffalo River's species except two minor ones.)

• National Speleological Society. Publications about caves (see page 425).

• Ozark Interpretive Association, Box 1279, Mountain View, AR 72560; (870)757-2674. Private nonprofit organization offering items related to natural and human history on the Ozark National Forest.

• Ozark Society Foundation, P.O. Box 3503, Little Rock, AR 72203. Books include Arkansas' most complete guides to wildflowers, and to trees, shrubs, and vines (prices are at www.ozarksociety.net).

• University of Arkansas Press, 201 Ozark Ave., Fayetteville, AR 72701; (479)575-3246. Some natural history, including comprehensive (large-sized) works on Arkansas birds, fishes, mammals, and reptiles.

Out-of-print materials can be seen or obtained at several places, including:

• Boone County Heritage Museum, 110 S. Cherry, Harrison, AR 72601; (870)741-3312. History of Missouri & North Arkansas Railroad.

• County libraries in Harrison, Marshall, Yellville, and Mountain Home. Local history materials not found elsewhere.

• Courthouses in Buffalo River counties. Old records of deeds, mortgages, tax payments, etc., that indicate land ownership and historic trends.

• Mullins Library, University of Arkansas, Fayetteville. Geological reports and historical records in Special Collections, U.S. government reports in Government Documents; other material in main library stacks.

• National Park Service, Buffalo National River, Harrison (see below). Collections of historical and other information available to qualified researchers needing answers to specific questions.

• Shiloh Museum, 118 W. Johnson, Springdale, AR 72764; (479)750-8165. Historic photographs, including some of the Buffalo River.

Public Agencies

• National Park Service   Telephone: (870)741-5443
   Buffalo National River   TDD/Hearing Impaired: (870)741-2884
   402 N. Walnut   Website: http://www.nps.gov/buff/
   Harrison, AR 72601   E-mail: buff_information@nps.gov

For newcomers to Buffalo National River, the Park Service can provide a free copy of *Currents*, a magazine having up-to-date information about the river's visitor facilities, concession services, and recreational opportunities.

For those wanting to float the river, updated information on rainfall and river level is available from the Park Service's Hydrologic Data System (www.buffaloriverandrain.com) having recording stations in the watershed. While the information is not guaranteed to be correct or complete and the user is responsible for judging its value, watching the data and becoming familiar with it over time could help in predicting high water. Current information on river levels can be obtained also by calling park headquarters.

For emergencies involving people on the river, calling 1-888-615-6580 toll-free reaches the Searcy County sheriff's office, and your call will then be relayed to park rangers.

• U.S. Forest Service   Telephone: (870)446-5122
   Buffalo Ranger District   The Upper Buffalo Wilderness
   Highway 7 North, P.O. Box 427   and Buffalo Scenic River
   Jasper, AR 72641   are on this district.
• U.S. Forest Service   Telephone: (870)269-3228
   Sylamore Ranger District   The Leatherwood Wilderness
   609 Sylamore Ave., P.O. Box 1279   is on this district.
   Mountain View, AR 72560

The Ozark National Forest's website (www.fs.fed.us/oonf) has the latest news releases and information about recreational opportunities.

Outdoor Groups

Private nonprofit, member-supported organizations having outdoor programs, conservation interests, and involvement with the Buffalo River:

• American Hiking Society, 1422 Fenwick Lane, Silver Spring, MD 20910; (301)565-6704; www.AmericanHiking.org Devoted to establishing, protecting, and maintaining foot trails in America. AHS-sponsored volunteer crews have built and repaired trails along the Buffalo. Quarterly magazine.

• Arkansas Archeological Society, 2475 N. Hatch Ave., Fayetteville, AR 72704-5590; (479)575-3556; www.arkarch.org Partners with Arkansas Archeological Survey; sponsors lectures, hands-on work with artifacts, annual excavations, training workshops. Local chapters in Arkansas. Bimonthly newsletter and annual bulletin.

• Arkansas Canoe Club, P.O. Box 1843, Little Rock, AR 72203; www.arkansascanoeclub.com Sponsors paddling trips, schools, clinics, whitewater rescue courses, river cleanups. Local chapters. Bimonthly newsletter.

• National Speleological Society, 2813 Cave Ave., Huntsville, AL 35810-4413; (256)852-1300; www.caves.org "To study, explore, and conserve caves." NSS publishes cave-related books, monthly newsletter, journal, members manual. Local grottoes (chapters) offer caving trips and more.

• Ozark Highlands Trail Association, HC 33 Box 50-A, Pettigrew, AR 72752-9501; www.HikeArkansas.com/ohta.html "To build, maintain, and enjoy the Ozark Highlands Trail." Sponsors day and overnight hikes, and work trips to build and repair trails. Bimonthly newsletter.

• Ozark Mountain Paddlers, Box 1581, Springfield, MO 65801. River trips, especially in Missouri Ozarks. American Canoe Association affiliate.

• Ozark Society, Box 2914, Little Rock, AR 72203; www.ozarksociety.net Works to protect wild and scenic rivers, wilderness, and unique natural areas in Ozark-Ouachita mountain region. The lead organization in promoting creation of Buffalo National River. Established Ozark Society Foundation to carry on nonprofit educational work. Society and local chapters sponsor river and trail trips. Society meetings, spring and fall; chapter meetings monthly. Quarterly newsletter, plus chapter newsletters.

• Sierra Club, 85 Second St., San Francisco, CA 94105; (415)977-5500; www.sierraclub.org "To explore, enjoy, and protect the planet." Arkansas Chapter sponsors hiking, backpacking, camping, river trips; campaigns nationally to protect forests and wilderness, locally to combat urban sprawl. Club battles in the political arena. Bimonthly magazine; chapter newsletter. Arkansas Chapter: http://arkansas.sierraclub.org

INDEX

At Gray Rock, 1982